W9-CJK-245

REPAIR MANUAL
FORD PROBE
1989

All U.S. and Canadian models of Ford Probe LX • GL • GT

Vice President and General Manager JOHN P. KUSHNERICK
Editor-in-Chief KERRY A. FREEMAN, S.A.E.
Managing Editor DEAN F. MORGANTINI, S.A.E.
Senior Editor RICHARD J. RIVELE, S.A.E.
Senior Editor W. CALVIN SETTLE, JR., S.A.E.
Editor RONALD T. WEBB

CHILTON BOOK COMPANY
Radnor, Pennsylvania
19089

CONTENTS

DRIVE TRAIN

SUSPENSION and STEERING

BRAKES

BODY

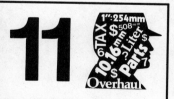

MECHANIC'S DATA

SAFETY NOTICE

Proper service and repair procedures are vital to the safe, reliable operation of all motor vehicles, as well as the personal safety of those performing repairs. This book outlines procedures for servicing and repairing vehicles using safe, effective methods. The procedures contain many NOTES, CAUTIONS and WARNINGS which should be followed along with standard safety procedures to eliminate the possibility of personal injury or improper service which could damage the vehicle or compromise its safety.

It is important to note that repair procedures and techniques, tools and parts for servicing motor vehicles, as well as the skill and experience of the individual performing the work vary widely. It is not possible to anticipate all of the conceivable ways or conditions under which vehicles may be serviced, or to provide cautions as to all of the possible hazards that may result. Standard and accepted safety precautions and equipment should be used during cutting, grinding, chiseling, prying, or any other process that can cause material removal or projectiles.

Some procedures require the use of tools specially designed for a specific purpose. Before substituting another tool or procedure, you must be completely satisfied that neither your personal safety, nor the performance of the vehicle will be endangered.

Although the information in this guide is based on industry sources and is as complete as possible at the time of publication, the possibility exists that the manufacturer made later changes which could not be included here. While striving for total accuracy, Chilton Book Company cannot assume responsibility for any errors, changes, or omissions that may occur in the compilation of this data.

PART NUMBERS

Part numbers listed in this reference are not recommendations by Chilton for any product by brand name. They are references that can be used with interchange manuals and aftermarket supplier catalogs to locate each brand supplier's discrete part number.

SPECIAL TOOLS

Special tools are recommended by the vehicle manufacturer to perform their specific job. Use has been kept to a minimum, but where absolutely necessary, they are referred to in the text by the part number of the tool manufacturer. These tools can be purchased, under the appropriate part number, from Owatonna Tool Company, Owatonna, MN 55060 or an equivalent tool can be purchased locally from a tool supplier or parts outlet. Before substituting any tool for the one recommended, read the SAFETY NOTICE at the top of this page.

ACKNOWLEDGMENTS

Chilton Book Company expresses its appreciation to the Ford Motor Company, Dearborn, Michigan for their generous assistance.

Chilton's Repair Manual: Ford Probe 1989
ISBN 0-8019-8012-7 pbk.
Library of Congress Catalog Card No.

General Information and Maintenance

HOW TO USE THIS BOOK

Chilton's Repair and Tune-Up Guide for the Ford Probe is intended to help you learn more about your car and save you money on its upkeep and operation.

The first two chapters will be the most used, since they contain basic maintenance procedures and tune-up information. Later chapters deal with the more complex systems of your car. Systems from the engine through the brakes are covered to the extent that the average do-it-yourselfer can perform seemingly difficult operations with confidence. It will give you detailed instructions to help you change your own brake pads and shoes, replace points and spark plugs, and do many more jobs that will save you money and help you avoid expensive problems. Such things as rebuilding the differential are not covered for the simple reason that the expertise required and the investment in special tools make such tasks uneconomical

This book can also be used as a reference for owners who want to understand their car and/or their mechanics better.

Before undertaking any repair, read through the entire procedure. This will give you the overall view of what tools and supplies will be required. Read ahead and plan ahead.

When overhauling a defective part is not considered practical, we tell you how to remove the part and how to install a new or rebuilt part. Rebuilt parts of excellent quality are, in many cases, readily available. These generally carry a guarantee similar to that of a new part. Since the price of these parts is usually much lower than that of a new part and the quality is often comparable, the option to purchase a rebuilt part should never by overlooked.

When working on your car, remember that whenever the left side of the car or engine is referred to, it is meant to specify the driver's side.

Conversely, the right side refers to the passenger's side.

Safety is always the most important rule, Constantly be aware of the dangers involved in working on or underneath any automobile and always take the proper precautions. (See the section in this chapter on Servicing Your Vehicle Safely and the SAFETY NOTICE on the acknowledgement page.)

Pay attention to the instructions provided. There are 3 common mistakes in mechanical work:

1. Incorrect order of assembly, disassembly or adjustment: When taking something apart or putting it together, doing things in the wrong order usually just costs you extra time; however, it can break something. Read the entire procedure before beginning disassembly. Do everything in the order in which the instructions say you should do it, even if you can't immediately see a reason for it. When you're taking apart something that is very intricate (for example, a carburetor), you might want to draw a picture of how it looks when assembled in order to make sure you get everything back in its proper position. We will supply exploded views whenever possible. When making adjustments, especially tune-up adjustments, do them in order. Occasionally one adjustment affects another and you cannot expect satisfactory results unless each adjustment is made only when it cannot be changed by any other.

2. Overtorquing (or undertorquing): While it is more common for overtorquing to cause damage, undertorquing can cause a fastener to vibrate loose causing serious damage. Especially when dealing with aluminum parts, pay attention to torque specifications and utilize a torque wrench in assembly. If a torque figure is not available, remember that if you are using the right tool to do the job, you will probably not have to strain yourself to get a fastener tight

enough. The pitch of most threads is so slight that the tension you put on the wrench will be multiplied many, many times in actual force on what you are tightening. A good example of how critical torque is can be seen in the case of spark plug installation, especially when you are putting the plug into an aluminum cylinder head. Too little torque can fail to crush the gasket, causing leakage of combustion gases and consequent loss of power and overheating of the plug and engine parts. Too much torque can damage the threads or distort the plug, which changes the spark gap.

There are many commercial products available for ensuring the fasteners won't come loose, even if they are not torqued just right (a very common brand is Loktite®). If you're worried about getting something together tight enough to hold, but loose enough to avoid mechanical damage during assembly, one of these products might offer substantial insurance. Read the label on the package and make sure the product is compatible with the materials, fluids, etc. involved.

3. Crossthreading: This occurs when a part such as a bolt is screwed into a nut or casting at the wrong angle and forced. Cross threading is more likely to occur if access is difficult. It helps to clean and lubricate fasteners, and to start threading the bolt, etc., to be installed as straight as possible. Start the bolt, spark plug, etc. with your fingers. If you encounter resistance, unscrew the part and start over again at a different angle until it can be inserted and turned several turns without much effort. Keep in mind that many parts, especially spark plugs, use tapered threads so that gentle turning will automatically bring the part you're threading to the proper angle if you don't force it or resist a change in angle. Don't put a wrench on the part until it's been turned a couple of turns by hand. If you suddenly encounter resistance, and the part has not seated fully, don't force it. Screw it back out and make sure it's clean and threading properly.

Always take your time and be patient; once you have some experience, working on your car can become an enjoyable, and money saving hobby.

TOOLS AND EQUIPMENT

The last thing you want to do is to rush out and buy an enormous set of tools on the theory that you may need one of them some day. The best approach is to proceed slowly, gathering together a set of those tools that are used most frequently. Don't be misled by the low cost of bargain tools. It is far better to spend the extra money and use quality, brand name, tools than to mangle your knuckles when one of your bargain sockets cracks and looses its grip. Some tools are guaranteed for life (that't right, life) which means you buy them once and only once, unless you lose them. Forged wrenches, 6 or 12 point sockets and fine tooth ratchets are far preferable than their less expensive counterparts.

Begin accumulating those tools that are used most frequently; those associated with routine maintenance and tune-up. In addition to the usual assortment of pliers and screwdrivers, you should have the following tools for routine maintenance jobs:

1. Metric (and SAE type if you are going to work on a domestic vehicle also) wrenches, sockets and combination open end/box end wrenches.
2. Jackstands, for safety and support.
3. Oil filter wrench.
4. Oil filler spout or funnel.
5. Grease gun, for chassis lubrication.
6. A low flat pan for draining oil.

The second list of tools is for tune-ups. While the tools involved here are slightly more sophisticated, they need not be outrageously expensive. There are several inexpensive tach/dwell meters (or, if the vehicle is equipped with an electronic ignition, a tachometer) on the market that are every bit as good as the expensive professional model. Just be sure that the meter goes to at least 1500 rpm on the tach scale and that it can be used on 4-,6- or 8-cylinder engines. Basic tune-up equipment should include:

1. Tachometer.
2. Spark plug wrench.
3. An inductive type DC timing light that works from the car's battery, and is compatible with electronic ignition, if equipped.
4. A set of flat feeler gauges.
5. A set of round wire spark plug gauges.

In addition to these basic tools there are a few other tools and gauges you may find useful but don't go out and buy them until you need them. These include:

1. A compression gauge. The screw in type is slower to use but it eliminates the possibility of a faulty reading due to escaping pressure.
2. A manifold vacuum gauge.
3. A 12V test light.
4. An induction meter. This is used for determining whether or not there is current flowing through a wire. These are handy for use if a wire is broken somewhere in a wiring harness.

As a final note, you will probably find a torque wrench necessary for all but the most basic work. The beam type models are perfectly adequate although the newer click types are more precise.

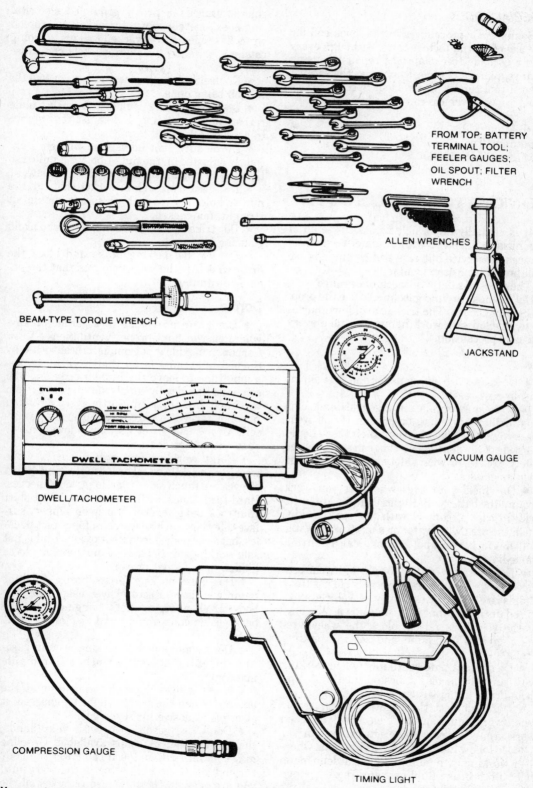

FROM TOP: BATTERY
TERMINAL TOOL;
FEELER GAUGES;
OIL SPOUT; FILTER
WRENCH

ALLEN WRENCHES

JACKSTAND

BEAM-TYPE TORQUE WRENCH

DWELL TACHOMETER

DWELL/TACHOMETER

VACUUM GAUGE

COMPRESSION GAUGE

TIMING LIGHT

You need only a basic assortment of hand tools and test instruments for most maintenance and repair jobs

SPECIAL TOOLS

Some repair procedures in this book call for the use of special factory tools. Although every effort is made to explain the repair job using your regular set of tools, sometimes the use of a special tool cannot be avoided. Special service tools for your vehicle can be ordered from:

Ford Motor Co.
Owatonna Tool Co.
Owatonna, MN 55060

SERVICING YOUR VEHICLE SAFELY

It is virtually impossible to anticipate all of the hazards involved with automotive maintenance and service but care and common sense will prevent most accidents.

The rules of safety for mechanics range from DON'T smoke around gasoline, to use the proper tool for the job. The trick to avoiding injuries is to develop safe work habits and take every possible precaution.

Do's

• Do keep a fire extinguisher and first aid kit within easy reach.

• Do wear safety glasses or goggles when cutting, drilling, grinding or prying. If you wear glasses for the sake of vision, then they should be made of hardened glass that can serve also as safety glasses, or wear safety goggles over your regular glasses.

• Do shield your eyes whenever you work around the battery. Batteries contain sulphuric acid; in case of contact with the eyes or skin, flush the area with water or a mixture of water and baking soda and get medical attention immediately.

• Do use safety stands for an under car service. Jacks are for raising vehicles; safety stands are for making sure the vehicle stays raised until you want it to come down. Whenever the vehicle is raised, block the wheels remaining on the ground and set the parking brake.

• Do use adequate ventilation when working with any chemicals. Asbestos dust resulting from brake lining wear can cause cancer.

• Do disconnect the negative battery cable when working on anything electrical, or when work around or near the electrical system.

• Do follow manufacturer's directions whenever working with potentially hazardous materials. Both brake fluid and antifreeze are poisonous if taken internally.

• Do properly maintain your tools. Loose hammerheads, mushroomed punches and chisels, frayed or poorly grounded electrical cords, excessively worn screwdrivers, spread wrenches (open end), cracked sockets, slipping ratchets, or faulty droplight sockets can cause accidents.

• Do use the proper size and type of tool for the job being done.

• Do when possible, pull on a wrench handle rather than push on it, and adjust your stance to prevent a fall.

• Do be sure that adjustable wrenches are tightly adjusted on the nut or bolt and pulled so that the face is on the side of the fixed jaw.

• Do select a wrench or socket that fits the nut or bolt. The wrench or socket should sit straight, not cocked.

• Do strike squarely with a hammer to avoid glancing blows.

• Do set the parking brake and block the drive wheels if the work requires that the engine be running.

Don'ts

• Don't run an engine in a garage or anywhere else without proper ventilation--EVER! Carbon monoxide is poisonous; it is absorbed by the body 400 times faster than oxygen; it takes a long time to leave the human body and you can build up a deadly supply of it in your system by simply breathing in a little every day. You may not realize you are slowly poisoning yourself. Always use power vents, windows, fans or open the garage doors.

• Don't work around moving parts while wearing a necktie or other loose clothing. Short sleeves are much safer than long, loose sleeves. Hard-toed shoes with neoprene soles protect your toes and give a better grip on slippery surfaces. Jewelry such as watches, fancy belt buckles, beads or body adornment of any kind is not safe working around a car. Long hair should be hidden under a hat or cap.

• Don't use pockets for toolboxes. A fall or bump can drive a screwdriver deep into your body. Even a wiping cloth hanging from the back pocket can wrap around a spinning shaft or fan.

• Don't smoke when working around gasoline, cleaning solvent or other flammable material.

• Don't smoke when working around the battery. When the battery is being charged, it gives off explosive hydrogen gas.

• Don't use gasoline to wash your hands; there are excellent soaps available. Gasoline may contain lead, and lead can enter the body through a cut, accumulating in the body until you are very ill. Gasoline also removes all the natural oils from the skin so that bone dry hands will suck up oil and grease.

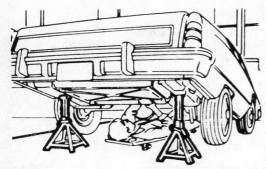

Always use jackstands when supporting the car, never use cinder blocks or tire changing jacks

• Don't service the air conditioning system unless you are equipped with the necessary tools and training. The refrigerant, R-12 is extremely cold and when exposed to the air, will instantly freeze any surface it comes in contact with, including your eyes. Although the refrigerant is normally non-toxic, R-12 becomes a deadly poisonous gas in the presence of an open flame. One good whiff of the vapors from burning refrigerant can be fatal.

SERIAL NUMBER IDENTIFICATION

Vehicle Identification Number

The vehicle identification number (VIN) plate is mounted on the instrument panel, adjacent to the lower corner of the windshield on the driver's side, and is visible through the windshield. See the following Vehicle Certification Label paragraph for an explanation of what the VIN means.

Vehicle Certification Label

The Vehicle Certification Label is attached on the left front door pillar. The upper half of the label contains the name of the manufacturer, month and year of manufacture, Gross Vehicle Weight Rating (GVWR), and Gross Axle Weight Rating (GAWR). The Vehicle Certification Label contains a 17-character Vehicle

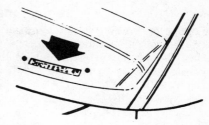

VIN number

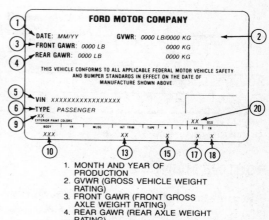

1. MONTH AND YEAR OF PRODUCTION
2. GVWR (GROSS VEHICLE WEIGHT RATING)
3. FRONT GAWR (FRONT GROSS AXLE WEIGHT RATING)
4. REAR GAWR (REAR AXLE WEIGHT RATING)
5. VIN (VEHICLE IDENTIFICATION NUMBER)
6. TYPE
9. EXTERIOR PAINT COLORS
10. BODY
13. INTERIOR TRIM
15. RADIO TYPE
17. AXLE RATIO
18. TRANSMISSION
20. DSO (SPECIAL ORDER CODE)

Vehicle certification label

Identification Number. The number is used for warranty identification of the vehicle and indicates: manufacturer, type of restraint system, line, series, body type, engine, model year and production serial number. The last six numbers of the VIN indicate the serial number of each unit built at each assembly plant.

The remaining information, on the label, consists of codes for: exterior color, body type, interior trim, radio type, axle, transmission and special order equipment.

Engine Identification

Year	Model	Engine Displacement cu. in. (liter)	Engine Series Identification (VIN)	No. of Cylinders	Engine Type
1989–90	Probe GL	133 (2.2)	C	4	OHC
	Probe LX	133 (2.2)	C	4	OHC
	Probe GT	133 (2.2)	L ①	4	OHC

OHC Overhead Cam
① Turbocharged engine

Vehicle Identification Chart

It is important for servicing and ordering parts to be certain of the vehicle and engine identification. The VIN (vehicle identification number) is a 17 digit number visible through the windshield on the driver's side of the dash and contains the vehicle and engine identification codes. The tenth digit indicates model year and the eighth digit indicates engine code. It can be interpreted as follows:

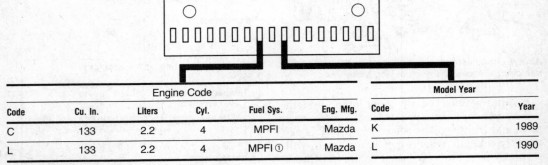

	Engine Code					Model Year	
Code	Cu. In.	Liters	Cyl.	Fuel Sys.	Eng. Mfg.	Code	Year
C	133	2.2	4	MPFI	Mazda	K	1989
L	133	2.2	4	MPFI ①	Mazda	L	1990

MPFI Multiport Fuel Injection
① Turbocharged engine

ROUTINE MAINTENANCE

Routine maintenance and driver's preventive maintenance are the most important steps that can be taken to extend the life of your car and avoid many expensive repairs.

Driver's preventive maintenance consists of taking only a minute every day (or so) to check the various fluid levels, hoses, belts, tire pressures and general visual condition of the engine and car body.

Routine maintenance calls for periodical service or replacement of parts and systems according to a schedule.

Air Cleaner

The air cleaner and duct system filters and delivers fresh air to the engine. The system con-

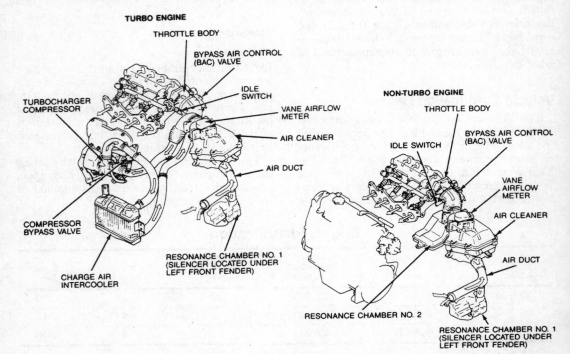

Air filter and duct system

sists of an air duct, resonance chamber (silencer), oil permeated filter element, vane airflow meter for measuring intake air, and a throttle body for controlling the amount of intake air. Never run the engine (other than for adjusting) without a filter element. The dirt and dust entering the engine can cause expensive damage to the pistons, bearings, etc.

Proper maintenance of the cleaner element is vital. A clogged filter element will fail to supply sufficient fresh air to induction system and engine, causing an over-rich fuel/air mixture. Such a condition will result in poor engine performance and economy. Periodical replacing of the filter element (refer to the maintenance chart) will help your car last longer and run better.

To replace the air cleaner filter element:

1. Disconnect the negative battery cable.
2. Disconnect the vane airflow meter (VAF) electrical meter.
3. Remove the air duct clamp and the duct from the VAF meter assembly.
4. Remove the cover mounting screws.
5. Remove the air filter cover and the filter element.
6. Inspect the filter element, cover and body for signs of dust or dirt leaking through the holes in the filter element or past the end seals.

Replace if necessary, or required for regular maintenance interval.

7. Install the filter element after cleaning the housing.
8. Place the cover in position and secure it with the mounting screws.
9. Install the air duct the VAF meter and secure the clamp. Connect the VAF meter electrical connector and connect the negative battery cable.

Fuel Filter

A replaceable high-pressure side fuel filter cartridge is located inside the engine compartment and filters the fuel between the fuel tank and the inlet of the fuel injector rail.

REMOVAL AND INSTALLATION

CAUTION: *Before servicing any fuel system component, relieve the fuel system pressure. Start the engine. Disconnect the fuel pump relay. After the engine stops, turn the ignition switch OFF. Connect the fuel pump relay. The fuel system pressure is now relieved.*

1. Relieve the fuel system pressure.
2. Remove the clamp and fuel line at the inlet of the fuel filter. Plug the line to prevent spillage and/or dirt from entering the system.

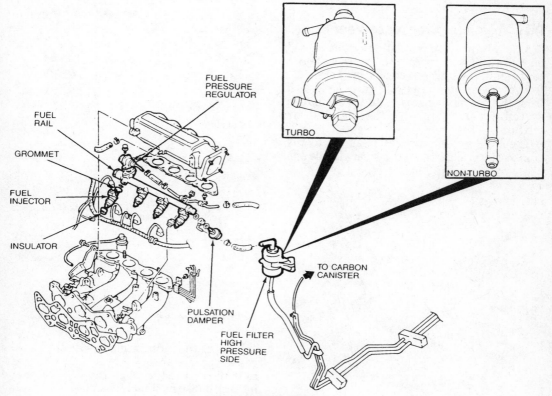

Fuel system and filters

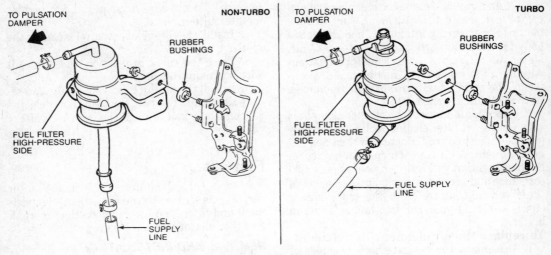

TO PULSATION
DAMPER

NON-TURBO

RUBBER
BUSHINGS

FUEL FILTER
HIGH-PRESSURE
SIDE

FUEL
SUPPLY
LINE

TO PULSATION
DAMPER

TURBO

RUBBER
BUSHINGS

FUEL FILTER
HIGH-PRESSURE
SIDE

FUEL SUPPLY
LINE

Fuel filter connections

3. Remove the clamp and fuel line from the outlet end of the fuel filter.

4. Remove the filter from the mounting clamp.

5. Install the fuel filter in the mounting clamp.

6. Unplug and connect the fuel lines to the filter. Tighten the clamps.

7. Start the engine and check for fuel leaks.

PCV Valve and Crankcase Vent Filter

A closed crankcase ventilation system is used on your car. The purpose of the closed system is to prevent blow-by gases, created by the engine, from escaping into the air. The gases are drawn from the engine crankcase into the air intake system for burning with the fuel and air mixture.

The PCV system supplies fresh air to the crankcase through the air cleaner. Inside the

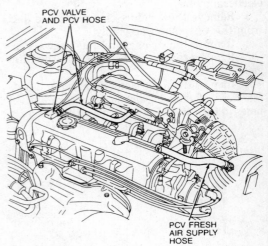

PCV VALVE
AND PCV HOSE

PCV FRESH
AIR SUPPLY
HOSE

PCV system

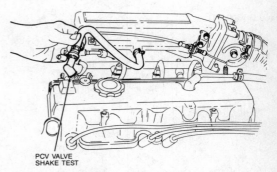

PCV VALVE
SHAKE TEST

PCV valve shake test

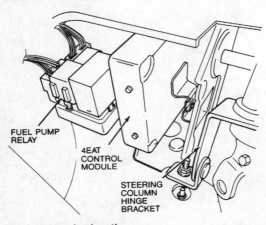

FUEL PUMP
RELAY

4EAT
CONTROL
MODULE

STEERING
COLUMN
HINGE
BRACKET

Fuel pump relay location

crankcase, the fresh air mixes with the blow-by gases. The mixture of fresh air and blow-by gases is then passed through the PCV valve and into the intake manifold. The PCV valve (usually mounted on the end of the valve cover) is a

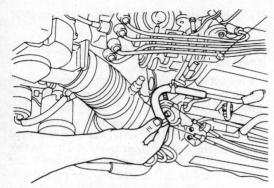

Place a finger over the opened end of the valve

metered orifice that reacts to intake manifold vacuum, and has an adequate capacity for all normal driving conditions. However, under heavy engine loads or high speed driving there is less intake manifold vacuum and the blow-by gases exceed the PCV valve's capacity. When this happens, the blow-by gases back up into the air cleaner through the front hose, mix with fresh air and are reburned in the engine.

REMOVAL AND INSTALLATION

1. Test the operation of the PCV valve, apply the parking brake, start the engine and allow it to operate at a normal idle speed.
2. Remove the PCV valve from the valve cover mounting. A hissing noise should be heard as air passes through the valve and a strong vacuum should be felt if you place a finger over the opened end of the valve.
3. To check the PCV valve with the engine not running, remove the PCV valve from the valve cover mounting. Shake the valve, if a rattling sound is heard, the valve is usually in operating condition.
4. If a rattling sound is not heard, or, suction is not felt when the engine is running, the valve is clogged.
5. Clean the valve and hose in solvent, check for air flow or rattle. Replace the valve and/or hose if necessary.

Evaporative Canister

The vapor canister is part of the Evaporative (EVAP) emission control system. The system prevents the escape of fuel tank vapors under hot engine soak and engine off conditions by storing them in the evaporative carbon canister. When the engine is running and warmed up, the system controls the vapors and purges them from the canister into the fuel/air intake system. Service of the canister is required only if it should become clogged and not allow purging.

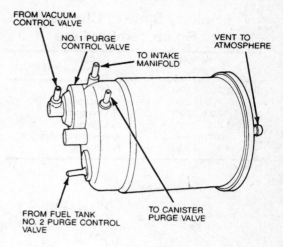

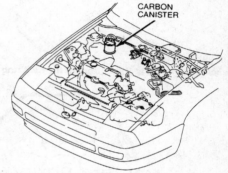

Carbon canister location

Battery

Loose, dirty, or corroded battery terminals are a major cause of "no-start." Every 3 months or so, remove the battery terminals and clean them, giving them a light coating of petroleum jelly when you are finished. This will help to retard corrosion.

Check the battery cables for signs of wear or chafing and replace any cable or terminal that looks marginal. Battery terminals can be easily cleaned and inexpensive terminal cleaning tools are an excellent investment that will pay for themselves many times over. They can usually be purchased from any well-equipped auto store or parts department. Side terminal batteries require a different tool to clean the threads in the battery case. The accumulated white powder and corrosion can be cleaned from the top of the battery with an old toothbrush and a solution of baking soda and water.

Unless you have a maintenance-free battery, check the electrolyte level (see Battery under Fluid Level Checks in this chapter) and check the specific gravity of each cell. Be sure that the vent holes in each cell cap are not blocked by grease or dirt. The vent holes allow hydrogen

Battery State of Charge at Room Temperature

Specific Gravity Reading	Charged Condition
1.260–1.280	Fully Charged
1.230–1.250	¾ Charged
1.200–1.220	½ Charged
1.170–1.190	¼ Charged
1.140–1.160	Almost no Charge
1.110–1.130	No Charge

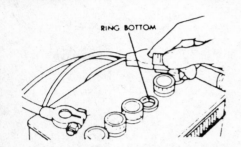

Fill each battery cell to the bottom of the split ring

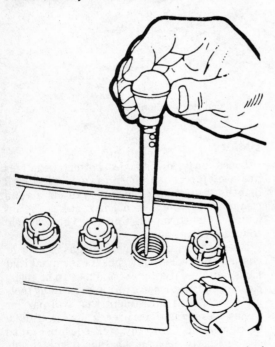

The specific gravity of the battery can be checked with a simple float hydrometer

gas, formed by the chemical reaction in the battery, to escape safely.

REPLACEMENT BATTERIES

The cold power rating of a battery measures battery starting performance and provides an approximate relationship between battery size and engine size. The cold power rating of a re-placement battery should match or exceed your engine size in cubic inches.

FLUID LEVEL (EXCEPT MAINTENANCE FREE BATTERIES)

Check the battery electrolyte level at least once a month, or more often in hot weather or during periods of extended car operation. The level can be checked through the case on translucent polypropylene batteries; the cell caps must be removed on other models. The electrolyte level in each cell should be kept filled to the split ring inside, or the line marked on the outside of the case.

If the level is low, add only distilled water, or colorless, odorless drinking water, through the opening until the level is correct. Each cell is completely separate from the others, so each must be checked and filled individually.

If water is added in freezing weather, the car should be driven several miles to allow the water to mix with the electrolyte. Otherwise, the battery could freeze.

SPECIFIC GRAVITY (EXCEPT MAINTENANCE FREE BATTERIES)

At least once a year, check the specific gravity of the battery. It should be between 1.20 and 1.26 at room temperature.

The specific gravity can be checked with the use of an hydrometer, an inexpensive instrument available from many sources, including auto parts stores. The hydrometer has a squeeze bulb at one end and nozzle at the other. Battery electrolyte is sucked into the hydrometer until the float is lifted from its seat. The specific gravity is then read by noting the position of the float. Generally, if after charging, the specific gravity between any two cells varies more than 50 points (0.050), the battery is bad and should be replaced.

Charging Rate Amps	Time
75	40 min
50	1 hr
25	2 hr
10	5 hr

Temperature (°F)	Minimum Voltage
70 or above	9.6
60	9.5
50	9.4
40	9.3
30	9.1
20	8.9
10	8.7
0	8.5

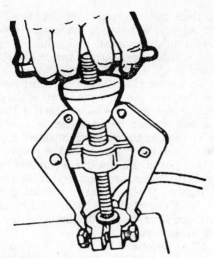

Pullers make clamp removal easier

It is not possible to check the specific gravity in this manner on sealed (maintenance free) batteries. Instead, the indicator built into the top of the case must be relied on to display any signs of battery deterioration. If the indicator is dark, the battery can be assumed to be OK. If the indicator is light, the specific gravity is low, and the battery should be charged or replaced.

CABLES AND CLAMPS

Once a year, the battery terminals and the cable clamps should be cleaned.

1. Loosen the clamps and remove the cables, negative cable first. On batteries with posts on top, the use of a puller specially made for the purpose is recommended. These are inexpensive, and available in auto parts stores.

2. Clean the cable clamps and the battery terminal with a wire brush, until all corrosion, grease, etc. is removed and the metal is shiny. It is especially important to clean the inside of the clamp thoroughly, since a small deposit of foreign material or oxidation there will prevent a sound electrical connection and inhibit either

Clean the inside of the clamps with a wire brush, or the special tool

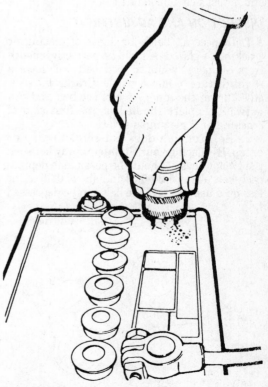

Clean the posts with a wire brush, or a terminal cleaner made for the purpose

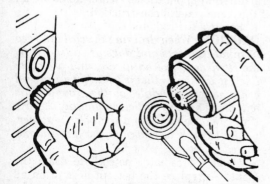

Special tools are also available for cleaning the posts and clamps on side terminal batteries

starting or charging. Special tools are available for cleaning these parts, one type for conventional batteries and another type for side terminal batteries.

3. Before installing the cables, loosen the battery hold-down clamp or strap, remove the battery and check the battery tray. Clear it of any debris, and check it for soundness. Rust should be wire brushed away, and the metal given a coat of anti-rust paint. Replace the battery and tighten the hold-down clamp or strap securely, but be careful not to overtighten, which will crack the battery case.

4. After the clamps and terminals are clean, install the cables, positive cable first; do not hammer on the clamps to install. Tighten the clamps securely, but do not distort them. Give the clamps and terminals a thin external coat of grease after installation, to retard corrosion.

5. Check the cables at the same time that the terminals are cleaned. If the cable insulation is cracked or broken, or if the ends are frayed, the cable should be replaced with a new cable of the same length and gauge.

Belts

At engine tune-up, or at least once a year, check the condition of the drive belts and check and adjust belt tension as below:

INSPECTION AND ADJUSTMENT

1. Inspect all belts for signs of glazing or cracking. A glazed belt will be perfectly smooth from slippage, while a good belt will have a slight texture of fabric visible. Cracks will usually start at the inner edge of the belt and run outward. Replace the belt at the first sign of cracking or if glazing is severe.

2. Belt tension does not refer to play or droop. By placing your thumb midway between the two pulleys, it should be possible to depress each belt about 0.24-0.31 in., about 0.35 in. or less on a used belt. If the belt can be depressed

more than this, or cannot be depressed this much, adjust the tension. Inadequate tension will result in slippage and wear, while excessive tension will damage bearings and cause belts to fray and crack.

3. To adjust the tension on components, loosen the pivot and mounting bolts of the component, or idler pulley, which the belt is driving. Use a soft wooden hammer handle, a broomstick, or the like to pry the component toward or away from the engine until the proper tension is achieved. Do not use a screwdriver or other metal device, such as a prybar, as a lever.

4. Tighten the component mounting bolts securely. If a new belt has been installed, check the tension after about 200 miles of driving. Adjust if necessary.

5. If belt tension at the idler pulley bracket is incorrect, loosen the locknut, then turn the adjusting bolt to move the idler pulley up or down until the belt tension is correct. Tighten the locknut securely and recheck the adjustment.

Hoses
INSPECTION

Inspect the condition of the radiator and heater hoses periodically. Early spring and at the beginning of the fall or winter, when you are performing other maintenance, are good times. Make sure the engine and cooling system are cold. Visually inspect for cracking, rotting or collapsed hoses, replace as necessary. Run your hand along the length of the hose. If a weak or swollen spot is noted when squeezing the hose wall, replace the hose.

REMOVAL AND INSTALLATION

Radiator hoses are generally of two constructions, the preformed (molded) type, which is custom made for a particular application, and the spring-loaded type, which is made to fit several different applications. Heater hoses are all of the same general construction.

1. Remove the radiator cap.

CAUTION: *When draining the coolant, keep in mind that cats and dogs are attracted by the ethylene glycol antifreeze, and are quite likely to drink any that is left in an uncovered container or in puddles on the ground. This will prove fatal in sufficient quantity. Always drain the coolant into a sealable container. Coolant should be reused unless it is contaminated or several years old.*

2. Open the radiator petcock to drain the coolant. To replace the bottom hose drain all the radiator coolant. If only the top hose is to be replaced drain just enough fluid to bring the

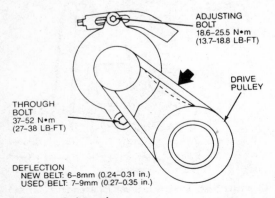

ADJUSTING BOLT
18.6–25.5 N•m
(13.7–18.8 LB-FT)

DRIVE PULLEY

THROUGH BOLT
37–52 N•m
(27–38 LB-FT)

DEFLECTION
NEW BELT: 6–8mm (0.24–0.31 in.)
USED BELT: 7–9mm (0.27–0.35 in.)

Alternator belt tension

HOW TO SPOT WORN V-BELTS

V-Belts are vital to efficient engine operation—they drive the fan, water pump and other accessories. They require little maintenance (occasional tightening) but they will not last forever. Slipping or failure of the V-belt will lead to overheating. If your V-belt looks like any of these, it should be replaced.

This belt has deep cracks, which cause it to flex. Too much flexing leads to heat build-up and premature failure. These cracks can be caused by using the belt on a pulley that is too small. Notched belts are available for small diameter pulleys.

Cracking or weathering

Oil and grease on a belt can cause the belt's rubber compounds to soften and separate from the reinforcing cords that hold the belt together. The belt will first slip, then finally fail altogether.

Softening (grease and oil)

Glazing is caused by a belt that is slipping. A slipping belt can cause a run-down battery, erratic power steering, overheating or poor accessory performance. The more the belt slips, the more glazing will be built up on the surface of the belt. The more the belt is glazed, the more it will slip. If the glazing is light, tighten the belt.

Glazing

The cover of this belt is worn off and is peeling away. The reinforcing cords will begin to wear and the belt will shortly break. When the belt cover wears in spots or has a rough jagged appearance, check the pulley grooves for roughness.

Worn cover

This belt is on the verge of breaking and leaving you stranded. The layers of the belt are separating and the reinforcing cords are exposed. It's just a matter of time before it breaks completely.

Separation

HOW TO SPOT BAD HOSES

Both the upper and lower radiator hoses are called upon to perform difficult jobs in an inhospitable environment. They are subject to nearly 18 psi at under hood temperatures often over 280°F., and must circulate nearly 7500 gallons of coolant an hour—3 good reasons to have good hoses.

Swollen hose

A good test for any hose is to feel it for soft or spongy spots. Frequently these will appear as swollen areas of the hose. The most likely cause is oil soaking. This hose could burst at any time, when hot or under pressure.

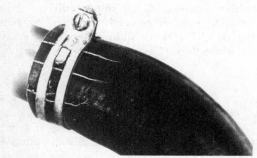

Cracked hose

Cracked hoses can usually be seen but feel the hoses to be sure they have not hardened; a prime cause of cracking. This hose has cracked down to the reinforcing cords and could split at any of the cracks.

Frayed hose end (due to weak clamp)

Weakened clamps frequently are the cause of hose and cooling system failure. The connection between the pipe and hose has deteriorated enough to allow coolant to escape when the engine is hot.

Debris in cooling system

Debris, rust and scale in the cooling system can cause the inside of a hose to weaken. This can usually be felt on the outside of the hose as soft or thinner areas.

level down below the level of the top hose. If the coolant is over a year old discard it.

3. Remove the hose clamps and remove the hose.

4. Use new hose clamps if the old ones are badly rusted or damaged. Slide the hose clamps over each end of the new hose then slide the hose over the hose connections.

5. Position each clamp about ¼ in. from the end of the hose and tighten.

6. Close the petcock and refill with the old fluid if it is less than a year old or with a new mixture of 50/50, coolant/water.

7. Start the engine and idle it for 15 minutes with the radiator cap off and check for leaks. Add coolant if necessary and install the radiator cap.

Air Conditioning System

GENERAL SERVICING PROCEDURES

The most important aspect of air conditioning service is the maintenance of pure and adequate charge of refrigerant in the system. A refrigeration system cannot function properly if a significant percentage of the charge is lost. Leaks are common because the severe vibration encountered in an automobile can easily cause a sufficient cracking or loosening of the air conditioning fittings. As a result, the extreme operating pressures of the system force refrigerant out.

The problem can be understood by considering what happens to the system as it is operated with a continuous leak. Because the expansion valve regulates the flow of refrigerant to the evaporator, the level of refrigerant there is fairly constant. The receiver/drier stores any excess of refrigerant, and so a loss will first appear there as a reduction in the level of liquid. As this level nears the bottom of the vessel, some refrigerant vapor bubbles will begin to appear in the stream of liquid supplied to the expansion valve. This vapor decreases the capacity of the expansion valve very little as the valve opens to compensate for its presence. As the quantity of liquid in the condenser decreases, the operating pressure will drop there and throughout the high side of the system. As the R-12 continues to be expelled, the pressure available to force the liquid through the expansion valve will continue to decrease, and, eventually, the valve's orifice will prove to be too much of a restriction for adequate flow even with the needle fully withdrawn.

At this point, low side pressure will start to drop, and severe reduction in cooling capacity, marked by freeze-up of the evaporator coil, will result. Eventually, the operating pressure of the evaporator will be lower than the pressure of the atmosphere surrounding it, and air will be drawn into the system wherever there are leaks in the low side.

Because all atmospheric air contains at least some moisture, water will enter the system and mix with the R-12 and the oil. Trace amounts of moisture will cause sludging of the oil, and corrosion of the system. Saturation and clogging of the filter/drier, and freezing of the expansion valve orifice will eventually result. As air fills the system to a greater and greater extend, it will interfere more and more with the normal flows of refrigerant and heat.

SAFETY

Precautions

There are two particular hazards associated with air conditioning systems and they both relate to the refrigerant gas.

First, the refrigerant gas is an extremely cold substance. When exposed to air, it will instantly freeze any surface it comes in contact with, including your eyes.

The second hazard relates to fire. Although normally non-toxic, refrigerant gas becomes highly poisonous in the presence of an open flame. One good whiff of the vapor formed by burning refrigerant can be fatal. Keep all forms of fire (including cigarettes) well clear of the air conditioning system.

Any repair work to an air conditioning system should be approached with caution. If there is any doubt concerning correct servicing, have it done professional. Do not, under any circumstances, attempt to loosen or tighten any fittings or perform any work other than that outlined here.

SYSTEM INSPECTION

Refrigerant leaks show up as oil areas on the various components because the compressor oil is transported around the entire system along with the refrigerant. Look for oily spots on all the hoses and lines, and especially on the hose and tubing connections. If there are oily deposits, the system may have a leak, and you should have it checked by a qualified repairman.

NOTE: *A small area of oil on the front of the compressor is normal and no cause for alarm.*

Periodically inspect the front of the condenser for bent fins or foreign material (dirt, bugs, leaves, etc.) If any cooling fins are bent, straighten them carefully with needle-nosed pliers. You can remove any debris with a stiff bristle brush or hose.

A lot of air conditioning problems can be avoided by simply running the air conditioner a least once a week, regardless of the season. Simply let the system run at least 5 minutes a week (even in the winter) and you'll keep the internal parts lubricated as well as preventing the hoses from hardening.

ADDITIONAL PREVENTIVE MAINTENANCE CHECKS

Antifreeze

In order to prevent heater core freeze-up during A/C operation, it is necessary to maintain permanent type antifreeze protection of $+15°F$ ($-9°C$) or lower. A reading of $-15°F$ ($-26°C$) is ideal since this protection also supplies sufficient corrosion inhibitors for the protection of the engine cooling system.

WARNING: *Do not use antifreeze longer than specified by the manufacturer.*

Radiator Cap

For efficient operation of an air conditioned truck's cooling system, the radiator cap should have a holding pressure which meets manufacturer's specifications. A cap which fails to hold these pressure should be replaced.

Condenser

Any obstruction of or damage to the condenser configuration will restrict the air flow which is essential to its efficient operation. It is therefore, a good rule to keep this unit clean and in proper physical shape.

NOTE: *Bug screens are regarded as obstructions.*

Condensation Drain Tube

This single molded drain tube expels the condensation, which accumulates on the bottom of

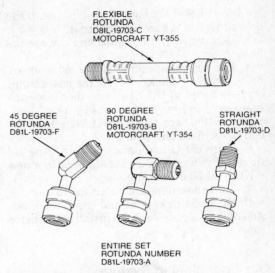

FLEXIBLE ROTUNDA D8IL-19703-C MOTORCRAFT YT-355

45 DEGREE ROTUNDA D81L-19703-F

90 DEGREE ROTUNDA D81L-19703-B MOTORCRAFT YT-354

STRAIGHT ROTUNDA D81L-19703-D

ENTIRE SET ROTUNDA NUMBER D81L-19703-A

Manifold gauge hose adapters

the evaporator housing, into the engine compartment.

If this tube is obstructed, the air conditioning performance can be restricted and condensation buildup can spill over onto the vehicle's floor.

GAUGE SETS

Servicing, such as discharging and charging the system, and all other work that requires opening the sealed system requires the use of a set of two gauges. The required set consists of a high (head) pressure gauge, for the pressure side of the system; and a low (suction) pressure gauge for the low pressure side of the system.

The low side gauge records both pressure and

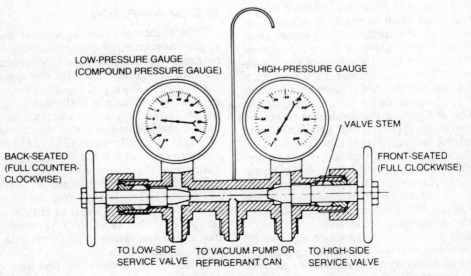

LOW-PRESSURE GAUGE (COMPOUND PRESSURE GAUGE)

HIGH-PRESSURE GAUGE

VALVE STEM

BACK-SEATED (FULL COUNTER-CLOCKWISE)

FRONT-SEATED (FULL CLOCKWISE)

TO LOW-SIDE SERVICE VALVE

TO VACUUM PUMP OR REFRIGERANT CAN

TO HIGH-SIDE SERVICE VALVE

Typical manifold gauge set

vacuum. Vacuum readings are calibrated from 0 to 30 inches and the pressure graduations read from 0 to no less the 150 psi.

The high side gauge measures pressure from 0 to at least 300 psi.

Both gauges are threaded into a manifold that contains two hand shut-off valves. Proper manipulation of the valves, and the use of the attached hoses allow the user to perform the following services. Test high and low side pressures. Remove air, moisture, and contaminated refrigerant. Purge the system (of refrigerant). Charge the system (with refrigerant).

The manifold gauges are designed so they have no direct effect on gauge readings, but serve only to provide for, or cut off, flow of refrigerant through the manifold. During all testing and hook-up operations, the valves are kept in the closed position to avoid disturbing the refrigeration system. The valves are opened only to purge the system or to charge it.

When purging the system, the center hose is uncapped at the lower end, and both valves are cracked open slightly. This allows refrigerant pressure to force the entire contents of the system out through the center hose. During charging, the valve on the high side is closed, and the valve on the low side is cracked open. Under these conditions, the low pressure in the evaporator will draw refrigerant from the relatively warm refrigerant storage container into the system.

NOTE: *A special adapter Rotunda D81L-19703A, or Motorcraft YT-354 or 355, or equivalent is necessary to connect the manifold gauge set to the high pressure service gauge port valve. If the manifold gauge set hoses are not equipped with valve depressing pins, install fitting adapters T71P-19703S or R, or equivalent, which have pins on the high and low pressure manifold hoses.*

DISCHARGING THE SYSTEM

1. Operate the air conditioning system for at least 10 minutes.

2. Shut off the engine and attach the gauge set.

3. Place a container (coffee can, for instance) or a rag at the outlet of the center manifold hose. The discharging refrigerant and system lubricating oil will be discharged through the hose into the container or rag in a controlled manner which will avoid uncontrolled exposure and possible harm from the refrigerant.

4. Open the low side manifold control slightly. Open the high side manifold control slightly.

NOTE: *Too rapid a discharge process is identified by the appearance of oily foam, close both valves slightly until the foaming stops.*

5. Close both valves on the gauge set when the pressures read 0, all of the refrigerant should be discharged from the system.

CHARGING THE SYSTEM

One pound cans of R12 refrigerant are available from auto parts and various retail stores. Always follow the manufacturer's instructions on the can when charging the systems.

CAUTION: *Never use one pound cans to charge into the high pressure side of the system (compressor discharge side) or into a system that is at high pressure High system pressures could be transferred onto the charging can causing it to explode.*

1. Attach the gauge set to the proper service port valves.

2. Install a R12 can dispensing valve to the center manifold hose (be sure the can puncturing needle is fully raised). Carefully attach a one pound can of refrigerant to the dispensing valve. The can of R12 MUST remain in the upright position so that gas and NOT liquid refrigerant enters the low side of the system.

3. Screw in the dispensing valve to puncture the can and then open the valve fully to permit the R12 to enter the center hose.

4. Loosen the center hose to gauge manifold slightly to purge the hose. Tighten the connector. Open the low side control valve slightly and loosen the low side connecter at the service port slightly to purge the hose. Tighten the connector and close the manifold control valve.

5. Roll down the car windows, start the engine and place the air conditioning controls to the full maximum position(s).

6. On models that are equipped with a low pressure cut-off switch mounted on the receiver-dryer, connect a jumper wire to the switch terminals so that the compressor clutch will remain engaged.

7. Open the low side manifold control valve to start charging the system. Adjust the valve so that the charging pressure does not exceed 40 psi. Too sudden a surge of refrigerant may permit unwanted liquid to enter the system and freeze block it.

8. Adjust the engine speed to a fast idle of about 1200 to 1500 rpm to help charge the system.

NOTE: *Placing the refrigerant can into a container of hot water of no more than 125°F will speed charging.*

9. The air conditioning system holds approximately 40 ounces of refrigerant. When changing cans, close the low side valve. After the system is completely charged, close the manifold gauge set valve, shut off the engine and remove the hoses and jumper wire.

Troubleshooting Basic Air Conditioning Problems

Problem	Cause	Solution
There's little or no air coming from the vents (and you're sure it's on)	• The A/C fuse is blown • Broken or loose wires or connections • The on/off switch is defective	• Check and/or replace fuse • Check and/or repair connections • Replace switch
The air coming from the vents is not cool enough	• Windows and air vent wings open • The compressor belt is slipping • Heater is on • Condenser is clogged with debris • Refrigerant has escaped through a leak in the system • Receiver/drier is plugged	• Close windows and vent wings • Tighten or replace compressor belt • Shut heater off • Clean the condenser • Check system • Service system
The air has an odor	• Vacuum system is disrupted • Odor producing substances on the evaporator case • Condensation has collected in the bottom of the evaporator housing	• Have the system checked/repaired • Clean the evaporator case • Clean the evaporator housing drains
System is noisy or vibrating	• Compressor belt or mountings loose • Air in the system	• Tighten or replace belt; tighten mounting bolts • Have the system serviced

Sight glass condition
  Constant bubbles, foam or oil streaks
  Clear sight glass, but no cold air
  Clear sight glass, but air is cold
  Clouded with milky fluid
	• Undercharged system
	
	• No refrigerant at all
	• System is OK
	• Receiver drier is leaking dessicant
		• Charge the system
		
		• Check and charge the system
		
		• Have system checked

Large difference in temperature of lines	• System undercharged	• Charge and leak test the system
Compressor noise	• Broken valves • Overcharged • Incorrect oil level • Piston slap • Broken rings • Drive belt pulley bolts are loose	• Replace the valve plate • Discharge, evacuate and install the correct charge • Isolate the compressor and check the oil level. Correct as necessary. • Replace the compressor • Replace the compressor • Tighten with the correct torque specification
Excessive vibration	• Incorrect belt tension • Clutch loose • Overcharged • Pulley is misaligned	• Adjust the belt tension • Tighten the clutch • Discharge, evacuate and install the correct charge • Align the pulley
Condensation dripping in the passenger compartment	• Drain hose plugged or improperly positioned • Insulation removed or improperly installed	• Clean the drain hose and check for proper installation • Replace the insulation on the expansion valve and hoses
Frozen evaporator coil	• Faulty thermostat • Thermostat capillary tube improperly installed • Thermostat not adjusted properly	• Replace the thermostat • Install the capillary tube correctly • Adjust the thermostat
Low side low—high side low	• System refrigerant is low • Expansion valve is restricted	• Evacuate, leak test and charge the system • Replace the expansion valve
Low side high—high side low	• Internal leak in the compressor—worn	• Remove the compressor cylinder head and inspect the compressor. Replace the valve plate assembly if necessary. If the compressor pistons, rings or

Troubleshooting Basic Air Conditioning Problems (cont.)

Problem	Cause	Solution
Low side high—high side low (cont.)		cylinders are excessively worn or scored replace the compressor
	• Cylinder head gasket is leaking	• Install a replacement cylinder head gasket
	• Expansion valve is defective	• Replace the expansion valve
	• Drive belt slipping	• Adjust the belt tension
Low side high—high side high	• Condenser fins obstructed	• Clean the condenser fins
	• Air in the system	• Evacuate, leak test and charge the system
	• Expansion valve is defective	• Replace the expansion valve
	• Loose or worn fan belts	• Adjust or replace the belts as necessary
Low side low—high side high	• Expansion valve is defective	• Replace the expansion valve
	• Restriction in the refrigerant hose	• Check the hose for kinks—replace if necessary
	• Restriction in the receiver/drier	• Replace the receiver/drier
	• Restriction in the condenser	• Replace the condenser
Low side and high side normal (inadequate cooling)	• Air in the system	• Evacuate, leak test and charge the system
	• Moisture in the system	• Evacuate, leak test and charge the system

Windshield Wipers

For maximum effectiveness and longest element life, the windshield and wiper blades should be kept clean. Dirt, tree sap, road tar and so on will cause streaking, smearing and blade deterioration if left on the glass. It is advisable to wash the windshield carefully with a commercial glass cleaner at least once a month. Wipe off the rubber blades with the wet rag afterwards. Do not attempt to move the wipers by hand; damage to the motor and drive mechanism will result.

If the blades are found to be cracked, broken or torn, they should be replaced immediately. Replacement intervals will vary with usage, although ozone deterioration usually limits blade life to about one year. If the wiper pattern is smeared or streaked, or if the blade chatters across the glass, the elements should be replaced. It is easiest and most sensible to replace the elements in pairs.

There are basically three different types of refills, which differ in their method of replacement. One type has two release buttons, approximately one-third of the way up from the ends of the blade frame. Pushing the buttons down releases a lock and allows the rubber filler to be removed from the frame. The new filler slides back into the frame and locks in place.

The second type of refill has two metal tabs which are unlocked by squeezing them together. The rubber filler can then be withdrawn from the frame jaws. A new refill is installed by inserting the refill into the front frame jaws and sliding it rearward to engage the remaining frame jaws. There are usually four jaws; be certain when installing, that the refill is engaged in all of them. At the end of its travel, the tabs will lock into place on the front jaws of the wiper blade frame.

The third type is a refill made from polycarbonate. The refill has a simple locking device at one end which flexes downward out of the groove into which the jaws of the holder fit, allowing easy release. By sliding the new refill through all the jaws and pushing through the slight resistance when it reaches the end of its travel, the refill will lock into position.

Regardless of the type of refill used, make sure that all of the frame jaws are engaged as the refill is pushed into place and locked. The metal blade holder and frame will scratch the glass if allowed to touch it.

Tires and Wheels
MAINTENANCE

Buy a tire pressure gauge and keep it in the glovebox of your car. Service station air gauges are generally either not working or inaccurate and should not be relied upon. The decal on the back of the glove box door or on the door frame panel gives the recommended air pressures for the standard tires. If you are driving on replacement tires of a different type, follow the inflation recommendations of the manufacturer and never exceed the maximum pressure stated on

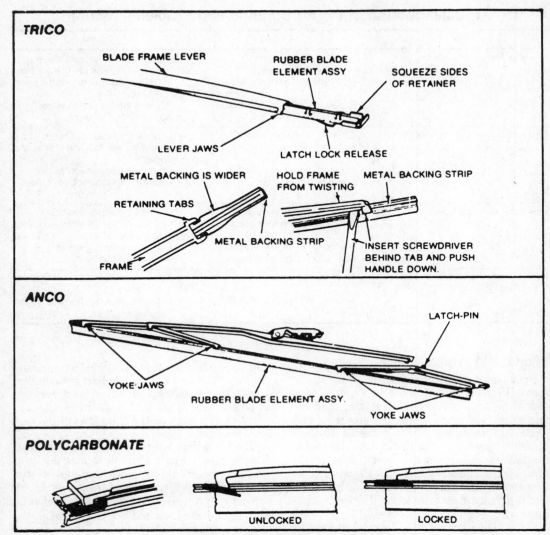

The three types of wiper blade refill retention

the sidewall. Always check tire pressure when the tires are cool because air pressure increases with heat and readings will be 4-6 psi higher after the tire has been run. For continued expressway driving, increase the tire pressure by a few pounds in each tire. Never mix tires of different construction on your car. When replacing tires, ensure that the new tire(s) are the same size and type as those which will be remaining on the car. Intermixing bias ply tires with radial or bias belted can result in unpredictable and treacherous handling.

ROTATION

Rotate the tires on your car every 8,000 miles or as recommended in your owners manual. The rotation pattern shown will result in all five tires wearing out at about the same time. If you plan on replacing the original equipment tires with duplicate types, don't use the spare and rotate only the four road wheels in the correct pattern according to tire type. When you buy new tires, you'll only require three—the spare will be fresh and you can use a worn tire as the spare. The tire size chart can be used for selecting replacement tires of a different size or construction.

When removing studded snow tires in the Spring, mark them left or right with chalk so that they can be returned to the same side. Studded tires take a set and noise and wear will increase if they are installed on the opposite side from which they were removed, in addition to the possibility of losing studs. Always tighten the wheel nuts in a criss-cross pattern. Tightening torque is 50-58 ft. lbs.

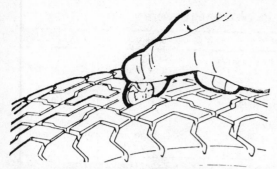

A penny works as well as anything for checking tire tread depth; when you can see the top of Lincoln's head, it's time for a new tire

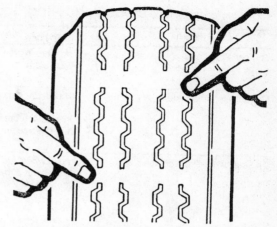

Tread wear indicators will appear when the tire is worn out

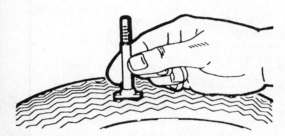

Tread depth can be checked with an inexpensive gauge

TIRE USAGE

The tires on your car were selected to provide the best all around performance for normal operation when inflated as specified. Oversize tires will not increase the maximum carrying capacity of the vehicle, although they will provide an extra margin of tread life. Be sure to check overall height before using larger size tires which may cause interference with suspension components or wheel wells. When replacing conventional tire sizes with other tire size designations, be sure to check the manufacturer's recommendations. Interchangeability is not always possible because of differences in load ratings, tire dimensions, wheel well clearances, and rim size. Also due to differences in handling characteristics, 70 Series and 60 Series tires should be used only in pairs on the same axle; radial tires should be used only in sets of four.

The wheels must be the correct width for the tire. Tire dealers have charts of tire and rim compatibility. A mismatch can cause sloppy handling and rapid tread wear. The old rule of thumb is that the tread width should match the rim width (inside bead to inside bead) within an inch. For radial tires, the rim width should be 80% or less of the tire (not tread) width.

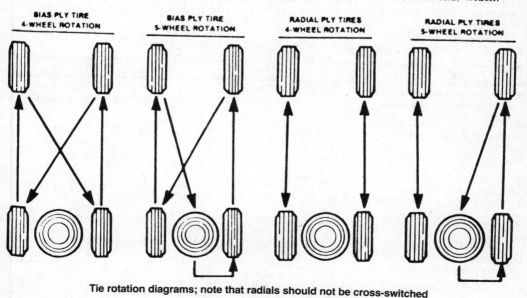

Tie rotation diagrams; note that radials should not be cross-switched

Troubleshooting Basic Wheel Problems

Problem	Cause	Solution
The car's front end vibrates at high speed	• The wheels are out of balance • Wheels are out of alignment	• Have wheels balanced • Have wheel alignment checked/ adjusted
Car pulls to either side	• Wheels are out of alignment • Unequal tire pressure • Different size tires or wheels	• Have wheel alignment checked/ adjusted • Check/adjust tire pressure • Change tires or wheels to same size
The car's wheel(s) wobbles	• Loose wheel lug nuts • Wheels out of balance • Damaged wheel • Wheels are out of alignment • Worn or damaged ball joint • Excessive play in the steering linkage (usually due to worn parts) • Defective shock absorber	• Tighten wheel lug nuts • Have tires balanced • Raise car and spin the wheel. If the wheel is bent, it should be replaced • Have wheel alignment checked/ adjusted • Check ball joints • Check steering linkage • Check shock absorbers
Tires wear unevenly or prematurely	• Incorrect wheel size • Wheels are out of balance • Wheels are out of alignment	• Check if wheel and tire size are compatible • Have wheels balanced • Have wheel alignment checked/ adjusted

The height (mounted diameter) of the new tires can greatly change speedometer accuracy, engine speed at a given road speed, fuel mileage, acceleration, and ground clearance. Tire manufacturers furnish full measurement specifications. Speedometer drive gears are available for correction.

NOTE: *Dimensions of tires marked the same size may vary significantly, even among tires from the same manufacturer.*

The spare tire should be of the same size, construction and design as the tires on the vehicle.

It's not a good idea to carry a spare of a different contstruction.

TIRE DESIGN

For maximum satisfaction, tires should be used in sets of five. Mixing or different types (radial, bias-belted, fiberglass belted) should be avoided. Conventional bias tires are constructed so that the cords run bead-to-bead at an angle. Alternate plies run at an opposite angle. This type of construction gives rigidity to both tread and sidewall. Bias-belted tires are similar

Troubleshooting Basic Tire Problems

Problem	Cause	Solution
The car's front end vibrates at high speeds and the steering wheel shakes	• Wheels out of balance • Front end needs aligning	• Have wheels balanced • Have front end alignment checked
The car pulls to one side while cruising	• Unequal tire pressure (car will usually pull to the low side) • Mismatched tires • Front end needs aligning	• Check/adjust tire pressure • Be sure tires are of the same type and size • Have front end alignment checked
Abnormal, excessive or uneven tire wear See "How to Read Tire Wear"	• Infrequent tire rotation • Improper tire pressure • Sudden stops/starts or high speed on curves	• Rotate tires more frequently to equalize wear • Check/adjust pressure • Correct driving habits
Tire squeals	• Improper tire pressure • Front end needs aligning	• Check/adjust tire pressure • Have front end alignment checked

Tire Size Comparison Chart

"Letter" sizes			Inch Sizes	Metric-inch Sizes		
"60 Series"	"70 Series"	"78 Series"	1965–77	"60 Series"	"70 Series"	"80 Series"
		Y78-12	5.50-12, 5.60-12 6.00-12	165/60-12	165/70-12	155-12
		W78-13 Y78-13	5.20-13 5.60-13 6.15-13	165/60-13 175/60-13 185/60-13	145/70-13 155/70-13 165/70-13	135-13 145-13 155-13, P155/80-13
A60-13 B60-13	A70-13 B70-13	A78-13 B78-13	6.40-13 6.70-13 6.90-13	195/60-13 205/60-13	175/70-13 185/70-13	165-13 175-13
C60-13 D60-13 E60-13	C70-13 D70-13 E70-13	C78-13 D78-13 E78-13	7.00-13 7.25-13 7.75-13	215/60-13	195/70-13	185-13
						195-13
			5.20-14 5.60-14 5.90-14	165/60-14 175/60-14	145/70-14 155/70-14	135-14 145-14
A60-14	A70-14 B70-14 C70-14	A78-14 B78-14 C78-14	6.15-14 6.45-14 6.95-14	185/60-14 195/60-14 205/60-14	165/70-14 175/70-14 185/70-14	155-14 165-14 175-14
D60-14 E60-14 F60-14 G60-14 H60-14 J60-14 L60-14	D70-14 E70-14 F70-14 G70-14 H70-14 J70-14 L70-14	D78-14 E78-14 F78-14, F83-14 G77-14, G78-14 H78-14 J78-14	7.35-14 7.75-14 8.25-14 8.55-14 8.85-14 9.15-14	215/60-14 225/60-14 235/60-14 245/60-14 255/60-14 265/60-14	195/70-14 200/70-14 205/70-14 215/70-14 225/70-14 235/70-14	185-14 195-14 205-14 215-14 225-14
B60-15 C60-15	A70-15 B70-15 C70-15 D70-15	A78-15 B78-15 C78-15 D78-15	5.60-15 6.35-15 6.85-15	185/60-15 195/60-15 205/60-15	165/70-15 175/70-15 185/70-15	155-15 165-15 175-15
E60-15 F60-15 G60-15 H60-15 J60-15 L60-15	E70-15 F70-15 G70-15 H70-15 J70-15 K70-15 L70-15 M70-15	E78-15 F78-15 G78-15 H78-15 J78-15 L78-15, L84-15 M78-15 N78-15	7.35-15 7.75-15 8.15-15/8.25-15 8.45-15/8.55-15 8.85-15/8.90-15 9.00-15 9.15-15	215/60-15 225/60-15 235/60-15 245/60-15 255/60-15 265/60-15	195/70-15 205/70-15 215/70-15 225/70-15 235/70-15 245/70-15	185-15 195-15 205-15 215-15 225-15 230-15 235-15 255-15

Note: Every size tire is not listed and many size comparisons are approximate, based on load ratings. Wider tires than those supplied new with the vehicle, should always be checked for clearance.

in construction to conventional bias ply tires. Belts run at an angle and also at a 90° angle to the bead, as in the radial tire. Tread life is improved considerably over the conventional bias tire. The radial tire differs in construction, but instead of the carcass plies running at an angle of 90° to each other, they run at an angle of 90° to the bead. This gives the tread a great deal of rigidity and the sidewall a great deal of flexibility and accounts for the characteristic bulge associated with radial tires.

When radial tires are used, tire sizes and wheel diameters should be selected to maintain ground clearance and tire load capacity equivalent to the minimum specified tire. Radial tires should always be used in sets of five, but in an emergency, radial tires can be used with cau-

tion on the rear axle only. If this is done, both tires on the rear should be of radial design.

WARNING: *Radial tires should never be used on only the front axle!*

FLUIDS AND LUBRICANTS

Fuel and Oil Recommendations

All models equipped with a catalytic converter--MUST use unleaded gasoline. Regular unleaded gasoline with an anti-knock index of at least 87 is usually satisfactory, although using a higher octane may enhance vehicle performance, especially with turbocharged equipped models.

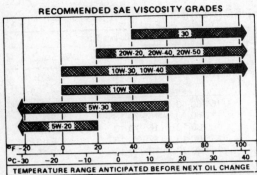

RECOMMENDED SAE VISCOSITY GRADES

NOTICE: Do not use SAE 5W-20 oils for continuous high-speed driving.

Oil viscosity chart

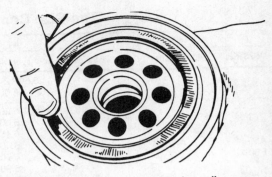

Coat the new oil filter gasket with clean oil

Oil must be selected with regard to the anticipated temperatures during the period before the next oil change. Using the chart, select the oil viscosity for the lowest expected temperature and you will be assured of easy cold starting and sufficient engine protection. The oil you pour into your engine should have the designation SG marked on the top of its container. For maximum fuel economy benefits, use an oil with the Roman Numeral II next to the words Energy Conserving in the API Service Symbol.

Engine
OIL LEVEL CHECK

Checking the engine oil level at every full tank fuel stop is probably a good habit to have. Check the engine oil as follows:

1. Park the car on the level.
2. The engine may be either hot or cold when checking oil level. However, if it is hot, wait for a few minutes after the engine has been shut off to allow the oil to drain back into the crankcase. If the engine is cold, do not start it before checking the oil level.
3. Open the hood and locate the dipstick. Pull the dipstick from its tube, wipe it clean, and reinsert it.
4. Pull the dipstick again and, holding it horizontally, read the oil level. The oil should be between the top (F) and bottom (L) mark. If the oil is below the (L) mark, add oil of the proper viscosity through the capped opening of the valve cover.
5. Insert the dipstick, and check the level again after adding any oil. Be careful not to overfill the crankcase. Approximately one quart of oil will raise the level from the low mark to the high mark. Excess oil will generally be consumed at an accelerated rate even if no damage to the engine seals occurs.

OIL AND FILTER CHANGE

Oil changes should be performed at intervals as described in your owners manual. However, it is a good idea to change the oil and oil filter at least twice a year, and to change the filter each time the oil is changed. If your car is being used under dusty conditions, change the oil and filter sooner. The same thing goes for cars being driven in stop and go city traffic, where acid and sludge buildup is a problem. The oil should also be changed more frequently in cars which are constantly driven at high speeds on expressways. The relatively high engine speeds associated with turnpike driving mean higher operating temperatures and a greater instance of oil foaming.

Always drain the oil after the engine has been run long enough to bring it to the normal operating temperature. Hot oil will flow easier and more contaminants will be removed with the oil than if it were drained cold. A large capacity drain pan, which can be purchased at any automotive supply store, will be more than paid back by savings from do-it-yourself oil changes. Another necessity is containers for the used oil. You will find that plastic bleach containers make excellent storage bottles.

Oil Change

1. Run the engine until it reaches the normal operating temperature. Raise and safely support the front of the car.

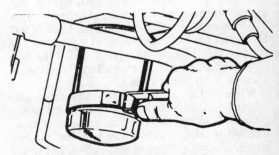

Remove the oil filter with a strap wrench

2. Slide a drain pan under the oil pan drain plug.

CAUTION: *The EPA warns that prolonged contact with used engine oil may cause a number of skin disorders, including cancer! You should make every effort to minimize your exposure to used engine oil. Protective gloves should be worn when changing the oil. Wash your hands and any other exposed skin areas as soon as possible after exposure to used engine oil. Soap and water, or waterless hand cleaner should be used.*

3. Loosen the drain plug with a socket or box wrench, and then remove it by hand. Push in on the plug as you turn it out, so that no oil escapes until the plug is completely removed.

4. Allow the oil to drain into the pan.

5. Clean and install the drain plug , making sure that the gasket is still on the plug.

6. Refill the engine with oil. Start the engine and check for leaks.

Oil Filter Change

The car manufacturer recommends changing the oil filter at every other oil change, but it is more beneficial to replace the filter every time the oil is changed.

CAUTION: *Prolonged and repeated skin contact with used engine oil, with no effort to remove the oil, may be harmful. Follow these simple precautions when handling used motor oil. Avoid prolonged skin contact with used motor oil. Remove oil from skin by washing thoroughly with soap and water or waterless hand cleaner. Do not use gasoline, thinners or solvents. Avoid prolonged skin contact with oil-soaked clothing.*

1. Drain the oil as already described.

CAUTION: *The EPA warns that prolonged contact with used engine oil may cause a number of skin disorders, including cancer! You should make every effort to minimize your exposure to used engine oil. Protective gloves should be worn when changing the oil. Wash your hands and any other exposed skin areas as soon as possible after exposure to used engine oil. Soap and water, or waterless hand cleaner should be used.*

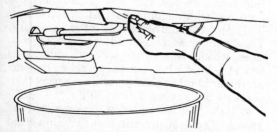

By keeping inward pressure on the plug as you unscrew it, oil won't escape past the threads

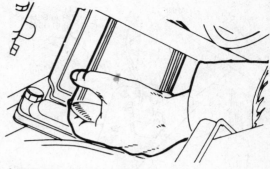

Install the oil filter by hand

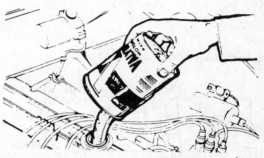

Add oil through the capped opening in the rocker (valve) cover

2. Remove the lower splash shield, if necessary for clearance.

3. Slide a drain pan under the oil filter. Slowly turn the filter off with an oil filter wrench.

4. Clean the oil filter adapter on the engine with a clean rag.

5. Oil the rubber seal on the replacement filter and install it. Tighten it until the seal is flush and then give it an additional ½–¾ turn (check the filter manufacturer's recommendations).

6. Install the splash pan, if equipped. Fill the engine with the proper amount of oil. Start the engine and check for leaks.

Manual Transaxle

FLUID RECOMMENDATIONS

Motorcraft MERCON® (DEXRON®II) automatic transmission fluid (Ford part number E4AZ-19582B is required.

LEVEL CHECK

1. Park the car on a level surface. Apply the parking brake.

2. On vehicles equipped with a digital instrument cluster, disconnect the harness from the speed sensor assembly located on the transaxle housing.

3. On vehicles equipped with an analog in-

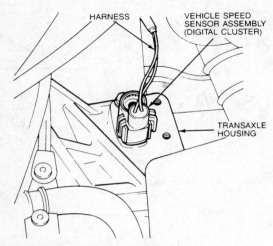

Speed sensor-digital cluster

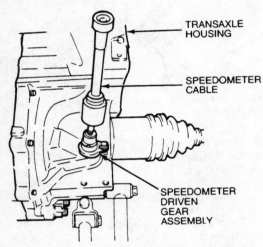

Analog cluster, speedometer cable removal and installation

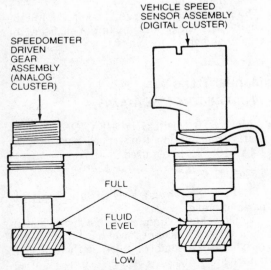

Checking the fluid level in the manual transaxle

strument cluster, disconnect the speedometer cable from the speedometer driven gear assembly located on the transaxle housing.

4. Remove the retaining bolt and pry out the speedometer driven gear assembly or the vehicle speed sensor from the transaxle housing.

5. Check the fluid level on the speedometer drive gear. The level should be just above the gear teeth.

6. Pour the necessary amount of fluid through the gear or sensor opening in the transaxle housing and check the level.

7. Install the speedometer drive gear or speed sensor and connections.

DRAIN AND REFILL

1. Raise and safely support the vehicle.

2. Slide a drain pan under the transaxle. Remove the speedometer driven gear or speed sensor on the top of the transaxle case.

3. Remove the drain plug on the bottom of the transaxle case.

4. When the fluid has been completely drained, install the drain plug.

5. Fill the transaxle to the proper level on the gear.

6. Install the speedometer drive gear or speed sensor. Lower the vehicle.

Automatic Transaxle

FLUID RECOMMONDATIONS

Motorcraft MERCON® (DEXRON®II) automatic transmission fluid (Ford part number E4AZ-19582B is required.

LEVEL CHECK

Check the level of the automatic transmission fluid every 2,000 miles.

CAUTION: *The electric cooling fan, on models equipped, may switch an any time the engine is running. Keep hands away.*

1. Park the car on a level surface with the engine idling. Apply the parking brake.

2. Shift the transaxle through all ranges and return the lever to the PARK position.

3. Remove the dipstick wipe it clean, then insert it firmly. Be certain that it has been pushed fully home. Remove the dipstick and check the fluid level while holding the dipstick horizontally. The level should be at or near the high mark. The dipstick has a high and low mark on both sides, which are accurate for level indications when the fluid is hot (normal operating temperature), or at other than normal operating temperature but not lower than 50°F.

4. If the fluid level is below the low mark, add Mercon® type automatic transmission fluid through the dipstick tube, one half pint at a time. This is more easily accomplished with the

aid of a funnel and hose. Check the level often between additions, being careful not to overfill the transmission. Overfilling will cause slippage, seal damage, and overheating.

DRAIN AND REFILL

1. Raise and safely support the vehicle.
2. Slide a drain pan under the transaxle and remove the drain plug. If not equipped with a drain plug, loosen the oil pan bolts a little at at time, separate the pan from the case and allow the fluid to drain.
3. Install the drain plug. Or, clean all gasket mounting surfaces. Install the oil pan and new gasket. Tighten the mounting bolts to 69-95 in. lbs. Fill the transaxle with the required amount of Mercon® (DEXRON®II) fluid. Start the engine and allow to idle for at least two minutes. With the parking brake applied, move the selector to each position ending in PARK.
4. Add sufficient fluid to bring the level to the lower dipstick mark. Check the fluid level after the transmission is up to normal operating temperature.

PAN AND FILTER SERVICE

Drain the transaxle. With the oil pan removed, inspect the filter. If mileage servicing, or a clogged condition exists, remove the filter. Install a new filter and tighten the mounting bolts to 69-95 in. lbs. Install the oil pan and fill the transaxle with the proper amount of fluid.

Cooling System

At least once every 2 years, the engine cooling system should be inspected, flushed, and refilled with fresh coolant. If the coolant is left in the system too long, it loses its ability to prevent rust and corrosion. If the coolant has too much water, it won't protect against freezing.

The pressure cap should be looked at for signs of age or deterioration. Fan belt and other drive belts should be inspected and adjusted to the proper tension.

Hose clamps should be tightened, and soft or cracked hoses replaced. Damp spots, or accumulations of rust or dye near hoses, water pump or other areas, indicate possible leakage, which must be corrected before filling the system with fresh coolant.

While you are checking the coolant level, check the radiator cap for a worn or cracked gasket. If the cap doesn't seal properly, fluid will be lost and the engine will overheat. Worn caps should be replaced with a new one.

Periodically clean any debris — leaves, paper, insects, etc. — from the radiator fins. Pick the large pieces off by hand. The smaller pieces can be washed away with water pressure from a hose.

Carefully straighten any bent radiator fins with a pair of needle nose pliers. Be careful--the fins are very soft. Don't wiggle the fins back and forth too much. Straighten them once and try not to move them again.

FLUID RECOMMONDITIONS

Coolant used (depending on winter temperatures) is usually a 50/50 mixture of ethylene glycol and water for year round use. Use a good quality antifreeze with water pump lubricants, rust inhibitors and other corrosion inhibitors along with acid neutralizers. Use only cooling system fluid (anti-freeze) that is SAFE FOR USE WITH AN ALUMINUM RADIATOR.

LEVEL CHECKS

All models are equipped with an recovery/expansion tank, check the level visually in the tank. It should be above the low mark. Never fill the tank over the upper mark.

DRAIN AND REFILL

CAUTION: *When draining the coolant, keep in mind that cats and dogs are attracted by the ethylene glycol antifreeze, and are quite likely to drink any that is left in an uncovered container or in puddles on the ground. This will prove fatal in sufficient quantity. Always drain the coolant into a sealable container. Coolant should be reused unless it is contaminated or several years old.*

Completely draining and refilling the cooling system every two years at least will remove accumulated rust, scale and other deposits.

1. Drain the existing antifreeze and coolant. Open the radiator and engine drain petcocks, or disconnect the bottom radiator hose, at the radiator outlet.

NOTE: *Before opening the radiator petcock, spray it with some penetrating lubricant*

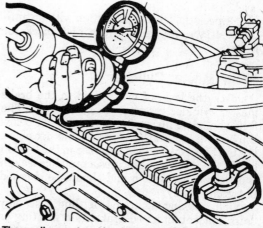

The cooling system should be pressure tested at least once a year

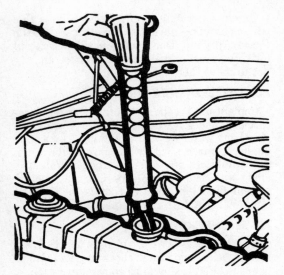

Coolant protection can be checked with a simple float type tester

2. Close the petcock or re-connect the lower hose and fill the system with water. Move the dash control to the hot position.

3. Add a can of quality radiator flush.

4. Idle the engine until the upper radiator hose gets hot.

5. Drain the system again.

6. Repeat this process until the drained water is clear and free of scale.

7. Close all petcocks and connect all the hoses.

8. Flush the recovery/expansion reservoir with water and leave empty.

9. Determine the capacity of your cooling system (see capacities specifications). Add a 50/50 mix of quality antifreeze (ethylene glycol) and water to provide the desired protection.

10. Run the engine to operating temperature.

11. Stop the engine and check the coolant level.

12. Check the level of protection with an antifreeze tester, replace the cap and check for leaks.

Brake Master Cylinder

Check the level of brake fluid in the brake master cylinder reservoir every 2 weeks. The fluid should be maintained to a level not below the bottom line on the reservoir and not above the top line. Any sudden decrease in the level in any of the reservoir indicates a probable leak in that particular system and should be checked out immediately.

When making additions of fluid, use only fresh, uncontaminated brake fluid meeting or exceeding DOT 3 standards. Be careful not to spill any brake fluid on painted surfaces, be-

cause it eats paint. Do not allow the fluid container or master cylinder reservoirs to remain open any longer than necessary; brake fluid absorbs moisture from the air, reducing its effectiveness and causing brake and clutch line corrosion.

Power Steering Pump
FLUID RECOMMENDATIONS

Type F automatic transmission fluid should be used.

LEVEL CHECK

The power steering pump reservoir is equipped with a cap mounted dipstick. The level should be between the high and low marks provided. Start the engine and turn the steering wheel back and forth several times. Turn off the engine and check the dipstick for a fluid level reading. Add fluid as required, but no higher than the upper full mark.

Chassis Greasing

Your car requires no regular chassis greasing.

Body Lubrication

The hood latch, auxiliary catch, door, hatchback and liftgate hinges should be lubricated with Multi-Purpose Polyethylene Grease at regular intervals. Door and window weatherstripping may be lubricated with Silicone Lube.

Rear Wheel Bearings
PACKING AND ADJUSTMENT

NOTE: *Sodium-based grease is not compatible with lithium-based grease. Read the package labels and be careful not to mix the two types. If there is any doubt as to the type of grease used, completely clean the old grease from the bearing and hub before replacing.*

Before handling the bearings, there are a few things that you should remember to do and not to do.

Remember to DO the following:

• Remove all outside dirt from the housing before exposing the bearing.

• Treat a used bearing as gently as you would a new one.

• Work with clean tools in clean surroundings.

• Use clean, dry canvas gloves, or at least clean, dry hands.

• Clean solvents and flushing fluids are a must.

• Use clean paper when laying out the bearings to dry.

JUMP STARTING A DEAD BATTERY

The chemical reaction in a battery produces explosive hydrogen gas. This is the safe way to jump start a dead battery, reducing the chances of an accidental spark that could cause an explosion.

Jump Starting Precautions

1. Be sure both batteries are of the same voltage.
2. Be sure both batteries are of the same polarity (have the same grounded terminal).
3. Be sure the vehicles are not touching.
4. Be sure the vent cap holes are not obstructed.
5. Do not smoke or allow sparks around the battery.
6. In cold weather, check for frozen electrolyte in the battery. Do not jump start a frozen battery.
7. Do not allow electrolyte on your skin or clothing.
8. Be sure the electrolyte is not frozen.
CAUTION: *Make certain that the ignition key, in the vehicle with the dead battery, is in the OFF position. Connecting cables to vehicles with on-board computers will result in computer destruction if the key is not in the OFF position.*

Jump Starting Procedure

1. Determine voltages of the two batteries; they must be the same.
2. Bring the starting vehicle close (they must not touch) so that the batteries can be reached easily.
3. Turn off all accessories and both engines. Put both cars in Neutral or Park and set the handbrake.
4. Cover the cell caps with a rag—do not cover terminals.
5. If the terminals on the run-down battery are heavily corroded, clean them.
6. Identify the positive and negative posts on both batteries and connect the cables in the order shown.
7. Start the engine of the starting vehicle and run it at fast idle. Try to start the car with the dead battery. Crank it for no more than 10 seconds at a time and let it cool off for 20 seconds in between tries.
8. If it doesn't start in 3 tries, there is something else wrong.
9. Disconnect the cables in the reverse order.
10. Replace the cell covers and dispose of the rags.

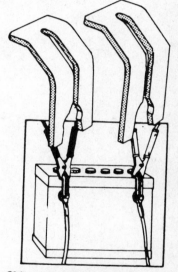

Side terminal batteries occasionally pose a problem when connecting jumper cables. There frequently isn't enough room to clamp the cables without touching sheet metal. Side terminal adaptors are available to alleviate this problem and should be removed after use.

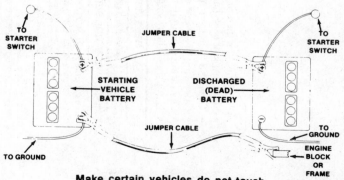

Make certain vehicles do not touch

This hook-up for negative ground cars only

Customer Maintenance Schedule A

Follow maintenance Schedule A if your driving habits **FREQUENTLY** include one or more of the following conditions:
- Short trips of less than 10 miles (16 km) when outside temperatures remain below freezing.
- Towing a trailer, or using a car top carrier.
- Operating in severe dust conditions.
- Operating during hot weather in stop-and-go "rush hour" traffic.
- Extensive idling, such as police, taxi or door-to-door delivery service.

Miles X (000)	3	6	9	12	15	18	21	24	27	30	33	36	39	42	45	48	51	54	57	60
Kilometers X (000)	4.8	9.6	14.	19.	24.	28.	33.	38.	43.	48.	52.	57.	62.	67.	72.	76.	81.	86.	91.	96.
EMISSION CONTROL SERVICE																				
Change Engine Oil & Oil Filter (whichever occurs first) Every 3 Months or	X	X	X	X	X	X	X	X	X	X	X	X	X	X	X	X	X	X	X	X
Replace Spark Plugs: Turbocharged					③					③					③					③
Non-turbocharged										X										X
Inspect Cooling System Every 12 Months or					X					X					X					X
Replace Engine Coolant Every 36 Months or										X										X
Inspect Accessory Drive Belts										X										X
Air Cleaner Element: Inspect/Clean					③										③					
Replace ②										X										X
Replace Fuel Filter																				X

Replace Engine Timing Belt ①			X
GENERAL MAINTENANCE			
Inspect Brake Lines, Connections & Hoses	X	X	X
Inspect Front Disc Brakes	X	X	X
Inspect Rear Drum Brakes	X		X
Tighten Bolts & Nuts on Chassis & Body	X	X	X
Inspect Steering Operations and Linkage	X		X
Inspect Front Suspension Ball Joints	X		X
Inspect Drive Shaft Dust Boots	X		X
Inspect Exhaust System Heat Shield	X		X
Inspect Fuel Lines	③		X
Change automatic transaxle fluid	④		④

① Replacement of the timing belt is required at every 60,000 miles (96,000 km). Failure to replace the timing belt may result in damage to the engine.

② If operating in severe dust, more frequent intervals may be required. Consult your dealer.

③ This item not required to be performed, however, Ford recommends that you perform maintenance on this item in order to achieve best vehicle operation. Failure to perform this recommended maintenance will not invalidate the vehicle emissions warranty or manufacturer recall liability.

④ Change automatic transaxle fluid if your driving habits frequently include one or more of the following conditions:
- Operation during hot weather (above 90°F, 32°C) carrying heavy loads and in hilly terrain.
- Towing a trailer or using a car top carrier.
- Police, taxi or door-to-door delivery service.

Customer Maintenance Schedule B

Follow this Schedule if, generally, you drive your car on a daily basis for several miles and **NONE OF THE DRIVING CONDITIONS SHOWN IN SCHEDULE A APPLY TO YOUR DRIVING HABITS.**

	Miles X (000)	7.5	15	22.5	30.0	37.5	45.0	52.5	60.0
	Kilometers X (000)	12	24	36	48	60	72	84	96
EMISSION CONTROL SERVICE									
Non-Turbocharged Change Engine Oil & Oil Filter		X	X	X	X	X	X	X	X
Turbocharged Replace Engine Oil & Oil Filter		EVERY 5,000 MILES (8,000 km) OR 6 MONTHS, WHICHEVER OCCURS FIRST							
Replace Spark Plugs: Turbocharged			③				③		
Non-Turbocharged									X
Inspect Cooling System Every 12 Months or			X		X		X		X
Replace Engine Coolant Every 36 Months or					X				X
Inspect Accessory Drive Belts					X				X
Replace Air Cleaner Element ②					X				X
Replace Fuel Filter									X
Replace Engine Timing Belt ①					③				①
GENERAL MAINTENANCE									
Inspect Brake Lines and Connections			X		X		X		X
Inspect Front Disc Brakes			X		X		X		X
Inspect Drum Brakes					X				X
Tighten Bolts & Nuts on Chassis & Body			X				X		
Inspect Steering Operation & Gear Linkage					X				X
Inspect Front Suspension Ball Joints					X				X
Inspect Driveshaft Dust Boots					X				X
Inspect Exhaust System Heat Shield					X				X
Inspect Fuel Lines									X

① Replacement of the timing belt is required at every 60,000 miles (96,000 km). Failure to replace the timing belt may result in damage to the engine.
② If operating in severe dust, more frequent intervals may be required. Consult your dealer.
③ This item not required to be performed, however, Ford recommends that you perform maintenance on this item in order to achieve best vehicle operation. Failure to perform this recommended maintenance will not invalidate the vehicle emissions warranty or manufacturer recall liability.

- Protect disassembled bearings from rust and dirt. Cover them up.
- Use clean rags to wipe bearings.
- Keep the bearings in oil-proof paper when they are to be stored or are not in use.
- Clean the inside of the housing before replacing the bearing.

Do NOT do the following:

- Don't work in dirty surroundings.
- Don't use dirty, chipped or damaged tools.
- Try not to work on wooden work benches or use wooden mallets.
- Don't handle bearings with dirty or moist hands.
- Do not use gasoline for cleaning; use a safe solvent.
- Do not spin-dry bearings with compressed air. They will be damaged.
- Do not spin dirty bearings.
- Avoid using cotton waste or dirty cloths to wipe bearings.
- Try not to scratch or nick bearing surfaces.
- Do not allow the bearing to come in contact with dirt or rust at any time.

1. Raise and safely support the rear of the vehicle. Remove the wheel assembly.

2. Remove the center hub cover. Use a chisel and unstake the hub nut. Remove and discard the hub nut.

3. Remove the brake drum or rotor assembly.

4. Pry the graese seal from the brake drum. Remove the snapring that retains the rear wheel bearing. Press the bearing from the hub.

5. Press a new bearing into position and install the snapring.

6. Lubricate the lips of a new grease retainer and install the retainer,

7. Install the drum or rotor assembly. Install a new hub retaining bolt and tighten it to 73-101 ft. lbs. Stake the nut using a blunt chisel.

8. Install the hub cover. Install the wheel assembly. Lower the vehicle.

PUSHING AND TOWING

Manual transaxle equipped cars may be started by pushing, in the event of a dead battery. But push starting IS NOT RECOMMENDED because of possible damage to the catalytic converter. If you must push start, ensure that the push car bumper doesn't override the bumper of your car. Depress the clutch pedal. Select Second or Third gear. Switch the ignition ON. When the car reaches a speed of approximately 10 mph, release the clutch to start the engine.

If towing is required, the vehicle should be flat bedded, or towed with the front wheels off of the ground.

JACKING

The vehicle is supplied with a scissors jack for emergency road repairs. The scissors jack may be used to raise the car via the notches on either side at the front and rear of the doors. Do not attempt to use the jack in any other places. Always block the diagonally opposite wheel when using a jack.

When using stands, use the side members at the front or trailing axle front mounting crossmember at the back for placement points.

henever you plan to work under the car, you must support it on jackstands or ramps. Never use cinder blocks or stacks of wood to support the car, even if you're only going to be under it for a few minutes. Never crawl under the car when it is supported only by the tire-changing jack.

Small hydraulic, screw, or scissors jacks are satisfactory for raising the car. Drive-on trestles or ramps are also a handy and safe way to both raise and support the car. These can be bought or constructed from wood or steel. Never support the car on any suspension member or underbody panel.

Capacities

Year	Model	VIN	No. Cylinder Displacement cu. in. (liter)	Engine Crankcase		Transmission (pts.)			Drive Axle (pts.)	Fuel Tank (gal.)	Cooling System (qts.)
				With Filter	Without Filter	4-Spd	5-Spd	Auto.			
1989–90	Probe	C	4-133 (2.2)	5.4	4.9	—	7.1	14.4	—	15.1	7.9
	Probe	L	4-133 (2.2)	5.4	4.9	—	7.7	—	—	15.1	7.9

Engine Performance and Tune-Up

2

Gasoline Engine Tune-Up Specifications

| Year | VIN | No. Cylinder Displacement cu. in. (liter) | Spark Plugs | | Ignition Timing (deg.) | | Compression Pressure (psi) | Fuel Pump (psi) | Idle Speed (rpm) | | Valve Clearance | |
			Type	Gap (in.)	MT	AT			MT	AT	In.	Ex.
1989–90	C	4-133 (2.2)	AGSP-33C	0.040	5–7 ①	5–7 ① ③	—	36	725– 775	③ ④	Hyd.	Hyd.
	L	4-133 (2.2)	AGSP-33C	0.040	8–10 ②	—	—	36	725– 775	—	Hyd.	Hyd.

① Distributor vacuum hoses disconnected and plugged
② Test connector grounded
③ Transaxle in Park
④ 725–775 rpm

TUNE-UP PROCEDURES

A tune-up is performed periodically to make a complete check of the operation of the engine and several associated systems, to bring various minor adjustments to the best possible position. The tune-up is a good time to perform a general preventive maintenance check-out on everything in the engine compartment. Look for things like loose or damaged wiring, fuel leaks, frayed drive belts, etc.

Refer to the maintenance interval chart (Chapter 1) for the recommended intervals between tune-ups. After one or two tune-ups, according to the vehicle's performance, you can determine your own tune-up interval. Whether it is 10,000, 15,000, 20,000 miles, or once every year; set up a definite schedule for your car and follow it religiously. Regular tuning will head off disappointing performance and help prevent roadside breakdowns.

Spark Plugs

A typical spark plug consists of a metal shell surrounding a ceramic insulator. A metal electrode extends downward through the center of the insulator and protrudes a small distance. Located at the end of the plug and attached to the side of the outer metal shell is the side electrode. The side electrode bends in at a 90° angle so that its tip is even with, and parallel to, the tip of the center electrode. The distance between these two electrodes (measured in thousandths of an inch) is called the spark plug gap. The spark plug in no way produces a spark but merely provides a gap across which the current can arc. The coil produces anywhere from 20,000 to 40,000 volts which travels to the distributor where it is distributed through the spark plug wires to the spark plugs. The current passes along the center electrode and jumps the gap to the side electrode, and, in do doing, ignites the air/fuel mixture in the combustion chamber.

Spark plugs ignite the air and fuel mixture in the cylinder as the piston reaches the top of the compression stroke. The controlled explosion that results forces the piston down, turning the crankshaft and the rest of the drive train.

The average life of a spark plug is dependent on a number of factors: the mechanical condi-

Troubleshooting Engine Performance

Problem	Cause	Solution
Hard starting (engine cranks normally)	• Binding linkage, choke valve or choke piston	• Repair as necessary
	• Restricted choke vacuum diaphragm	• Clean passages
	• Improper fuel level	• Adjust float level
	• Dirty, worn or faulty needle valve and seat	• Repair as necessary
	• Float sticking	• Repair as necessary
	• Faulty fuel pump	• Replace fuel pump
	• Incorrect choke cover adjustment	• Adjust choke cover
	• Inadequate choke unloader adjustment	• Adjust choke unloader
	• Faulty ignition coil	• Test and replace as necessary
	• Improper spark plug gap	• Adjust gap
	• Incorrect ignition timing	• Adjust timing
	• Incorrect valve timing	• Check valve timing; repair as necessary
Rough idle or stalling	• Incorrect curb or fast idle speed	• Adjust curb or fast idle speed
	• Incorrect ignition timing	• Adjust timing to specification
	• Improper feedback system operation	• Refer to Chapter 4
	• Improper fast idle cam adjustment	• Adjust fast idle cam
	• Faulty EGR valve operation	• Test EGR system and replace as necessary
	• Faulty PCV valve air flow	• Test PCV valve and replace as necessary
	• Choke binding	• Locate and eliminate binding condition
	• Faulty TAC vacuum motor or valve	• Repair as necessary
	• Air leak into manifold vacuum	• Inspect manifold vacuum connections and repair as necessary
	• Improper fuel level	• Adjust fuel level
	• Faulty distributor rotor or cap	• Replace rotor or cap
	• Improperly seated valves	• Test cylinder compression, repair as necessary
	• Incorrect ignition wiring	• Inspect wiring and correct as necessary
	• Faulty ignition coil	• Test coil and replace as necessary
	• Restricted air vent or idle passages	• Clean passages
	• Restricted air cleaner	• Clean or replace air cleaner filler element
	• Faulty choke vacuum diaphragm	• Repair as necessary
Faulty low-speed operation	• Restricted idle transfer slots	• Clean transfer slots
	• Restricted idle air vents and passages	• Clean air vents and passages
	• Restricted air cleaner	• Clean or replace air cleaner filter element
	• Improper fuel level	• Adjust fuel level
	• Faulty spark plugs	• Clean or replace spark plugs
	• Dirty, corroded, or loose ignition secondary circuit wire connections	• Clean or tighten secondary circuit wire connections
	• Improper feedback system operation	• Refer to Chapter 4
	• Faulty ignition coil high voltage wire	• Replace ignition coil high voltage wire
	• Faulty distributor cap	• Replace cap
Faulty acceleration	• Improper accelerator pump stroke	• Adjust accelerator pump stroke
	• Incorrect ignition timing	• Adjust timing
	• Inoperative pump discharge check ball or needle	• Clean or replace as necessary
	• Worn or damaged pump diaphragm or piston	• Replace diaphragm or piston

Troubleshooting Engine Performance (cont.)

Problem	Cause	Solution
Faulty acceleration (cont.)	• Leaking carburetor main body cover gasket	• Replace gasket
	• Engine cold and choke set too lean	• Adjust choke cover
	• Improper metering rod adjustment (BBD Model carburetor)	• Adjust metering rod
	• Faulty spark plug(s)	• Clean or replace spark plug(s)
	• Improperly seated valves	• Test cylinder compression, repair as necessary
	• Faulty ignition coil	• Test coil and replace as necessary
	• Improper feedback system operation	• Refer to Chapter 4
Faulty high speed operation	• Incorrect ignition timing	• Adjust timing
	• Faulty distributor centrifugal advance mechanism	• Check centrifugal advance mechanism and repair as necessary
	• Faulty distributor vacuum advance mechanism	• Check vacuum advance mechanism and repair as necessary
	• Low fuel pump volume	• Replace fuel pump
	• Wrong spark plug air gap or wrong plug	• Adjust air gap or install correct plug
	• Faulty choke operation	• Adjust choke cover
	• Partially restricted exhaust manifold, exhaust pipe, catalytic converter, muffler, or tailpipe	• Eliminate restriction
	• Restricted vacuum passages	• Clean passages
	• Improper size or restricted main jet	• Clean or replace as necessary
	• Restricted air cleaner	• Clean or replace filter element as necessary
	• Faulty distributor rotor or cap	• Replace rotor or cap
	• Faulty ignition coil	• Test coil and replace as necessary
	• Improperly seated valve(s)	• Test cylinder compression, repair as necessary
	• Faulty valve spring(s)	• Inspect and test valve spring tension, replace as necessary
	• Incorrect valve timing	• Check valve timing and repair as necessary
	• Intake manifold restricted	• Remove restriction or replace manifold
	• Worn distributor shaft	• Replace shaft
	• Improper feedback system operation	• Refer to Chapter 4
Misfire at all speeds	• Faulty spark plug(s)	• Clean or replace spark plug(s)
	• Faulty spark plug wire(s)	• Replace as necessary
	• Faulty distributor cap or rotor	• Replace cap or rotor
	• Faulty ignition coil	• Test coil and replace as necessary
	• Primary ignition circuit shorted or open intermittently	• Troubleshoot primary circuit and repair as necessary
	• Improperly seated valve(s)	• Test cylinder compression, repair as necessary
	• Faulty hydraulic tappet(s)	• Clean or replace tappet(s)
	• Improper feedback system operation	• Refer to Chapter 4
	• Faulty valve spring(s)	• Inspect and test valve spring tension, repair as necessary
	• Worn camshaft lobes	• Replace camshaft
	• Air leak into manifold	• Check manifold vacuum and repair as necessary
	• Improper carburetor adjustment	• Adjust carburetor
	• Fuel pump volume or pressure low	• Replace fuel pump
	• Blown cylinder head gasket	• Replace gasket
	• Intake or exhaust manifold passage(s) restricted	• Pass chain through passage(s) and repair as necessary
	• Incorrect trigger wheel installed in distributor	• Install correct trigger wheel

Troubleshooting Engine Performance (cont.)

Problem	Cause	Solution
Power not up to normal	• Incorrect ignition timing	• Adjust timing
	• Faulty distributor rotor	• Replace rotor
	• Trigger wheel loose on shaft	• Reposition or replace trigger wheel
	• Incorrect spark plug gap	• Adjust gap
	• Faulty fuel pump	• Replace fuel pump
	• Incorrect valve timing	• Check valve timing and repair as necessary
	• Faulty ignition coil	• Test coil and replace as necessary
	• Faulty ignition wires	• Test wires and replace as necessary
	• Improperly seated valves	• Test cylinder compression and repair as necessary
	• Blown cylinder head gasket	• Replace gasket
	• Leaking piston rings	• Test compression and repair as necessary
	• Worn distributor shaft	• Replace shaft
	• Improper feedback system operation	• Refer to Chapter 4
Intake backfire	• Improper ignition timing	• Adjust timing
	• Faulty accelerator pump discharge	• Repair as necessary
	• Defective EGR CTO valve	• Replace EGR CTO valve
	• Defective TAC vacuum motor or valve	• Repair as necessary
	• Lean air/fuel mixture	• Check float level or manifold vacuum for air leak. Remove sediment from bowl
Exhaust backfire	• Air leak into manifold vacuum	• Check manifold vacuum and repair as necessary
	• Faulty air injection diverter valve	• Test diverter valve and replace as necessary
	• Exhaust leak	• Locate and eliminate leak
Ping or spark knock	• Incorrect ignition timing	• Adjust timing
	• Distributor centrifugal or vacuum advance malfunction	• Inspect advance mechanism and repair as necessary
	• Excessive combustion chamber deposits	• Remove with combustion chamber cleaner
	• Air leak into manifold vacuum	• Check manifold vacuum and repair as necessary
	• Excessively high compression	• Test compression and repair as necessary
	• Fuel octane rating excessively low	• Try alternate fuel source
	• Sharp edges in combustion chamber	• Grind smooth
	• EGR valve not functioning properly	• Test EGR system and replace as necessary
Surging (at cruising to top speeds)	• Low carburetor fuel level	• Adjust fuel level
	• Low fuel pump pressure or volume	• Replace fuel pump
	• Metering rod(s) not adjusted properly (BBD Model Carburetor)	• Adjust metering rod
	• Improper PCV valve air flow	• Test PCV valve and replace as necessary
	• Air leak into manifold vacuum	• Check manifold vacuum and repair as necessary
	• Incorrect spark advance	• Test and replace as necessary
	• Restricted main jet(s)	• Clean main jet(s)
	• Undersize main jet(s)	• Replace main jet(s)
	• Restricted air vents	• Clean air vents
	• Restricted fuel filter	• Replace fuel filter
	• Restricted air cleaner	• Clean or replace air cleaner filter element
	• EGR valve not functioning properly	• Test EGR system and replace as necessary
	• Improper feedback system operation	• Refer to Chapter 4

tion of the engine; the type of engine; the type of fuel; driving conditions; and the driver.

When you remove the spark plugs, check their condition. They are a good indicator of the condition of the engine. It it a good idea to remove the spark plugs at regular intervals, such as every 2,000 or 3,000 miles, just so you can keep an eye on the mechanical state of your engine.

A small deposit of light tan or gray material on a spark plug that has been used for any period of time is to be considered normal.

The gap between the center electrode and the side or ground electrode can be expected to increase not more than 0.001 in. every 1,000 miles under normal conditions.

When a spark plug is functioning normally or, more accurately, when the plug is installed in an engine that is functioning properly, the plugs can be taken out, cleaned, regapped, and reinstalled in the engine without doing the engine any harm.

When, and if, a plug fouls and beings to misfire, you will have to investigate, correct the cause of the fouling, and either clean or replace the plug.

There are several reasons why a spark plug will foul and you can learn which is at fault by just looking at the plug. A few of the most common reasons for plug fouling, and a description of the fouled plug's appearance, are listed in the Color Section, which also offers solutions to the problems.

SPARK PLUG HEAT RANGE

Spark plug heat range is the ability of the plug to dissipate heat. The longer the insulator (or the farther it extends into the engine), the hotter the plug will operate; the shorter the insulator the cooler it will operate. A plug that absorbs little heat and remains too cool will quickly accumulate deposits of oil and carbon since it is not hot enough to burn them off. This leads to plug fouling and consequently to misfiring. A plug that absorbs too much heat will have no deposits, but, due to the excessive heat, the electrodes will burn away quickly and in some instances, preignition may result. Preignition takes place when plug tips get so hot that they glow sufficiently to ignite the fuel/air mixture before the actual spark occurs. This early ignition will usually cause a pinging during low speeds and heavy loads.

The general rule of thumb for choosing the correct heat range when picking a spark plug is: if most of your driving is long distance, high speed travel, use a colder plug; if most of your driving is stop and to, use a hotter plug. Original equipment plugs are compromise plugs, but most people never have occasion to change their

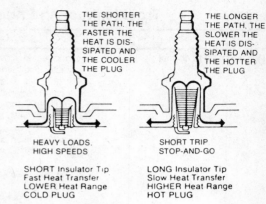

THE SHORTER THE PATH, THE FASTER THE HEAT IS DISSIPATED AND THE COOLER THE PLUG

THE LONGER THE PATH, THE SLOWER THE HEAT IS DISSIPATED AND THE HOTTER THE PLUG

HEAVY LOADS, HIGH SPEEDS

SHORT Insulator Tip
Fast Heat Transfer
LOWER Heat Range
COLD PLUG

SHORT TRIP STOP-AND-GO

LONG Insulator Tip
Slow Heat Transfer
HIGHER Heat Range
HOT PLUG

Spark plug heat range

plugs from the factory-recommended heat range.

REMOVAL AND INSTALLATION

1. If the spark plug wires are not numbered (by cylinder) place a piece of masking tape on each wire and number it.

2. Grasp each wire by the rubber boot. Twist and pull the boot and wire from the spark plug. Never pull on the plug wire alone--you may damage the conductor inside.

3. Use a spark plug socket, loosen the plugs slightly and wipe or blow all dirt away from around the plug base.

4. Unscrew and remove the spark plugs from the engine. Clean, regap or replace as necessary. If you do not number the plug wires and get mixed up on their correct location, refer to the firing order illustrations. Firing order is: 1-3-4-2.

5. If, after removing and examining the spark plugs you feel that cleaning and

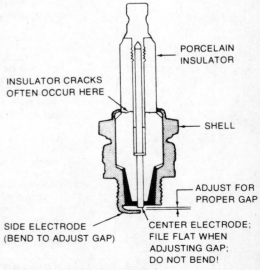

PORCELAIN INSULATOR

INSULATOR CRACKS OFTEN OCCUR HERE

SHELL

ADJUST FOR PROPER GAP

SIDE ELECTRODE (BEND TO ADJUST GAP)

CENTER ELECTRODE; FILE FLAT WHEN ADJUSTING GAP; DO NOT BEND!

Cross section of a spark plug

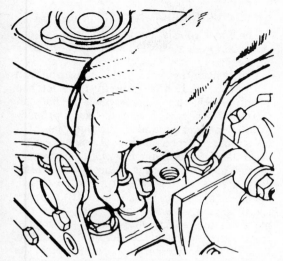

Twist and pull the rubber boot to remove the spark plug wires; never pull on the wire itself

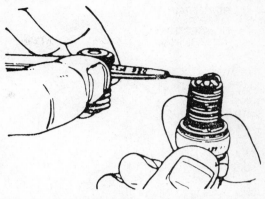

Always use a wire gauge to check the electrode gap

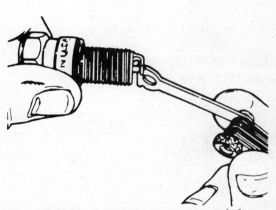

Adjust the electrode gap by bending the side electrode

regapping them is all that is necessary; use a stiff wire brush and clean all the carbon deposits from the electrodes and insulator or take the plugs to a service center and have them cleaned in a plug cleaning machine. New spark plugs come pre-gapped, however different models require different size gaps. Always check the gap and reset if necessary.

6. To set the gap on new or cleaned spark plug, use a spark plug wire feeler gauge. The wire gauge should pass through the electrodes with just a slight drag. Use the electrode bending tool on the end of the gauge to adjust the gap. Never attempt to adjust the center electrode.

7. Put a drop of oil on the base threads of the plug. Start the spark plug into the cylinder

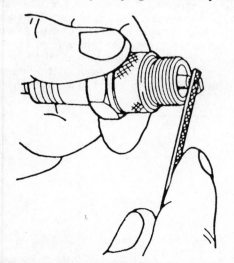

Plugs that are in good condition can be filed and reused

head by hand. Use a socket and tighten to no more than 21 ft. lbs.

Spark Plug Wires

Visually inspect the spark plug cables for burns, cuts, or breaks in the insulation. Check the spark plug boots and the nipples on the distributor cap and coil. Replace any damaged wiring. If no physical damage is obvious, the wires can be checked with an ohmmeter for excessive resistance and continuity. Resistance should be 5000Ω per one foot of cable. Measure the resistance with the plug wire still attached to the distributor cap.

When installing a new set of spark plug cables, replace the cables one at a time so there will be no mixup. Start by replacing the longest cable first. Install the boot firmly over the spark plug. Route the wire exactly the same as the original. Insert the nipple into the tower on the distributor cap. Repeat the process for each cable.

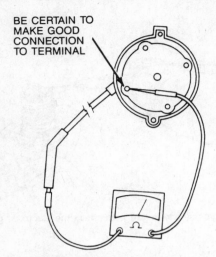

BE CERTAIN TO
MAKE GOOD
CONNECTION
TO TERMINAL

Measuring spark plug wire resistance

Distributor Cap and Rotor
REMOVAL AND INSTALLATION

1. Mark the plug wires to assure proper sequence during installation.

2. Remove the spark plug wires from the distributor cap. Remove the coil high tension wire from the distributor cap.

3. Remove the two cap to distributor mounting screws and remove the distribytor cap.

4. Remove the cover and the rotor. Remove the gasket from the cover.

5. Inspect the cap and rotor for carbon tracking and cracks, or wear. Peplace as necessary.

6. Install the gasket, cover and rotor.

7. Positon the cap on the distributor, be sure the locating tabs are in the correct location.

8. Secure the two mounting screws.

9. Install the spark plug wires in their corect locations. Install the coil high tension lead.

FIRING ORDER

To avoid confusion, replace spark plug wires one at a time.

Electronic Ignition System

The Ford Probe is equipped with an electronic ignition system controlled by the Ford EEC system.

The ignition system on the non-turbo is a transistorized, high-energy type with a vacuum/mechanical spark advance mechanism. Current flows to the ignition coil's primary winding and is grounded through the ECA (electronic control assembly). A magnetic pickup in the distributor aligns with the distributor sensor coil and current is induced which closes an electronic switch. With the switch closed, voltage is applied to both sides of the primary coil. Applying voltage to both sides of the primary winding effectively removes the ground from the winding and interrupts its current flow. When the current flow is interrupted, the high voltage induced in the coil's secondary winding grounds through the distributor to the spark plug.

The ignition system used on the turbo engine incorporates an ignition module and an electronic spark advance system controlled by the ECA (electronic control assembly). The ignition module is mounted to the side of the ignition coil. Current flows through the ignition coil's primary winding and is grounded through the ignition module. When the ECA sends an ignition signal to the ignition module, an electronic switch in the module opens and interrupts current flow through the primary winding. With the current flow interrupted, the high voltage induced in the ignition coil's secondary winding grounds through the distributor to the spark plug.

The Electronic Engine Control (EEC) System is a controlling system designed to optimize tailpipe emissions, fuel economy, driveability, and performance. This is accomplished by means of an onboard Electronic Control Assembly (ECA) which receives inputs from various sensors. The ECA makes computations based on these inputs, and then sends controlling signals to various components to achieve desired

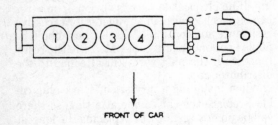

FRONT OF CAR

Ford Motor Co. (Mazda) 2.2L OHC engine
Firing order: 1-3-4-2
Non-turbocharged engine

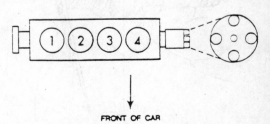

FRONT OF CAR

Ford Motor Co. (Mazda) 2.2L OHC engine
Firing order: 1-3-4-2
Turbocharged engine

Firing Order: 1-3-4-2

air/fuel ratio, ignition, EGR and idle speed operations. The 2.2L engine, in the Probe, uses an electronic fuel injection (EFI) system that is classified as a multi-point, pulse time, mass airflow, injection system. Fuel is supplied by an electric fuel pump/sender unit. With the ignition switch in Start or Run, battery voltage is applied to one coil of the Fuel Pump Relay through the Neutral Safety Switch (ATX) or the Start Interlock Switch (MTX) when they are closed. When the second coil of the Fuel Pump Relay receives a ground through the

ECA, battery voltage is applied through the Inertia Switch to the pump of the Fuel Pump/Sender Unit.

EEC System inputs consist of a Knock Sensor (turbo only) which detects engine knock and sends a signal to the Knock Control Unit and ECA so that ignition timing and/or Turbocharger Control Valve position can be adjusted. The EGR Position Sensor detects the position of the EGR Control Valve and relays this information to the ECA (turbo and Calif. models). The Electrical Load Unit detects when an elec-

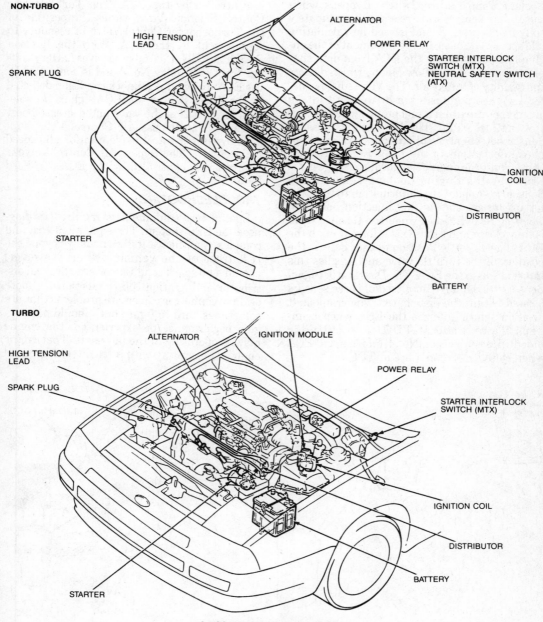

Ignition system components

trical load is been applied and signals the ECA to maintain proper idle speed with the engine load. The Power Steering Pressure Switch informs the ECA of power steering pump operation when the steering wheel is turned. The Neutral Gear Switch (MTX) signals the ECA when the gear selector is in the neutral position. The Clutch Switch (MTX) informs the ECA when the clutch is depressed. The Exhaust Gas Oxygen (EGO) Sensor sends a voltage signal to the ECA which indicates the oxygen content in the exhaust gases. Radiator coolant temperature is detected by the Engine Coolant Temperature Switch. It opens when the coolant temperature reaches approximately sixty-two degrees F. and is used for calculating idle speed. The basic fuel requirement of the engine is determined by the ECA from data supplied by the Vane Airflow Meter, which detects the quanity of intake air. The Vane Airflow Meter also incorporates a sensor to detect intake air temperature and a fuel pump switch to control the fuel pump. The Barometric Pressure Sensor detects atmospheric pressure and supplies information to the ECA. Engine coolant throughout the engine temperature range is detected by the Engine Coolant Temperature Sensor. It supplies this information to the ECA for use in calculating fuel injection amounts. The Idle Switch closes when the throttle valve is fully closed and sends this information to the ECA. The Throttle Position Sensor detects the position of the throttle valve and supplies this information to the ECA. The Distributor Signal Sensors (turbo) are comprised of three sensors located within the distributor. The crankshaft position sensor informs the ECA when cylinders 1 and 3 are at TDC. The cylinder indentification sensor No. 4 informs the ECA when cylinders 2 and 4 are at TDC.

Electronic Control Assembly controlled components are; the EGR Control Solenoid Valve which controls the amount of vacuum applied to the EGR control valve. With the Ignition Switch in RUN, the valve receives battery voltage from EFI Relay No. 2 and is controlled by the ECA. The Pressure Regulator Control Solenoid Valve controls the vacuum to the fuel pressure regulator. It prevents percolation of the fuel during idle or after the engine is restarted when it is at normal operating temperature. With the Ignition Switch in RUN, this valve receives battery voltage from EFI Relay No.2 and is controlled by the ECA. The Turbocharger Control Solenoid Valve varies the position of the Turbocharger Contol Valve in response to signals sent by the ECA. With the Ignition Switch in RUN, this valve receives battery voltage from EFI Relay No. 2 and is controlled by the ECA. In event of a knock condition detected by the Knock Sensor, the ECA signals the solenoid to reposition the valve and decrease boost pressure. The Bypass Air Control Valve supplies bypass air into the plenum for idle speed maintenance. The Bypass Air Control Valve is electronically controlled by the ECA. (@ Ford Motor Co.).

TROUBLESHOOTING

Special test equipment is required to diagnose the EEC system. The equipment cost and complexity of the testing are usually beyond the resources of the vehicle owner. However, should a no spark condition occur: check all distributor and ignition coil connections. A loose or dirty connector can create problems that are sometimes hard to figure out. Should poor engine performance be experienced; the engine may be operating in the fail mode. That is, the engine is operating with a fixed ten degree be-

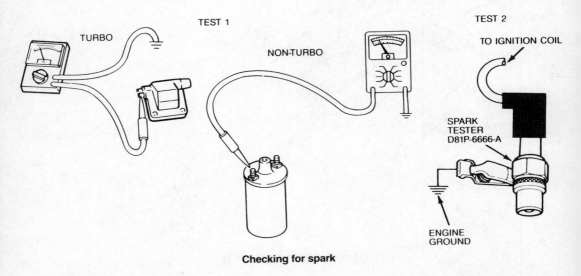

TEST 1

TURBO

NON-TURBO

TEST 2

TO IGNITION COIL

SPARK TESTER D81P-6666-A

ENGINE GROUND

Checking for spark

fore top dead center spark timing, and the EGR system is not operating. If this case exists, EEC system servicing is required. To check for spark, connect a test spark plug to the coil wire and crank the engine briefly. If spark jumps the air gap it is all right. If no spark, the ignition coil, ignition module or high tension wire should be suspect. See Chapter 3 for coil resistance testing.

Ignition Timing

Ignition timing is the measurement, in degrees of crankshaft rotation, of the point at which the spark plugs fire in each of the cylinders. It is measured in degrees before or after Top Dead Center (TDC) of the compression stroke. Base ignition timing is controlled by the distributor body location on the engine.

Ideally, the air/fuel mixture in the cylinder will be ignited by the spark plug just as the piston passes TDC of the compression stroke. If this happens, the piston will be beginning the power stroke just as the compressed and ignited air/fuel mixture starts to expand. The expansion of the air/fuel mixture then forces the piston down on the power stroke and turns the crankshaft.

Because it takes a fraction of a second for the spark plug to ignite the mixture in the cylinder, and the spark plug must fire a little before the piston reaches TDC. Otherwise, the mixture will not be completely ignited as the piston passes TDC and the full power of the explosion will not be used by the engine.

The timing measurement is given in degrees of crankshaft rotation before the piston reaches TDC (BTDC). If the setting for the ignition times is 5 degrees BTDC, each spark plug must fire 5 degrees before each piston reaches TDC.

This only holds true, however, when the engine is at idle speed.

As the engine speed increases, the pistons go faster. The spark plugs have to ignite the fuel even sooner if it is to be completely ignited when the piston reaches TDC. To do this, the distributor has a means to advance the timing of the spark as the engine speed increases. This is sometimes accomplished by centrifugal weights within the distributor and a vacuum diaphragm mounted on the side of the distributor. Or, in some cases, is controlled by an electronic control unit that receives engine performance information from various sensors and sets the ignition timing to meet the engine's requirements.

If the ignition is set too far advanced (BTDC), the ignition and expansion of the fuel in the cylinder will occur too soon and tend to force the piston down while it is still traveling up. This causes engine ping. If the ignition spark is set too far retarded after TDC (ATDC), the piston will have already passed TDC and started on its way down when the fuel is ignited. This will cause the piston to be forced down for only a portion of its travel. This will result in poor engine performance and lack of power.

The ignition timing is checked with an inductive timing light. This device is connected in series with the No. 1 spark plug or the coil wire, depending on type of timing light. The current that fires the spark plug also causes the timing light to flash.

CAUTION: *When making any adjustments with the engine running, or with the ignition switch ON, and the engine not running: be careful of the electric cooling fan blades and component drive belts.*

Ignition timing should always be checked as a part of any tune-up.

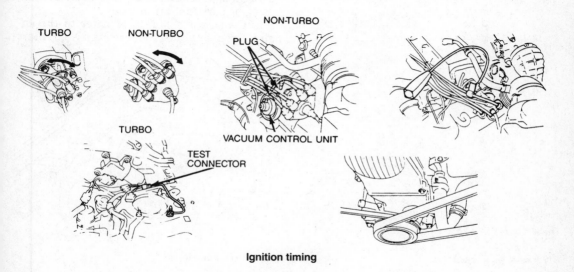

Ignition timing

To adjust ignition timing:

1. Attach the timing light according to the instructions that came with the light.

2. Locate the timing tab on the front of the engine near the crankshaft pulley. Mark the appropriate line (check tune-up specifications), and the notch in the crankshaft pulley with chalk so they will be more visible.

3. Disconnect and plug the hoses to the vacuum advance unit on the distributor on non-turbo models. On turbo equipped models, connect a jumper wire between the test connector pin No. 1 and ground.

4. Make sure all accessories are turned off. Start the engine and allow it to reach operating temperature. Make sure the idle rpm is correct.

5. Shine the timing light at the crankshaft pulley marks. The marked line should align with pulley notch.

6. If the marks do not align, loosen the distributor mounting bolts and rotate the distributor slowly in either direction to align the timing marks. Timing is:

- Non-turbo — 5–7° BTDC
- Turbo models — 8–10° BTDC

7. Tighten the mounting bolts when the ignition timing is correct. Shut off engine and remove timing light.

Valve Lash

Valve adjustment determines how far the valves enter the cylinder and how long they stay open and closed.

If the valve clearance is too large, part of the lift of the camshaft will be used in removing the excessive clearance. Consequently, the valve will not be opening as far as it should. This condition has two effects: the valve train components will emit a tapping sound as they take up the excessive clearance and the engine will perform poorly because the valves don't open fully and allow the proper amount of gases to flow into and out of the engine.

If the valve clearance is too small, the intake valve and the exhaust valves will open too far and they will not fully seat on the cylinder head when they close. When a valve seats itself on the cylinder head, it does two things: it seals the combustion chamber so that none of the gases in the cylinder escape and it cools itself by transferring some of the heat it absorbs from the combustion in the cylinder to the cylinder head and to the engine's cooling system. If the valve clearance is too small, the engine will run poorly because of the gases escaping from the combustion chamber. The valves will also become overheated and will warp, since they cannot transfer heat unless they are touching the valve seat in the cylinder head.

VALVE ADJUSTMENT

Hydraulic lash adjusters are incorporated in the valve rocker arms. No manual adjustment is required or possible. Service is by replacement.

Idle Speed and Mixture Adjustments

Mixture adjustment is factory set and controlled by the EEC system, adjustment should not be attempted.

IDLE SPEED

1. Turn all accessories OFF.

2. Firmly set the parking brake and position the gear shift selector in neutral (manual transaxle), or park (auto transaxle).

3. Connect a digital tachometer to the engine. Ground the test connector pin No. 1. Start

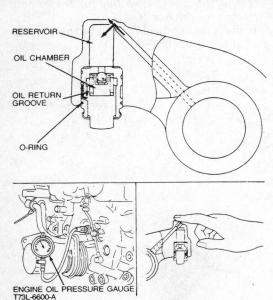

ENGINE OIL PRESSURE GAUGE
T73L-6600-A

Hydraulic lash adjuster

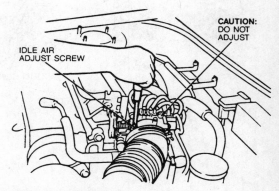

Idle speed adjustment

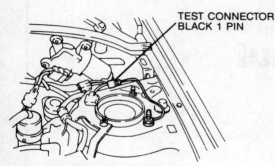

TEST CONNECTOR
BLACK 1 PIN

Ground black number one pin

and operate the engine at 2500–3000 rpm for three minutes.

4. Check the idle speed, it should be between 725–750 rpm.

5. Adjust the idle speed as required by turning the air adjusting screw located on the throttle body.

6. After adjustment is completed, shut off the engine and remove the test equipment and jumper wire.

Engine and Engine Overhaul

3

ENGINE ELECTRICAL

Understanding the Engine Electrical System

The engine electrical system can be broken down into three separate and distinct systems:

1. The starting system.
2. The charging system.
3. The ignition system.

BATTERY AND STARTING SYSTEM

Basic Operating Principles

The battery is the first link in the chain of mechanisms which work together to provide cranking of the automobile engine. In most modern cars, the battery is a lead/acid electrochemical device consisting of six 2v subsections connected in series so the unit is capable of producing approximately 12v of electrical pressure. Each subsection, or cell, consists of a series of positive and negative plates held a short distance apart in a solution of sulfuric acid and water. The two types of plates are of dissimilar metals. This causes a chemical reaction to be set up, and it is this reaction which produces current flow from the battery when its positive and negative terminals are connected to an electrical appliance such as a lamp or motor. The continued transfer of electrons would eventually convert the sulfuric acid in the electrolyte to water, and make the two plates identical in chemical composition. As electrical energy is removed from the battery, its voltage output tends to drop. Thus, measuring battery voltage and battery electrolyte composition are two ways of checking the ability of the unit to supply power. During the starting of the engine, electrical energy is removed from the battery. However, if the charging circuit is in good condition and the operating conditions are normal, the power removed from the battery will be replaced by the generator (or alternator) which will force electrons back through the battery, reversing the normal flow, and restoring the battery to its original chemical state.

The battery and starting motor are linked by very heavy electrical cables designed to minimize resistance to the flow of current. Generally, the major power supply cable that leaves the battery goes directly to the starter, while other electrical system needs are supplied by a smaller cable. During starter operation, power flows from the battery to the starter and is grounded through the car's frame and the battery's negative ground strap.

The starting motor is a specially designed, direct current electric motor capable of producing a very great amount of power for its size. One thing that allows the motor to produce a great deal of power is its tremendous rotating speed. It drives the engine through a tiny pinion gear (attached to the starter's armature), which drives the very large flywheel ring gear at a greatly reduced speed. Another factor allowing it to produce so much power is that only intermittent operation is required of it. This, little allowance for air circulation is required, and the windings can be built into a very small space.

The starter solenoid is a magnetic device which employs the small current supplied by the starting switch circuit of the ignition switch. This magnetic action moves a plunger which mechanically engages the starter and electrically closes the heavy switch which connects it to the battery. The starting switch circuit consists of the starting switch contained within the ignition switch, a transmission neutral safety switch or clutch pedal switch, and the wiring necessary to connect these in series with the starter solenoid or relay.

A pinion, which is a small gear, is mounted to a one-way drive clutch. This clutch is splined to the starter armature shaft. When the ignition switch is moved to the **start** position, the solenoid plunger slides the pinion toward the flywheel ring gear via a collar and spring. If the teeth on the pinion and flywheel match properly, the pinion will engage the flywheel immediately. If the gear teeth butt one another, the spring will be compressed and will force the gears to mesh as soon as the starter turns far enough to allow them to do so. As the solenoid plunger reaches the end of its travel, it closes the contacts that connect the battery and starter and then the engine is cranked.

As soon as the engine starts, the flywheel ring gear begins turning fast enough to drive the pinion at an extremely high rate of speed. At this point, the one-way clutch begins allowing the pinion to spin faster than the starter shaft so that the starter will not operate at excessive speed. When the ignition switch is released from the starter position, the solenoid is de-energized, and a spring contained within the solenoid assembly pulls the gear out of mesh and interrupts the current flow to the starter.

Some starter employ a separate relay, mounted away from the starter, to switch the motor and solenoid current on and off. The relay thus replaces the solenoid electrical switch, buy does not eliminate the need for a solenoid mounted on the starter used to mechanically engage the starter drive gears. The relay is used to reduce the amount of current the starting switch must carry.

THE CHARGING SYSTEM

Basic Operating Principles

The automobile charging system provides electrical power for operation of the vehicle's ignition and starting systems and all the electrical accessories. The battery services as an electrical surge or storage tank, storing (in chemical form) the energy originally produced by the engine driven generator. The system also provides a means of regulating generator output to protect the battery from being overcharged and to avoid excessive voltage to the accessories.

The storage battery is a chemical device incorporating parallel lead plates in a tank containing a sulfuric acid/water solution. Adjacent plates are slightly dissimilar, and the chemical reaction of the two dissimilar plates produces electrical energy when the battery is connected to a load such as the starter motor. The chemical reaction is reversible, so that when the generator is producing a voltage (electrical pressure) greater than that produced by the battery, electricity is forced into the battery, and the battery is returned to its fully charged state.

The vehicle's generator is driven mechanically, through V-belts, by the engine crankshaft. It consists of two coils of fine wire, one stationary (the stator), and one movable (the rotor). The rotor may also be known as the armature, and consists of fine wire wrapped around an iron core which is mounted on a shaft. The electricity which flows through the two coils of wire (provided initially by the battery in some cases) creates an intense magnetic field around both rotor and stator, and the interaction between the two fields creates voltage, allowing the generator to power the accessories and charge the battery.

There are two types of generators: the earlier is the direct current (DC) type. The current produced by the DC generator is generated in the armature and carried off the spinning armature by stationary brushes contacting the commutator. The commutator is a series of smooth metal contact plates on the end of the armature. The commutator is a series of smooth metal contact plates on the end of the armature. The commutator plates, which are separated from one another by a very short gap, are connected to the armature circuits so that current will flow in one directions only in the wires carrying the generator output. The generator stator consists of two stationary coils of wire which draw some of the output current of the generator to form a powerful magnetic field and create the interaction of fields which generates the voltage. The generator field is wired in series with the regulator.

Newer automobiles use alternating current generators or alternators, because they are more efficient, can be rotated at higher speeds, and have fewer brush problems. In an alternator, the field rotates while all the current produced passes only through the stator winding. The brushes bear against continuous slip rings rather than a commutator. This causes the current produced to periodically reverse the direction of its flow. Diodes (electrical one-way switches) block the flow of current from traveling in the wrong direction. A series of diodes is wired together to permit the alternating flow of the stator to be converted to a pulsating, but unidirectional flow at the alternator output. The alternator's field is wired in series with the voltage regulator.

The regulator consists of several circuits. Each circuit has a core, or magnetic coil of wire, which operates a switch. Each switch is connected to ground through one or more resistors. The coil of wire responds directly to system voltage. When the voltage reaches the required level, the magnetic field created by the winding of wire closes the switch and inserts a resistance into the generator field circuit, thus reducing the output. The contacts of the switch cycle open and close many times each second to precisely control voltage.

While alternators are self-limiting as far as maximum current is concerned, DC generators employ a current regulating circuit which responds directly to the total amount of current flowing through the generator circuit rather than to the output voltage. The current regulator is similar to the voltage regulator except that all system current must flow through the energizing coil on its way to the various accessories.

Ignition Coil

TESTING

The fastest way to check is by substituting a know good coil. If a coil is not on hand, proceed with one or more of the following tests.

1. With the ignition switch on the ON position measure the voltage at the negative terminal of the ignition coil. If zero volts are shown, there is an open circuit in the coil.

2. On non-turbo models; check the ignition coil resistance. If the engine will run allow it to reach normal operating temperature (the ignition coil should be hot). Shut off the engine and disconnect the high tension lead (coil wire) from the coil tower.

3. Measure primary resistance with an ohmmeter, connecting the coil minus and plus primary terminals. Resistance should be; 1.04–1.27Ω.

4. Measure the secondary resistance by connecting the ohnmeter between the contacts in the coil tower and the plus primary terminal. Resistance should be; 7.1-9.7kΩ.

5. Replace the coil if the voltage tests show zero volts or the resistances are not within specs.

6. On turbo models; check resistance at the ignition coil connector. Check the primary resistance between the BL to BL/W. Resistance should be 0.72–0.88Ω. Check the secondary resistance between the BK/W to secondary and BK/W to case (see illustration). Secondary resistance should be 10.3-13.9kΩ. Case resistance should be 10MΩ minimum for both turbo and non-turbo.

REMOVAL AND INSTALLATION

1. On non-turbo models, disconnect the negative battery cable.

2. Remove the high tension lead from the coil in a twisting pulling manner.

3. Remove the distributor wiring harness from the coil making note of its position for correct installation.

4. Remove the mounting nuts and the coil and bracket assembly.

System	Resistance @ 20ºC (68ºF)	
	Turbo	Non-Turbo
Primary	0.72 to 0.88 ohm	1.04 to 1.27 ohm
Secondary	10.3 to 13.9 K ohm	7.1 to 9.7 K ohm
Case	10 M ohm min.	10 M ohm min.

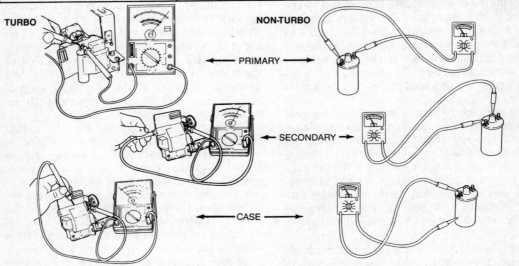

Checking coil resistance

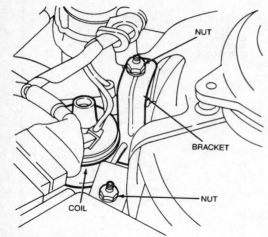

Non-turbo coil mounting

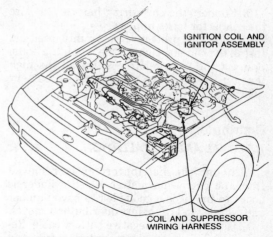

Turbo coil and component location

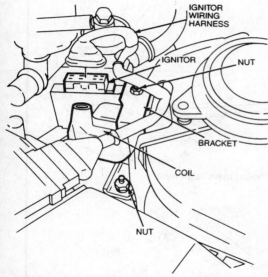

Turbo coil mounting

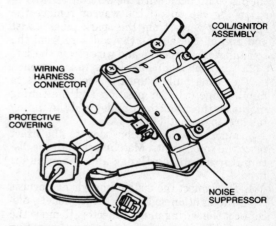

Turbo coil and igniter assembly

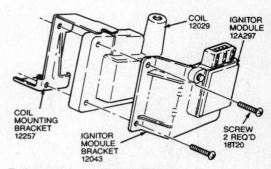

Turbo module to coil assembly

5. Place the coil and bracket assembly in position and secure with the mounting screws. Connect the distributor wiring harness and high tension lead. Connect the negative battery cable.

6. On turbo models; Disconnect the negative battery cable.

7. Remove the high tension lead from the coil in a twisting pulling manner.

8. Disconnect the igniter wiring harness and remove the mounting nuts.

9. Lift the coil and igniter assembly to gain access to the coil and noise suppressor harness. Disconnect the harness.

10. Slide the protective cover back to gain access to the wiring harness connector. Disconnect the coil wiring harness. Remove the noise suppressor.

11. Remove the mounting screws and the igniter module.

12. Remove the igniter module mounting bracket and the coil.

13. Install the coil and igniter module with their mounting screws.

14. Install the ignition module and the noise suppressor.

15. Connect the coil wiring harness, be sure the connector locks in place.

16. Slide the protective cover into position. Install the coil and tighten the mounting bolts. Connect the ignitor harness. Install the high tension lead. Connect the negative battery cable.

Distributor

REMOVAL AND INSTALLATION

Although the distributor can be removed from the engine no matter which cylinder is about to fire, it is a good idea to have number one cylinder at TDC before distributor removal.

1. Disconnect the negative battery cable. Remove the distributor cap mounting screws and the distributor cap, with the wires attached. Position the cap out of the way or remove the spark plug wires from the spark plugs (twist and pull on the boots), the coil wire from the coil and remove the cap and wires from the car.

2. Turn the engine clockwise (use a wrench on the crank pulley) until the rotor points to number one cylinder position and the timing marks on the crankshaft pulley and the timing tab are aligned at TDC.

3. Mark the distributor body to the exact place the rotor points. Matchmark both the distributor mounting flange and the cylinder head.

4. Disconnect the distributor wiring harness from the ignition coil or on turbo models, disconnect the wiring plug connector. Remove the vacuum lines from the advance unit (non-turbo). Loosen and remove the distributor to cylin-

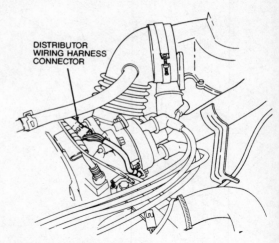

DISTRIBUTOR WIRING HARNESS CONNECTOR

Distributor harness removal-turbo

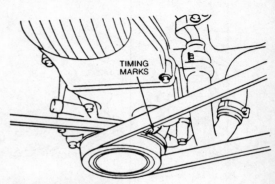

TIMING MARKS

Timing mark alignment

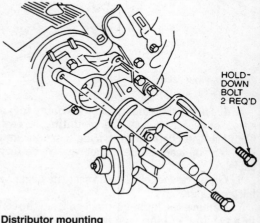

HOLD-DOWN BOLT 2 REQ'D

Distributor mounting

der head retaining bolts. Lift the distributor straight away from the cylinder head.

5. If the engine has not been disturbed, i.e. the crankshaft was not turned, then install the distributor by placing the rotor in the same positon it was in when the distributor was removed, carefully align the matchmarks and and position the distributor into the cylinder head

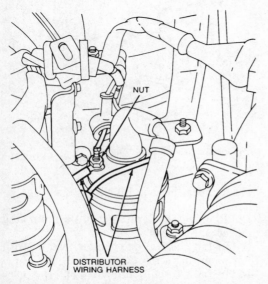

NUT

DISTRIBUTOR WIRING HARNESS

Distributor wiring harness removal; non-turbo

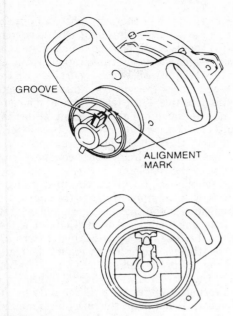

GROOVE

ALIGNMENT
MARK

Distributor alignment

adaptor. Install the mounting bolts. Always check the ignition timing whenever the distributor has been removed.

6. If the engine has been disturbed, i.e. rotated while the distributor was out, proceed as follows:

7. Turn the crankshaft so that the No. 1 piston is on the compression stroke and the timing marks are aligned.

8. Turn the distributor shaft so that the rotor points to the line you marked on the distributor. If you did not mark the distributor, line up the groove and alignment mark on the bottom of the distributor.

9. Insert the distributor into the cylinder head adapter and install the mounting bolts. Do not tighten the retaining bolts, you still have to check the engine timing.

10. Install the rotor, cap, plug wires, coil lead, primary lead (or harness) and connect the vacuum hoses. Connect the negative battery cable. Start the engine, allow it to reach operating temperature and check the ignition timing.

Alternator

The alternator charging system is a negative (−) ground system which consists of an alternator, a regulator, a charge indicator, a storage battery and wiring connecting the components, and fuse link wire.

The alternator is belt-driven from the engine. Energy is supplied from the alternator/regulator system to the rotating field through two brushes to two slip-rings. The slip-rings are mounted on the rotor shaft and are connected to the field coil. This energy supplied to the rotating field from the battery is called excitation current and is used to initially energize the field to begin the generation of electricity. Once the alternator starts to generate electricity, the excitation current comes from its own output rather than the battery.

The alternator produces power in the form of alternating current. The alternating current is rectified by 6 diodes into direct current. The direct current is used to charge the battery and power the rest of the electrical system.

When the ignition key is turned on, current flows from the battery, through the charging system indicator light on the instrument panel, to the voltage regulator, and to the alternator. Since the alternator is not producing any current, the alternator warning light comes on. When the engine is started, the alternator begins to produce current and turns the alternator light off. As the alternator turns and produces current, the current is divided in two ways: part to the battery to charge the battery and power the electrical components of the vehicle, and part is returned to the alternator to enable it to increase its output. In this situation, the alternator is receiving current from the battery and from itself. A voltage regulator is wired into the current supply to the alternator to prevent it from receiving too much current which would cause it to put out too much current. Conversely, if the voltage regulator does not allow the alternator to receive enough current, the battery will not be fully charged and will eventually go dead.

The battery is connected to the alternator at all times, whether the ignition key is turned on or not. If the battery were shorted to ground, the alternator would also be shorted. This would damage the alternator. To prevent this, a fuse link is installed in the wiring between the battery and the alternator. If the battery is shorted, the fuse link is melted, protecting the alternator.

PRECAUTIONS

Your car is equipped with an alternator. Unlike the direct current (DC) generators used on many old cars, there are several precautions which must be strictly observed in order to avoid damaging the unit. They are:

1. Always observe proper polarity of the battery connections; be especially careful when jump starting the car. (See chapter one for jump starting procedures).

2. Never ground or short out the alternator or alternator regulator terminals.

3. Never operate the alternator with any of its or the battery's lead wires disconnected.

4. Always remove the battery or at least disconnect the ground cable while charging.

5. Always disconnect the battery ground cable while repairing or replacing an electrical component.

6. Never use a fast battery charger to jump start a dead battery.

7. Never attempt to polarize an alternator.

8. Never subject the alternator to excessive heat or dampness (for instance, steam cleaning the engine).

9. Never use arc welding equipment on the car with the alternator connected.

CHARGING SYSTEM TROUBLESHOOTING

There are many possible ways in which the charging system can malfunction. Often the source of a problem is difficult to diagnose, requiring special equipment and a good deal of experience. This is usually not the case, however, where the charging system fails completely and causes the dash board warning light to come on or the battery to become dead. To troubleshoot a complete system failure only two pieces of equipment are needed: a test light, to determine that current is reaching a certain point; and a current indicator (ammeter), to determine the direction of the current flow and its measurement in amps.

This test works under three assumptions:

1. The battery is known to be good and fully charged.

2. The alternator belt is in good condition and adjusted to the proper tension.

3. All connections in the system are clean and tight.

NOTE: *In order for the current indicator to give a valid reading, the car must be equipped with battery cables which are of the same gauge size and quality as original equipment battery cables.*

1. Turn off all electrical components on the car. Make sure the doors of the car are closed. If the car is equipped with a clock, disconnect the clock by removing the lead wire from the rear of the clock. Disconnect the positive battery cable from the battery and connect the ground wire on a test light to the disconnected positive battery cable. Touch the probe end of the test light to the positive battery post. The test light should not light. If the test light does light, there is a short or open circuit on the car.

2. Disconnect the voltage regulator wiring harness connector at the voltage regulator. Turn on the ignition key. Connect the wire on a test light to a good ground (engine bolt). Touch the probe end of a test light to the ignition wire connector into the voltage regulator wiring connector. This wire corresponds to the I terminal on the regulator. If the test light goes on, the charging system warning light circuit is complete. If the test light does not come on and the warning light on the instrument panel is on, either the resistor wire, which is parallel with the warning light, or the wiring to the voltage regulator, is defective. If the test light does not come on and the warning light is not on, either the bulb is defective or the power supply wire form the battery through the ignition switch to the bulb has an open circuit. Connect the wiring harness to the regulator.

3. Examine the fuse link wire in the wiring harness from the starter relay to the alternator. If the insulation on the wire is cracked or split, the fuse link may be melted. Connect a test light to the fuse link by attaching the ground wire on the test light to an engine bolt and touching the probe end of the light to the bottom of the fuse link wire where it splices into the alternator output wire. If the bulb in the test light does not light, the fuse link is melted.

4. Start the engine and place a current indicator on the positive battery cable. Turn off all electrical accessories and make sure the doors are closed. If the charging system is working properly, the gauge will show a draw of less than 5 amps. If the system is not working properly, the gauge will show a draw of more than 5 amps. A charge moves the needle toward the battery, a draw moves the needle away from the battery. Turn the engine off.

5. Disconnect the wiring harness from the voltage regulator at the regulator at the regulator connector. Connect a male spade terminal (solderless connector) to each end of a jumper wire. Insert one end of the wire into the wiring harness connector which corresponds to the A terminal on the regulator. Insert the other end of the wire into the wiring harness connector which corresponds to the F terminal on the regulator. Position the connector with the jumper wire installed so that it cannot contact any metal surface under the hood. Position a current indicator gauge on the positive battery cable. Have an assistant start the engine. Observe the reading on the current indicator. Have your assistant slowly raise the speed of the engine to about 2,000 rpm or until the current indicator needle stops moving, whichever comes first. Do not run the engine for more than a short period of time in this condition. If the wiring harness connector or jumper wire becomes excessively hot during this test, turn off the engine and check for a grounded wire in the regulator wiring harness. If the current indicator shows a charge of about three amps less than the output of the alternator, the alternator is working properly. If the previous tests showed a draw, the voltage regulator is defective. If the gauge

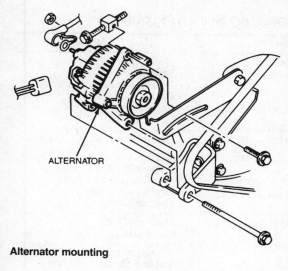

Alternator mounting

does not show the proper charging rate, the alternator is defective.

REMOVAL AND INSTALLATION

1. Disconnect the negative battery cable. Raise and safely support the front of the vehicle.

2. Remove the catalytic converter as follows: remove the flange nuts and washers from both ends. remove the resonator pipe to body insulators. push the exhaust system rearward and remove the converter.

3. Depress the locking tab at the rear of the alternator and remove the wiring harness.

4. Loosen the alternator through bolt and adjustment locking bolt and remove the drive belt.

5. Remove the mounting bolts and the alternator.

6. Place the alternator in position and install the mounting and adjustment bolts loosely. Install and tension the drive belt. Secure the alternator mounting and adjustment bolts. Through bolt torque is 27-38 ft. lbs. Adjusting bolt torque is 13-18 ft. lbs.

7. Connect the alternator wiring harness.

8. Install the catalytic converter using new mounting gaskets.

9. Lower the vehicle. Connect the negative battery cable.

Regulator

The electronic voltage regulator is of the IC (integrated circuit) type and is an internal part of the alternator rotor, brush and brush holder assembly. No adjustment is possible.

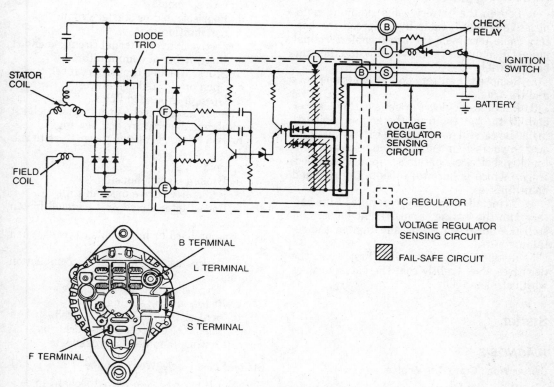

Alternator internal circuits

Troubleshooting Basic Charging System Problems

Problem	Cause	Solution
Noisy alternator	• Loose mountings • Loose drive pulley • Worn bearings • Brush noise • Internal circuits shorted (High pitched whine)	• Tighten mounting bolts • Tighten pulley • Replace alternator • Replace alternator • Replace alternator
Squeal when starting engine or accelerating	• Glazed or loose belt	• Replace or adjust belt
Indicator light remains on or ammeter indicates discharge (engine running)	• Broken fan belt • Broken or disconnected wires • Internal alternator problems • Defective voltage regulator	• Install belt • Repair or connect wiring • Replace alternator • Replace voltage regulator
Car light bulbs continually burn out— battery needs water continually	• Alternator/regulator overcharging	• Replace voltage regulator/alternator
Car lights flare on acceleration	• Battery low • Internal alternator/regulator problems	• Charge or replace battery • Replace alternator/regulator
Low voltage output (alternator light flickers continually or ammeter needle wanders)	• Loose or worn belt • Dirty or corroded connections • Internal alternator/regulator problems	• Replace or adjust belt • Clean or replace connections • Replace alternator or regulator

Battery

REMOVAL AND INSTALLATION

1. Loosen the battery cable clamping nuts, negative (ground) cable first. Spread the battery cable terminals (or use a cable terminal puller). Remove the negative cable and then the positive cable.

2. Remove the battery hold-down frame nuts and the frame.

3. Put on work gloves or use a battery carrier and lift the battery from the engine compartment. Be careful not to tip the battery and spill acid on yourself or the car during removal. Automotive batteries contain a sulphuric acid electrolyte which is harmful to skin, clothing and paint finishes.

4. To install the battery; carefully fit the battery into the engine compartment holder. Install the holddown frame and tighten the retaining nuts.

5. Install the positive cable first, then the negative cable. Lightly coat the battery cables with petroleum jelly.

Starter

DIAGNOSIS

Starter Won't Crank The Engine

1. Dead battery.
2. Open starter circuit, such as:

   a. Broken or loose battery cables.

   b. Inoperative starter motor solenoid.

   c. Broken or loose wire from ignition switch to solenoid.

   d. Poor solenoid or starter ground.

   e. Bad ignition switch.

3. Defective starter internal circuit, such as:

   a. Dirty or burnt commutator.

   b. Stuck, worn or broken brushes.

   c. Open or shorted armature.

   d. Open or grounded fields.

4. Starter motor mechanical faults, such as:

   a. Jammed armature end bearings.

   b. Bad bearings, allowing armature to rub fields.

   c. Bent shaft.

   d. Broken starter housing.

   e. Bad starter drive mechanism.

   f. Bad starter drive or flywheel-driven gear.

5. Engine hard or impossible to crank, such as:

   a. Hydrostatic lock, water in combustion chamber.

   b. Crankshaft seizing in bearings.

   c. Piston or ring seizing.

   d. Bent or broken connecting rod.

   e. Seizing of connecting rod bearings.

   f. Flywheel jammed or broken.

Starter Spins Freely, Won't Engage

1. Sticking or broken drive mechanism.
2. Damaged ring gear.

REMOVAL AND INSTALLATION

1. Disconnect the negative battery ground cable from the battery. Raise and safely support the front of the vehicle.

2. If equipped with a manual transaxle, remove the exhaust pipe bracket.

3. Remove the transaxle-to-engine bracket and the intake manifold-to-engine bracket.

4. Disconnect the electrical connections at the starter and remove the wiring.

5. Remove the starter-to-engine mounting bolts and remove the starter.

6. Install the starter and torque the bolts to 23-34 ft. lbs.

7. Connect the wiring to the starter. Torque the starter cable to 90-110 in. lbs.

8. Install the intake manifold-to-engine bracket and torque the mounting bolts to 14-22 ft. lbs.

9. On automatic transaxle models; install the transaxle-to-bell housing bracket and torque the bolt to 66-86 ft. lbs. Tighten all other bolts to 27-38 ft. lbs.

10. On manual transaxle models; torque the transaxle-to-engine bracket bolts to 33-45 ft. lbs. and the exhaust bracket bolts to 32–45 ft. lbs.

11. Lower the vehicle and connect the battery cable.

OVERHAUL

Gear Reduction Type

NOTE: *Starter removed from car.*

1. Remove the wire connecting the starter solenoid to the starter.

2. Remove the two screws holding the solenoid to the starter. Pull the solenoid from the starter. Retain the mounting shims.

3. Scribe an alignment mark on the front cover and body of the starter. Remove the

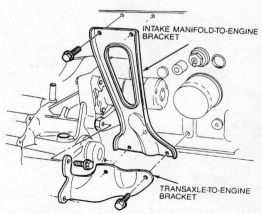

Starter motor bracket removal

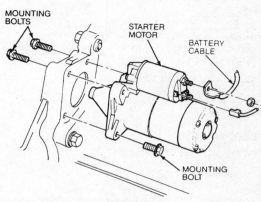

Starter motor mounting bolts

brush plate screws and the two through bolts from the front of the starter.

4. Remove the end cover and brush holder assembly.

5. Remove the armature and field frame. Take care not to loose the ball that is located in the gear assembly.

6. Remove the internal gear gasket, planetary gears, solenoid cover plate and seal and pull the gear assembly from the housing.

7. Pay attention to the direction the drive yoke is facing. Remove the drive yoke from the assembly.

8. Remove the retaining ring from the gear assembly. Remove the drive pinion, internal gear and washer from the driveshaft.

9. Remove the brushes from the brush plate.

10. Service and test the components as required.

11. Lubricate the armature shaft gear, internal and planetary gears, plunger, drive yoke thrust surfaces and the driveshaft splines with Lubriplate 777® or equivalent.

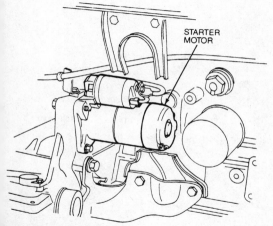

Starter motor mounting

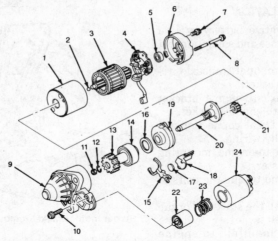

1. FIELD FRAME HOUSING	7. BRUSH PLATE SCREW	13. DRIVE PINION	19. INTERNAL GEAR
2. BALL	8. THROUGH-BOLT	14. OVERRUNNING CLUTCH	20. DRIVESHAFT
3. ARMATURE	9. DRIVE END HOUSING	15. DRIVE YOKE	21. PLANETARY GEAR
4. BRUSH PLATE	10. SOLENOID SCREW	16. WASHER	22. PLUNGER
5. BEARING	11. COLLAR	17. SEAL	23. SPRING
6. END COVER	12. SNAP RING	18. PLATE	24. SOLENOID

Exploded view of the starter motor assembly

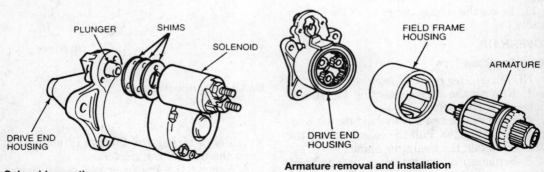

Solenoid mounting

Armature removal and installation

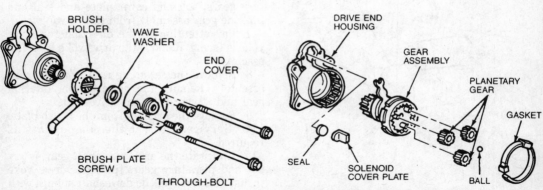

End cover removal and installation

Starter drive removal and installation

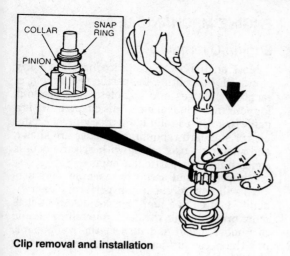

Clip removal and installation

12. Install the brushes in the brush holder. Install the washer, internal gear, drive pinion and collar onto the armature shaft.
13. Install the retaining ring. Press the collar

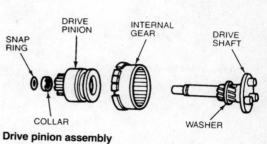

Drive pinion assembly

Troubleshooting Basic Starting System Problems

Problem	Cause	Solution
Starter motor rotates engine slowly	• Battery charge low or battery defective	• Charge or replace battery
	• Defective circuit between battery and starter motor	• Clean and tighten, or replace cables
	• Low load current	• Bench-test starter motor. Inspect for worn brushes and weak brush springs.
	• High load current	• Bench-test starter motor. Check engine for friction, drag or coolant in cylinders. Check ring gear-to-pinion gear clearance.
Starter motor will not rotate engine	• Battery charge low or battery defective	• Charge or replace battery
	• Faulty solenoid	• Check solenoid ground. Repair or replace as necessary.
	• Damage drive pinion gear or ring gear	• Replace damaged gear(s)
	• Starter motor engagement weak	• Bench-test starter motor
	• Starter motor rotates slowly with high load current	• Inspect drive yoke pull-down and point gap, check for worn end bushings, check ring gear clearance
	• Engine seized	• Repair engine
Starter motor drive will not engage (solenoid known to be good)	• Defective contact point assembly	• Repair or replace contact point assembly
	• Inadequate contact point assembly ground	• Repair connection at ground screw
	• Defective hold-in coil	• Replace field winding assembly
Starter motor drive will not disengage	• Starter motor loose on flywheel housing	• Tighten mounting bolts
	• Worn drive end busing	• Replace bushing
	• Damaged ring gear teeth	• Replace ring gear or driveplate
	• Drive yoke return spring broken or missing	• Replace spring
Starter motor drive disengages prematurely	• Weak drive assembly thrust spring	• Replace drive mechanism
	• Hold-in coil defective	• Replace field winding assembly
Low load current	• Worn brushes	• Replace brushes
	• Weak brush springs	• Replace springs

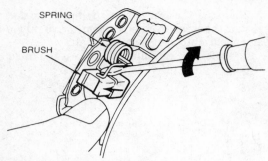

Brush removal and installation

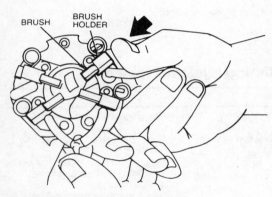

Make sure the brushes move freely

over the ring. Install the drive yoke on the gear assembly (be sure the yoke is facing in the correct direction).

14. Install the gasket on the internal gear. Slide the gear assembly into the drive end housing and install the solenoid cover plate seal and plate.

15. Install the planetary gears and ball. Connect the field frame housing to the drive end housing. Make sure the alignment marks match.

16. Load the brushes into their holders. Position the brush springs so that they will not interfere with assembly.

17. Install the brush plate assembly over the armature. Set the brushes against the commutator.

18. Slide the armature and brush plate assembly into the field frame housing, aligning the marks.

19. Install and tighten the starter motor through bolts and the brush plate end cover.

20. Connect the plunger and spring to the drive yoke. Install the solenoid.

21. Install the starter motor.

ENGINE MECHANICAL

Engine Overhaul Tips

Most engine overhaul procedures are fairly standard. In addition to specific parts replacement procedures and complete specifications for your individual engine, this chapter also is a guide to accepted rebuilding procedures. Examples of standard rebuilding practice are shown and should be used along with specific details concerning your particular engine.

Competent and accurate machine shop services will ensure maximum performance, reliability and engine life. In most instances it is more profitable for the do-it-yourself mechanic to remove, clean and inspect the component, buy the necessary parts and deliver these to a shop for actual machine work.

On the other hand, much of the rebuilding work (crankshaft, block, bearings, piston, rods, and other components) is still within the scope of the do-it-yourself mechanic.

TOOLS

The tools required for an engine overhaul or parts replacement will depend on the depth of your involvement. With a few exceptions, they will be the tools found in a mechanic's tool kit (see Chapter 1). More in-depth work will require any or all of the following: A dial indicator (reading in thousandths) mounted on a universal base. Micrometers and telescope gauges. Jaw and screw-type pullers. A scraper. A valve spring compressor. A ring groove cleaner. A piston ring expander and compressor. A ridge reamer. Cylinder hone or glaze breaker. Plastigage®. An engine stand. Use of most of these tools is illustrated in this chapter. Many can be rented for a one-time use from a local parts jobber or tool supply house specializing in automotive work.

Occasionally, the use of special tools is called for. See the information on Special Tools and the Safety Notice in the front of this book before substituting another tool.

INSPECTION TECHNIQUES

Procedures and specifications are given in this chapter for inspecting, cleaning and assessing the wear limits of most major components. Other procedures such as Magnaflux® and Zyglo® can be used to locate material flaws and stress cracks. Magnaflux® is a magnetic process applicable only to ferrous materials. The Zyglo® process coats the material with a flourescent dye penetrant and can be used on any material. Check for suspected surface cracks can be more readily made using spot check dye. The dye is sprayed onto the suspected area, wiped off and area sprayed with a developer. Cracks will show up brightly.

Aluminum Engine Components

Aluminum has become extremely popular for use in engines, due to its low weight. Observe the following precautions when handling aluminum parts:

Never hot tank aluminum parts (the caustic hot-tank solution will eat the aluminum).

Remove all aluminum parts (identification tag, etc) from engine parts prior to hot-tanking.

Always coat threads lightly with engine oil or anti-seize compounds before installation, to prevent seizure.

Never over-torque bolts or spark plugs, especially in aluminum threads. Stripped threads in any component can be repaired using any of several commercial repair kits (Heli-Coil®, Microdot®, Keenserts®, etc.)

When assembling the engine, any parts that will be in frictional contact must be prelubed to provide lubrication at initial startup. Any product specifically formulated for this purpose can be used, but engine oil is not recommended as a pre-lube.

When semi-permanent (locked, but removable) installation of bolts or nuts is desired, threads should be cleaned and coated with Loctite® or other similar, commercial non-hardening sealant.

Repairing Damaged Threads

Several methods of repairing damaged threads are available. Heli-Coil® (shown hers), Keenserts® and Microdot® are among the most widely used. All involve basically the same principle--drilling out stripped threads, tapping the hole and installing prewound insert--making welding, plugging and oversize fasteners unnecessary.

Two types of thread repair inserts are usually

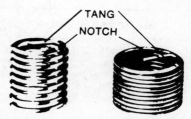

Standard thread repair insert (left), and spark plug thread insert

Drill out the damaged threads with specified drill. Drill completely through the hole or to the bottom of a blind hole

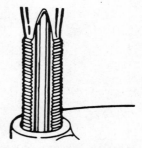

With the tap supplied, tap the hole to receive the thread insert. Keep the tap well oiled and back it out frequently to aovid clogging the threads

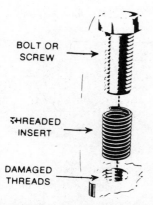

Damaged bolt holes threads can be replaced with thread repair inserts

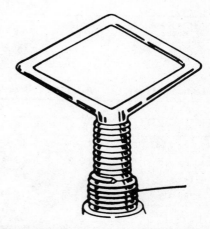

Screw the threaded insert onto the installer tool until the tang engages the slot. Screw the insert into the tapped hole until it is ¼ or ½ turn below the top surface. After installation break off the tang with a hammer and punch

Standard Torque Specifications and Fastener Markings

In the absence of specific torques, the following chart can be used as a guide to the maximum safe torque of a particular size/grade of fastener.

- There is no torque difference for fine or coarse threads.
- Torque values are based on clean, dry threads. Reduce the value by 10% if threads are oiled prior to assembly.
- The torque required for aluminum components or fasteners is considerably less.

U.S. Bolts

SAE Grade Number	1 or 2			5			6 or 7		
Number of lines always 2 less than the grade number.									
Bolt Size (Inches)—(Thread)	Maximum Torque			Maximum Torque			Maximum Torque		
	Ft. Lbs.	Kgm	Nm	Ft. Lbs.	Kgm	Nm	Ft. Lbs.	Kgm	Nm
¼ — 20	5	0.7	6.8	8	1.1	10.8	10	1.4	13.5
— 28	6	0.8	8.1	10	1.4	13.6			
5⁄16 — 18	11	1.5	14.9	17	2.3	23.0	19	2.6	25.8
— 24	13	1.8	17.6	19	2.6	25.7			
⅜ — 16	18	2.5	24.4	31	4.3	42.0	34	4.7	46.0
— 24	20	2.75	27.1	35	4.8	47.5			
7⁄16 — 14	28	3.8	37.0	49	6.8	66.4	55	7.6	74.5
— 20	30	4.2	40.7	55	7.6	74.5			
½ — 13	39	5.4	52.8	75	10.4	101.7	85	11.75	115.2
— 20	41	5.7	55.6	85	11.7	115.2			
9⁄16 — 12	51	7.0	69.2	110	15.2	149.1	120	16.6	162.7
— 18	55	7.6	74.5	120	16.6	162.7			
⅝ — 11	83	11.5	112.5	150	20.7	203.3	167	23.0	226.5
— 18	95	13.1	128.8	170	23.5	230.5			
¾ — 10	105	14.5	142.3	270	37.3	366.0	280	38.7	379.6
— 16	115	15.9	155.9	295	40.8	400.0			
⅞ — 9	160	22.1	216.9	395	54.6	535.5	440	60.9	596.5
— 14	175	24.2	237.2	435	60.1	589.7			
1 — 8	236	32.5	318.6	590	81.6	799.9	660	91.3	894.8
— 14	250	34.6	338.9	660	91.3	849.8			

Metric Bolts

Relative Strength Marking	4.6, 4.8			8.8		
Bolt Markings						
Bolt Size Thread Size x Pitch (mm)	Maximum Torque			Maximum Torque		
	Ft. Lbs.	Kgm	Nm	Ft. Lbs.	Kgm	Nm
6 x 1.0	2–3	2–4	3–4	3–6	.4–8	5–8
8 x 1.25	6–8	.8–1	8–12	9–14	1.2–1.9	13–19
10 x 1.25	12–17	1.5–2.3	16–23	20–29	2.7–4.0	27–39
12 x 1.25	21–32	2.9–4.4	29–43	35–53	4.8–7.3	47–72
14 x 1.5	35–52	4.8–7.1	48–70	57–85	7.8–11.7	77–110
16 x 1.5	51–77	7.0–10.6	67–100	90–120	12.4–16.5	130–160
18 x 1.5	74–110	10.2–15.1	100–150	130–170	17.9–23.4	180–230
20 x 1.5	110–140	15.1–19.3	150–190	190–240	26.2–46.9	160–320
22 x 1.5	150–190	22.0–26.2	200–260	250–320	34.5–44.1	340–430
24 x 1.5	190–240	26.2–46.9	260–320	310–410	42.7–56.5	420–550

The screw in compression gauge is more accurate

supplied--a standard type for most Inch Coarse, Inch Fine, Metric Coarse and Metric Fine thread sizes and a spark plug type to fit most spark plug port sizes. Consult the individual manufacturer's catalog to determine exact applications. Typical thread repair kits will contain a selection of prewound threaded inserts a tap (corresponding to the outside diameter threads of the insert) and an installation tool. Spark plug inserts usually differ because they require a tap equipped with pilot threads and combined reamer/tap section. Most manufacturers also supply blister-packed thread repair inserts separately in addition to a master kit containing a variety of taps and inserts plus installation tools.

Before effecting a repair to a threaded hole, remove any snapped, broken or damaged bolts or studs. Penetrating oil can be used to free frozen threads; the offending item can be removed with locking pliers or with a screw or stud extractor. After the hole is clear, the thread can be repaired, as follows:

CHECKING ENGINE COMPRESSION

A noticeable lack of engine power, excessive oil consumption and/or poor fuel mileage measured over an extended period are all indicators of internal engine wear. Worn piston rings, scored or worn cylinder bores, blown head gaskets, sticking or burnt valves and worn valve seats are all possible culprits. here. A check of each cylinder's compression will help you locate the problems.

As mentioned in the Tools and equipment section of Chapter 1, a screw-in type compression gauge is more accurate than the type you simply hold against the spark plug hole, although it takes slightly longer to use. It's worth it to obtain a more accurate reading.

1. Warm up the engine to normal operating temperature.
2. Remove all spark plugs.
3. Disconnect the high-tension lead from the ignition coil.
4. Disconnect the cold start valve and all injector connections.
5. Screw the compression gauge into the No. 1 spark plug hold until the fitting is snug.
NOTE: *Be careful not to crossthread the plug hold. On aluminum cylinder heads use extra care, as the threads in these heads are easily ruined.*
6. Ask an assistant to depress the accelerator pedal fully. Then, while you read the compression gauge, ask the assistant to crank the engine two or three times in short bursts using the ignition switch.
7. Read the compression gauge at the end of each series of cranks, and record the highest of these readings. Repeat this procedure for each of the engine's cylinders.
8. A cylinder's compression pressure is usually acceptable if it is not less than 80% of maximum. The difference between each cylinder should be no more than 12-14 pounds.
9. If a cylinder is unusually low, pour a tablespoon of clean engine oil into the cylinder through the spark plug hold and repeat the compression test. If the compression comes up after adding the oil, it appears that that cylinder's piston rings or bore are damaged or worn. If the pressure remains low, the valves may not be seating properly (a valve job is needed), or the head gasket may be blown near that cylinder. If compression in any two adjacent cylinders is low, and if the addition of oil doesn't help the compression, there is leakage past the head gasket. Oil and coolant water in the combustion chamber can result from this problem. There may be evidence of water droplets on the engine dipstick when a head gasket has blown.

General Engine Specifications

Year	VIN	No. Cylinder Displacement cu. in. (liter)	Fuel System Type	Net Horsepower @ rpm	Net Torque @ rpm (ft. lbs.)	Bore x Stroke (in.)	Compression Ratio	Oil Pressure @ rpm
1989–90	C	4-133 (2.2)	MPFI	110 @ 4700	130 @ 3000	3.39 x 3.75	8.6 : 1	57 @ 3000
	L	4-133 (2.2)	MPFI	145 @ 4300	190 @ 3500	3.39 x 3.75	7.8 : 1	57 @ 3000

MPFI Multiport Fuel Injection

Troubleshooting Engine Mechanical Problems

Problem	Cause	Solution
External oil leaks	• Fuel pump gasket broken or improperly seated	• Replace gasket
	• Cylinder head cover RTV sealant broken or improperly seated	• Replace sealant; inspect cylinder head cover sealant flange and cylinder head sealant surface for distortion and cracks
	• Oil filler cap leaking or missing	• Replace cap
	• Oil filter gasket broken or improperly seated	• Replace oil filter
	• Oil pan side gasket broken, improperly seated or opening in RTV sealant	• Replace gasket or repair opening in sealant; inspect oil pan gasket flange for distortion
	• Oil pan front oil seal broken or improperly seated	• Replace seal; inspect timing case cover and oil pan seal flange for distortion
	• Oil pan rear oil seal broken or improperly seated	• Replace seal; inspect oil pan rear oil seal flange; inspect rear main bearing cap for cracks, plugged oil return channels, or distortion in seal groove
	• Timing case cover oil seal broken or improperly seated	• Replace seal
	• Excess oil pressure because of restricted PCV valve	• Replace PCV valve
	• Oil pan drain plug loose or has stripped threads	• Repair as necessary and tighten
	• Rear oil gallery plug loose	• Use appropriate sealant on gallery plug and tighten
	• Rear camshaft plug loose or improperly seated	• Seat camshaft plug or replace and seal, as necessary
	• Distributor base gasket damaged	• Replace gasket
Excessive oil consumption	• Oil level too high	• Drain oil to specified level
	• Oil with wrong viscosity being used	• Replace with specified oil
	• PCV valve stuck closed	• Replace PCV valve
	• Valve stem oil deflectors (or seals) are damaged, missing, or incorrect type	• Replace valve stem oil deflectors
	• Valve stems or valve guides worn	• Measure stem-to-guide clearance and repair as necessary
	• Poorly fitted or missing valve cover baffles	• Replace valve cover
	• Piston rings broken or missing	• Replace broken or missing rings
	• Scuffed piston	• Replace piston
	• Incorrect piston ring gap	• Measure ring gap, repair as necessary
	• Piston rings sticking or excessively loose in grooves	• Measure ring side clearance, repair as necessary
	• Compression rings installed upside down	• Repair as necessary
	• Cylinder walls worn, scored, or glazed	• Repair as necessary
	• Piston ring gaps not properly staggered	• Repair as necessary
	• Excessive main or connecting rod bearing clearance	• Measure bearing clearance, repair as necessary
No oil pressure	• Low oil level	• Add oil to correct level
	• Oil pressure gauge, warning lamp or sending unit inaccurate	• Replace oil pressure gauge or warning lamp
	• Oil pump malfunction	• Replace oil pump
	• Oil pressure relief valve sticking	• Remove and inspect oil pressure relief valve assembly
	• Oil passages on pressure side of pump obstructed	• Inspect oil passages for obstruction

Troubleshooting Engine Mechanical Problems (cont.)

Problem	Cause	Solution
No oil pressure (cont.)	• Oil pickup screen or tube obstructed	• Inspect oil pickup for obstruction
	• Loose oil inlet tube	• Tighten or seal inlet tube
Low oil pressure	• Low oil level	• Add oil to correct level
	• Inaccurate gauge, warning lamp or sending unit	• Replace oil pressure gauge or warning lamp
	• Oil excessively thin because of dilution, poor quality, or improper grade	• Drain and refill crankcase with recommended oil
	• Excessive oil temperature	• Correct cause of overheating engine
	• Oil pressure relief spring weak or sticking	• Remove and inspect oil pressure relief valve assembly
	• Oil inlet tube and screen assembly has restriction or air leak	• Remove and inspect oil inlet tube and screen assembly. (Fill inlet tube with lacquer thinner to locate leaks.)
	• Excessive oil pump clearance	• Measure clearances
	• Excessive main, rod, or camshaft bearing clearance	• Measure bearing clearances, repair as necessary
High oil pressure	• Improper oil viscosity	• Drain and refill crankcase with correct viscosity oil
	• Oil pressure gauge or sending unit inaccurate	• Replace oil pressure gauge
	• Oil pressure relief valve sticking closed	• Remove and inspect oil pressure relief valve assembly
Main bearing noise	• Insufficient oil supply	• Inspect for low oil level and low oil pressure
	• Main bearing clearance excessive	• Measure main bearing clearance, repair as necessary
	• Bearing insert missing	• Replace missing insert
	• Crankshaft end play excessive	• Measure end play, repair as necessary
	• Improperly tightened main bearing cap bolts	• Tighten bolts with specified torque
	• Loose flywheel or drive plate	• Tighten flywheel or drive plate attaching bolts
	• Loose or damaged vibration damper	• Repair as necessary
Connecting rod bearing noise	• Insufficient oil supply	• Inspect for low oil level and low oil pressure
	• Carbon build-up on piston	• Remove carbon from piston crown
	• Bearing clearance excessive or bearing missing	• Measure clearance, repair as necessary
	• Crankshaft connecting rod journal out-of-round	• Measure journal dimensions, repair or replace as necessary
	• Misaligned connecting rod or cap	• Repair as necessary
	• Connecting rod bolts tightened improperly	• Tighten bolts with specified torque
Piston noise	• Piston-to-cylinder wall clearance excessive (scuffed piston)	• Measure clearance and examine piston
	• Cylinder walls excessively tapered or out-of-round	• Measure cylinder wall dimensions, rebore cylinder
	• Piston ring broken	• Replace all rings on piston
	• Loose or seized piston pin	• Measure piston-to-pin clearance, repair as necessary
	• Connecting rods misaligned	• Measure rod alignment, straighten or replace
	• Piston ring side clearance excessively loose or tight	• Measure ring side clearance, repair as necessary
	• Carbon build-up on piston is excessive	• Remove carbon from piston

Troubleshooting Engine Mechanical Problems (cont.)

Problem	Cause	Solution
Valve actuating component noise	• Insufficient oil supply	• Check for: (a) Low oil level (b) Low oil pressure (c) Plugged push rods (d) Wrong hydraulic tappets (e) Restricted oil gallery (f) Excessive tappet to bore clearance
	• Push rods worn or bent	• Replace worn or bent push rods
	• Rocker arms or pivots worn	• Replace worn rocker arms or pivots
	• Foreign objects or chips in hydraulic tappets	• Clean tappets
	• Excessive tappet leak-down	• Replace valve tappet
	• Tappet face worn	• Replace tappet; inspect corresponding cam lobe for wear
	• Broken or cocked valve springs	• Properly seat cocked springs; replace broken springs
	• Stem-to-guide clearance excessive	• Measure stem-to-guide clearance, repair as required
	• Valve bent	• Replace valve
	• Loose rocker arms	• Tighten bolts with specified torque
	• Valve seat runout excessive	• Regrind valve seat/valves
	• Missing valve lock	• Install valve lock
	• Push rod rubbing or contacting cylinder head	• Remove cylinder head and remove obstruction in head
	• Excessive engine oil (four-cylinder engine)	• Correct oil level

Valve Specifications

Year	VIN	No. Cylinder Displacement cu. in. (liter)	Seat Angle (deg.)	Face Angle (deg.)	Spring Test Pressure (lbs.)	Spring Installed Height (in.)	Stem-to-Guide Clearance (in.)		Stem Diameter (in.)	
							Intake	Exhaust	Intake	Exhaust
1989–90	C	4-133 (2.2)	45	45	—	—	0.008	0.008	0.2744–0.2750	0.2742–0.2748
	L	4-133 (2.2)	45	45	—	—	0.008	0.008	0.2744–0.2750	0.2742–0.2748

Camshaft Specifications

All measurements given in inches.

Year	VIN	No. Cylinder Displacement cu. in. (liter)	Journal Diameter					Lobe Lift		Bearing Clearance	Camshaft End Play
			1	2	3	4	5	In.	Ex.		
1989–90	C	4-133 (2.2)	1.2575–1.2585	1.2563–1.2573	1.2563–1.2573	1.2563–1.2573	1.2575–1.2585	—	—	①	0.003–0.006
	L	4-133 (2.2)	1.2575–1.2585	1.2563–1.2573	1.2563–1.2573	1.2563–1.2573	1.2575–1.2585	—	—	①	0.003–0.006

① Front and rear—0.0014–0.0030 in.
  Center journals—0.0026–0.0045 in.

Troubleshooting the Cooling System

Problem	Cause	Solution
High temperature gauge indication—overheating	• Coolant level low	• Replenish coolant
	• Fan belt loose	• Adjust fan belt tension
	• Radiator hose(s) collapsed	• Replace hose(s)
	• Radiator airflow blocked	• Remove restriction (bug screen, fog lamps, etc.)
	• Faulty radiator cap	• Replace radiator cap
	• Ignition timing incorrect	• Adjust ignition timing
	• Idle speed low	• Adjust idle speed
	• Air trapped in cooling system	• Purge air
	• Heavy traffic driving	• Operate at fast idle in neutral intermittently to cool engine
	• Incorrect cooling system component(s) installed	• Install proper component(s)
	• Faulty thermostat	• Replace thermostat
	• Water pump shaft broken or impeller loose	• Replace water pump
	• Radiator tubes clogged	• Flush radiator
	• Cooling system clogged	• Flush system
	• Casting flash in cooling passages	• Repair or replace as necessary. Flash may be visible by removing cooling system components or removing core plugs.
	• Brakes dragging	• Repair brakes
	• Excessive engine friction	• Repair engine
	• Antifreeze concentration over 68%	• Lower antifreeze concentration percentage
	• Missing air seals	• Replace air seals
	• Faulty gauge or sending unit	• Repair or replace faulty component
	• Loss of coolant flow caused by leakage or foaming	• Repair or replace leaking component, replace coolant
	• Viscous fan drive failed	• Replace unit
Low temperature indication—undercooling	• Thermostat stuck open	• Replace thermostat
	• Faulty gauge or sending unit	• Repair or replace faulty component
Coolant loss—boilover	• Overfilled cooling system	• Reduce coolant level to proper specification
	• Quick shutdown after hard (hot) run	• Allow engine to run at fast idle prior to shutdown
	• Air in system resulting in occasional "burping" of coolant	• Purge system
	• Insufficient antifreeze allowing coolant boiling point to be too low	• Add antifreeze to raise boiling point
	• Antifreeze deteriorated because of age or contamination	• Replace coolant
	• Leaks due to loose hose clamps, loose nuts, bolts, drain plugs, faulty hoses, or defective radiator	• Pressure test system to locate source of leak(s) then repair as necessary
	• Faulty head gasket	• Replace head gasket
	• Cracked head, manifold, or block	• Replace as necessary
	• Faulty radiator cap	• Replace cap
Coolant entry into crankcase or cylinder(s)	• Faulty head gasket	• Replace head gasket
	• Crack in head, manifold or block	• Replace as necessary
Coolant recovery system inoperative	• Coolant level low	• Replenish coolant to FULL mark
	• Leak in system	• Pressure test to isolate leak and repair as necessary
	• Pressure cap not tight or seal missing, or leaking	• Repair as necessary
	• Pressure cap defective	• Replace cap
	• Overflow tube clogged or leaking	• Repair as necessary
	• Recovery bottle vent restricted	• Remove restriction

Troubleshooting the Cooling System (cont.)

Problem	Cause	Solution
Noise	• Fan contacting shroud	• Reposition shroud and inspect engine mounts
	• Loose water pump impeller	• Replace pump
	• Glazed fan belt	• Apply silicone or replace belt
	• Loose fan belt	• Adjust fan belt tension
	• Rough surface on drive pulley	• Replace pulley
	• Water pump bearing worn	• Remove belt to isolate. Replace pump.
	• Belt alignment	• Check pulley alignment. Repair as necessary.
No coolant flow through heater core	• Restricted return inlet in water pump	• Remove restriction
	• Heater hose collapsed or restricted	• Remove restriction or replace hose
	• Restricted heater core	• Remove restriction or replace core
	• Restricted outlet in thermostat housing	• Remove flash or restriction
	• Intake manifold bypass hole in cylinder head restricted	• Remove restriction
	• Faulty heater control valve	• Replace valve
	• Intake manifold coolant passage restricted	• Remove restriction or replace intake manifold

NOTE: *Immediately after shutdown, the engine enters a condition known as heat soak. This is caused by the cooling system being inoperative while engine temperature is still high. If coolant temperature rises above boiling point, expansion and pressure may push some coolant out of the radiator overflow tube. If this does not occur frequently it is considered normal.*

Crankshaft and Connecting Rod Specifications
All measurements are given in inches.

Year	VIN	No. Cylinder Displacement cu. in. (liter)	Crankshaft				Connecting Rod		
			Main Brg. Journal Dia.	Main Brg. Oil Clearance	Shaft End-play	Thrust on No.	Journal Diameter	Oil Clearance	Side Clearance
1989–90	C	4-133 (2.2)	2.3597–2.3604	①	0.0031–0.0071	3	2.0055–2.0061	0.0011–0.0026	0.0004–0.0103
	L	4-133 (2.2)	2.3597–2.3604	①	0.0031–0.0071	3	2.0055–2.0061	0.0011–0.0026	0.0004–0.0103

① No. 1, 2, 4 and 5—0.0010–0.0017 in.
  No. 3—0.0012–0.0019 in.

Piston and Ring Specifications
All measurements are given in inches.

Year	VIN	No. Cylinder Displacement cu. in. (liter)	Piston Clearance	Ring Gap			Ring Side Clearance		
				Top Compression	Bottom Compression	Oil Control	Top Compression	Bottom Compression	Oil Control
1989–90	C	4-133 (2.2)	0.0014–0.0030	0.008–0.014	0.006–0.012	0.012–0.035	0.001–0.003	0.001–0.003	—
	L	4-133 (2.2)	0.0014–0.0030	0.008–0.014	0.006–0.012	0.006–0.014	0.001–0.003	0.001–0.003	—

Troubleshooting the Serpentine Drive Belt

Problem	Cause	Solution
Tension sheeting fabric failure (woven fabric on outside circumference of belt has cracked or separated from body of belt)	• Grooved or backside idler pulley diameters are less than minimum recommended • Tension sheeting contacting (rubbing) stationary object • Excessive heat causing woven fabric to age • Tension sheeting splice has fractured	• Replace pulley(s) not conforming to specification • Correct rubbing condition • Replace belt • Replace belt
Noise (objectional squeal, squeak, or rumble is heard or felt while drive belt is in operation)	• Belt slippage • Bearing noise • Belt misalignment • Belt-to-pulley mismatch • Driven component inducing vibration • System resonant frequency inducing vibration	• Adjust belt • Locate and repair • Align belt/pulley(s) • Install correct belt • Locate defective driven component and repair • Vary belt tension within specifications. Replace belt.
Rib chunking (one or more ribs has separated from belt body)	• Foreign objects imbedded in pulley grooves • Installation damage • Drive loads in excess of design specifications • Insufficient internal belt adhesion	• Remove foreign objects from pulley grooves • Replace belt • Adjust belt tension • Replace belt
Rib or belt wear (belt ribs contact bottom of pulley grooves)	• Pulley(s) misaligned • Mismatch of belt and pulley groove widths • Abrasive environment • Rusted pulley(s) • Sharp or jagged pulley groove tips • Rubber deteriorated	• Align pulley(s) • Replace belt • Replace belt • Clean rust from pulley(s) • Replace pulley • Replace belt
Longitudinal belt cracking (cracks between two ribs)	• Belt has mistracked from pulley groove • Pulley groove tip has worn away rubber-to-tensile member	• Replace belt • Replace belt
Belt slips	• Belt slipping because of insufficient tension • Belt or pulley subjected to substance (belt dressing, oil, ethylene glycol) that has reduced friction • Driven component bearing failure • Belt glazed and hardened from heat and excessive slippage	• Adjust tension • Replace belt and clean pulleys • Replace faulty component bearing • Replace belt
"Groove jumping" (belt does not maintain correct position on pulley, or turns over and/or runs off pulleys)	• Insufficient belt tension • Pulley(s) not within design tolerance • Foreign object(s) in grooves • Excessive belt speed • Pulley misalignment • Belt-to-pulley profile mismatched • Belt cordline is distorted	• Adjust belt tension • Replace pulley(s) • Remove foreign objects from grooves • Avoid excessive engine acceleration • Align pulley(s) • Install correct belt • Replace belt
Belt broken (Note: identify and correct problem before replacement belt is installed)	• Excessive tension • Tensile members damaged during belt installation • Belt turnover • Severe pulley misalignment • Bracket, pulley, or bearing failure	• Replace belt and adjust tension to specification • Replace belt • Replace belt • Align pulley(s) • Replace defective component and belt

Troubleshooting the Serpentine Drive Belt (cont.)

Problem	Cause	Solution
Cord edge failure (tensile member exposed at edges of belt or separated from belt body)	• Excessive tension • Drive pulley misalignment • Belt contacting stationary object • Pulley irregularities • Improper pulley construction • Insufficient adhesion between tensile member and rubber matrix	• Adjust belt tension • Align pulley • Correct as necessary • Replace pulley • Replace pulley • Replace belt and adjust tension to specifications
Sporadic rib cracking (multiple cracks in belt ribs at random intervals)	• Ribbed pulley(s) diameter less than minimum specification • Backside bend flat pulley(s) diameter less than minimum • Excessive heat condition causing rubber to harden • Excessive belt thickness • Belt overcured • Excessive tension	• Replace pulley(s) • Replace pulley(s) • Correct heat condition as necessary • Replace belt • Replace belt • Adjust belt tension

Torque Specifications
All readings in ft. lbs.

Year	VIN	No. Cylinder Displacement cu. in. (liter)	Cylinder Head Bolts	Main Bearing Bolts	Rod Bearing Bolts	Crankshaft Sprocket Bolts	Flywheel Bolts	Manifold Intake	Manifold Exhaust	Spark Plugs
1989–90	C	4-133 (2.2)	59–64	61–65	48–51	108–116	71–76	14–22	16–21	11–17
	L	4-133 (2.2)	59–64	61–65	48–51	108–116	71–76	14–22	16–21	11–17

Engine

REMOVAL AND INSTALLATION

NOTE: *The air conditioning system must be discharged during the following procedure. Have it do professionally if you are not equipped to do it yourself.*

1. Release the fuel pressure and disconnect the negative battery cable. Raise and safely support the front of the vehicle.

2. Mark the hood hinge-to-hood locations and remove the hood.

3. Drain the cooling system, the engine oil and the transaxle fluid.

CAUTION: *When draining the coolant, keep in mind that cats and dogs are attracted by the ethylene glycol antifreeze, and are quite likely to drink any that is left in an uncovered container or in puddles on the ground. This will prove fatal in sufficient quantity. Always drain the coolant into a sealable container. Coolant should be reused unless it is contaminated or several years old.*

The EPA warns that prolonged contact with used engine oil may cause a number of skin disorders, including cancer! You should make every effort to minimize your exposure to used engine oil. Protective gloves should be worn when changing the oil. Wash your hands and any other exposed skin areas as soon as possible after exposure to used engine oil. Soap and water, or waterless hand cleaner should be used.

4. Remove the battery, battery tray and the fuse holder.

5. Remove the air filter assembly and ducts. Disconnect the accelerator and speed control cable (if equipped).

6. Label and disconnect the electrical connectors from the electronic fuel injection system, the ignition coil, the thermostat housing sensors, the exhaust oxygen sensor, the radiator sensors and the cooling fan assembly.

7. Disconnect the transaxle fluid cooler lines from the radiator (ATX). Plug the lines. Remove the radiator cooling fan assembly and the radiator.

8. Remove the clutch release cylinder (MTX) an place it out of the way.

9. Disconnect the front exhaust pipe and converter from the exhaust manifold.

10. Discharge the air conditioning system. Remove the air conditioning lines from the compressor. Disconnect the electrical wiring from the compressor.

11. Disconnect and plug the power steering

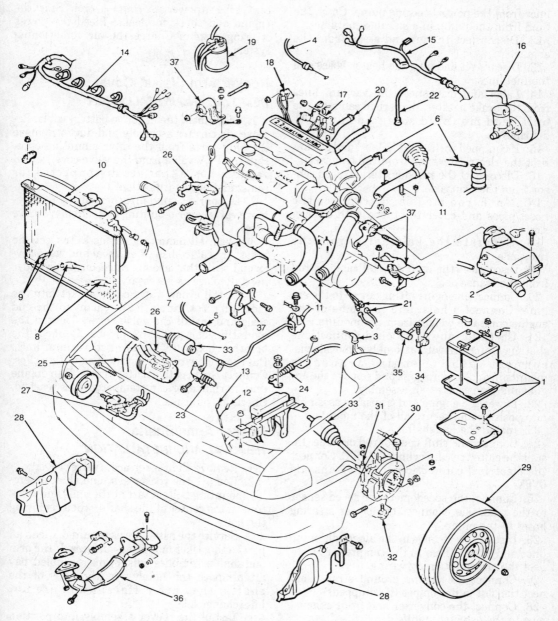

1. BATTERY AND BATTERY CARRIER
2. AIR CLEANER ASSEMBLY
3. HIGH TENSION LEAD
4. ACCELERATOR CABLE
5. THROTTLE CABLE (ATX)
6. FUEL HOSE
7. RADIATOR HOSE
8. ATF HOSE (ATX)
9. RADIATOR HARNESS
10. RADIATOR AND ELECTRIC FAN
11. INTERCOOLER PIPE AND HOSE (TURBO)
12. HEAT GAUGE UNIT CONNECTOR
13. WATER THERMO SWITCH CONNECTOR
14. EGI HARNESS
15. ENGINE HARNESS
16. BRAKE VACUUM HOSE
17. THREE-WAY SOLENOID ASSEMBLY
18. EGR SOLENOID ASSEMBLY (TURBO)
19. CANISTER HOSE
20. HEATER HOSE
21. TRANSAXLE HARNESS
22. SPEEDOMETER CABLE
23. CLUTCH RELEASE CYLINDER (MTX)
24. CONTROL CABLE (ATX)
25. DRIVE BELT
26. A/C COMPRESSOR AND BRACKET
27. P/S OIL PUMP
28. INNER FENDER SPLASH GUARDS
29. FRONT WHEEL
30. TIE ROD END
31. STABILIZER CONTROL ROD
32. LOWER ARM BUSHING
33. DRIVESHAFT
34. CHANGE ROD (MTX)
35. EXTENSION BAR (MTX)
36. EXHAUST PIPE
37. ENGINE MOUNT

Engine removal and installation

lines from the power steering pump. Catch the fluid from the pump in a suitable container.

12. Disconnect the ground strap from the engine.

13. Disconnect and plug the heater hoses and the fuel lines.

14. Label and disconnect the vacuum lines from the brake booster, the carbon canister, the bulkhead mounted solenoids and the distributor.

15. If equipped with an ATX, label and disconnect the electrical wiring from the transaxle.

16. Disconnect the speedometer or speed sensor from the transaxle.

17. On Turbo models; disconnect the hoses/pipes and cover the turbo with a clean rag.

18. Separate the halfshafts from the transaxle.

19. Disconnect the shift control cable or rod from the transaxle.

20. Connect an engine lifting device to the engine. Connect a hoist and lift some of the engine/transaxle weight from the mounts.

21. Check for any overlooked connections that may interfere with assembly removal. Disconnect the engine/transaxle mounts/insulators/brackets and remove the engine and transaxle as an assembly.

22. Lower the engine and transaxle assembly into position and secure all of the mounts.

23. Install the halfshafts.

24. Connect the shift control rod or cable. Install the clutch release cylinder (MTX). Connect the electrical connections to the transaxle (ATX).

25. Connect the speedometer or speed sensor to the transaxle. Connect the power steering hoses to the pump.

26. Install new O-rings in the air conditioning lines and attach them to the compressor. Connect the air conditioning wiring.

27. Connect the engine ground strap. Connect the Turbo lines/pipes (if equipped).

28. Connect the converter and front exhaust pipe to the exhaust manifold.

29. Install the radiator and cooling fan assembly. Connect the wiring. Connect the cooler lines if ATX.

30. Connect all vacuum lines to the carbon canister, bulkhead solenoids, brake booster, fuel injection, and thermostat housing.

31. Connect all of the electrical wiring connectors to the various sensors and controls. Connect the fuel lines, heater and radiator hoses.

32. Install the accelerator and speed control cables. Install the air filter assembly and ducts.

33. Fill the cooling system, transaxle and engine with the proper amount of coolant or lubri-

cant. Fill the power steering reservoir. Start the engine and check for leaks. Bleed the power steering system. Charge the air conditioning system.

Rocker Arm (Valve) Cover
REMOVAL AND INSTALLATION

1. Disconnect the negative battery cable. Remove air cleaner assembly and ducts. Remove the plug wires from the their mounting clips. Pull the PCV valve from the valve cover. Label vacuum hoses that are disconnected for reinstallation identification.

2. Disconnect any breather hoses and remove valve cover mounting bolts. Remove valve cover.

3. Clean all mounting surfaces. Inspect the breather seal, camshaft end seal and valve cover end seals that are mounted on the cylinder head. Replace as necessary.

4. Install a new valve cover gasket into the mounting slot. Apply RTV sealant to the end seals and install the valve cover. Tighten the mounting bolt to 52-69 in. lbs. Connect the breather hoses, PCV valve and vacuum lines. Put the plug wires back in their mounting clips. Connect the negative battery cable. Run engine until normal operating temperature is reached. Check for oil leaks.

Rocker Arms/Shafts
REMOVAL AND INSTALLATION

1. Remove the rocker arm (valve) cover.

2. Remove the rocker arm and shaft assembly mounting bolts. Start at the ends and work toward the center of the shafts, when removing the bolts.

3. Service the assembly as required. Clean all parts and gasket mounting surfaces. If the arm and shaft assemblies must be disassembled, pay attention to the notches at the ends of the shafts, they are different and are not interchangeable.

4. Install the rocker assembly into position and secure with the mounting bolts. Tighten the bolts in sequence working from the center outward. Torque the bolts to 13-20 ft. lbs. Tighten in two steps.

5. Install the rocker arm (valve) cover.

Thermostat
REMOVAL AND INSTALLATION

1. Disconnect the negative battery cable.

2. Drain the cooling system to a point below the thermostat housing.

CAUTION: *When draining the coolant, keep in mind that cats and dogs are attracted by*

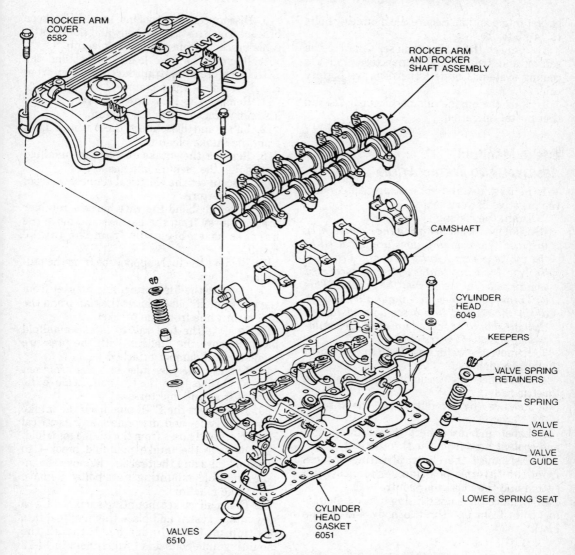

ROCKER ARM COVER 6582

ROCKER ARM AND ROCKER SHAFT ASSEMBLY

CAMSHAFT

CYLINDER HEAD 6049

KEEPERS

VALVE SPRING RETAINERS

SPRING

VALVE SEAL

VALVE GUIDE

LOWER SPRING SEAT

CYLINDER HEAD GASKET 6051

VALVES 6510

Rocker arm cover, shaft and camshaft removal and installation

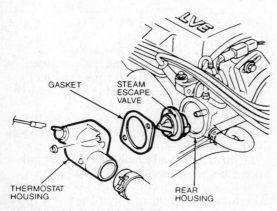

GASKET

STEAM ESCAPE VALVE

THERMOSTAT HOUSING

REAR HOUSING

Thermostat removal and installation

the ethylene glycol antifreeze, and are quite likely to drink any that is left in an uncovered container or in puddles on the ground. This will prove fatal in sufficient quantity. Always drain the coolant into a sealable container. Coolant should be reused unless it is contaminated or several years old.

3. Disconnect the water thermo switch and the temperature gauge sending unit.

4. Remove the upper radiator hose at the thermostat housing.

5. Remove the housing mounting bolts. Remove the housing and thermostat.

6. Clean all gasket surfaces.

7. Install the thermostat, housing and new

gasket into position. Secure the mounting bolts to 14-22 ft. lbs.

8. Connect the radiator hose. Connect the sensor and temp gauge connectors. Fill the cooling system. Connect the negative battery cable.

9. Start the engine and check for leaks and thermostat operation.

Intake Manifold

REMOVAL AND INSTALLATION

1. Relieve fuel system pressure. Disconnect the negative battery cable.

2. Drain the cooling system.

CAUTION: *When draining the coolant, keep in mind that cats and dogs are attracted by the ethylene glycol antifreeze, and are quite likely to drink any that is left in an uncovered container or in puddles on the ground. This will prove fatal in sufficient quantity. Always drain the coolant into a sealable container. Coolant should be reused unless it is contaminated or several years old.*

3. Remove the water hose from the bottom of the intake manifold.

4. Disconnect the accelerator cable from the throttle body.

5. Remove the air duct from the throttle body.

6. Label and disconnect the vacuum lines and coolant hose from the throttle body.

7. Disconnect the electrical wiring harness from the throttle position sensor, the idle switch and the bypass air control valve.

8. Remove the engine lifting bracket mounting bolts from the throttle body and engine block.

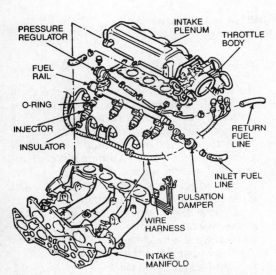

Non-turbo intake plenum removal and installation

9. Disconnect the coolant line, EGR hose bracket from the throttle body and the throttle cable brackets from the intake plenum.

10. Remove the wire loom bracket and the EGR back-pressure transducer bracket from the right side of the plenum.

11. Remove the PCV hose and vacuum line assembly bracket from the plenum.

12. Label and disconnect the vacuum lines from the intake plenum.

13. Remove the intake to plenum manifold nuts/bolts, the plenum and gasket.

14. Disconnect the electrical connectors from the fuel injectors.

15. Carefully bend the wire harness retainer brackets away from the harness and move the harness assembly away from the intake manifold.

16. Remove the fuel supply tube from the pulsation damper.

17. Remove the fuel return line bracket from the intake manifold. Remove the clamp and the fuel return line from the bracket.

18. Remove the fuel rail to intake manifold bolts. Remove the fuel rail with the pressure regulator and damper attached.

19. Remove the fuel injectors, the grommet and the O-rings from the fuel rail. Remove the O-rings from the injectors.

20. Disconnect the EGR pipe from the intake manifold. Label and disconnect any electrical connectors and hoses from the intake manifold.

21. Remove the intake manifold bracket to manifold nuts and the bracket. Remove the intake manifold mounting nuts/bolts. Remove the intake manifold.

22. Clean all gasket mounting surfaces. Use a new intake gasket and place the manifold into position on the cylinder head. Install the mounting nuts/bolts and torque them to 14-22 ft. lbs.

23. Install the intake manifold to engine bracket. Torque the mounting nuts/bolts to 14-22 ft. lbs.

24. Lubricate new injector mounting O-rings with engine oil and install them on the injectors.

25. Install the injectors on the fuel rail.

26. Install the injectors and fuel rail assembly into the intake manifold. Torque the mounting bolts to 14-19 ft. lbs. Connect the electrical wiring connectors to the injectors.

27. Install the fuel return bracket onto the intake manifold and attach the line at the bracket with a clamp.

28. Install the fuel supply line onto the pulsation damper and secure with a clamp.

29. Use a new mounting gasket and secure the intake plenum to the intake manifold. Torque the mounting nuts/bolts to 14-19 ft. lbs.

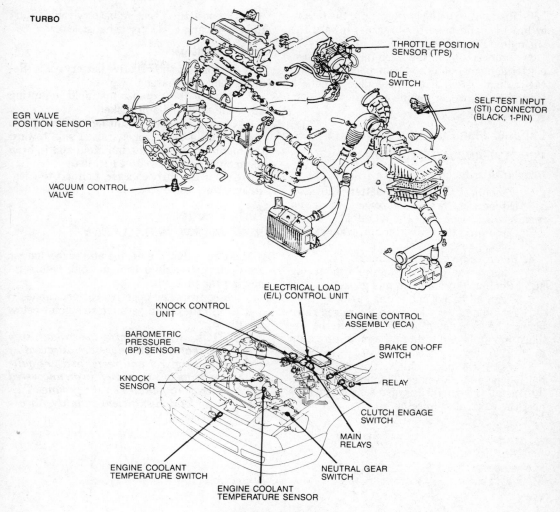

TURBO

THROTTLE POSITION
SENSOR (TPS)

IDLE
SWITCH

SELF-TEST INPUT
(STI) CONNECTOR
(BLACK, 1-PIN)

EGR VALVE
POSITION SENSOR

VACUUM CONTROL
VALVE

ELECTRICAL LOAD
(E/L) CONTROL UNIT

KNOCK CONTROL
UNIT

ENGINE CONTROL
ASSEMBLY (ECA)

BAROMETRIC
PRESSURE
(BP) SENSOR

BRAKE ON-OFF
SWITCH

KNOCK
SENSOR

RELAY

CLUTCH ENGAGE
SWITCH

MAIN
RELAYS

ENGINE COOLANT
TEMPERATURE SWITCH

NEUTRAL GEAR
SWITCH

ENGINE COOLANT
TEMPERATURE SENSOR

Turbo intake system

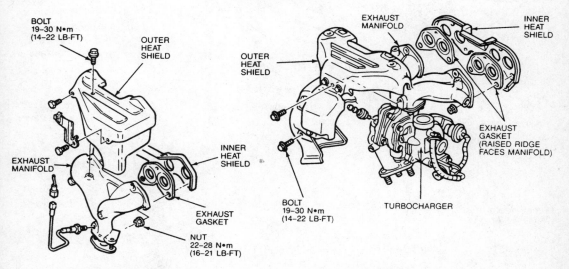

BOLT
19–30 N•m
(14–22 LB-FT)

OUTER
HEAT
SHIELD

EXHAUST
MANIFOLD

INNER
HEAT
SHIELD

OUTER
HEAT
SHIELD

EXHAUST
GASKET
(RAISED RIDGE
FACES MANIFOLD)

INNER
HEAT
SHIELD

EXHAUST
MANIFOLD

EXHAUST
GASKET

BOLT
19–30 N•m
(14–22 LB-FT)

TURBOCHARGER

NUT
22–28 N•m
(16–21 LB-FT)

NON-TURBOCHARGED

TURBOCHARGED

Exhaust manifold removal and installation

30. Install the wiring harness onto the retainer brackets and bend the brackets toward the wiring harness.

31. Connect all of the vacuum lines, hose, electrical connections and control cables. Refill the cooling system. Start the engine and check for leaks and proper engine operation.

Exhaust Manifold

REMOVAL AND INSTALLATION

Without Turbocharger

1. Disconnect the negative battery cable.
2. Disconnect the exhaust oxygen sensor and remove the sensor from the manifold.
3. Disconnect the converter and exhaust pipe from the exhaust manifold.
4. Remove the outer heat shield.
5. Remove the exhaust manifold mounting nuts. Remove the manifold and gaskets.
6. Clean all gasket mounting surfaces.
7. Install a new gasket with the raised ridge facing the exhaust manifold. Install the exhaust manifold and tighten the mounting nuts to 16-21 ft. lbs.
8. Install the outer shield. Connect the exhaust pipe and converter. Tighten to 23-34 ft. lbs. Install the exhaust oxygen sensor and connect the electrial connector.

9. Connect the negative battery cable. Start the engine and check for exhaust leaks.

With Turbocharger

1. Disconnect the negative battery cable. Remove the turbocharger.
2. Remove the exhaust manifold mounting nuts, the manifold and gasket.
3. Clean all gasket mounting surfaces.
4. Install a new gasket, raised side toward the manifold. Install the manifold and tighten the mounting nuts to 16-21 ft. lbs.
5. Install the turbocharger. Connect the negative battery cable.

Turbocharger

REMOVAL AND INSTALLATION

Make sure that the engine and turbocharger are cold, preferably overnight cold, before removing the unit.

1. Disconnect the negative battery cable.
2. Drain the cooling system to a point below the turbo.

CAUTION: *When draining the coolant, keep in mind that cats and dogs are attracted by the ethylene glycol antifreeze, and are quite likely to drink any that is left in an uncovered container or in puddles on the ground. This will prove fatal in sufficient quantity. Always*

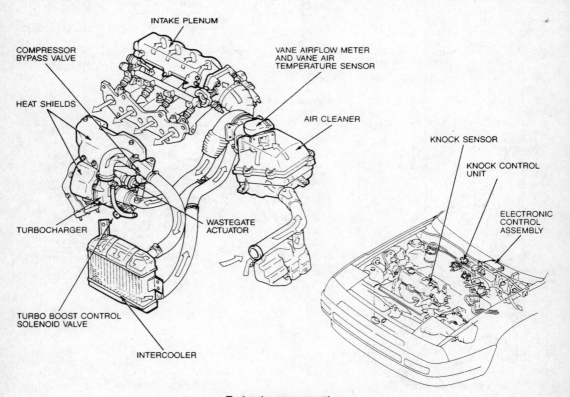

Turbocharger mounting

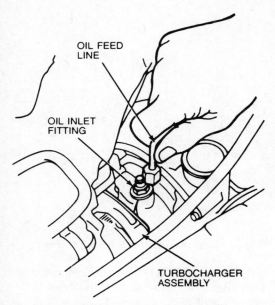

Turbo oil feed line, removal and installation

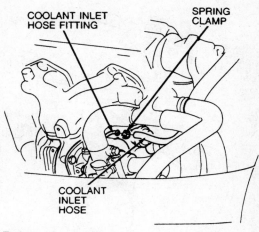

Turbo coolant inlet line

drain the coolant into a sealable container. Coolant should be reused unless it is contaminated or several years old.

3. Remove the air inlet and outlet hoses from the turbocharger compressor.

4. Remove the heat shields from the exhaust manifold and turbo.

5. From above the distributor, disconnect the exhaust gas oxygen sensor (EGO) connector and place the wire over the front of the vehicle away from the heat shield.

6. From the top of the turbocharger, remove the oil feed line. From the lower region of the turbo, remove the oil return line and gasket.

7. Label and disconnect the coolant inlet and outlet lines from the turbocharger.

8. From the exhaust manifold, remove the EGR tube. From the air by-pass valve joint pipe area, disconnect the turbo boost control solenoid electrical lead.

9. Remove the air tube from the turbo boost control solenoid valve.

10. Remove the retaining bracket from under the turbo.

11. Discharge the air conditioning system. Remove the compressor line from the head of the compressor.

12. Remove the exhaust oxygen sensor from the exhaust manifold.

13. Disconnect the exhaust pipe from the tur-

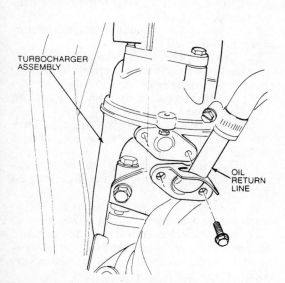

Turbo oil return line, removal and installation

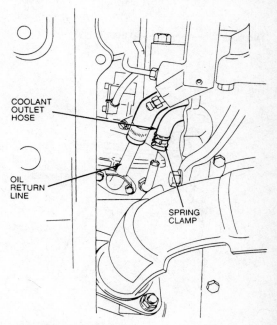

Turbo coolant outlet line

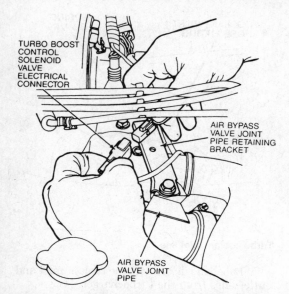

Turbo boost control solenoid, removal and installation

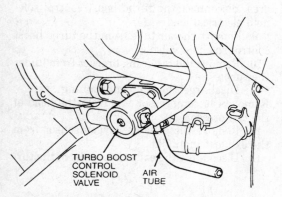

Turbo air tube, removal and installation

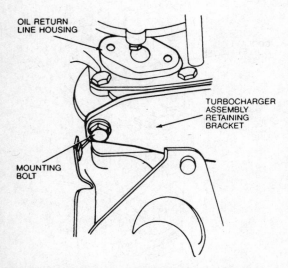

Remove/install the mounting bolt under the turbo

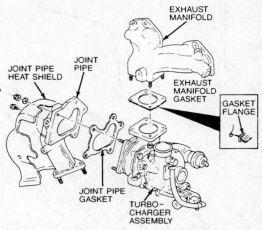

Remove/install the manifold and components

bo. Remove the exhaust manifold mounting bolts. Remove the exhaust manifold and turbocharger unit.

14. Remove the turbocharger to exhaust manifold nuts. Remove the exhaust manifold. Remove the joint pipe from the turbo.

15. Clean all gasket mounting surfaces.

16. Install the joint pipe to the turbo, with a new gasket. Torque the nuts to 27-46 ft. lbs.

17. Install the exhaust manifold to the turbo with a new gasket. Torque the nuts to 20-29 ft. lbs.

18. Install the manifold and turbocharger to the cylinder head with a new gasket. Torque the nuts to 15-21 ft. lbs.

19. Install the exhaust a new gasket. Torque the nuts to 23-34 ft. lbs.

20. Install the coolant lines and oil return line to the turbo. Connect the oil feed line. Insert 25mL of engine oil into the turbo before connecting the oil feed line.

21. Connect the various sensors, vacuum lines and electrical connectors.

22. Connect the EGR tube and solenoid. Charge the air conditioning system after connecting the compressor line.

23. Refill the cooling system. Connect the negative battery cable.

24. After replacing the turbocharger, perform the following to prime the turbo with oil and coolant.

25. Disconnect the electrical connector from the coil. Crank the engine for approximately 20 seconds.

26. Connect the coil harness. Start the engine and operate it at idle for about 30 seconds.

27. Stop the engine, disconnect the negative battery cable and depress the brake pedal for at least 5 seconds to cancel the malfunction mode. Connect the negative battery cable.

28. Start the engine, allow it to reach normal

operating temperature. Check for leaks and engine performance.

Intercooler

REMOVAL AND INSTALLATION

1. Remove the front facia from the vehicle. Remove the front bumper.
2. Disconnect the air hoses at the intercooler.
3. Remove the intercooler bracket bolts and the bolt securing the intercooler to the bracket.
4. Remove the intercooler.
5. Check the fins for damage or bending. Check, also, for cracks or other damage.
6. Place the intercooler into position and secure it. Connect the hoses. Install the front bumper and fasica.

Air Conditioning Compressor

REMOVAL AND INSTALLATION

1. Disconnect the negative battery cable. Discharge the air conditioning system. Remove the drive belt.
2. Remove the suction and discharge manifold assembly from the compressor.
3. Remove the mounting bolts from the upper compressor mounting bracket.
4. Remove the belt tensioner adjustment bolt. Remove the attaching nut from the compressor upper mounting bracket.
5. Remove the upper through bolt and remove the upper compressor mounting bracket.
6. Disconnect the field coil electrical connector.
7. Remove the lower through bolt form the compressor to chassis mounting bracket.
8. Remove the compressor, front mounting bracket and rear mounting bracket as an assembly.
9. Remove the brackets from the compressor.
10. Install the mounting brackets on the front and rear of the compressor.
11. Place the compressor and bracket assembly into position and install the lower through bolt.
12. Install the upper through bolt, adjuster bolt and upper bracket bolts. Install the drive belt and tension.
13. Install the suction and discharge manifold.
14. Connect the negative battery cable. Charge the air conditioning system.

Radiator

REMOVAL AND INSTALLATION

1. Disconnect the negative battery cable. Drain the cooling system.

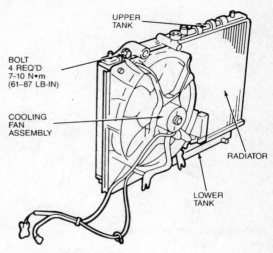

UPPER TANK

BOLT
4 REQ'D
7–10 N•m
(61–87 LB-IN)

COOLING FAN ASSEMBLY

RADIATOR

LOWER TANK

Remove/install the radiator

CAUTION: *When draining the coolant, keep in mind that cats and dogs are attracted by the ethylene glycol antifreeze, and are quite likely to drink any that is left in an uncovered container or in puddles on the ground. This will prove fatal in sufficient quantity. Always drain the coolant into a sealable container. Coolant should be reused unless it is contaminated or several years old.*

2. Disconnect the cooling fan wiring harness.
3. Disconnect the overflow tube from the radiator filler neck. Disconnect the upper and lower radiator hoses. Disconnect the tranaxle fluid cooler line (ATX).
4. Disconnect the coolant temperature sensor wires from the lower radiator tank.
5. Remove the upper bolts that attach the radiator upper tank brackets.
6. Remove the radiator and cooling fan as an assembly.
7. Remove the cooling fan and shroud from the radiator.
8. Install the fan and shroud assembly to the radiator. Install the radiator assembly into the vehicle.
9. Connect the coolant sensor wiring. the radiator hoses, cooler lines, hoses and overflow line. Connect the cooling fan wiring and the negative battery cable. Fill the cooling system.

Air Conditioning Condenser

REMOVAL AND INSTALLATION

1. Discharge the air conditioning system. Disconnect the negative battery cable.
2. Remove the radiator.
3. Remove the condenser mounting bolts after disconnecting the air conditioning lines.
4. Remove the condenser.

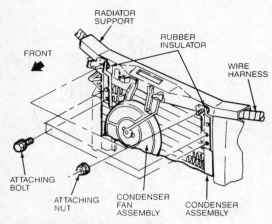

Remove/install the AC condenser

5. Install and secure the condenser. Connect the air conditioning lines. Install the radiator.

6. Connect the negative battery cable. Charge the air conditioning system.

Water Pump

REMOVAL AND INSTALLATION

The water pump is located on the front of the engine behind the timing belt cover.

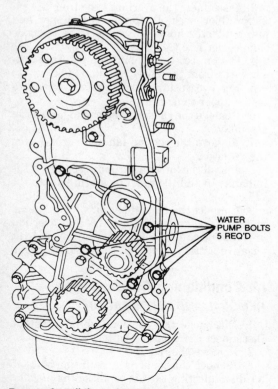

Remove/install the water pump

1. Disconnect the negative battery cable. Drain the cooling system.

CAUTION: *When draining the coolant, keep in mind that cats and dogs are attracted by the ethylene glycol antifreeze, and are quite likely to drink any that is left in an uncovered container or in puddles on the ground. This will prove fatal in sufficient quantity. Always drain the coolant into a sealable container. Coolant should be reused unless it is contaminated or several years old.*

2. Remove the timing belt.

3. Remove the timing belt tensioner pulley spring and the tensioner pulley.

4. Remove the water pump mounting bolts. Remove the water pump and mounting O-ring.

5. Clean all gasket and O-ring mounting surfaces.

6. Install a new mounting O-ring on the water pump. Place the pump into position and secure it with the mounting bolts. Torque the bolts to 14-19 ft. lbs.

7. Install the timing belt tensioner and spring. Install the timing belt.

8. Fill the cooling system. Connect the negative battery cable.

Cylinder Head

REMOVAL AND INSTALLATION

1. Disconnect the negative battery cable. Drain the cooling system.

CAUTION: *When draining the coolant, keep in mind that cats and dogs are attracted by the ethylene glycol antifreeze, and are quite likely to drink any that is left in an uncovered container or in puddles on the ground. This*

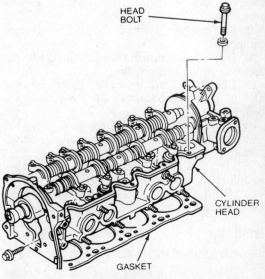

Remove/install the cylinder head

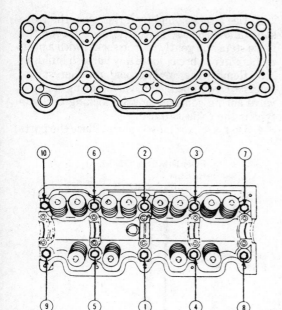

Cylinder head mounting bolt torque sequence

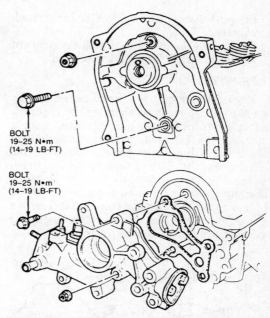

BOLT
19–25 N•m
(14–19 LB-FT)

BOLT
19–25 N•m
(14–19 LB-FT)

Remove/install the front and rear housings to the cylinder head

will prove fatal in sufficient quantity. Always drain the coolant into a sealable container. Coolant should be reused unless it is contaminated or several years old.

2. Remove all drive belts. Remove the crankshaft belt pulley. Remove the timing belt cover.

3. Remove the timing belt. Remove the rocker arm (valve) cover.

4. Remove the exhaust and intake manifolds.

5. Remove the spark plugs. Remove the distributor.

6. Remove the front and rear engine lifting eyes. Disconnect the engine grounding wire.

7. Disconnect the electrical wiring at the thermostat housing. Remove the upper radiator hose and by-pass hose.

8. Remove the rocker arm and shaft assemblies. Remove the cylinder head mounting bolts. Start at the outer edges of the head and work toward the center. Remove the cylinder head.

9. Remove the front and rear housings from the cylinder head.

10. Clean all gasket mounting surfaces.

11. Service the cylinder head as required.

12. Install the cylinder head with a new gasket. Tighten the head bolts in sequence working from the center toward the outer edges. Torque in two equal steps to 59-64 ft. lbs.

13. Install the front and rear housings with new gaskets. Torque the mounting bolts to 14-19 ft. lbs.

14. Install the lifting eyes, the distributor, thermostat housing (if removed), intake and exhaust manifolds, engine ground wire, rocker arm and shaft assembly, rocker cover, timing belt, timing belt cover, crank drive belt pulley and drive belts.

15. Fill the cooling system. Connect the negative battery cable.

CLEANING AND INSPECTION

NOTE: *With the cylinder head removed from the engine, the rocker arm assemblies and camshaft removed, the valves, valve springs and valve stem oil seals can not be serviced.*

Since the machining of valve seats and valves, and the insertion of new valve guides or valve seats may tax the experience and equipment resources of the car owner, it is suggested that the cylinder head be taken to an automotive machine shop for rebuilding.

1. Remove the cylinder head from the car engine (see Cylinder Head Removal). Place the head on a workbench and remove any manifolds that are still connected. Remove all rocker arm assembly parts, if still installed and the camshaft (see Camshaft Removal).

2. Turn the cylinder head over so that the mounting surface is facing up and support evenly on wooden blocks.

3. Use a scraper and remove all of the gasket material and carbon stuck to the head mounting surface. Mount a wire carbon removal brush in an electric drill and clean away the carbon on the valve heads and head combustion chambers.

NOTE: *When scraping or decarbonizing the cylinder head, take car not to damage or nick the gasket mounting surface or combustion chamber.*

4. Number the valve heads with a permanent felt-tipped marker for cylinder location.

RESURFACING

If the cylinder head is warped, resurfacing by an automotive machine shop, will be required. After cleaning the gasket surface, place a straight-edge across the mounting surface of the head. Using feeler gauges, determine the clearance at the center and along the length between the head and straight-edge. Measure clearance at the center and along the lengths of both diagonals. If warpage exceeds 0.003 in. in a 6 in. span, or 0.006 in. over the total length the cylinder head must be resurfaced.

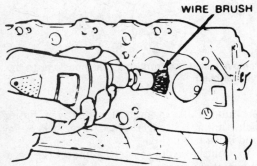

Removing the carbon from the cylinder head with a wire brush and an electric drill

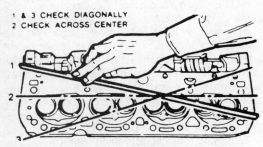

Checking the cylinder head for flatness

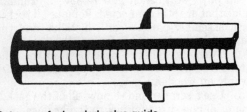

Cutaway of a knurled valve guide

Valves and Springs

REMOVAL AND INSTALLATION

1. Block the head on its side, or install a pair of head-holding brackets made especially for valve removal.

2. Use a socket slightly larger than the valve stem and keepers, place the socket over the valve stem and gently hit the socket with a plastic hammer to break loose any varnish buildup.

3. Remove the valve keepers, retainer, spring shield (if equipped) and valve spring using a valve spring compressor (the locking C-clamp type is the easiest to use).

4. Do not mix removed parts. Place the parts

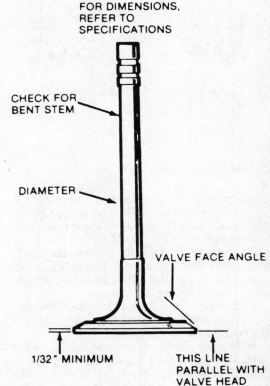

Critical valve dimensions

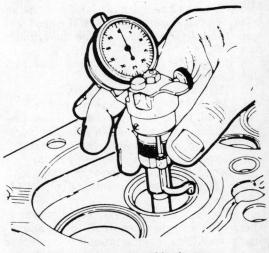

Checking the valve stem to guide clearance

from each valve in a separate container, numbered and identified for the valve and cylinder.

5. Remove and discard the valve stem oil seal, a new seal will be used at assembly time.

6. Remove the valve from the cylinder head and place, in order, through holes punched in a stiff piece of cardboard or stick in case the numbers marked on the valve head gets rubbed off.

7. Use an electric drill and rotary wire brush to clean the intake and exhaust valve ports, combustion chamber and valve seats. In some cases, the carbon build-up will have to be chipped away. Use a blunt pointed drift for carbon chipping, be careful around valve seat areas.

NOTE: *When using a wire brush to clean carbon on the valve parts, valves,etc., be sure the deposits are actually removed, rather than burnished.*

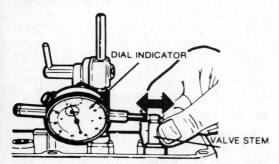

Have a machine shop check the valve seat concentricity

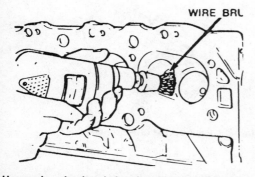

Use a wire wheel and electric drill to remove carbon from the combustion chambers and valve ports

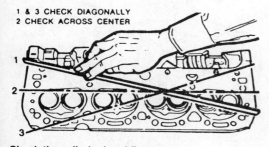

Check the cylinder head flatness

8. Use a valve guide cleaning brush and safe solvent to clean the valve guides.

9. Clean the valves with a revolving wire brush. Heavy carbon deposits may be removed with blunt drift.

10. Wash and clean all valve springs, keepers, retaining caps etc., in safe solvent. Remember to keep parts from each valve separate.

11. Check the cylinder head for cracks. Cracks usually start around the exhaust valve seat because it is the hottest part of the combustion chamber. If a crack is suspected but cannot be detected visually, have the area checked with a dye penetrant or other method by the machine shop.

12. After all cylinder head parts are reasonably clean check the valve stem-to-guide clearance. If a dial indicator is not on hand, a visual inspection can give you a fairly good idea if the guide, valve stem or both are worn.

13. Insert the valve into the guide until slightly away from the valve seat. Wiggle the valve sideways. A small amount of wobble is normal, excessive wobble means a worn guide and/or

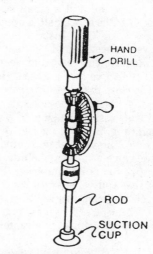

Home made lapping tool

Lapping the valves by hand

valve stem. If a dial indicator is on hand, mount the indicator so that gauge stem is 90° to the valve stem as close to the top of the valve guide as possible. Move the valve from the seat, and measure the valve guide-to-stem clearance by rocking the stem back and forth to actuate the dial indicator. Measure the valve stem using a micrometer and compare to specifications to determine whether stem or guide is causing excessive clearance.

14. The valve guide, if worn, must be repaired before the valve seats can be resurfaced. A new valve guide should be installed or, in some cases, knurled. Consult the automotive machine shop.

15. Valve faces and valve seats should be machined to specifications; the machine shop can handle the job for you. Only enough material to clean up any pits or grooves should be removed. The valve seat should not be too wide or too narrow. The valve face should contact the seat on their respective centers. The valve seat can be narrowed or widened as required.

16. After the valves and valve seats have been machined, they should be hand lapped. Use valve grinding compound and a small suction cupped valve stick. Place a small amount of compound on the valve face. Install the valve and rotate the valve face against the seat with the valve stick. Remove the valve and clean the compound from the valve face and seat. If the contact ring is too close to the outer edge of the valve face, narrow the seat; if too close to the inner edge widen the seat. If the edge of a valve head, after machining, is $\frac{1}{32}$ in. or less replace the valve. The tip of the valve stem should also be dressed on the valve grinding machine, however do not remove too much material.

17. After all valve and valve seats have been machined, check the remaining valve train parts (springs, retainers, keepers, etc.) for wear. Check the valve springs for straightness and tension.

18. Assemble the head using new valve stem guide seals. Lubricate the valve stems before installation. Check the valve spring installed height, shim or replace necessary.

CHECKING VALVE SPRINGS

Place the valve spring on a flat surface next to a carpenters square. Measure the height of the spring, and rotate the spring against the edge of the square to measure distortion. If the spring height varies (by comparison) by more than $\frac{1}{16}$ in. or if the distortion exceeds $\frac{1}{16}$ in., replace the spring.

Have the valve springs tested for spring pressure at the installed and compressed (installed height minus valve lift) height using a valve spring tester. Springs should be within one

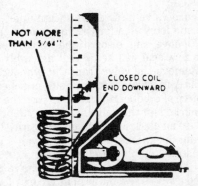

Check the valve spring free length and squareness

pound, plus or minus each other. Replace springs as necessary.

VALVE SPRING INSTALLED HEIGHT

After installing the valve spring, measure the distance between the spring mounting pad and the lower edge of the spring retainer. Compare the measurement to specifications. If the installed height is incorrect, add shim washers between the mounting pad and the base of the spring. Use only washers designed for spring shimming; available at parts houses.

VALVE STEM OIL SEALS

Positive valves seals are used. The seal fits over to top of the valve guide. Always install new valve stem seals when reassembling the cylinder head.

Have the valve spring pressure checked

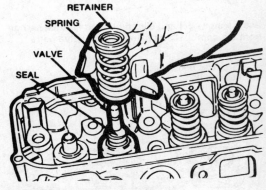

Installing valve stem oil seals

Valve Seats

The valve seat inserts are replaceable on all these engines.

1. With the valve removed, check the seat for wear, cracks, damage or uneven contact with the valve. If the damage or contact problem is slight, the valve may be refaced with a lapping compound and lapping tool. The compound is spread on the seat face and the valve inserted. The valve is then ground against the seat with the lapping tool, removing a small amount of metal and creating a polished surface.

2. If the damage or contact problem cannot be rectified by lapping, the insert can be cut with a special seat cutter which will remove the damaged material and cut the correct angle.

3. If the seat insert is cracked, too thin, or burnt, it must be replaced. An automotive machine shop can handle the job for you.

Oil Pan

REMOVAL AND INSTALLATION

1. Disconnect the negative battery cable. Raise and safely support the front of the vehicle.

2. Remove the right front wheel and the right inner splash panel. Drain the oil.

CAUTION: *The EPA warns that prolonged contact with used engine oil may cause a number of skin disorders, including cancer!*

You should make every effort to minimize your exposure to used engine oil. Protective gloves should be worn when changing the oil. Wash your hands and any other exposed skin areas as soon as possible after exposure to used engine oil. Soap and water, or waterless hand cleaner should be used.

3. Remove the engine to flywheel housing support bracket. Remove the flywheel housing lower cover.

4. Remove the front exhaust pipe and support bracket.

5. Remove the oil pan mounting bolts. Remove the oil pan, the oil pump pickup tube and the stiffener bracket.

6. Clean all gasket mounting surfaces.

7. Use silicone sealer and apply a continuous bead on both sides of the stiffener along the inside of the bolt holes.

8. Install the oil pump pickup tube and gasket, the stiffener and oil pan.

9. Tighten the oil pan mounting bolts to 69-104 in. lbs.

10. Install the flywheel housing lower cover, the support bracket, the exhaust pipe and brace and the splash shield and wheel.

11. Fill the engine with the proper amount of motor oil. Connect the negative battery cable and lower the vehicle.

Oil Pump

REMOVAL AND INSTALLATION

The oil pump is mounted on the front of the engine and houses the front oil seal.

1. Disconnect the negative battery cable. Remove the timing belt, crankshaft sprocket and the engine oil pan.

2. Remove the oil pump mounting bolts and disconnect the oil pump pickup tube and screen.

3. Remove the oil pump from the front of the engine.

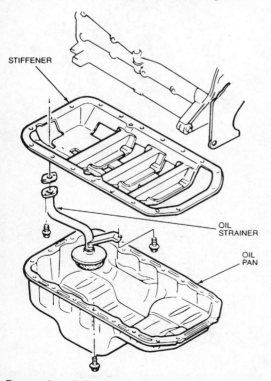

STIFFENER

OIL STRAINER

OIL PAN

Remove/install the oil pan

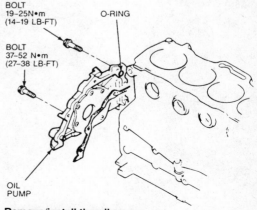

BOLT 19–25N•m (14–19 LB-FT)

O-RING

BOLT 37–52 N•m (27–38 LB-FT)

OIL PUMP

Remove/install the oil pump

4. Clean all gasket mounting surfaces.

5. Install a new seal in the oil pump.

6. Apply a continuous bead of silicone sealer to the mounting surface of the oil pump. Install the pump to the engine. Torque the upper bolts to 14-19 ft. lbs. Torque the lower bolts to 27-38 ft. lbs.

7. Install the pickup tube and oil pan.

8. Install the crankshaft sprocket and timing belt. Fill the engine with the correct amount of motor oil. Connect the negative battery cable. Lower the vehicle.

Timing Belt Cover

REMOVAL AND INSTALLATION

1. The engine is equipped with a two piece timing belt cover.

2. Disconnect the negative battery cable.

3. To remove the upper cover: remove the upper cover mounting bolts. Remove the cover and gasket.

4. Install the gasket and timing cover. Secure the cover with the mounting bolts.

5. To remove the lower timing belt cover: remove the upper cover.

6. Remove the air conditioning compressor and alternator drive belts.

7. Raise and safely support the front of the vehicle.

8. Remove the right front wheel. Remove the right inner splash shield.

9. Remove the crankshaft drive belt pulley.

10. Remove the lower timing belt cover mounting bolts and the timing cover.

11. Install the timing belt cover and mounting bolts.

12. Install the crankshaft drive belt pulley. Torque the mounting bolts to 109-112 in. lbs.

13. Install the right splash panel and wheel. Lower the vehicle.

14. Install and adjust the drive belts. Connect the negative battery cable.

Timing Belt and Tensioner

REMOVAL AND INSTALLATION

1. Bring the engine to top dead center (TDC) for No. 1 piston. The timing marks should be aligned on the front cover and pointer. Disconnect the negative battery cable. Removal all drive belts.

2. Remove the crankshaft drive belt pulley.

3. Remove the timing belt covers.

4. Remove the timing belt tensioner spring and retaining bolt.

5. Remove the idler pulley retaining bolt.

6. Mark an arrow on the timing belt in the direction of engine rotation.

7. Remove the timing belt from the sprockets.

8. Align the camshaft sprocket mark with the mark on the upper front inner cover. Align the crankshaft sprocket mark with the mark on the lower inner fron cover.

9. Install the timing belt (old belt with the arrow facing in the engine rotation direction), be sure the camshaft and crankshaft sprocket timing marks are aligned with the inner cover marks. Place the tensioner and spring in position. Temporarily secure the tensioner with the spring fully extended.

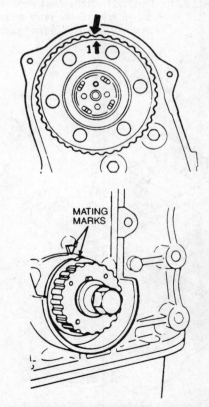

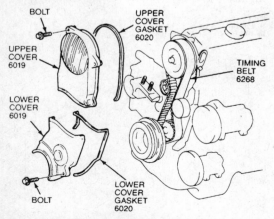

Remove/install the timing belt cover

Align the camshaft and crankshaft sprocket timing marks with the engine front marks

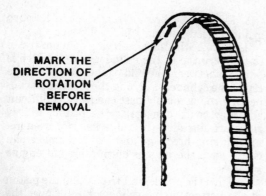

MARK THE
DIRECTION OF
ROTATION
BEFORE
REMOVAL

Mark an arrow on the old timing belt for rotation direction

Timing Sprockets and Oil Seals
REMOVAL AND INSTALLATION

1. Remove the timing belt.
2. Loosen and remove the retaining bolt for the camshaft or crankshaft drive sprocket.
3. To loosen the camshaft sprocket bolt, insert a prybar through a hole in the sprocket against the inner cover raised boss to prevent the shaft from turning when loosening the bolt. To loosen the crankshaft sprocket bolt: if equipped with a manual transaxle, place the vehicle in gear and apply the parking brake. Loos-

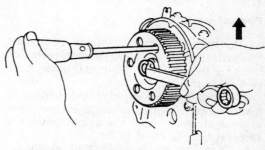

Camshaft sprocket removal

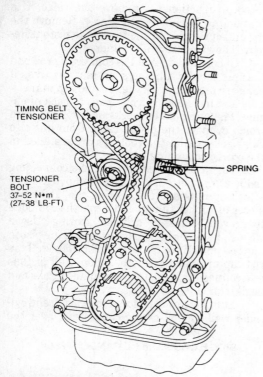

TIMING BELT
TENSIONER

TENSIONER
BOLT
37–52 N•m
(27–38 LB-FT)

SPRING

Timing belt installation

10. Install the timing belt around the sprockets. Make sure there is no looseness at the water pump pulley and idler side.
11. Loosen the tensioner bolt and allow the tension to be applied to the timing belt.
12. Turn the crankshaft around twice in the normal direction of rotation. Align the timing marks. If the marks are aligned, torque the tensioner bolt to 27–38 ft. lbs. If the marks are not aligned, repeat the belt installation procedure.
13. Install the timing belt covers, the crankshaft drive belt pulley, the inner splash shield and wheel. Lower the vehicle. Install the drive belts. Connect the negative battery cable.

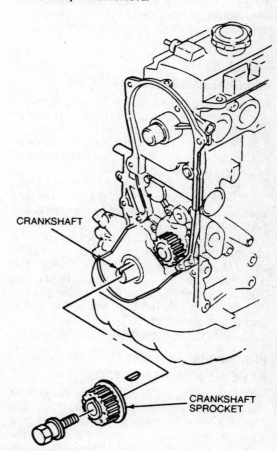

CRANKSHAFT

CRANKSHAFT
SPROCKET

Remove/install the crankshaft

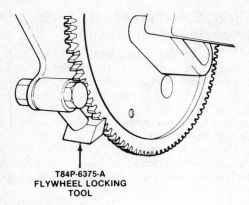

T84P-6375-A
**FLYWHEEL LOCKING
TOOL**

Flywheel holder tool

en the bolt. If equipped with an automatic transaxle: remove the lower flywheel cover and block the flywheel with a special flywheel holder. Loosen the sprocket bolt.

4. Install the drive sprocket and tighten the mounting bolt. Secure the unit as in the removal procedure to tighten the bolt. Tighten the sprocket bolts to 35-48 ft. lbs.

5. To replace the camshaft front oil seal, removed the front inner case. The crankshaft front oil seal is mounted in the oil pump case (refer to the oil pump servicing procedure.

Camshaft
REMOVAL AND INSTALLATION

1. Disconnect the negative battery cable.
2. Remove the timing belt. Remove the rocker cover, rocker arm and shaft assemblies.
3. Remove the distributor. Remove the camshaft drive sprocket. Remove the front and rear housings from the cylinder head.
4. Remove the camshaft and bearing caps.
5. Clean all gasket mounting surfaces. Inspect all components, replace as necessary. Replace any worn oil seals.
6. Install the camshaft and bearing caps. The camshaft bearing caps and rocker arm shafts share the same mounting bolts. Install the rocker arm and shaft assemblies. Install the front and rear housing to the cylinder head.
7. Install the distributor, the rocker cover, timing belt and cover.
8. Connect the negative battery cable.

Pistons and Connecting Rods
REMOVAL AND INSTALLATION

NOTE: *Although, in most cases, the pistons and connecting rods can be removed from the engine (after the cylinder head and oil pan are removed) while the engine is still in the car; it is far easier to work on the engine when removed from the car.*

1. Remove the engine from the car. Remove cylinder head, oil pan and front cover.
2. Because the top piston ring does not travel to the very top of the cylinder bore, a ridge is built up between the end of the travel and the top of the cylinder. Pushing the piston and connecting rod assembly past the ridge is difficult and may cause damage to the piston. If new rings are installed the ridge has not been removed, ring breakage and piston damage can occur when the ridge is encountered at engine speed.
3. Turn the crankshaft to position the piston at the bottom of the cylinder bore. Cover the top of the piston with a rag. Install a ridge reamer in the bore and follow the manufacture's instructions to remove the ridge. Use caution, avoid cutting too deeply. Remove the rag and cutting from the top of the piston. Remove the ridge from all cylinders.
4. Check the edges of the connecting rod and bearing cap for numbers or matchmarks, if none are present mark the rod and cap numerically and in sequence from front to back of engine. The numbers or marks not only tell from which cylinder the piston came from but also helps ensure that the rod caps are installed in the correct matching position.
5. Turn the crankshaft until the connecting rod is at the bottom of travel. Remove the two attaching nuts and the bearing cap. Take two pieces of rubber tubing and cover the rod bolts to prevent crank or cylinder scoring. Use a wooden hammer handle to help push the piston and rod up and out of the cylinder. Reinstall the rod cap in proper position. Remove all pistons and connecting rods. Inspect cylinder walls and deglaze or hone as necessary.
6. Lubricate each piston, rod bearing and cylinder wall. Install a ring compressor over the

RIDGE CAUSED BY CYLINDER WEAR

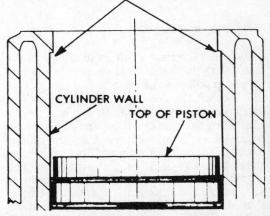

CYLINDER WALL

TOP OF PISTON

The cylinder wall upper ridge must be removed before the pistons are removed

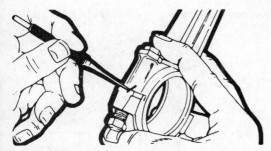

Match connecting rods to their caps with a scribe mark

piston, position the piston with mark toward front of engine and carefully install it into engine. Tap the piston into the bore with a wooden hammer handle or rubber hammer. Position connecting rod with bearing insert installed over the crank journal. Install the rod cap with bearing in proper position. Secure with rod nuts and torque to proper specifications. Install all of the remaining piston assemblies.

CLEANING AND INSPECTION

1. Use a piston ring expander and remove the rings from the piston.

2. Clean the ring grooves using an appropriate cleaning tool, exercise care to avoid cutting too deeply.

3. Clean all varnish and carbon from the piston with a safe solvent. Do not use a wire brush or caustic solution on the pistons.

4. Inspect the pistons for scuffing, scoring, cracks, pitting or excessive ring groove wear. If wear is evident, the piston must be replaced.

5. Have the piston and connecting rod assembly checked by a machine shop for correct

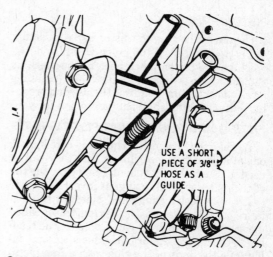

USE A SHORT PIECE OF 3/8" HOSE AS A GUIDE

Cut rubber hoses and place on connecting rod bolts for crankshaft protection when installing the connecting rod and piston assembly

alignment, piston pin wear and piston diameter. If the piston had Collapsed it will have to be replaced or knurled to restore original diameter. Connecting rod bushing replacement, piston pin fitting and piston changing can be handled by the machine shop.

CYLINDER BORE

Check the cylinder bore for wear using a telescope gauge and a micrometer, measure the cylinder bore diameter perpendicular to the piston pin at a point 2½ in. below the top of the engine block. Measure the piston skirt perpendicular to the piston pin. The difference between the two measurements is the piston clearance. If the clearance is within specifications, finish honing or glaze breaking is all that is required. If clearance is excessive a slightly oversize piston may be required. If greatly oversize, the engine will have to be bored and 0.010 in. or larger oversized pistons installed.

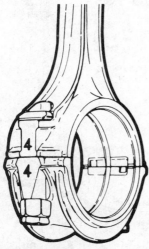

Match the connecting rods to their cylinders with a number stamp

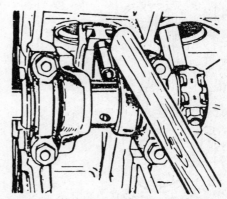

Carefully tap the piston and rod out with a wooden hammer handle

PISTON PINS

The pin connecting the piston and connecting rod is press fitted. If too much free play develops take the piston assemblies to the machine shop and have oversize pins installed. Installing new rods or pistons requires the use of a press--have the machine shop handle the job for you.

FITTING AND POSITIONING PISTON RINGS

1. Take the new piston rings and care install, one at a time into the cylinder that they will be used in. Push the ring about 1 in. below the top of the cylinder block using an inverted piston.

2. Use a feeler gauge and measure the distance between the ends of the ring, this is called measuring the ring end-gap. Compare the reading to the one called for in the specifications table. File the ends of the ring with a fine file to obtain necessary clearance.

NOTE: *If inadequate ring end-gap is utilized, ring breakage will result.*

3. Inspect the ring grooves on the piston for excessive wear or taper. If necessary have the grooves recut for use with a standard ring and spacer. The machine shop can handle the job for you.

4. Check the ring groove by rolling the new piston ring around the groove to check for burrs or carbon deposits. If any are found, remove with a fine file. Hold the ring in the groove and measure side clearance with a feeler gauge. If clearance is excessive, spacer(s) will have to be added.

NOTE: *Always add spacers above the piston ring.*

5. Install the rings on the piston, lower ring first using a ring installing tool. Consult the in-

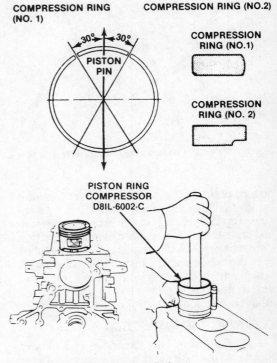

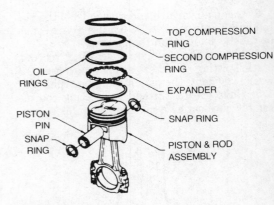

Piston ring and piston installation

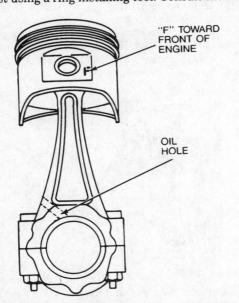

"F" TOWARD FRONT OF ENGINE

OIL HOLE

F faces the front of the engine

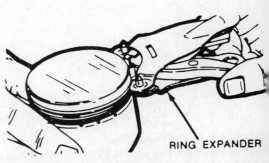

TOP COMPRESSION RING

SECOND COMPRESSION RING

OIL RINGS

EXPANDER

PISTON PIN

SNAP RING

SNAP RING

PISTON & ROD ASSEMBLY

Piston rings and wrist pin

RING EXPANDER

Removing the piston rings

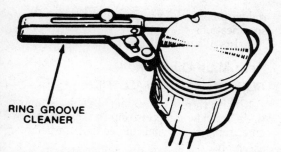

RING GROOVE
CLEANER

Clean the piston ring grooves using a ring groove cleaner tool

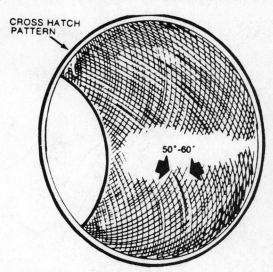

CROSS HATCH PATTERN

50°-60°

Cylinder bore cross-hatching after honing

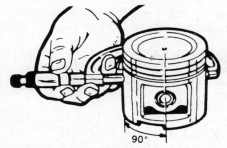

90°

Measuring the piston prior to fitting

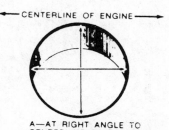

← CENTERLINE OF ENGINE →

A—AT RIGHT ANGLE TO CENTERLINE OF ENGINE
B—PARALLEL TO CENTERLINE OF ENGINE

Cylinder bore measuring points

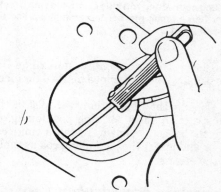

Checking piston ring end gap with a feeler gauge

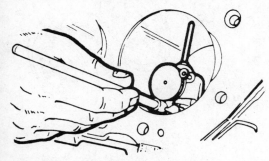

Measuring the cylinder bore with a dial indicator

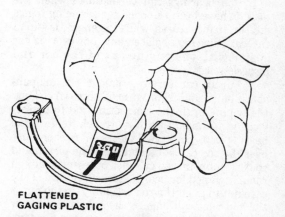

FLATTENED
GAGING PLASTIC

Checking the rod bearing clearance with Plastigage® or equivalent

struction sheet that comes with the rings to be sure they are installed with the correct side up. A mark on the ring usually faces upward.

6. When installing oil rings; install the center spreader (ring) in the groove. Hold the ends of the ring butted together (they must not overlap) and install the bottom rail (scraper) with the end about 1 in. away from the butted end of the control ring. Install the top rail about 1 in. away from the butted end of the control but on the opposite side from the lower rail.

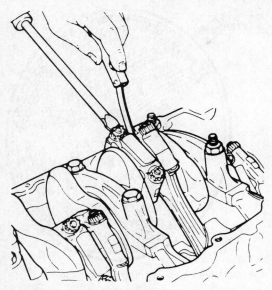

Checking connecting rod side clearance with a feeler gauge. Use a small pry bar to carefully spread the connecting rods

7. Install the two compression rings (the rings usually have a stamped marked that faces up).

8. Consult the illustration with piston ring set instruction sheet for ring positioning, arrange the rings as shown, install a ring compressor and insert the piston and rod assembly into the engine.

ROD BEARING REPLACEMENT

1. Rod bearings can be installed when the pistons have been removed for servicing (rings etc.) or, in most cases, while the engine is still in the car. Bearing replacement, however, is far easier with the engine out of the car and disassembled.

2. For in car service, remove the oil pan, spark plugs and front cover if necessary, Turn the engine until the connecting rod to be serviced is at the bottom of its travel. Remove the bearing cap, place two pieces of rubber hose over the rod cap bolts and push the piston and rod assembly up the cylinder bore until enough room is gained for bearing insert removal. Take care not to push the rod assembly up too far or the top ring will engage the cylinder ridge or come out of the cylinder and require head removal for reinstallation.

3. Clean the rod journal, the connecting rod end and the bearing cap after removing the old bearing inserts. Install the new inserts in the rod and bearing cap, lubricate them with oil. Position the rod over the crankshaft journal and install the rod cap. Make sure the cap and

rod numbers match, torque the rod nuts to specifications.

4. Install the front cover, oil pan, etc.

Rear Main Oil Seal

REMOVAL AND INSTALLATION

1. With the engine out of the vehicle, remove the seal holder adapter from the rear of the engine, replace the seal and install the adapter assembly.

2. With the engine in the vehicle, it is necessary to remove the transaxle.

3. After the transaxle has been removed, remove the clutch and flywheel or flexplate.

4. Remove the seal holder adapter. Remove the seal.

5. Clean all surfaces, install a new seal with the hollow side toward the engine. Install a new mounting gasket and install the adapter to the engine. Torque the mounting bolts to 69-104 in. lbs.

6. Install the clutch and flywheel or flexplate. Tighten the bolts to 71-76 ft. lbs.

7. Install the flexplate.

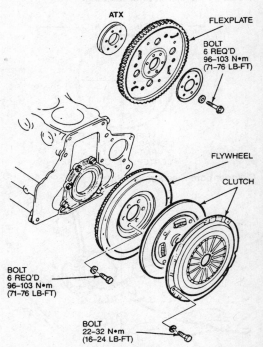

Rear main oil seal and flywheel

Crankshaft and Main Bearings

REMOVAL AND INSTALLATION

1. With the engine out of the car, remove the intake manifold, cylinder head, front cover, timing belt, oil pan, oil pump and flywheel.

2. Remove the piston and rod assemblies. Re-

move the main bearing caps after marking them for position and direction.

3. Remove the crankshaft, bearing inserts and a rear main oil seal. Clean the engine block and cap bearing saddles. Clean the crankshaft and inspect for wear. Check the bearing journals with a micrometer for out-of-round condition and to determine what size rod and main bearing inserts to install.

4. Install the main bearing upper inserts and rear main oil seal half into the engine block.

5. Lubricate the bearing inserts and the crankshaft journals. Slowly and carefully lower the crankshaft into position.

6. Install the bearing inserts and rear main seal into the bearing caps, install the caps working from the middle out. Torque cap bolts to specifications in stages, rotate the crankshaft after each torque stage.

7. Remove the bearing caps, one at a time and check the oil clearance with Plastigage®. Reinstall if clearance is within specifications. Check the crankshaft end-play, if within specifications install connecting rod and piston assemblies with new rod bearing inserts. Check connecting rod bearing oil clearance and rod side play, if correct, assemble the rest of the engine.

BEARING OIL CLEARANCE

Remove the cap from the bearing to be checked. Using a clean, dry rag, thoroughly clean all of the oil from the crankshaft journal and bearing insert.

NOTE: *Plastigage® is soluble in oil; therefore, oil on the journal or bearing could result in erroneous readings.*

Place a piece of Plastigage® along the width of the bearing insert, install the cap, and torque to specifications.

Remove the bearing cap, and determine the bearing clearance by comparing the squished width of Plastigage® to the scale on the Plastigage® envelope. Journal taper is determined by comparing the width of the Plastigage® strip near its ends. Rotate the crankshaft 90° by hand and retest, to determine journal eccentricity.

NOTE: *Do not rotate the crankshaft with the Plastigage® installed. If bearing insert and journal appear intact, and are within tolerances, no further main bearing service is required. If bearing or journal appear defective, cause of failure should be determined before replacement.*

CRANKSHAFT END-PLAY/CONNECTING ROD SIDE PLAY

Place a pry bar between a main bearing cap and crankshaft casting taking care not to dam-

age any journals. Pry backward and forward measure the distance between the thrust bearing (center main) and crankshaft with a feeler gauge. Compare reading with specifications. If too great a clearance is determined, a larger thrust bearing or crank machining may be required. Check with an automotive machine shop for their advice.

Connecting rod clearance between the rod and crankthrow casting can be checked with a feeler gauge. Pry the rod carefully to one side as far as possible and measure the distance on the other side of the rod.

CRANKSHAFT REPAIRS

If a journal is damaged on the crankshaft, repair is possible by having the crankshaft machined, after removal from engine to a standard undersize. Consult the machine shop for their advice.

Flywheel/Flex Plate

NOTE: *Flex plate is the term for a flywheel used with an automatic transaxle. The ring gear on a flex plate is note replaceable. If the ring gear is damaged beyond use, the flex plate must be replaced.*

REMOVAL AND INSTALLATION

1. Raise and support the car on jackstands.
2. Remove the transaxle.
3. Remove the clutch, if equipped, or torque converter from the flywheel. The flywheel bolts should be loosened a little at a time in a cross pattern to avoid warping the flywheel. On cars with manual transmission, replace the pilot bearing in the end of the crankshaft if replacing the flywheel.
4. The flywheel should be checked for cracks and glazing. It can be resurfaced by a machine shop.
5. If the ring gear is to be replaced, drill a hole in the gear between two teeth, being careful not to contact the flywheel surface. Using a cold chisel at this point, crack the ring gear and remove it.
6. Polish the inner surface of the new ring gear and heat it in an oven to about 600°F. Quickly place the ring gear on the flywheel and tap it into place, making sure that it is fully seated.

NOTE: *Never heat the ring gear past 800°F, or the tempering will be destroyed.*

7. Installation is the reverse of removal. Tighten the flywheel/flex plate bolts an little at a time in a criss-cross pattern, to 71-76 ft. lbs.

EXHAUST SYSTEM

Safety Precautions

For a number of reasons, exhaust system work can be the most dangerous type of work you can do on your car. Always observe the following precautions:

• Support the car extra securely. Not only will you often be working directly under it, but you'll frequently be using a lot of force, say, heavy hammer blows, to dislodge rusted parts. This can cause a car that's improperly supported to shift and possibly fall.

• Wear goggles. Exhaust system parts are always rusty. Metal chips can be dislodged, even when you're only turning rusted bolts. Attempting to pry pipes apart with a chisel makes the chips fly even more frequently.

• If you're using a cutting torch, keep it a great distance from either the fuel tank or lines. Stop what you're doing and feel the temperature of the fuel bearing pipes on the tank frequently. Even slight heat can expand and/or vaporize fuel, resulting in accumulated vapor, or even a liquid leak, near your torch.

• Watch where your hammer blows fall and make sure you hit squarely. You could easily tap a brake or fuel line when you hit an exhaust system part with a glancing blow. Inspect all lines and hoses in the area where you've been working.

CAUTION: *Be very careful when working on or near the catalytic converter! External temperatures can reach 1,500°F (816°C) and more, causing severe burns. Removal or installation should be performed only on a cold exhaust system.*

Special Tools

A number of special exhaust system tools can be rented from auto supply houses or local stores that rent special equipment. A common one is a tail pipe expander, designed to enable you to join pipes of identical diameter.

It may also be quite helpful to use solvents designed to loosen rusted bolts or flanges. Soaking rusted parts the night before you do the job can speed the work of freeing rusted parts considerably. Remember that these solvents are often flammable. Apply only to parts after they are cool!

INSPECTION

Once or twice a year, check the muffler(s) and pipes for signs of corrosion and damage. Check the hangers and, or O-ring suspensions for wear, cracks or hardening. Check the heat shields (models equipped) for corrosion or damage. Replace components as necessary.

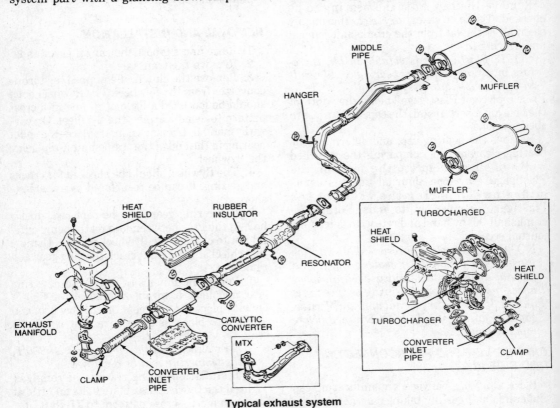

Typical exhaust system

Most models usually are equipped with a catalytic converter(s), which is attached to the front exhaust pipe. The exhaust system is usually bolted together. Replacement parts are usually the same as the original system, with the exception of some mufflers. The original system usually has the muffler and the inlet and tailpipe welded together. Some replacement companies supply the system in three pieces that are clamped together during installation. Splash shield removal will be required, in some cases, for removal and installation clearance.

Use only the proper size sockets or wrenches when unbolting system components. Do not tighten completely until all components are attached, aligned, and suspended. Check the system for leaks after the installation is completed.

Converter Inlet Pipe (Front Exhaust Pipe)
REMOVAL AND INSTALLATION

1. Disconnect the negative battery cable. Raise and safely support the front of the vehicle.
2. Remove the clamp securing the heat shield.
3. Remove the nuts that attach the front pipe to the exhaust manifold and to the front of the catalytic converter.

4. Push the converter rearward and remove the front pipe and mounting gaskets.
5. Clean the exhaust manifold and converter gasket mounting flange surfaces.
6. Position a new mounting gasket on the converter flange and loosely attach the inlet pipe.
7. Position a new mounting gasket on the exhaust manifold flange and loosely install the inlet pipe.
8. Tighten the exhaust manifold to inlet pipe nuts first. Tighten to 26-36 ft. lbs.
9. Tighten the inlet pipe to converter nuts to 40-59 ft. lbs. Install the heat shield clamp. Connect the negative battery cable. Start the engine and check for exhaust leaks. Shut off the engine and lower the vehicle.

Catalytic Converter
REMOVAL AND INSTALLATION

1. Disconnect the negative battery cable. Raise and safely support the front of the vehicle.
2. Place a support under the resonator pipe assembly.
3. Remove the mounting nuts from the front and rear of the converter.
4. Remove the front resonator pipe hanger from the mounting grommets. Push the assembly toward the rear and remove the converter.
5. Clean the mounting flanges. Install a

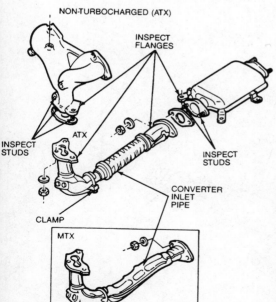

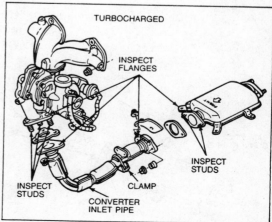

Remove/install the inlet pipe

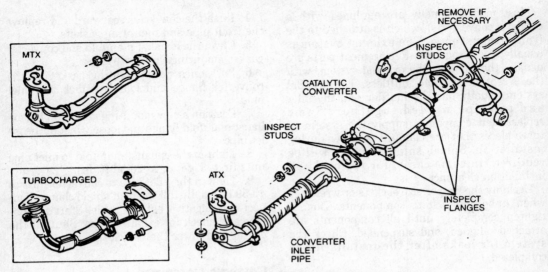

Remove/install the catalytic converter

front gasket to the converter and loosely install the front of the converter to the inlet pipe.

6. Install a gasket on the rear of the converter and loosely attach the resonator pipe assembly. Secure the resonator pipe assembly front mounting bracket into the mounting grommets.

7. Check the assembly for proper body clearance. Tighten the front mounting nuts to 40-59 ft. lbs. Tighten the rear resonator pipe assembly mounting nuts to 23-34 ft. lbs.

8. Connect the negative battery cable. Start the engine and check for exhaust leaks. Shut off the engine and lower the vehicle.

Resonator
REMOVAL AND INSTALLATION

1. Disconnect the negative battery cable. Raise and safely support the rear of the vehicle.

2. Support the converter. Remove the front and rear resonator pipe mounting nuts.

3. Remove the resonator from the body

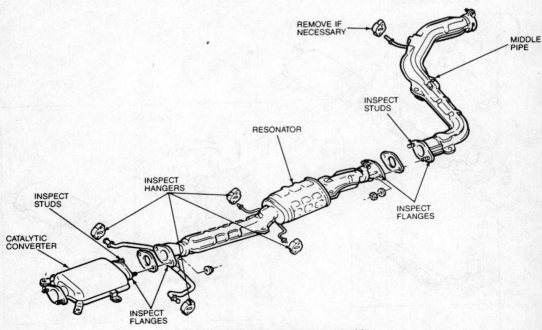

Remove/install the resonator assembly

mounting grommets. Push the assembly rearward and remove the resonator.

4. Clean the flange surfaces. Check all hardware and hangers, replace as necessary.

5. Install new gaskets on the flanges and loosely install the resonator assembly. Mount the brackets into the body grommets.

6. Check the body clearance and tighten the front mounting nuts to 23-34 ft. lbs. Tighten the rear flange mounting nuts to 25-38 ft. lbs. Remove the converter support.

7. Connect the negative battery cable. Start the engine and check for exhaust leaks. Shut off the engine and lower the vehicle.

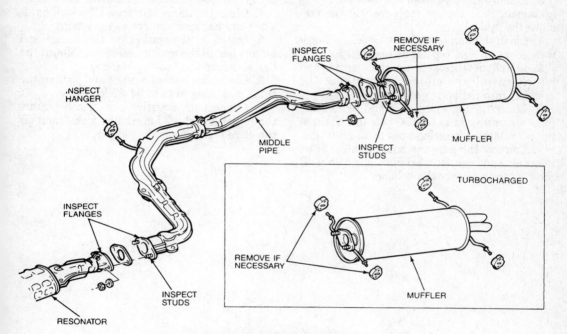

Remove/install the middle pipe

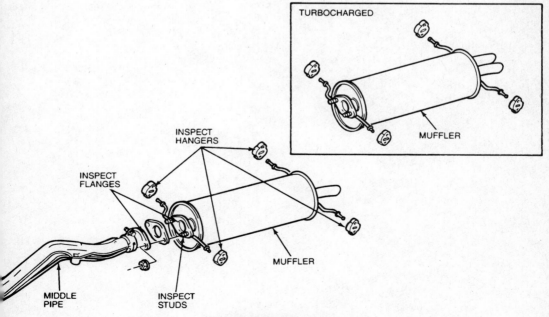

Remove/install the muffler

Middle Pipe
REMOVAL AND INSTALLATION

1. Disconnect the negative battery cable. Raise and safely support the rear of the vehicle.

2. Remove the front and rear pipe mounting nuts.

3. Remove the pipe from the body mounting grommets. Push the assembly rearward and remove the middle pipe.

4. Clean the flange surfaces. Check all hardware and hangers, replace as necessary.

5. Install new gaskets on the flanges and loosely install the middle pipe. Mount the brackets into the body grommets.

6. Check the body clearance and tighten the front mounting nuts to 23-34 ft. lbs. Tighten the rear flange mounting nuts to 25-38 ft. lbs.

7. Connect the negative battery cable. Start the engine and check for exhaust leaks. Shut off the engine and lower the vehicle.

Muffler
REMOVAL AND INSTALLATION

1. Disconnect the negative battery cable. Raise and safely support the rear of the vehicle.

2. Remove the front flange mounting nuts.

3. Remove the muffler from the body mounting grommets. Remove the muffler assembly.

4. Clean the flange surfaces. Check all hardware and hangers, replace as necessary.

5. Install a new gasket on the flange and loosely install the muffler assembly. Mount the brackets into the body grommets.

6. Check the body clearance and tighten the front mounting nuts to 34-52 ft. lbs.

7. Connect the negative battery cable. Start the engine and check for exhaust leaks. Shut off the engine and lower the vehicle.

EMISSION CONTROLS

Crankcase Ventilation System

OPERATION

A closed-type crankcase ventilation system is used to prevent engine blow-by-gases from escaping into the atmosphere.

The PCV valve is generally located in the hose from the rocker cover. A larger hose is connected from the front of the rocker arm cover to the air cleaner assembly. Under light to medium carburetor throttle opening, the blow-by-gases are drawn through the PCV valve. Under heavy acceleration, both the PCV valve and the large hose route the gases into the engine.

SERVICE

To check for a clogged PCV valve; with the engine running, remove the valve from its mounting. A hissing sound should be heard and vacuum should be felt from the inlet (bottom) side of the valve. Turn off the engine, shake the valve. A clicking sound should come from the valve when it is skaken. If the valve fails either of thes tests, replace it.

REMOVAL AND INSTALLATION

Remove the valve from its mounting. Disconnect the hose(s) from the valve. Install a new valve into the hose(s) and push the valve into the mounting.

Evaporative Emmission Controls

OPERATION

This system is designed to prevent hydrocarbons from escaping into the atmosphere from the fuel tank, due to normal evaporation. Some parts of the typical system are:

1. Canister Purge Regulator (CPR) Solenoid Valve: The CPR controls the vacuum applied to the canister purge valve. When the CPR Solenoid is energized, vacuum is supplied to the canister purge valve which regulates second stage purge from the carbon canister to the intake manifold. When de-energized, the vacuum is vented to the atmosphere through the valve air filter. The CPR Solenoid Valve is controlled by a signal from the Electronic Control Assembly (ECA).

2. Canister Purge Valve: The purge valve

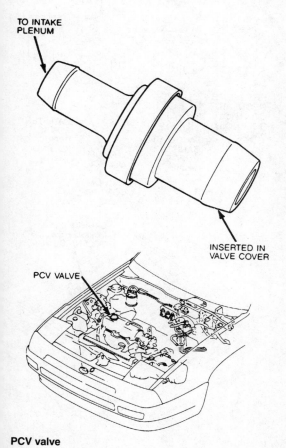

TO INTAKE PLENUM

INSERTED IN VALVE COVER

PCV VALVE

PCV valve

regulates evaporate fumes from the carbon canister to the intake manifold. The valve is controlled by the CPR as determined by an ECA signal. The valve is located near the vacuum tubing assembly behind the intake manifold.

3. Carbon Canister: The fuel vapors from the fuel tank are stored in the carbon canister until the vehicle is operated, at which time, the vapors will be purged from the canister into the engine. The canister is mounted in the rear left corner of the engine compartment.

4. Vacuum Control Valve: The vacuum control valve controls vacuum applied to No. 1 purge control valve and to canister purge regulator solenoid valve. The vacuum control valve senses engine coolant temperature and opens vacuum line above 129°F (54°C). The valve is threaded into the bottom of the intake manifold.

SERVICE

Be sure that all hoses are clamped and not dry-rotted or broken. Check the valves for cracks, signs of gasoline leakage, and proper operating condition.

Visually inspect the engine compartment to ensure that all intake air hoses, vacuum lines and wiring are properly routed and securely connected. Check all hoses, vacuum lines, wiring, connectors, and othe components for evidence of looseness, cracks, restrictions or other damage.

Inspect the air cleaner body, cover and connecting parts for damage, looseness, missing

TURBO ENGINE

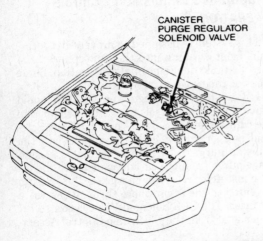

NON-TURBO ENGINE

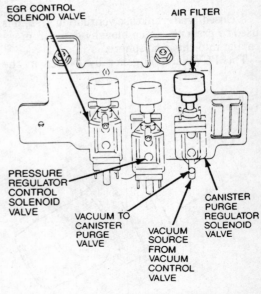

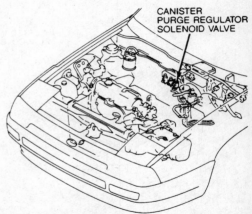

CPR and sensor locations

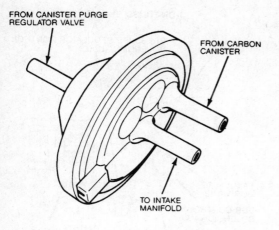

FROM CANISTER PURGE REGULATOR VALVE

FROM CARBON CANISTER

TO INTAKE MANIFOLD

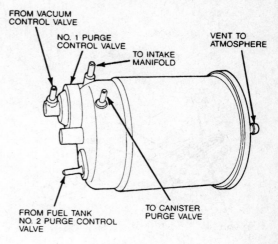

FROM VACUUM CONTROL VALVE

NO. 1 PURGE CONTROL VALVE

TO INTAKE MANIFOLD

VENT TO ATMOSPHERE

FROM FUEL TANK NO. 2 PURGE CONTROL VALVE

TO CANISTER PURGE VALVE

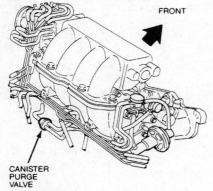

FRONT

CANISTER PURGE VALVE

Canister purge valve

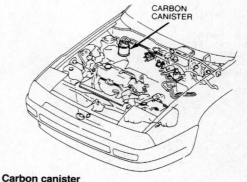

CARBON CANISTER

Carbon canister

fasteners, and for filter misfit. Remove the air cleaner cover and inspect the air filter element for dirt.

Exhaust Gas Recirculation System
OPERATION

The EGR system recirculates part of the exhaust gases into the combustion chambers. This dilutes the air/fuel mixture, reducing formation of oxides of nitrogen in the exhaust gases by lowering the peak combustion temperatures. Some parts of the EGR system are:

1. EGR Back Pressure Variable Transducer: The transducer modulates the EGR vacuum so that the amount of gas flow is proportional to throttle opening. It does this by sensing the exhaust back pressure and bleeding off some of the vacuum when back pressure is low. Since exhaust pressure depends on engine load, it is the equivalent of a throttle opening signal. The transducer is mounted above the EGR valve.

2. EGR Control Solenoid Valve: Two differnt control solenoid valves are used. One type on the non-turbo engine, a different type on the turbo engine. The non-turbo engine uses a sin-

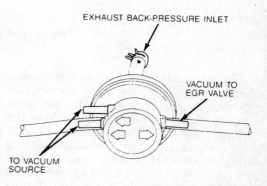

EXHAUST BACK-PRESSURE INLET

VACUUM TO EGR VALVE

TO VACUUM SOURCE

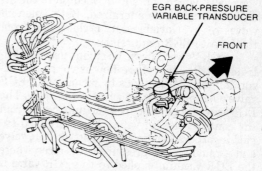

EGR BACK-PRESSURE VARIABLE TRANSDUCER

FRONT

Back pressure variable transducer

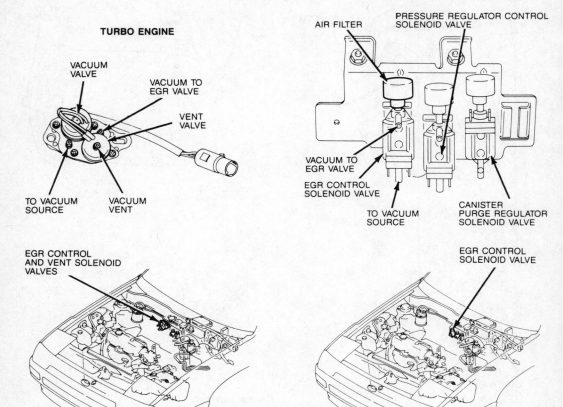

EGR control solenoid valve

gle control solenoid valve. The solenoid supplies vacuum to the EGR valve when de-energized and vents vacuum through its air filter when energized. It also receives a signal from the ECA according to EGR requirements. The turbo engine uses a dual type solenoid. One is a vacuum valve which supplies vacuum to the EGR valve when energized, and the second is a vent valve which vents EGR vacuum to the atmosphere when de-energized. Both solenoid valves receive variable duty cycle signals from the ECA to EGR requirements.

3. EGR Valve; The turbo engine uses an electronic EGR valve where flow is controlled according to ECA demands by means of an EGR valve position sensor attached to the valve. The EGR valve is operated by a vacuum signal from the control solenoid valve. The non-turbo engine incorporates a modified ported EGR valve and a remote back pressure transducer where the EGR vacuum applied to the EGR valve is modulated by sensing exhaust back pressure.

This provides EGR flow proportional to engine load. Vacuum is supplied to the EGR transducer is controlled by an EGR control solenoid valve.

EGR MAINTENANCE

1. Check all vacuum hoses for cracks, breakage and correct installation.
2. Check EGR valve operation by applying vacuum to the EGR valve vacuum nipple with the engine idling. The idle should become rough.
3. Check the passages in the cylinder head and intake manifold for clogging. Clean as necessary.
4. Cold start the engine. The EGR port nipple should be open. When the coolant is warmed to over 131°F (55°C), the port should be closed.

Check Engine Light

A Check Engine light is located on the lower right side of the instrument cluster. The ligh

TURBO ENGINE

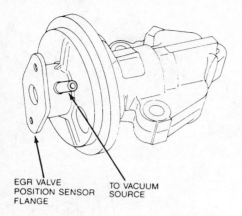

EGR VALVE
POSITION SENSOR
FLANGE

TO VACUUM
SOURCE

NON-TURBO ENGINE

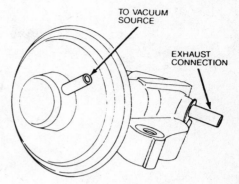

TO VACUUM
SOURCE

EXHAUST
CONNECTION

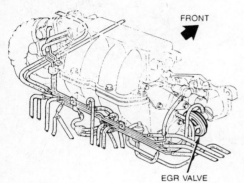

FRONT

EGR VALVE

BACK-PRESSURE
TRANSDUCER

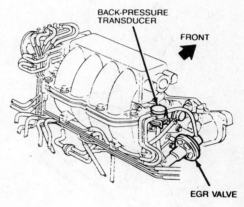

FRONT

EGR VALVE

EGR valve

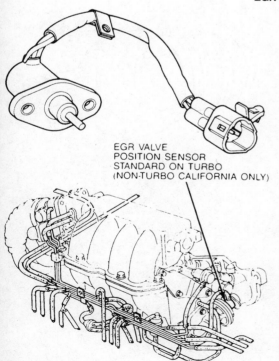

EGR VALVE
POSITION SENSOR
STANDARD ON TURBO
(NON-TURBO CALIFORNIA ONLY)

EGR position sensor

turns on to signal the driver the ECA system is malfunctioning. It is normal for the light to come on when the ignition switch is turned on, but should go out when the engine is started. If the light fails to go out or comes on while the vehicle is operating, a failure or proble is indicated. Servicing is required as soon as possible.

When the self-test input STI), located in the engine compartment near the driver's side strut tower, connector is grounded, the light provides a flashing signal indicating the test mode condition.

The self test output (STO) six-pin connector, is used to retrieve service codes which were stored while the vehicle was in normal operation.

To eliminate the codes from memory, disconnect the negative battery cable, depress the brake pedal for five to ten seconds, connect the battery cable and check to see that the codes are elimated. The Check Engine light will turn off when the malfunction is corrected.

Exhaust Oxygen Sensor

The oxygen sensor is mounted in the exhaust manifold. The output signal from the sensor,

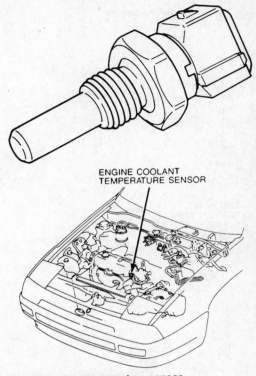

Engine coolant temperature sensor

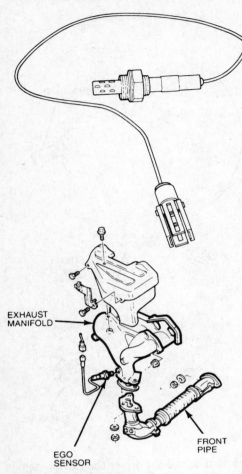

EXHAUST MANIFOLD

EGO SENSOR

FRONT PIPE

Exhaust gas oxygen sensor

which varies with the oxygen content of the exhaust gas stream, is provided to the ECA.

Coolant Temperature Sensor/Switch

Several coolant temperature sensor/switches are installed. The sensors provide data to the ECA for use in controlling fuel delivery and secondary air management.

Barometric Pressure (BP) Sensor

The BPS is used to sense changes in barometric pressure, allowing the ECA to sense the altitude at which the vehicle is operating. The signal from the BP affects; air/fuel ratio and idle speed.

Bypass Air Control (BAC) Valve

The BAC valve mounts on the throttle body and controls idle smoothness by regulating the throttle plate bypass air.

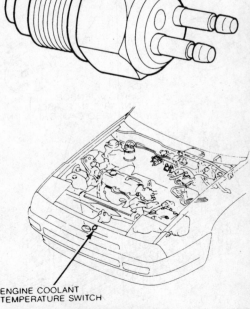

ENGINE COOLANT TEMPERATURE SWITCH

Engine coolant temperature switch

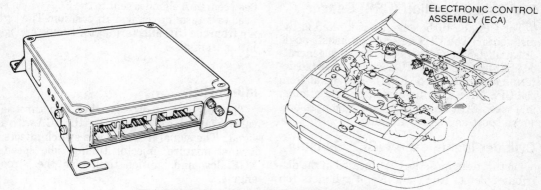

The ECA is located on the floor panel behind the center console

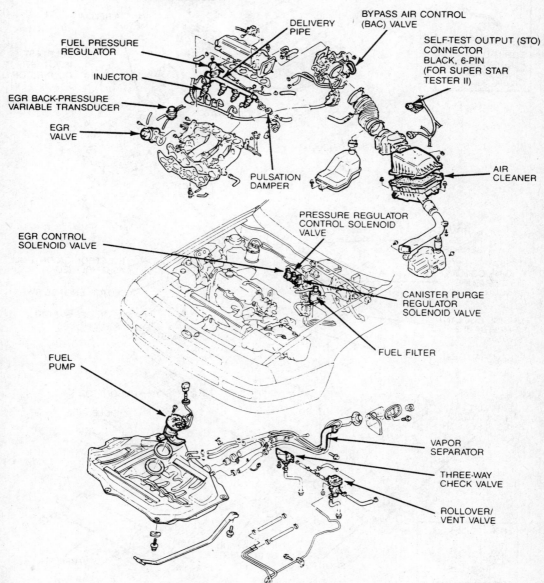

ELECTRONIC CONTROL ASSEMBLY (ECA)

DELIVERY PIPE

BYPASS AIR CONTROL (BAC) VALVE

FUEL PRESSURE REGULATOR

SELF-TEST OUTPUT (STO) CONNECTOR BLACK, 6-PIN (FOR SUPER STAR TESTER II)

INJECTOR

EGR BACK-PRESSURE VARIABLE TRANSDUCER

EGR VALVE

PULSATION DAMPER

AIR CLEANER

PRESSURE REGULATOR CONTROL SOLENOID VALVE

EGR CONTROL SOLENOID VALVE

CANISTER PURGE REGULATOR SOLENOID VALVE

FUEL FILTER

FUEL PUMP

VAPOR SEPARATOR

THREE-WAY CHECK VALVE

ROLLOVER/ VENT VALVE

Non-turbo fuel/emissions component locations

Crankshaft Position (CPS) Sensor

The CPS, on turbo engines, is located in the distributor. The CPS detects crankshaft angle at equally spaced intervals. A signal is generated and supplied to the ECA which is used to determine engine speed (RPM). The signal from the CPS affects; air/fuel ratio, injector timing, idle speed,EGR flow, purge flow, fuel pressure, turbo boost and ignition timing.

Cylinder Identification (CID) Sensors

On turbo engines, the CID, located in the distributor detect No. 1 and No. 4 cylinders top

dead center. A signal is sent to the ECA which is used to determine crankshaft position. The signal from the CID affects; injector timing and ignition timing.

Idle Switch

The idle switch detects when the throttle valve is fully closed and supplies the ECA with a signal. The signal from the idle switch affects; air/fuel mixture, injector timing, idle speed, EGR flow and ignition timing on the turbo engine.

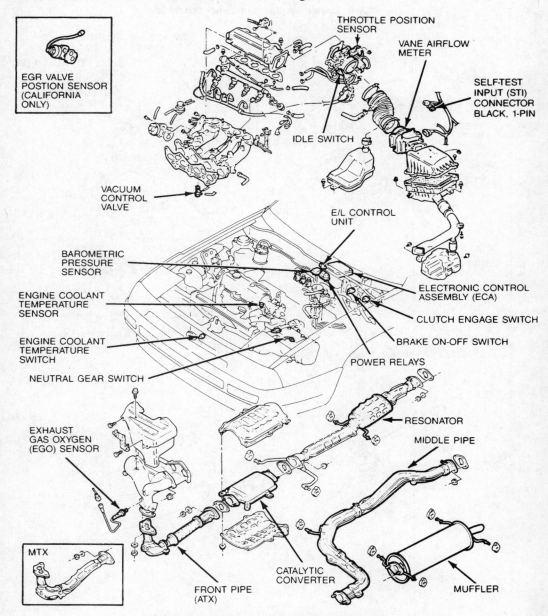

Non-turbo exhaust and input devices locations

Knock Control Unit

The knock control detects when vibration in the engine occurs, voltage is generated by the knock sensor and a signal is sent to the knock control unit. The unit determines whether the signal is preignition or other vibration. A signal is sent to the ECA and timing is retarded as required.

Throttle Position Sensor

The TP detects throttle plate opening angle. It supplies the ECA with a signal proportional to plate angle. The signal from the TP affects; air/fuel ratio, injector timing, idle speed, EGR flow, fuel pressure and ignition timing on the turbo engine.

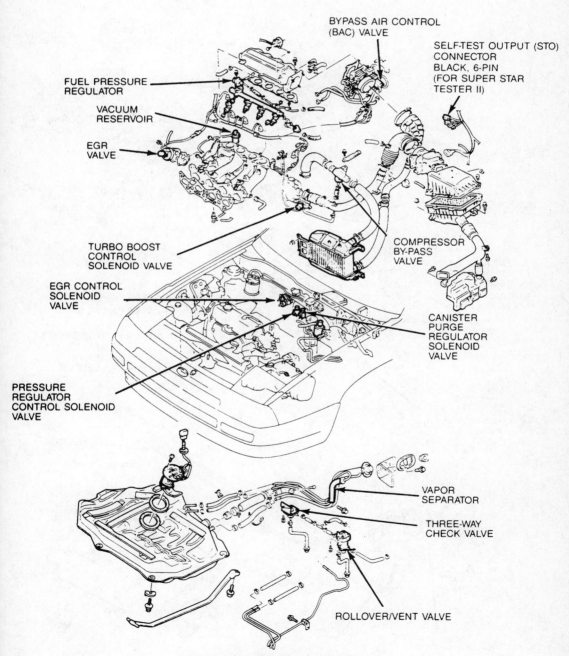

Turbo fuel/output devices locations

Vane Air Temperature (VAT) Sensor

The VAT is an integral part of the Vane Air-flow Meter. The sensor measures incoming air temperature and sends a signal to the ECA. The signal affects; air/fuel ratio, idle speed, fuel pressure and turbo boost.

MALFUNCTION SELF-TEST

Malfunction Indication Light and Testing

The Malfunction Indication Light provides a visual signal to the driver when an ECA input device malfunctions.

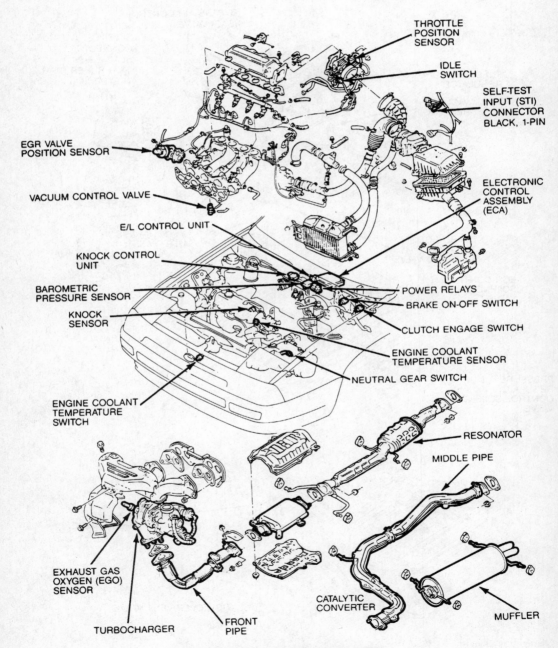

THROTTLE POSITION SENSOR

IDLE SWITCH

SELF-TEST INPUT (STI) CONNECTOR BLACK, 1-PIN

ELECTRONIC CONTROL ASSEMBLY (ECA)

EGR VALVE POSITION SENSOR

VACUUM CONTROL VALVE

E/L CONTROL UNIT

KNOCK CONTROL UNIT

BAROMETRIC PRESSURE SENSOR

KNOCK SENSOR

POWER RELAYS

BRAKE ON-OFF SWITCH

CLUTCH ENGAGE SWITCH

ENGINE COOLANT TEMPERATURE SENSOR

NEUTRAL GEAR SWITCH

ENGINE COOLANT TEMPERATURE SWITCH

RESONATOR

MIDDLE PIPE

EXHAUST GAS OXYGEN (EGO) SENSOR

TURBOCHARGER

FRONT PIPE

CATALYTIC CONVERTER

MUFFLER

Turbo exhaust and input devices locations

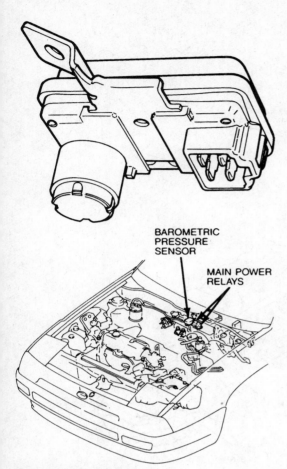

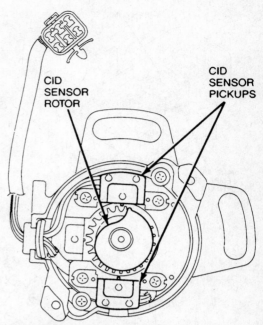

Cylinder identification (CID) sensors

Barometric pressure sensor

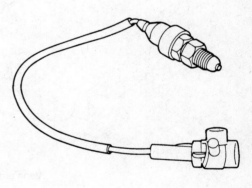

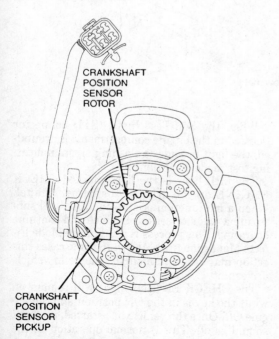

Crankshaft position sensor

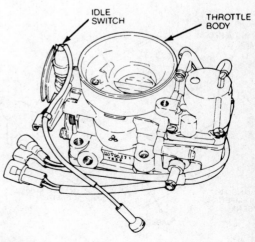

Idle switch

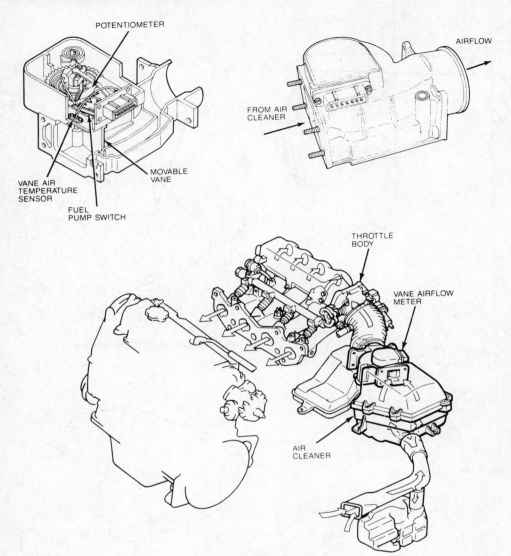

Vane airflow meter

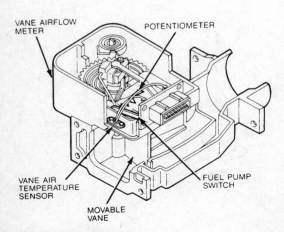

Vane air temperature sensor

When the Self-Test Input (STI) connector (located in the engine compartment) is grounded, the light provides a flashing signal indicating test mode condition.

The MIL light is the light marked CHECK ENGINE on the driver's instrument panel. When a malfunction occurs, the ECA will substitute a value or series of values and continue operating. This process is call Failure Mode Effects Management (FMEM). In some cases this action may result in a slight change in vehicle driveability.

The CHECK ENGINE light will remain on while the key is in the ON position and the engine Off. Once the vehicle has started, the light should go off. This is normal operation. If the light should remain on after the engine has started, run the Key On, Engine Off tests that follow. The CHECK ENGINE light only warns the driver of an input device malfunction. When in the Self-Test mode the CHECK ENGINE light will flash the service codes.

KEY ON ENGINE OFF SELF-TEST

To activate the MIL (CHECK ENGINE), connect a jumper wire from the Self-Test input (STI) connector to ground and place the ignition switch in the ON position.

The Self-Test Input Connector (STI) is the 1 pin connector under the hood behind the driver's side strut tower.

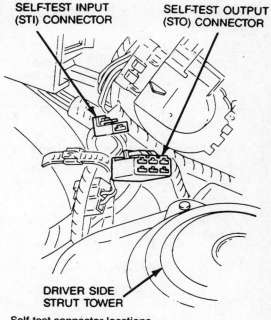

SELF-TEST INPUT (STI) CONNECTOR

SELF-TEST OUTPUT (STO) CONNECTOR

DRIVER SIDE STRUT TOWER

Self-test connector locations

ANALOG

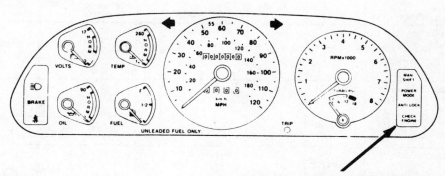

MALFUNCTION INDICATOR LIGHT (MIL)

DIGITAL

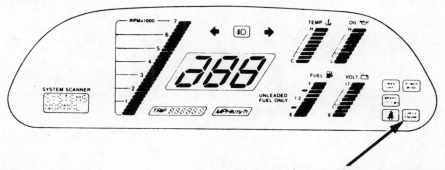

MALFUNCTION INDICATOR LIGHT (MIL)

Malfunction indicator light locations

DESCRIPTION

FMEM is an alternate system strategy in the ECA, designed to allow improved vehicle drive should one or more sensor inputs fail.

When a sensor input is perceived to be out-of-limits by the ECA, an alternative strategy will be initiated.

The ECA will substitute a fixed in-limit sensor value and will continue to monitor the faulty sensor input. If the faulty sensor operates within limits, the ECA will return to the normal engine running strategy.

MIL Check Engine Light will remain on when FMEM is in effect.

A code indication without MIL illumination prior to activating Self-Test indicated a past failure that is not present at the time of testing, these codes should only be addressed if the code(s) can be recreated in continuous testing.

	Engine			Malfunction Display	
Sensor or Sub-system	2.2L EFI	2.2L EFI TC	FMEM	Malfunction Code No.	MIL Output Signal Pattern
Ignition Pulse	X	X	—	01	
Crankshaft Position Sensor		X	—	02	
Cylinder Identification Sensor A		X	ECA uses only 1 sensor if 1 fails	03	
Cylinder Identification Sensor B		X		04	
Knock Sensor or Knock Control Unit		X	Retards ignition timing 6 deg. in heavy-load condition. TBC solenoid opens earlier	05	

Self test codes and light flash patterns

| Sensor or Sub-system | Engine | | FMEM | Malfunction Display | |
	2.2L EFI	2.2L EFI TC		Malfunction Code No.	MIL Output Signal Pattern
Vane Airflow Meter	X	X	Maintains basic signal at preset value of midrange vane position	08	
Engine Coolant Temperature Sensor	X	X	Maintains constant command — 35°C (95°F) fuel. 50°C (122°F) for ISC control use	09	
Vane Air Temperature Sensor	X	X	Maintains constant 20°C (68°F) command	10	
Throttle Position Sensor	X	X	Maintains constant command of throttle valve fully open	12	
Barometric Pressure Sensor	X	X	Maintains constant command of sea level pressure	14	
EGO Sensor	X	X	Cancels feedback operation	15	
EGR Valve Position Sensor	California Only	X	Cuts-off EGR	16	

Self test codes and light flash patterns

| Sensor or Sub-system | Engine | | FMEM | Service Code Display | |
	2.2L EFI	2.2L EFI TC		Service Code No.	MIL Output Signal Pattern
Pressure Regulator Control	X	X	—	25	
Canister Purge Solenoid Valve	X	X	—	26	
EGR Control Solenoid Valve	X	X	—	28	
EGR Vent Solenoid Valve		X	—	29	
Idle Speed Control Solenoid Valve	X	X	—	34	
Turbocharger Boost Control Solenoid Valve		X	—	42	

CAUTION:

a) If there is more than one service code present, the lowest number malfunction code is displayed first. The remaining codes are displayed in order.

b) After repairing a failure, turn off the ignition switch and disconnect the negative battery cable. Depress the brake pedal for at least five seconds to erase the memory of a malfunction code.

Self test codes and light flash patterns

VACUUM DIAGRAMS

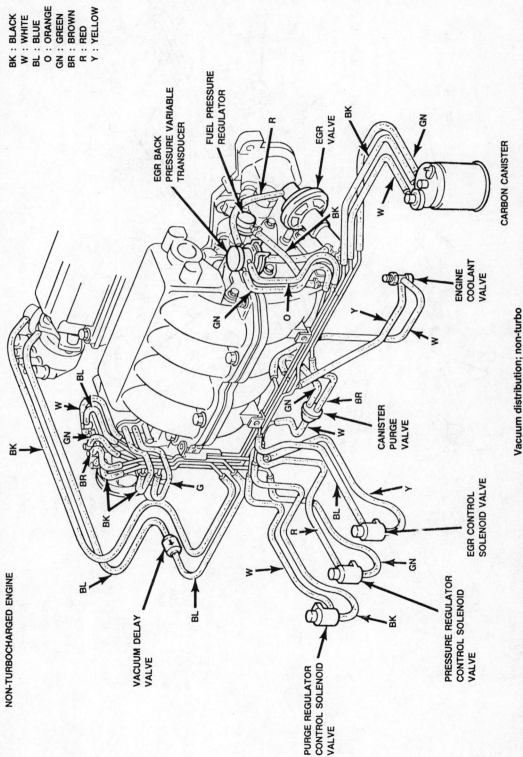

BK : BLACK
W : WHITE
BL : BLUE
O : ORANGE
GN : GREEN
BR : BROWN
R : RED
Y : YELLOW

NON-TURBOCHARGED ENGINE

EGR BACK PRESSURE VARIABLE TRANSDUCER

FUEL PRESSURE REGULATOR

EGR VALVE

CARBON CANISTER

ENGINE COOLANT VALVE

CANISTER PURGE VALVE

EGR CONTROL SOLENOID VALVE

PRESSURE REGULATOR CONTROL SOLENOID VALVE

PURGE REGULATOR CONTROL SOLENOID VALVE

VACUUM DELAY VALVE

Vacuum distribution; non-turbo

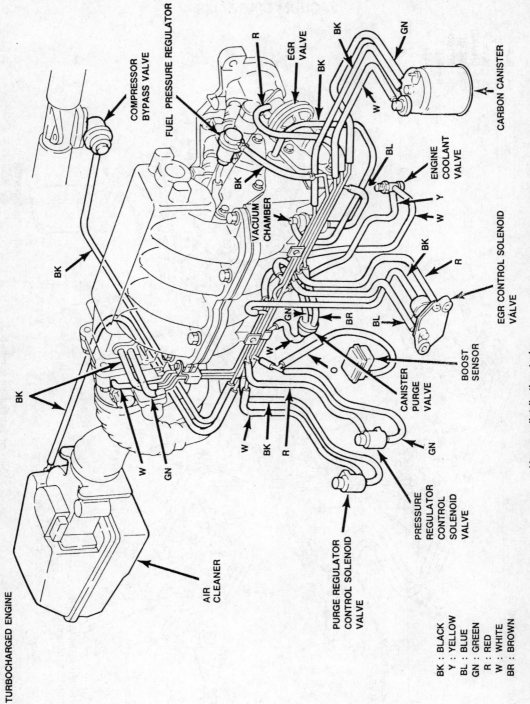

TURBOCHARGED ENGINE

COMPRESSOR BYPASS VALVE

FUEL PRESSURE REGULATOR

EGR VALVE

CARBON CANISTER

VACUUM CHAMBER

ENGINE COOLANT VALVE

EGR CONTROL SOLENOID VALVE

BOOST SENSOR

CANISTER PURGE VALVE

PRESSURE REGULATOR CONTROL SOLENOID VALVE

PURGE REGULATOR CONTROL SOLENOID VALVE

AIR CLEANER

BK : BLACK
Y : YELLOW
BL : BLUE
GN : GREEN
R : RED
W : WHITE
BR : BROWN

Vacuum distribution; turbo

Fuel System

5

FUEL INJECTION SYSTEM

The fuel system supplies fuel to the injectors at constant pressure in the correct volume for efficient combustion. The major components of the system include the fuel tank, connecting lines, fuel pump, fuel filter, pressure regulator, solenoid, pulsation damper, delivery pipe, injectors, fuel pump switch and a fuel relay. The electronic control assembly (ECA) controls the rate of fuel injection in response to signals received from various sensors and switches. It corrects the fuel rate for all major operating modes including basic injection rate, acceleration, power enrichment, feedback, deceleration, vehicle or engine overspeed cut, turbo overboost cut, and air conditioning start-up. The rate at which the air/fuel ratio is changed from one operating mode to another is preset in the ECA.

NOTE: *This book contains some testing and service procedures for your car's fuel injection system. More comprehensive testing and diagnosis procedures may be found in* CHILTON'S GUIDE TO FUEL INJECTION AND FEEDBACK CARBURETORS, *book part number 7488, available at your local retailer.*

CAUTION: *The injection fuel system is supplied fuel under high pressure. The pressure must be relieved before servicing the fuel system. Working around gasoline is extremely dangerous unless precautions are taken! NEVER smoke! Make sure the electrical system is disconnected. Avoid prolonged contact of gasoline with the skin. Wear safety glasses. Avoid prolonged breathing of gasoline vapors.*

Releasing Fuel System Pressure

1. Start the engine. Disconnect the fuel pump relay. The relay is located under the dash, near the clutch pedal or pedal supports.

2. After the engine shuts off, turn off the ignition and install the fuel pump relay. System pressure is now relieved.

3. Whenever a fuel line is opened, cover the fitting with a rag prior to loosening to prevent fuel spray.

CAUTION: *Never smoke when working around gasoline! Avoid all sources of sparks or ignition. Gasoline vapors are EXTREMELY volatile!*

Electric Fuel Pump
REMOVAL AND INSTALLATION

The fuel pump is mounted on the fuel sending unit assembly inside the fuel tank.

1. RELIEVE THE FUEL SYSTEM PRESSURE!

2. Disconnect the negative battery cable.

3. Remove the rear seat cushion. Disconnect the sending unit electrical connector.

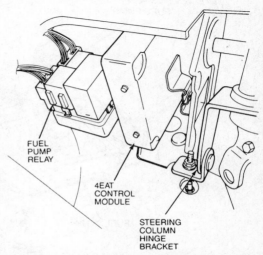

FUEL PUMP RELAY

4EAT CONTROL MODULE

STEERING COLUMN HINGE BRACKET

Remove the fuel pump relay while relieving system pressure

4. Remove the mounting screws retaining the sending unit.

CAUTION: *Never smoke when working around gasoline! Avoid all sources of sparks or ignition. Gasoline vapors are EXTREMELY volatile!*

5. Remove the sending unit cover. Remove the clamps securing the fuel supply and return line hoses. Remove the hoses from the sending unit.

6. Remove all of the screws from the sending unit and remove the unit.

NON-TURBO

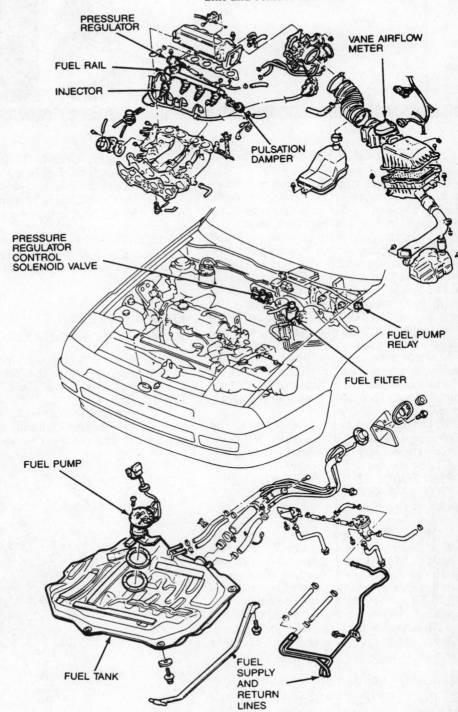

Fuel system; non-turbo

TURBO

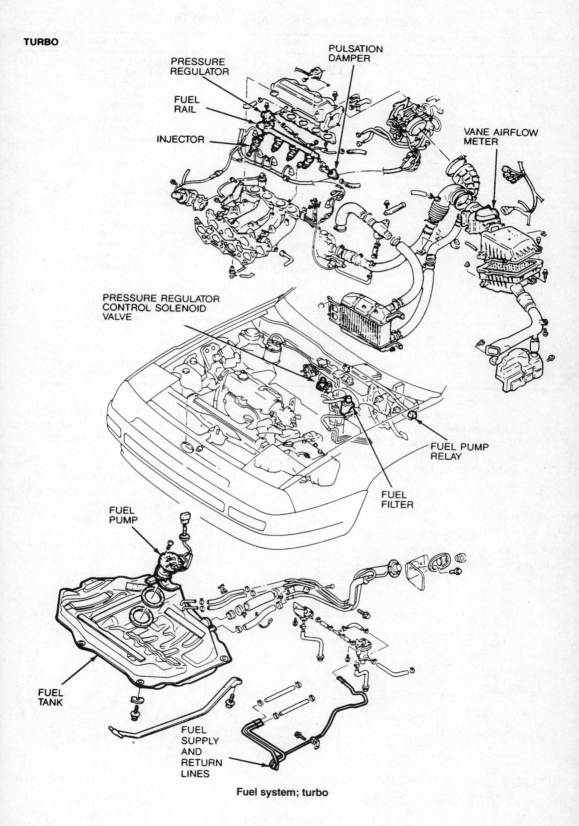

PRESSURE
REGULATOR

PULSATION
DAMPER

FUEL
RAIL

INJECTOR

VANE AIRFLOW
METER

PRESSURE REGULATOR
CONTROL SOLENOID
VALVE

FUEL PUMP
RELAY

FUEL
FILTER

FUEL
PUMP

FUEL
TANK

FUEL
SUPPLY
AND
RETURN
LINES

Fuel system; turbo

Troubleshooting Basic Fuel System Problems

Problem	Cause	Solution
Engine cranks, but won't start (or is hard to start) when cold	• Empty fuel tank • Incorrect starting procedure • Defective fuel pump • No fuel in carburetor • Clogged fuel filter • Engine flooded • Defective choke	• Check for fuel in tank • Follow correct procedure • Check pump output • Check for fuel in the carburetor • Replace fuel filter • Wait 15 minutes; try again • Check choke plate
Engine cranks, but is hard to start (or does not start) when hot— (presence of fuel is assumed)	• Defective choke	• Check choke plate
Rough idle or engine runs rough	• Dirt or moisture in fuel • Clogged air filter • Faulty fuel pump	• Replace fuel filter • Replace air filter • Check fuel pump output
Engine stalls or hesitates on acceleration	• Dirt or moisture in the fuel • Dirty carburetor • Defective fuel pump • Incorrect float level, defective accelerator pump	• Replace fuel filter • Clean the carburetor • Check fuel pump output • Check carburetor
Poor gas mileage	• Clogged air filter • Dirty carburetor • Defective choke, faulty carburetor adjustment	• Replace air filter • Clean carburetor • Check carburetor
Engine is flooded (won't start accompanied by smell of raw fuel)	• Improperly adjusted choke or carburetor	• Wait 15 minutes and try again, without pumping gas pedal • If it won't start, check carburetor

7. Position the sending unit and attach. Connect the hoses and install the cover.

8. Connect the electrical connection. Install the rear seat cushion. Connect the negative battery cable. Start the vehicle and check operation.

TESTING

1. If a fuel feed problem is suspected: Visually inspect the fuel delivery system and components including the fuel tank and connecting lines, pressure regulator, fuel rail, injectors, vacuum and electrical lines for leaks, cracks, looseness, pinching, grounding, corrosion, or other damage.

2. Check for an empty fuel tank.

3. Check the 15 amp engine fuse.

4. Check the fuel system pressure with a special fuel pressure test kit connected in front of the fuel filter to the feed line. Pressure should be 27–40 psi.

CAUTION: *Never smoke when working around gasoline! Avoid all sources of sparks*

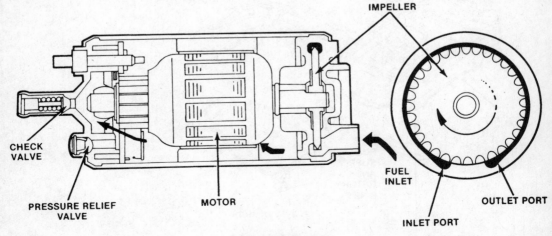

CHECK VALVE

PRESSURE RELIEF VALVE

MOTOR

IMPELLER

FUEL INLET

INLET PORT

OUTLET PORT

Electric fuel pump

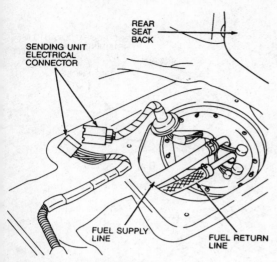

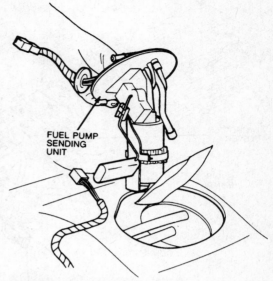

Fuel tank sending unit location

Remove/install the sending unit

or ignition. Gasoline vapors are EXTREME-LY volatile!

5. Has the inertia shut off switch been activated: Open the cover in the luggage compartment and reset the inertia switch by pushing the reset button.

6. Check the fuel pump relay connection, does the relay click when the ignition is turned on.

7. The fuel pump may be suspect if checking reveals no other problems.

Throttle Body

REMOVAL AND INSTALLATION

1. RELIEVE THE FUEL SYSTEM PRESSURE!
CAUTION: *Never smoke when working*

around gasoline! Avoid all sources of sparks or ignition. Gasoline vapors are EXTREME-LY volatile!

2. Disconnect the negative battery cable.

3. Remove the accelerator cables from the throttle body.

4. Remove the air duct from the throttle body.

5. Label and remove all vacuum lines and hoses from the throttle body.

6. Disconnect the throttle position sensor connector, idle switch connector, and by-pass air control valve connector. Remove the engine lifting bracket mounting bolt from the throttle body.

7. Remove the coolant line/EGR hose bracket from the throttle body.

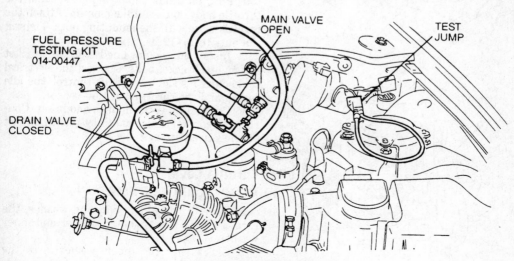

Pressure test kit installation

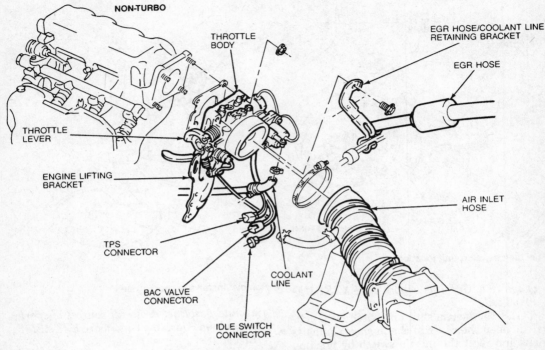

Remove/install the throttle body

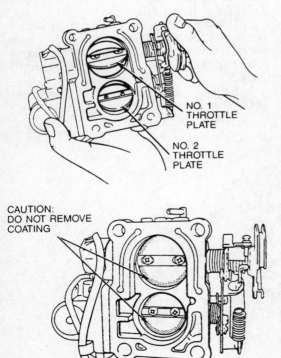

NO. 1 THROTTLE PLATE

NO. 2 THROTTLE PLATE

CAUTION: DO NOT REMOVE COATING

Throttle plate identification

8. Remove the throttle body mounting nuts and remove the throttle body.

NOTE: *The No. 2 throttle plate is factory set to begin opening after the No. 1 plate. Do not attempt to adjust. Do not remove the thin sealing coating from the edges of the throttle plates.*

9. Position a new mounting gasket and the throttle body on the intake plenum. Attach the throttle plate with the mounting nuts. Tighten the nuts to 14–19 ft. lbs.

10. Install the coolant line/EGR hose bracket and engine bracket bolts. Connect the electrical connectors for the by-pass air control, the idle switch and the throttle position sensor.

11. Connect all vacuum lines and hoses. Connect the control cables and inlet duct. Connect the negative battery cable.

Throttle Lever

REMOVAL AND INSTALLATION

1. Remove the nut and spring washer, the throttle lever, spacer, outer washer and inner washer.

2. Check that the inner washer is in the proper position. Assemble the spacer and outer

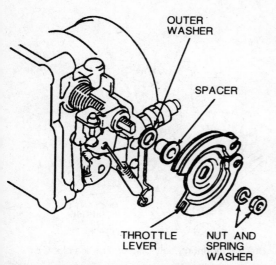

Remove the throttle lever and attaching components in this sequence

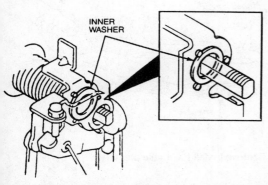

When installing the throttle lever make sure the inner washer is in the proper position

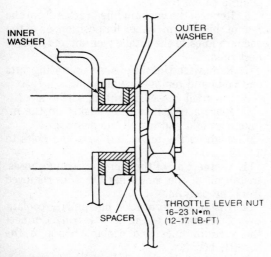

Throttle lever installed

washer, place them into position. Install the throttle lever and nut. When tightening the nut, hold the throttle blades fully closed to prevent bending the stopper lever.

3. Tighten the nut to 12–17 ft. lbs. Check that the throttle plates open and close smoothly.

By-pass Air Control (BAC) Valve
REMOVAL AND INSTALLATION

1. Remove the four mounting screws from the BAC valve after disconnecting the electrical connector.

2. Remove the BAC from the throttle body.

3. Clean all mounting surfaces. Apply sealer to both sides of a new gasket and put the gasket and BAC, in position, on the throttle body. Tighten the mounting screws.

4. Blow air through the valve port (A) and check that the air comes out of port (B) when the BAC is cold. If the air flow is restricted, replace the BAC.

5. Connect a volt/ohmmeter to the BAC electrical connector. Resistance at cold engine temperature should be 6.3–9.9Ω. Replace the BAC if the resistance is not within specs.

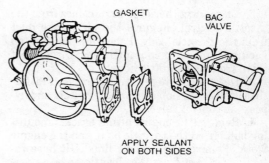

Remove/install the BAC

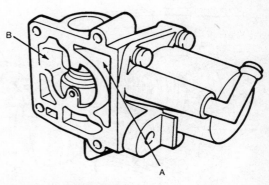

Airflow through the BAC

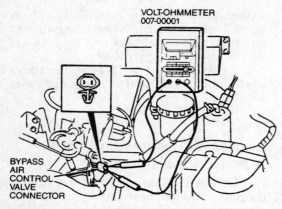

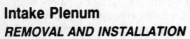

Checking the BAC electrical resistance

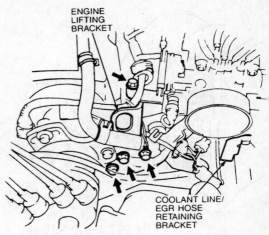

Bracket mounting bolt locations on the plenum

Intake Plenum

REMOVAL AND INSTALLATION

1. Disconnect the negative battery cable. Drain the cooling system.

CAUTION: *When draining the coolant, keep in mind that cats and dogs are attracted by the ethylene glycol antifreeze, and are quite likely to drink any that is left in an uncovered container or in puddles on the ground. This will prove fatal in sufficient quantity. Always drain the coolant into a sealable container. Coolant should be reused unless it is contaminated or several years old.*

2. Disconnect the accelerator cables from the throttle control. Remove the air intake duct from the throttle body. Label, for position, all vacuum lines and coolant hoses, disconnect them from the throttle body.

3. Disconnect the electrical connectors for; the throttle position sensor, idle switch, and by-pass air control valve.

4. Remove the engine lifting bracket mounting bolts from the throttle body and the engine block. Remove the coolant line/EGR hose retaining bracket from the throttle body.

5. Remove the throttle cable mounting brackets from the intake plenum. Remove the

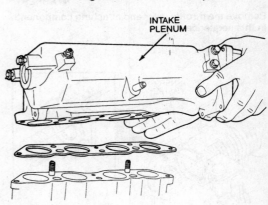

Remove/install the intake plenum

mounting brackets for the wire loom and EGR back-pressure transducer from the right side of the plenum. Remove the PCV hose from the plenum connector.

6. Remove the vacuum line bracket from the rear of the plenum. Label, for position, all of the vacuum lines to the intake plenum and disconnect them.

7. Remove the intake plenum mounting nuts and bolts and remove the plenum.

8. Clean all gasket mounting surfaces.

9. Place a new mounting gasket on the intake manifold and install the plenum.

10. Tighten the mounting nuts and bolts to 14–19 ft. lbs.

11. Connect all of the plenum vacuum hoses. Install all of the mounting brackets removed from the plenum.

12. Install the lift bracket bolt and the coolant hose/EGR bracket to the throttle body. Connect the vacuum lines and coolant hoses to the throttle body.

13. Connect the throttle position sensor, idle

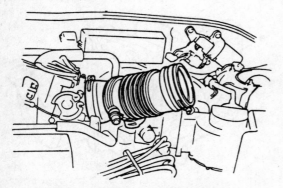

Disconnect the intake air duct from the plenum

switch and bypass air control valve electrical connectors.

14. Attach the throttle/accelerator cable. Install the intake air duct. Connect the negative battery cable. Fill the cooling system.

Vane Airflow Meter
REMOVAL AND INSTALLATION

1. Disconnect the negative battery cable.

2. Disconnect airflow meter electrical connector. Remove the air duct from the air filter cover and remove the air cleaner cover mounting bolts.

3. Remove the air cleaner cover. Remove the vane airflow meter mounting nuts from inside the air cleaner cover. Remove the meter.

4. Place the vane airflow meter into positon on the air cleaner cover. Install the attaching nuts. Install the air cleaner cover and the duct hose.

5. Connect the vane airflow meter electrical connector. Connect the negative battery cable.

Fuel Injectors
REMOVAL AND INSTALLATION

1. RELIEVE THE FUEL SYSTEM PRESSURE!

CAUTION: *Never smoke when working around gasoline! Avoid all sources of sparks or ignition. Gasoline vapors are EXTREMELY volatile!*

2. Disconnect the negative battery cable.

3. Remove the intake plenum.

4. Disconnect the electrical connectors from the fuel injectors. On models equipped with an automatic transaxle, disconnect the engine coolant temperature switch.

5. Carefully bend the wire retaining brackets

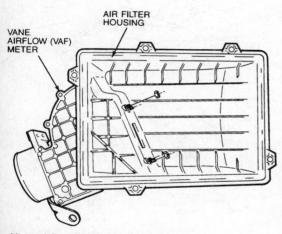

Vane airflow (VAF) meter location

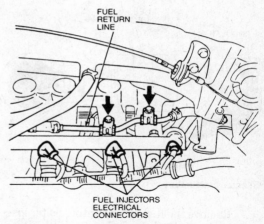

Fuel return line and injector wiring harness

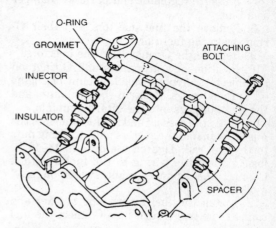

Fuel rail and injectors

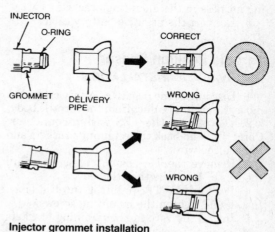

Injector grommet installation

away from the injector wiring harness. Move the harness away from the intake manifold.

6. Disconnect the fuel supply line from the pulsation damper. Remove the fuel return line bracket from the intake manifold. Disconnect the fuel return line.

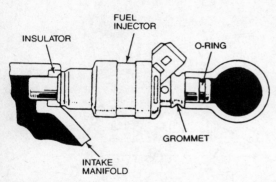

Injector installation

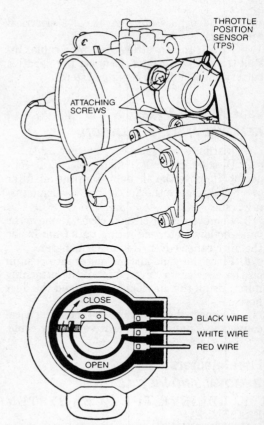

Throttle position sensor removal and installation

7. Remove the fuel rail mounting bolts, spacers, insulators, and the fuel rail with the injectors, pressure regulator and pulsation damper as a unit.

8. Remove the fuel injectors and their O-rings from the fuel rail.

9. Remove the O-rings from the injectors.

10. Position new grommets and O-rings on the injectors. Apply a small amount of engine oil to the O-rings. Position the insulators and the fuel injectors into the intake manifold.

11. Place the spacers and the fuel rail onto the injectors. Install the spacers and attaching nuts to the fuel rail. Tighten the nuts to 14–19 ft. lbs. Connect the wiring to the fuel injectors. Connect the engine coolant switch on ATX models.

12. Install the fuel return line bracket and connect the fuel return line. Connect the fuel supply line.

13. Install the intake plenum. Secure the wiring harness in the mounting brackets

14. Connect the negative battery cable.

Throttle Position Sensor

REMOVAL AND INSTALLATION

1. Disconnect the negative battery cable. Remove the air intake duct from the throttle body.

2. Disconnect the TPS wiring connector. Carefully bend back the retaining brackets and remove the wire,

3. Remove the TPS mounting screws. Pull the sensor from the throttle body.

4. Position the TPS into the throttle body. Install and tighten the mounting screws.

5. Install the wire in the retaining brackets and connect the electrical connector.

6. Adjust the TPS as required. Install the air duct. Connect the negative battery cable.

TPS ADJUSTMENT

1. Remove the air duct from the throttle (if not already disconnected).

2. Disconnect the three pin connector at the

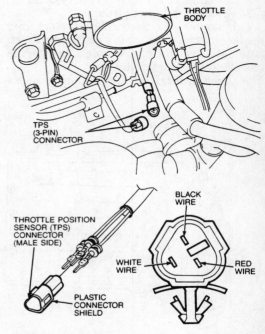

TPS connector

CHILTON'S
FUEL ECONOMY
& TUNE-UP TIPS

Tune-up • Spark Plug Diagnosis • Emission Controls

Fuel System • Cooling System • Tires and Wheels

General Maintenance

55 WAYS TO IMPROVE FUEL ECONOMY

CHILTON'S FUEL ECONOMY & TUNE-UP TIPS

Fuel economy is important to everyone, no matter what kind of vehicle you drive. The maintenance-minded motorist can save both money and fuel using these tips and the periodic maintenance and tune-up procedures in this Repair and Tune-Up Guide.

There are more than 130,000,000 cars and trucks registered for private use in the United States. Each travels an average of 10-12,000 miles per year, and, and in total they consume close to 70 billion gallons of fuel each year. This represents nearly ⅔ of the oil imported by the United States each year. The Federal government's goal is to reduce consumption 10% by 1985. A variety of methods are either already in use or under serious consideration, and they all affect you driving and the cars you will drive. In addition to "down-sizing", the auto industry is using or investigating the use of electronic fuel delivery, electronic engine controls and alternative engines for use in smaller and lighter vehicles, among other alternatives to meet the federally mandated Corporate Average Fuel Economy (CAFE) of 27.5 mpg by 1985. The government, for its part, is considering rationing, mandatory driving curtailments and tax increases on motor vehicle fuel in an effort to reduce consumption. The government's goal of a 10% reduction could be realized — and further government regulation avoided — if every private vehicle could use just 1 less gallon of fuel per week.

How Much Can You Save?

Tests have proven that almost anyone can make at least a 10% reduction in fuel consumption through regular maintenance and tune-ups. When a major manufacturer of spark plugs sur-

TUNE-UP

1. Check the cylinder compression to be sure the engine will really benefit from a tune-up and that it is capable of producing good fuel economy. A tune-up will be wasted on an engine in poor mechanical condition.

2. Replace spark plugs regularly. New spark plugs alone can increase fuel economy 3%.

3. Be sure the spark plugs are the correct type (heat range) for your vehicle. See the Tune-Up Specifications.

Heat range refers to the spark plug's ability to conduct heat away from the firing end. It must conduct the heat away in an even pattern to avoid becoming a source of pre-ignition, yet it must also operate hot enough to burn off conductive deposits that could cause misfiring.

The heat range is usually indicated by a number on the spark plug, part of the manufacturer's designation for each individual spark plug. The numbers in bold-face indicate the heat range in each manufacturer's identification system.

Manufacturer	Typical Designation
AC	R **45** TS
Bosch (old)	WA **145** T30
Bosch (new)	HR **8** Y
Champion	RBL **15** Y
Fram/Autolite	4**15**
Mopar	P-**62** PR
Motorcraft	BRF-**42**
NGK	BP **5** ES-15
Nippondenso	W **16** EP
Prestolite	14GR **5** 2A

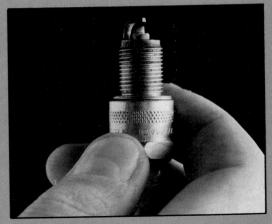

Periodically, check the spark plugs to be sure they are firing efficiently. They are excellent indicators of the internal condition of your engine.

On AC, Bosch (new), Champion, Fram/Autolite, Mopar, Motorcraft and Prestolite, a higher number indicates a hotter plug. On Bosch (old), NGK and Nippondenso, a higher number indicates a colder plug.

4. Make sure the spark plugs are properly gapped. See the Tune-Up Specifications in this book.

5. Be sure the spark plugs are firing efficiently. The illustrations on the next 2 pages show you how to "read" the firing end of the spark plug.

6. Check the ignition timing and set it to specifications. Tests show that almost all cars have incorrect ignition timing by more than 2°.

veyed over 6,000 cars nationwide, they found that a tune-up, on cars that needed one, increased fuel economy over 11%. Replacing worn plugs alone, accounted for a 3% increase. The same test also revealed that 8 out of every 10 vehicles will have some maintenance deficiency that will directly affect fuel economy, emissions or performance. Most of this mileage-robbing neglect could be prevented with regular maintenance.

Modern engines require that all of the functioning systems operate properly for maximum efficiency. A malfunction anywhere wastes fuel. You can keep your vehicle running as efficiently and economically as possible, by being aware of your vehicle's operating and performance characteristics. If your vehicle suddenly develops performance or fuel economy problems it could be due to one or more of the following:

PROBLEM	POSSIBLE CAUSE
Engine Idles Rough	Ignition timing, idle mixture, vacuum leak or something amiss in the emission control system.
Hesitates on Acceleration	Dirty carburetor or fuel filter, improper accelerator pump setting, ignition timing or fouled spark plugs.
Starts Hard or Fails to Start	Worn spark plugs, improperly set automatic choke, ice (or water) in fuel system.
Stalls Frequently	Automatic choke improperly adjusted and possible dirty air filter or fuel filter.
Performs Sluggishly	Worn spark plugs, dirty fuel or air filter, ignition timing or automatic choke out of adjustment.

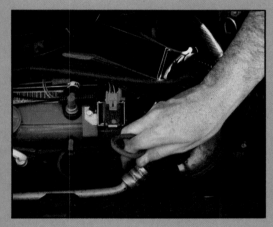

Check spark plug wires on conventional point type ignition for cracks by bending them in a loop around your finger.

Be sure that spark plug wires leading to adjacent cylinders do not run too close together. (Photo courtesy Champion Spark Plug Co.)

7. If your vehicle does not have electronic ignition, check the points, rotor and cap as specified.

8. Check the spark plug wires (used with conventional point-type ignitions) for cracks and burned or broken insulation by bending them in a loop around your finger. Cracked wires decrease fuel efficiency by failing to deliver full voltage to the spark plugs. One misfiring spark plug can cost you as much as 2 mpg.

9. Check the routing of the plug wires. Misfiring can be the result of spark plug leads to adjacent cylinders running parallel to each other and too close together. One wire tends to pick up voltage from the other causing it to fire "out of time".

10. Check all electrical and ignition circuits for voltage drop and resistance.

11. Check the distributor mechanical and/or vacuum advance mechanisms for proper functioning. The vacuum advance can be checked by twisting the distributor plate in the opposite direction of rotation. It should spring back when released.

12. Check and adjust the valve clearance on engines with mechanical lifters. The clearance should be slightly loose rather than too tight.

SPARK PLUG DIAGNOSIS

Normal

APPEARANCE: This plug is typical of one operating normally. The insulator nose varies from a light tan to grayish color with slight electrode wear. The presence of slight deposits is normal on used plugs and will have no adverse effect on engine performance. The spark plug heat range is correct for the engine and the engine is running normally.

CAUSE: Properly running engine.

RECOMMENDATION: Before reinstalling this plug, the electrodes should be cleaned and filed square. Set the gap to specifications. If the plug has been in service for more than 10-12,000 miles, the entire set should probably be replaced with a fresh set of the same heat range.

Oil Deposits

APPEARANCE: The firing end of the plug is covered with a wet, oily coating.

CAUSE: The problem is poor oil control. On high mileage engines, oil is leaking past the rings or valve guides into the combustion chamber. A common cause is also a plugged PCV valve, and a ruptured fuel pump diaphragm can also cause this condition. Oil fouled plugs such as these are often found in new or recently overhauled engines, before normal oil control is achieved, and can be cleaned and reinstalled.

RECOMMENDATION: A hotter spark plug may temporarily relieve the problem, but the engine is probably in need of work.

Incorrect Heat Range

APPEARANCE: The effects of high temperature on a spark plug are indicated by clean white, often blistered insulator. This can also be accompanied by excessive wear of the electrode, and the absence of deposits.

CAUSE: Check for the correct spark plug heat range. A plug which is too hot for the engine can result in overheating. A car operated mostly at high speeds can require a colder plug. Also check ignition timing, cooling system level, fuel mixture and leaking intake manifold.

RECOMMENDATION: If all ignition and engine adjustments are known to be correct, and no other malfunction exists, install spark plugs one heat range colder.

Photos Courtesy Fram Corporation

Carbon Deposits

APPEARANCE: Carbon fouling is easily identified by the presence of dry, soft, black, sooty deposits.

CAUSE: Changing the heat range can often lead to carbon fouling, as can prolonged slow, stop-and-start driving. If the heat range is correct, carbon fouling can be attributed to a rich fuel mixture, sticking choke, clogged air cleaner, worn breaker points, retarded timing or low compression. If only one or two plugs are carbon fouled, check for corroded or cracked wires on the affected plugs. Also look for cracks in the distributor cap between the towers of affected cylinders.

RECOMMENDATION: After the problem is corrected, these plugs can be cleaned and reinstalled if not worn severely.

MMT Fouled

APPEARANCE: Spark plugs fouled by MMT (Methycyclopentadienyl Maganese Tricarbonyl) have reddish, rusty appearance on the insulator and side electrode.

CAUSE: MMT is an anti-knock additive in gasoline used to replace lead. During the combustion process, the MMT leaves a reddish deposit on the insulator and side electrode.

RECOMMENDATION: No engine malfunction is indicated and the deposits will not affect plug performance any more than lead deposits (see Ash Deposits). MMT fouled plugs can be cleaned, regapped and reinstalled.

High Speed Glazing

APPEARANCE: Glazing appears as shiny coating on the plug, either yellow or tan in color.

CAUSE: During hard, fast acceleration, plug temperatures rise suddenly. Deposits from normal combustion have no chance to fluff-off; instead, they melt on the insulator forming an electrically conductive coating which causes misfiring.

RECOMMENDATION: Glazed plugs are not easily cleaned. They should be replaced with a fresh set of plugs of the correct heat range. If the condition recurs, using plugs with a heat range one step colder may cure the problem.

Ash (Lead) Deposits

APPEARANCE: Ash deposits are characterized by light brown or white colored deposits crusted on the side or center electrodes. In some cases it may give the plug a rusty appearance.

CAUSE: Ash deposits are normally derived from oil or fuel additives burned during normal combustion. Normally they are harmless, though excessive amounts can cause misfiring. If deposits are excessive in short mileage, the valve guides may be worn.

RECOMMENDATION: Ash-fouled plugs can be cleaned, gapped and reinstalled.

Detonation

APPEARANCE: Detonation is usually characterized by a broken plug insulator.

CAUSE: A portion of the fuel charge will begin to burn spontaneously, from the increased heat following ignition. The explosion that results applies extreme pressure to engine components, frequently damaging spark plugs and pistons.

Detonation can result by over-advanced ignition timing, inferior gasoline (low octane) lean air/fuel mixture, poor carburetion, engine lugging or an increase in compression ratio due to combustion chamber deposits or engine modification.

RECOMMENDATION: Replace the plugs after correcting the problem.

EMISSION CONTROLS

13. Be aware of the general condition of the emission control system. It contributes to reduced pollution and should be serviced regularly to maintain efficient engine operation.

14. Check all vacuum lines for dried, cracked or brittle conditions. Something as simple as a leaking vacuum hose can cause poor performance and loss of economy.

15. Avoid tampering with the emission control system. Attempting to improve fuel econ-

FUEL SYSTEM

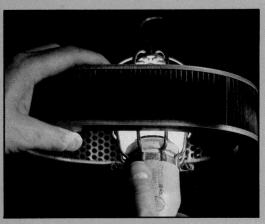

Check the air filter with a light behind it. If you can see light through the filter it can be reused.

Extremely clogged filters should be discarded and replaced with a new one.

18. Replace the air filter regularly. A dirty air filter richens the air/fuel mixture and can increase fuel consumption as much as 10%. Tests show that 1/3 of all vehicles have air filters in need of replacement.

19. Replace the fuel filter at least as often as recommended.

20. Set the idle speed and carburetor mixture to specifications.

21. Check the automatic choke. A sticking or malfunctioning choke wastes gas.

22. During the summer months, adjust the automatic choke for a leaner mixture which will produce faster engine warm-ups.

COOLING SYSTEM

29. Be sure all accessory drive belts are in good condition. Check for cracks or wear.

30. Adjust all accessory drive belts to proper tension.

31. Check all hoses for swollen areas, worn spots, or loose clamps.

32. Check coolant level in the radiator or expansion tank.

33. Be sure the thermostat is operating properly. A stuck thermostat delays engine warm-up and a cold engine uses nearly twice as much fuel as a warm engine.

34. Drain and replace the engine coolant at least as often as recommended. Rust and scale

TIRES & WHEELS

38. Check the tire pressure often with a pencil type gauge. Tests by a major tire manufacturer show that 90% of all vehicles have at least 1 tire improperly inflated. Better mileage can be achieved by over-inflating tires, but never exceed the maximum inflation pressure on the side of the tire.

39. If possible, install radial tires. Radial tires deliver as much as 1/2 mpg more than bias belted tires.

40. Avoid installing super-wide tires. They only create extra rolling resistance and decrease fuel mileage. Stick to the manufacturer's recommendations.

41. Have the wheels properly balanced.

omy by tampering with emission controls is more likely to worsen fuel economy than improve it. Emission control changes on modern engines are not readily reversible.

16. Clean (or replace) the EGR valve and lines as recommended.

17. Be sure that all vacuum lines and hoses are reconnected properly after working under the hood. An unconnected or misrouted vacuum line can wreak havoc with engine performance.

23. Check for fuel leaks at the carburetor, fuel pump, fuel lines and fuel tank. Be sure all lines and connections are tight.

24. Periodically check the tightness of the carburetor and intake manifold attaching nuts and bolts. These are a common place for vacuum leaks to occur.

25. Clean the carburetor periodically and lubricate the linkage.

26. The condition of the tailpipe can be an excellent indicator of proper engine combustion. After a long drive at highway speeds, the inside of the tailpipe should be a light grey in color. Black or soot on the insides indicates an overly rich mixture.

27. Check the fuel pump pressure. The fuel pump may be supplying more fuel than the engine needs.

28. Use the proper grade of gasoline for your engine. Don't try to compensate for knocking or "pinging" by advancing the ignition timing. This practice will only increase plug temperature and the chances of detonation or pre-ignition with relatively little performance gain.

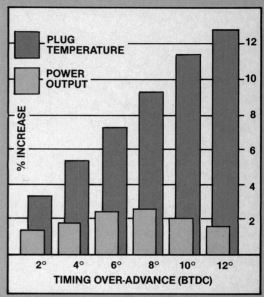

Increasing ignition timing past the specified setting results in a drastic increase in spark plug temperature with increased chance of detonation or preignition. Performance increase is considerably less. (Photo courtesy Champion Spark Plug Co.)

that form in the engine should be flushed out to allow the engine to operate at peak efficiency.

35. Clean the radiator of debris that can decrease cooling efficiency.

36. Install a flex-type or electric cooling fan, if you don't have a clutch type fan. Flex fans use curved plastic blades to push more air at low speeds when more cooling is needed; at high speeds the blades flatten out for less resistance. Electric fans only run when the engine temperature reaches a predetermined level.

37. Check the radiator cap for a worn or cracked gasket. If the cap does not seal properly, the cooling system will not function properly.

42. Be sure the front end is correctly aligned. A misaligned front end actually has wheels going in differed directions. The increased drag can reduce fuel economy by .3 mpg.

43. Correctly adjust the wheel bearings. Wheel bearings that are adjusted too tight increase rolling resistance.

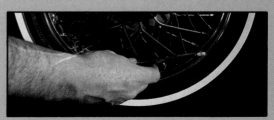

Check tire pressures regularly with a reliable pocket type gauge. Be sure to check the pressure on a cold tire.

GENERAL MAINTENANCE

Check the fluid levels (particularly engine oil) on a regular basis. Be sure to check the oil for grit, water or other contamination.

A vacuum gauge is another excellent indicator of internal engine condition and can also be installed in the dash as a mileage indicator.

44. Periodically check the fluid levels in the engine, power steering pump, master cylinder, automatic transmission and drive axle.

45. Change the oil at the recommended interval and change the filter at every oil change. Dirty oil is thick and causes extra friction between moving parts, cutting efficiency and increasing wear. A worn engine requires more frequent tune-ups and gets progressively worse fuel economy. In general, use the lightest viscosity oil for the driving conditions you will encounter.

46. Use the recommended viscosity fluids in the transmission and axle.

47. Be sure the battery is fully charged for fast starts. A slow starting engine wastes fuel.

48. Be sure battery terminals are clean and tight.

49. Check the battery electrolyte level and add distilled water if necessary.

50. Check the exhaust system for crushed pipes, blockages and leaks.

51. Adjust the brakes. Dragging brakes or brakes that are not releasing create increased drag on the engine.

52. Install a vacuum gauge or miles-per-gallon gauge. These gauges visually indicate engine vacuum in the intake manifold. High vacuum = good mileage and low vacuum = poorer mileage. The gauge can also be an excellent indicator of internal engine conditions.

53. Be sure the clutch is properly adjusted. A slipping clutch wastes fuel.

54. Check and periodically lubricate the heat control valve in the exhaust manifold. A sticking or inoperative valve prevents engine warm-up and wastes gas.

55. Keep accurate records to check fuel economy over a period of time. A sudden drop in fuel economy may signal a need for tune-up or other maintenance.

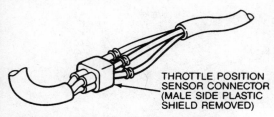

Shield removed from the TPS connector

Throttle plates closed/opened

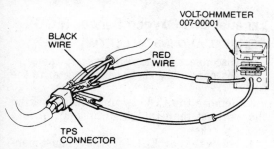

Red wire voltmeter connection

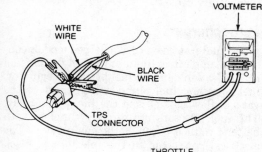

White wire voltmeter connection

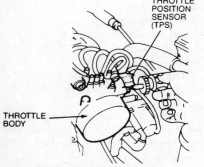

bottom of the throttle body. Remove the plastic shield from the male side of the TPS connector.

3. Connect the unshielded male side TPS connector to the female; be sure that the wire leads are in their proper locations.

WARNING: *TAKE CARE NOT TO ACCIDENTALLY GROUND THE EXPOSED WIRE LEADS!*

4. Turn the ignition switch to the ON position. Make sure both throttle plates are in their fully closed position.

RED/WHITE Wire Voltage Relationship Chart

Specification: Throttle valve fully closed position

RED wire voltage (V)	WHITE wire voltage (V)	RED wire voltage (V)	WHITE wire voltage (V)
4.50–4.59	0.37–0.54	5.10–5.19	0.42–0.61
4.60–4.69	0.38–0.55	5.20–5.29	0.43–0.62
4.70–4.79	0.39–0.56	5.30–5.39	0.44–0.63
4.80–4.89	0.40–0.57	5.40–5.49	0.44–0.64
4.90–4.99	0.40–0.58	5.50	0.44–0.66
5.00–5.09	0.41–0.60		

Specification: Throttle valve fully open position

RED wire voltage (V)	WHITE wire voltage (V)	RED wire voltage (V)	WHITE wire voltage (V)
4.50–4.59	3.58–4.23	5.10–5.19	4.05–4.79
4.60–4.69	3.66–4.32	5.20–5.29	4.13–4.88
4.70–4.79	3.74–4.41	5.30–5.39	4.21–4.98
4.80–4.89	3.82–4.51	5.40–5.49	4.29–5.07
4.90–4.99	3.90–4.60	5.50	4.29–5.17
5.00–5.09	3.97–4.70		

Inspection Steps
Step 1: Throttle valve fully closed position
1. Measure RED wire voltage.
2. Record RED wire voltage.
3. Measure WHITE wire voltage.
4. Verify that WHITE wire voltage is within the specified range.

Step 2: Throttle valve fully open position
5. Measure WHITE wire voltage.
6. Verify that WHITE wire voltage is within the specified range.

Adjustment
If the WHITE wire voltage measured in step 1 is not within specification range, adjust or replace the throttle position sensor (TPS).

Red/White wire resistance relationship

5. Use a digital voltmeter and connect the test leads between the BLACK and RED TPS wires. Record the voltage reading. Reading required RED wire (V): 4.5–5.5V.

6. Change the lead from the voltmeter to the WHITE TPS lead. Loosen, but do not remove the TPS mounting screws. Turn the TPS to adjust the WHITE wire voltage within the range specified for the recorded RED wire voltage. See voltage chart.

7. Tighten the TPS mounting screws and check that the WHITE wire voltage is within specification. If the WHITE wire cannot be adjusted to required specification, the TPS must be replaced and adjusted.

8. Hold the throttle valves wide opened. Measure the RED wire voltage and record the reading.

9. Check that the WHITE wire voltage is within specification. If not within specifications, the TPS must be replaced and adjusted.

10. Turn the ignition switch to OFF. Disconnect the voltmeter and replace the plastic shield on the male side of the TPS connector. Connect the TPS connector.

11. Disconnect the negative battery cable and depress the brake pedal for at least two seconds to eliminate the ECA malfunction memory. Connect the negative battery cable.

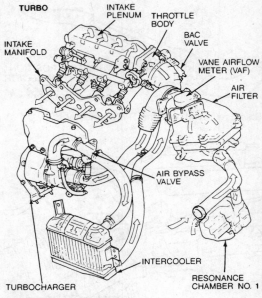

Turbo air induction system

Exhaust Gas Oxygen Sensor (EGO)
REMOVAL AND INSTALLATION

1. Disconnect the negative battery cable.
2. Disconnect the electrical connector to the EGO.
3. Remove the EGO by unscrewing it from the exhaust manifold with an appropriate wrench/socket.
4. Screw the new EGO into the exhaust manifold and connect the wiring. Connect the negative battery cable.

Turbocharger

The fuel system on turbocharged models consists of an electric fuel pump, fuel filters, fuel rail, pulsation damper, fuel pressure regulator, fuel injectors, fuel pump switch (part of the vane airflow meter), and the fuel pump relay. The fuel injectors are directly supplied with battery voltage through the main relay. The electrical connector to the injectors is black (non-turbo is blue). Fuel is metered and injected into the intake ports according to the injection signals received from the ECA. When injection signals are applied to the coil of the injector, the needle is pulled off its seat. Fuel is injected into the intake port. The amount of fuel supplied to the engine depends on the duration the injector stays open.

When the engine is in the cranking mode, fuel is supplied to all cylinders simultaneously by providing one injection per crankshaft rotation (two injections per cycle). Therefore one injection period supplies half of the fuel necessary

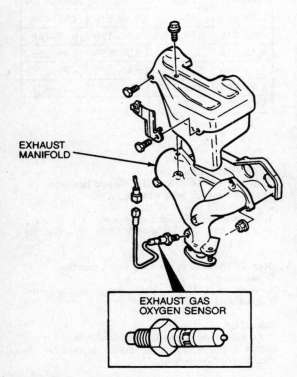

Exhaust gas oxygen sensor

for ideal combustion. Between idle and 6000 rpm, fuel is supplied through a two group injection by providing one injection per two crankshaft rotations (one injection per cycle). At the completion of the first crankshaft rotation, fuel is supplied to cylinders No.1 and 3 by determination of the cylinder identification sensors signal created in the distributor. After completion of the second crankshaft rotation, fuel is supplied to cylinders No. 2 and 4 by determination of the cylinder identification sensors signal also created in the distributor. To prevent engine

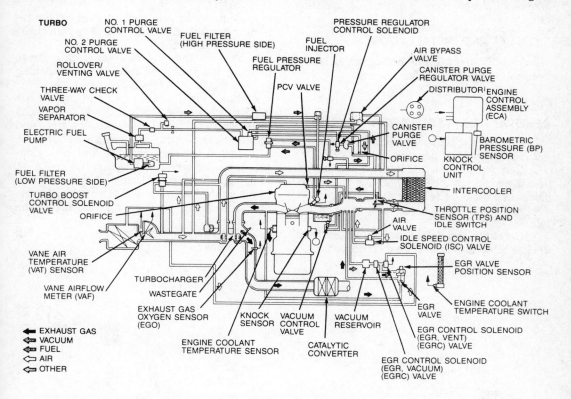

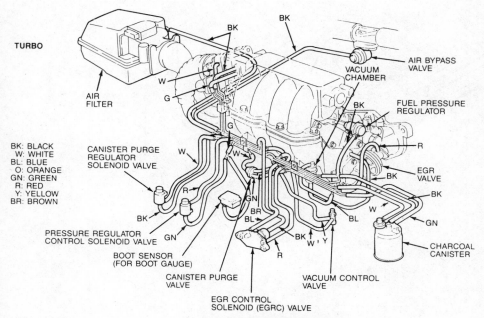

Turbo fuel injection system

overspeeding and possible damage, the fuel supply is cut off if engine speed continues over 6000 rpm for approximately 5 seconds. If engine speed momentarily exceeds 6300 rpm, fuel is cut until engine speed drops below 5800 rpm. In addition, the fuel supply is cut when the intake manifold pressure exceeds ECA specified value.

REMOVAL AND INSTALLATION

Refer to Chapter 3. The turbocharger is serviced by replacement only.

Fuel Tank

REMOVAL AND INSTALLATION

1. RELIEVE FUEL SYSTEM PRESSURE!
2. Disconnect the negative battery cable.
3. Remove the rear seat cushion and disconnect the wiring to the tank and fuel pump. Remove the hoses to the sending unit.
4. Raise and safely support the rear of the vehicle.
5. Carefully and safely drain the fuel from the gas tank into an approved container.

CAUTION: *Never smoke when working around gasoline! Avoid all sources of sparks or ignition. Gasoline vapors are EXTREMELY volatile!*

6. Remove the clamps and vapor hoses at the fuel filler neck. Remove the clamp and filler neck hose.
7. Remove the two parking brake cable retaining brackets from the chassis to gain clearance for tank removal.
8. Remove the fuel tank mounting strap. Support the tank and remove the attaching bolts and brackets. Lower the fuel tank.
9. Position the fuel tank and install the mounting bolts and brackets. Tighten the bolts to 16–24 ft. lbs. Install the mounting strap and tighten the mounting bolt to 32–45 ft. lbs.
10. Install the parking brake brackets. Connect the filler neck and hoses.
11. Tighten the tank drain plug to 9–13 ft. lbs. Lower the vehicle. Connect the hoses and wiring connectors to the sending unit. Install the seat cushion.
12. Connect the negative battery cable. Fill the gas tank.

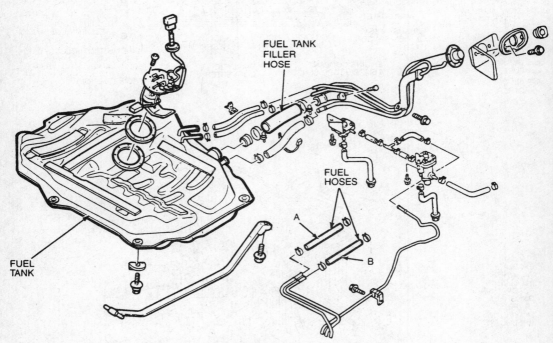

Fuel tank

Chassis Electrical

6

UNDERSTANDING AND TROUBLESHOOTING ELECTRICAL SYSTEMS

With the rate at which both import and domestic manufacturers are incorporating electronic control systems into their production lines, it won't be long before every new vehicle is equipped with one or more on-board computer. These electronic components (with no moving parts) should theoretically last the life of the vehicle, provided nothing external happens to damage the circuits or memory chips.

While it is true that electronic components should never wear out, in the real world malfunctions do occur. It is also true that any computer-based system is extremely sensitive to electrical voltages and cannot tolerate careless or haphazard testing or service procedures. An inexperienced individual can literally do major damage looking for a minor problem by using the wrong kind of test equipment or connecting test leads or connectors with the ignition switch ON. When selecting test equipment, make sure the manufacturers instructions state that the tester is compatible with whatever type of electronic control system is being serviced. Read all instructions carefully and double check all test points before installing probes or making any test connections.

The following section outlines basic diagnosis techniques for dealing with computerized automotive control systems. Along with a general explanation of the various types of test equipment available to aid in servicing modern electronic automotive systems, basic repair techniques for wiring harnesses and connectors is given. Read the basic information before attempting any repairs or testing on any computerized system, to provide the background of information necessary to avoid the most common and obvious mistakes that can cost both time and money. Although the replacement and testing procedures are simple in themselves, the systems are not, and unless one has a thorough understanding of all components and their function within a particular computerized control system, the logical test sequence these systems demand cannot be followed. Minor malfunctions can make a big difference, so it is important to know how each component affects the operation of the overall electronic system to find the ultimate cause of a problem without replacing good components unnecessarily. It is not enough to use the correct test equipment; the test equipment must be used correctly.

Safety Precautions

CAUTION: *Whenever working on or around any computer based microprocessor control system, always observe these general precautions to prevent the possibility of personal injury or damage to electronic components.*

● Never install or remove battery cables with the key ON or the engine running. Jumper cables should be connected with the key OFF to avoid power surges that can damage electronic control units. Engines equipped with computer controlled systems should avoid both giving and getting jump starts due to the possibility of serious damage to components from arcing in the engine compartment when connections are made with the ignition ON.

● Always remove the battery cables before charging the battery. Never use a high output charger on an installed battery or attempt to use any type of "hot shot" (24 volt) starting aid.

● Exercise care when inserting test probes into connectors to insure good connections without damaging the connector or spreading the pins. Always probe connectors from the rear (wire) side, NOT the pin side, to avoid accidental shorting of terminals during test procedures.

• Never remove or attach wiring harness connectors with the ignition switch ON, especially to an electronic control unit.

• Do not drop any components during service procedures and never apply 12 volts directly to any component (like a solenoid or relay) unless instructed specifically to do so. Some component electrical windings are designed to safely handle only 4 or 5 volts and can be destroyed in seconds if 12 volts are applied directly to the connector.

• Remove the electronic control unit if the vehicle is to be placed in an environment where temperatures exceed approximately 176°F (80°C), such as a paint spray booth or when arc or gas welding near the control unit location in the car.

ORGANIZED TROUBLESHOOTING

When diagnosing a specific problem, organized troubleshooting is a must. The complexity of a modern automobile demands that you approach any problem in a logical, organized manner. There are certain troubleshooting techniques that are standard:

1. Establish when the problem occurs. Does the problem appear only under certain conditions? Were there any noises, odors, or other unusual symptoms?

2. Isolate the problem area. To do this, make some simple tests and observations; then eliminate the systems that are working properly. Check for obvious problems such as broken wires, dirty connections or split or disconnected vacuum hoses. Always check the obvious before assuming something complicated is the cause.

3. Test for problems systematically to determine the cause once the problem area is isolated. Are all the components functioning properly? Is there power going to electrical switches and motors? Is there vacuum at vacuum switches and/or actuators? Is there a mechanical problem such as bent linkage or loose mounting screws? Doing careful, systematic checks will often turn up most causes on the first inspection without wasting time checking components that have little or no relationship to the problem.

4. Test all repairs after the work is done to make sure that the problem is fixed. Some causes can be traced to more than one component, so a careful verification of repair work is important to pick up additional malfunctions that may cause a problem to reappear or a different problem to arise. A blown fuse, for example, is a simple problem that may require more than another fuse to repair. If you don't look for a problem that caused a fuse to blow, for example, a shorted wire may go undetected.

Experience has shown that most problems tend to be the result of a fairly simple and obvious cause, such as loose or corroded connectors or air leaks in the intake system; making careful inspection of components during testing essential to quick and accurate troubleshooting. Special, hand held computerized testers designed specifically for diagnosing the EEC-IV system are available from a variety of aftermarket sources, as well as from the vehicle manufacturer, but care should be taken that any test equipment being used is designed to diagnose that particular computer controlled system accurately without damaging the control unit (ECU) or components being tested.

NOTE: *Pinpointing the exact cause of trouble in an electrical system can sometimes only be accomplished by the use of special test equipment. The following describes commonly used test equipment and explains how to put it to best use in diagnosis. In addition to the information covered below, the manufacturer's instructions booklet provided with the tester should be read and clearly understood before attempting any test procedures.*

TEST EQUIPMENT

Jumper Wires

Jumper wires are simple, yet extremely valuable, pieces of test equipment. Jumper wires are merely wires that are used to bypass sections of a circuit. The simplest type of jumper wire is merely a length of multistrand wire with an alligator clip at each end. Jumper wires are usually fabricated from lengths of standard automotive wire and whatever type of connector (alligator clip, spade connector or pin connector) that is required for the particular vehicle being tested. The well equipped tool box will have several different styles of jumper wires in several different lengths. Some jumper wires

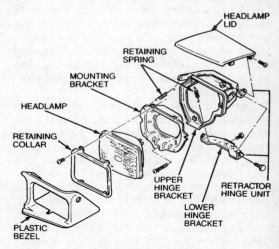

Headlamp beam removal/installation

HEADLAMP LID

RETAINING SPRING

MOUNTING BRACKET

HEADLAMP

RETAINING COLLAR

UPPER HINGE BRACKET

RETRACTOR HINGE UNIT

LOWER HINGE BRACKET

PLASTIC BEZEL

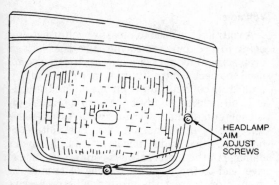

HEADLAMP
AIM
ADJUST
SCREWS

Headlamp alignment points

are made with three or more terminals coming from a common splice for special purpose testing. In cramped, hard-to-reach areas it is advisable to have insulated boots over the jumper wire terminals in order to prevent accidental grounding, sparks, and possible fire, especially when testing fuel system components.

Jumper wires are used primarily to locate open electrical circuits, on either the ground (-) side of the circuit or on the hot (+) side. If an electrical component fails to operate, connect the jumper wire between the component and a good ground. If the component operates only with the jumper installed, the ground circuit is open. If the ground circuit is good, but the component does not operate, the circuit between the power feed and component is open. You can sometimes connect the jumper wire directly from the battery to the hot terminal of the component, but first make sure the component uses 12 volts in operation. Some electrical components, such as fuel injectors, are designed to operate on about 4 volts and running 12 volts directly to the injector terminals can burn out the wiring. By inserting an inline fuseholder between a set of test leads, a fused jumper wire can be used for bypassing open circuits. Use a 5 amp fuse to provide protection against voltage spikes. When in doubt, use a voltmeter to check the voltage input to the component and measure how much voltage is being applied normally. By moving the jumper wire successively back from the lamp toward the power source, you can isolate the area of the circuit where the open is located. When the component stops functioning, or the power is cut off, the open is in the segment of wire between the jumper and the point previously tested.

CAUTION: *Never use jumpers made from wire that is of lighter gauge than used in the circuit under test. If the jumper wire is of too small gauge, it may overheat and possibly melt. Never use jumpers to bypass high resistance loads (such as motors) in a circuit. Bypassing resistances, in effect, creates a short*

circuit which may, in turn, cause damage and fire. Never use a jumper for anything other than temporary bypassing of components in a circuit.*

12 Volt Test Light

The 12 volt test light is used to check circuits and components while electrical current is flowing through them. It is used for voltage and ground tests. Twelve volt test lights come in different styles but all have three main parts; a ground clip, a probe, and a light. The most commonly used 12 volt test lights have pick-type probes. To use a 12 volt test light, connect the ground clip to a good ground and probe wherever necessary with the pick. The pick should be sharp so that it can penetrate wire insulation to make contact with the wire, without making a large hole in the insulation. The wrap-around light is handy in hard to reach areas or where it is difficult to support a wire to push a probe pick into it. To use the wrap around light, hook the wire to probed with the hook and pull the trigger. A small pick will be forced through the wire insulation into the wire core.

CAUTION: *Do not use a test light to probe electronic ignition spark plug or coil wires. Never use a pick-type test light to probe wiring on computer controlled systems unless specifically instructed to do so. Any wire insulation that is pierced by the test light probe should be taped and sealed with silicone after testing.*

Like the jumper wire, the 12 volt test light is used to isolate opens in circuits. But, whereas the jumper wire is used to bypass the open to operate the load, the 12 volt test light is used to locate the presence of voltage in a circuit. If the test light glows, you know that there is power up to that point; if the 12 volt test light does not glow when its probe is inserted into the wire or connector, you know that there is an open circuit (no power). Move the test light in successive steps back toward the power source until the light in the handle does glow. When it does glow, the open is between the probe and point previously probed.

NOTE: *The test light does not detect that 12 volts (or any particular amount of voltage) is present; it only detects that some voltage is present. It is advisable before using the test light to touch its terminals across the battery posts to make sure the light is operating properly.*

Self-Powered Test Light

The self-powered test light usually contains a 1.5 volt penlight battery. One type of self-powered test light is similar in design to the 12 volt test light. This type has both the battery and the light in the handle and pick-type probe tip. The second type has the light toward the open tip, so that the light illuminates the contact point. The self-powered test light is dual purpose piece of test equipment. It can be used to test for either open or short circuits when power is isolated from the circuit (continuity test). A powered test light should not be used on any computer controlled system or component unless specifically instructed to do so. Many engine sensors can be destroyed by even this small amount of voltage applied directly to the terminals.

Open Circuit Testing

To use the self-powered test light to check for open circuits, first isolate the circuit from the vehicle's 12 volt power source by disconnecting the battery or wiring harness connector. Connect the test light ground clip to a good ground and probe sections of the circuit sequentially with the test light. (start from either end of the circuit). If the light is out, the open is between the probe and the circuit ground. If the light is on, the open is between the probe and end of the circuit toward the power source.

Short Circuit Testing

By isolating the circuit both from power and from ground, and using a self-powered test light, you can check for shorts to ground in the circuit. Isolate the circuit from power and ground. Connect the test light ground clip to a good ground and probe any easy-to-reach test point in the circuit. If the light comes on, there is a short somewhere in the circuit. To isolate the short, probe a test point at either end of the isolated circuit (the light should be on). Leave the test light probe connected and open connectors, switches, remove parts, etc., sequentially, until the light goes out. When the light goes out, the short is between the last circuit component opened and the previous circuit opened.

NOTE: *The 1.5 volt battery in the test light does not provide much current. A weak battery may not provide enough power to illuminate the test light even when a complete circuit is made (especially if there are high resistances in the circuit). Always make sure that the test battery is strong. To check the battery, briefly touch the ground clip to the probe; if the light glows brightly the battery is strong enough for testing. Never use a self-powered test light to perform checks for opens or shorts when power is applied to the electrical system under test. The 12 volt vehicle power will quickly burn out the 1.5 volt light bulb in the test light.*

Voltmeter

A voltmeter is used to measure voltage at any point in a circuit, or to measure the voltage drop across any part of a circuit. It can also be used to check continuity in a wire or circuit by indicating current flow from one end to the other. Voltmeters usually have various scales on the meter dial and a selector switch to allow the selection of different voltages. The voltmeter has a positive and a negative lead. To avoid damage to the meter, always connect the negative lead to the negative (-) side of circuit (to ground or nearest the ground side of the circuit) and connect the positive lead to the positive (+) side of the circuit (to the power source or the nearest power source). Note that the negative voltmeter lead will always be black and that the positive voltmeter will always be some color other than black (usually red). Depending on how the voltmeter is connected into the circuit, it has several uses.

A voltmeter can be connected either in parallel or in series with a circuit and it has a very high resistance to current flow. When connected in parallel, only a small amount of current will flow through the voltmeter current path; the rest will flow through the normal circuit current path and the circuit will work normally. When the voltmeter is connected in series with a circuit, only a small amount of current can flow through the circuit. The circuit will not work properly, but the voltmeter reading will show if the circuit is complete or not.

Available Voltage Measurement

Set the voltmeter selector switch to the 20V position and connect the meter negative lead to the negative post of the battery. Connect the positive meter lead to the positive post of the battery and turn the ignition switch ON to provide a load. Read the voltage on the meter or digital display. A well charged battery should register over 12 volts. If the meter reads below 11.5 volts, the battery power may be insufficient to operate the electrical system properly. This test determines voltage available from the battery and should be the first step in any electrical trouble diagnosis procedure. Many electrical problems, especially on computer controlled systems, can be caused by a low state of charge in the battery. Excessive corrosion at the battery cable terminals can cause a poor contact that will prevent proper charging and full battery current flow.

Normal battery voltage is 12 volts when fully charged. When the battery is supplying current to one or more circuits it is said to be "under load". When everything is off the electrical system is under a "no-load" condition. A fully charged battery may show about 12.5 volts at no load; will drop to 12 volts under medium load; and will drop even lower under heavy load. If the battery is partially discharged the voltage decrease under heavy load may be excessive, even though the battery shows 12 volts or more at no load. When allowed to discharge further, the battery's available voltage under load will decrease more severely. For this reason, it is important that the battery be fully charged during all testing procedures to avoid errors in diagnosis and incorrect test results.

Voltage Drop

When current flows through a resistance, the voltage beyond the resistance is reduced (the larger the current, the greater the reduction in voltage). When no current is flowing, there is no voltage drop because there is no current flow. All points in the circuit which are connected to the power source are at the same voltage as the power source. The total voltage drop always equals the total source voltage. In a long circuit with many connectors, a series of small, unwanted voltage drops due to corrosion at the connectors can add up to a total loss of voltage which impairs the operation of the normal loads in the circuit.

INDIRECT COMPUTATION OF VOLTAGE DROPS

1. Set the voltmeter selector switch to the 20 volt position.
2. Connect the meter negative lead to a good ground.
3. Probe all resistances in the circuit with the positive meter lead.
4. Operate the circuit in all modes and observe the voltage readings.

DIRECT MEASUREMENT OF VOLTAGE DROPS

1. Set the voltmeter switch to the 20 volt position.
2. Connect the voltmeter negative lead to the ground side of the resistance load to be measured.
3. Connect the positive lead to the positive side of the resistance or load to be measured.
4. Read the voltage drop directly on the 20 volt scale.

Too high a voltage indicates too high a resistance. If, for example, a blower motor runs too slowly, you can determine if there is too high a resistance in the resistor pack. By taking voltage drop readings in all parts of the circuit, you can isolate the problem. Too low a voltage drop indicates too low a resistance. If, for example, a blower motor runs too fast in the MED and/or LOW position, the problem can be isolated in

the resistor pack by taking voltage drop readings in all parts of the circuit to locate a possibly shorted resistor. The maximum allowable voltage drop under load is critical, especially if there is more than one high resistance problem in a circuit because all voltage drops are cumulative. A small drop is normal due to the resistance of the conductors.

HIGH RESISTANCE TESTING

1. Set the voltmeter selector switch to the 4 volt position.
2. Connect the voltmeter positive lead to the positive post of the battery.
3. Turn on the headlights and heater blower to provide a load.
4. Probe various points in the circuit with the negative voltmeter lead.
5. Read the voltage drop on the 4 volt scale. Some average maximum allowable voltage drops are:

FUSE PANEL — 7 volts
IGNITION SWITCH — 5volts
HEADLIGHT SWITCH — 7 volts
IGNITION COIL (+) — 5 volts
ANY OTHER LOAD — 1.3 volts
NOTE: *Voltage drops are all measured while a load is operating; without current flow, there will be no voltage drop.*

Ohmmeter

The ohmmeter is designed to read resistance (ohms) in a circuit or component. Although there are several different styles of ohmmeters, all will usually have a selector switch which permits the measurement of different ranges of resistance (usually the selector switch allows the multiplication of the meter reading by 10, 100, 1000, and 10,000). A calibration knob allows the meter to be set at zero for accurate measurement. Since all ohmmeters are powered by an internal battery (usually 9 volts), the ohmmeter can be used as a self-powered test light. When the ohmmeter is connected, current from the ohmmeter flows through the circuit or component being tested. Since the ohmmeter's internal resistance and voltage are known values, the amount of current flow through the meter depends on the resistance of the circuit or component being tested.

The ohmmeter can be used to perform continuity test for opens or shorts (either by observation of the meter needle or as a self-powered test light), and to read actual resistance in a circuit. It should be noted that the ohmmeter is used to check the resistance of a component or wire while there is no voltage applied to the circuit. Current flow from an outside voltage source (such as the vehicle battery) can damage the ohmmeter, so the circuit or component should be isolated from the vehicle electrical system before any testing is done. Since the ohmmeter uses its own voltage source, either lead can be connected to any test point.

NOTE: *When checking diodes or other solid state components, the ohmmeter leads can only be connected one way in order to measure current flow in a single direction. Make sure the positive (+) and negative (-) terminal connections are as described in the test procedures to verify the one-way diode operation.*

In using the meter for making continuity checks, do not be concerned with the actual resistance readings. Zero resistance, or any resistance readings, indicate continuity in the circuit. Infinite resistance indicates an open in the circuit. A high resistance reading where there should be none indicates a problem in the circuit. Checks for short circuits are made in the same manner as checks for open circuits except that the circuit must be isolated from both power and normal ground. Infinite resistance indicates no continuity to ground, while zero resistance indicates a dead short to ground.

RESISTANCE MEASUREMENT

The batteries in an ohmmeter will weaken with age and temperature, so the ohmmeter must be calibrated or "zeroed" before taking measurements. To zero the meter, place the selector switch in its lowest range and touch the two ohmmeter leads together. Turn the calibration knob until the meter needle is exactly on zero.

NOTE: *All analog (needle) type ohmmeters must be zeroed before use, but some digital ohmmeter models are automatically calibrated when the switch is turned on. Self-calibrating digital ohmmeters do not have an adjusting knob, but its a good idea to check for a zero readout before use by touching the leads together. All computer controlled systems require the use of a digital ohmmeter with at least 10 meagohms impedance for testing. Before any test procedures are attempted, make sure the ohmmeter used is compatible with the electrical system or damage to the on-board computer could result.*

To measure resistance, first isolate the circuit from the vehicle power source by disconnecting the battery cables or the harness connector. Make sure the key is OFF when disconnecting any components or the battery. Where necessary, also isolate at least one side of the circuit to be checked to avoid reading parallel resistances. Parallel circuit resistances will always give a lower reading than the actual resistance of either of the branches. When measuring the resistance of parallel circuits, the total resistance will always be lower than the smallest resistance in the circuit. Connect the meter leads to both sides of the circuit (wire or component) and read the actual measured ohms on the meter scale. Make sure the selector switch is set to the proper ohm scale for the circuit being tested to avoid misreading the ohmmeter test value.

CAUTION: *Never use an ohmmeter with power applied to the circuit. Like the self-powered test light, the ohmmeter is designed to operate on its own power supply. The normal 12 volt automotive electrical system current could damage the meter.*

Ammeters

An ammeter measures the amount of current flowing through a circuit in units called amperes or amps. Amperes are units of electron flow which indicate how fast the electrons are flowing through the circuit. Since Ohms Law dictates that current flow in a circuit is equal to the circuit voltage divided by the total circuit resistance, increasing voltage also increases the current level (amps). Likewise, any decrease in resistance will increase the amount of amps in a circuit. At normal operating voltage, most circuits have a characteristic amount of amperes, called "current draw" which can be measured using an ammeter. By referring to a specified current draw rating, measuring the amperes, and comparing the two values, one can determine what is happening within the circuit to aid in diagnosis. An open circuit, for example, will not allow any current to flow so the ammeter reading will be zero. More current flows through a heavily loaded circuit or when the charging system is operating.

An ammeter is always connected in series with the circuit being tested. All of the current that normally flows through the circuit must also flow through the ammeter; if there is any other path for the current to follow, the ammeter reading will not be accurate. The ammeter itself has very little resistance to current flow and therefore will not affect the circuit, but it will measure current draw only when the circuit is closed and electricity is flowing. Excessive current draw can blow fuses and drain the battery, while a reduced current draw can cause motors to run slowly, lights to dim and other components to not operate properly. The ammeter can help diagnose these conditions by locating the cause of the high or low reading.

Multimeters

Different combinations of test meters can be built into a single unit designed for specific tests. Some of the more common combination test devices are known as Volt/Amp testers, Tach/Dwell meters, or Digital Multimeters. The Volt/Amp tester is used for charging system, starting system or battery tests and consists of a voltmeter, an ammeter and a variable resistance carbon pile. The voltmeter will usually have at least two ranges for use with 6, 12 and 24 volt systems. The ammeter also has more than one range for testing various levels of battery loads and starter current draw and the carbon pile can be adjusted to offer different amounts of resistance. The Volt/Amp tester has heavy leads to carry large amounts of current and many later models have an inductive ammeter pickup that clamps around the wire to simplify test connections. On some models, the ammeter also has a zero-center scale to allow testing of charging and starting systems without switching leads or polarity. A digital multimeter is a voltmeter, ammeter and ohmmeter combined in an instrument which gives a digital readout. These are often used when testing solid state circuits because of their high input impedance (usually 10 megohms or more).

The tach/dwell meter combines a tachometer and a dwell (cam angle) meter and is a specialized kind of voltmeter. The tachometer scale is marked to show engine speed in rpm and the dwell scale is marked to show degrees of distributor shaft rotation. In most electronic ignition systems, dwell is determined by the control unit, but the dwell meter can also be used to check the duty cycle (operation) of some electronic engine control systems. Some tach/dwell meters are powered by an internal battery, while others take their power from the car battery in use. The battery powered testers usually require calibration much like an ohmmeter before testing.

Special Test Equipment

A variety of diagnostic tools are available to help troubleshoot and repair computerized engine control systems. The most sophisticated of these devices are the console type engine analyzers that usually occupy a garage service bay, but there are several types of aftermarket electronic testers available that will allow quick circuit tests of the engine control system by plugging directly into a special connector located in the engine compartment or under the dashboard. Several tool and equipment manufacturers offer simple, hand held testers that measure various circuit voltage levels on command to check all system components for proper operation. Although these testers usually cost about $300-$500, consider that the average computer control unit (or ECM) can cost just as much and the money saved by not replacing perfectly good sensors or components in an attempt to correct

a problem could justify the purchase price of a special diagnostic tester the first time it's used.

These computerized testers can allow quick and easy test measurements while the engine is operating or while the car is being driven. In addition, the on-board computer memory can be read to access any stored trouble codes; in effect allowing the computer to tell you where it hurts and aid trouble diagnosis by pinpointing exactly which circuit or component is malfunctioning. In the same manner, repairs can be tested to make sure the problem has been corrected. The biggest advantage these special testers have is their relatively easy hookups that minimize or eliminate the chances of making the wrong connections and getting false voltage readings or damaging the computer accidentally.

NOTE: *It should be remembered that these testers check voltage levels in circuits; they don't detect mechanical problems or failed components if the circuit voltage falls within the preprogrammed limits stored in the tester PROM unit. Also, most of the hand held testes are designed to work only on one or two systems made by a specific manufacturer.*

A variety of aftermarket testers are available to help diagnose different computerized control systems. Owatonna Tool Company (OTC), for example, markets a device called the OTC Monitor which plugs directly into the assembly line diagnostic link (ALDL). The OTC tester makes diagnosis a simple matter of pressing the correct buttons and, by changing the internal PROM or inserting a different diagnosis cartridge, it will work on any model from full size to subcompact, over a wide range of years. An adapter is supplied with the tester to allow connection to all types of ALDL links, regardless of the number of pin terminals used. By inserting an updated PROM into the OTC tester, it can be easily updated to diagnose any new modifications of computerized control systems.

Wiring Harnesses

The average automobile contains about ½ mile of wiring, with hundreds of individual connections. To protect the many wires from damage and to keep them from becoming a confusing tangle, they are organized into bundles, enclosed in plastic or taped together and called wire harnesses. Different wiring harnesses serve different parts of the vehicle. Individual wires are color coded to help trace them through a harness where sections are hidden from view.

A loose or corroded connection or a replacement wire that is too small for the circuit will add extra resistance and an additional voltage drop to the circuit. A ten percent voltage drop can result in slow or erratic motor operation, for example, even though the circuit is complete. Automotive wiring or circuit conductors can be in any one of three forms:

1. Single strand wire
2. Multistrand wire
3. Printed circuitry

Single strand wire has a solid metal core and is usually used inside such components as alternators, motors, relays and other devices. Multistrand wire has a core made of many small strands of wire twisted together into a single conductor. Most of the wiring in an automotive electrical system is made up of multistrand wire, either as a single conductor or grouped together in a harness. All wiring is color coded on the insulator, either as a solid color or as a colored wire with an identification stripe. A printed circuit is a thin film of copper or other conductor that is printed on an insulator backing. Occasionally, a printed circuit is sandwiched between two sheets of plastic for more protection and flexibility. A complete printed circuit, consisting of conductors, insulating material and connectors for lamps or other components is called a printed circuit board. Printed circuitry is used in place of individual wires or harnesses in places where space is limited, such as behind instrument panels.

Wire Gauge

Since computer controlled automotive electrical systems are very sensitive to changes in resistance, the selection of properly sized wires is critical when systems are repaired. The wire gauge number is an expression of the cross section area of the conductor. The most common system for expressing wire size is the American Wire Gauge (AWG) system.

Wire cross section area is measured in circular mils. A mil is $\frac{1}{1000}$" (0.001"); a circular mil is the area of a circle one mil in diameter. For example, a conductor ¼" in diameter is 0.250 in. or 250 mils. The circular mil cross section area of the wire is 250 squared (250^2)or 62,500 circular mils. Imported car models usually use metric wire gauge designations, which is simply the cross section area of the conductor in square millimeters (mm^2).

Gauge numbers are assigned to conductors of various cross section areas. As gauge number increases, area decreases and the conductor becomes smaller. A 5 gauge conductor is smaller than a 1 gauge conductor and a 10 gauge is smaller than a 5 gauge. As the cross section area of a conductor decreases, resistance increases and so does the gauge number. A conductor with a higher gauge number will carry less current than a conductor with a lower gauge number.

NOTE: *Gauge wire size refers to the size of*

the conductor, not the size of the complete wire. It is possible to have two wires of the same gauge with different diameters because one may have thicker insulation than the other.

12 volt automotive electrical systems generally use 10, 12, 14, 16 and 18 gauge wire. Main power distribution circuits and larger accessories usually use 10 and 12 gauge wire. Battery cables are usually 4 or 6 gauge, although 1 and 2 gauge wires are occasionally used. Wire length must also be considered when making repairs to a circuit. As conductor length increases, so does resistance. An 18 gauge wire, for example, can carry a 10 amp load for 10 feet without excessive voltage drop; however if a 15 foot wire is required for the same 10 amp load, it must be a 16 gauge wire.

An electrical schematic shows the electrical current paths when a circuit is operating properly. It is essential to understand how a circuit works before trying to figure out why it doesn't. Schematics break the entire electrical system down into individual circuits and show only one particular circuit. In a schematic, no attempt is made to represent wiring and components as they physically appear on the vehicle; switches and other components are shown as simply as possible. Face views of harness connectors show the cavity or terminal locations in all multi-pin connectors to help locate test points.

If you need to backprobe a connector while it is on the component, the order of the terminals must be mentally reversed. The wire color code can help in this situation, as well as a keyway, lock tab or other reference mark.

NOTE: *Wiring diagrams are not included in this book. As trucks have become more complex and available with longer option lists, wiring diagrams have grown in size and complexity. It has become almost impossible to provide a readable reproduction of a wiring diagram in a book this size. Information on ordering wiring diagrams from the vehicle manufacturer can be found in the owner's manual.*

WIRING REPAIR

Soldering is a quick, efficient method of joining metals permanently. Everyone who has the occasion to make wiring repairs should know how to solder. Electrical connections that are soldered are far less likely to come apart and will conduct electricity much better than connections that are only "pig-tailed" together. The most popular (and preferred) method of soldering is with an electrical soldering gun. Soldering irons are available in many sizes and wattage ratings. Irons with higher wattage ratings deliver higher temperatures and recover lost heat faster. A small soldering iron rated for no more than 50 watts is recommended, especially on electrical systems where excess heat can damage the components being soldered.

There are three ingredients necessary for successful soldering; proper flux, good solder and sufficient heat. A soldering flux is necessary to clean the metal of tarnish, prepare it for soldering and to enable the solder to spread into tiny crevices. When soldering, always use a resin flux or resin core solder which is non-corrosive and will not attract moisture once the job is finished. Other types of flux (acid core) will leave a residue that will attract moisture and cause the wires to corrode. Tin is a unique metal with a low melting point. In a molten state, it dissolves and alloys easily with many metals. Solder is made by mixing tin with lead. The most common proportions are 40/60, 50/50 and 60/40, with the percentage of tin listed first. Low priced solders usually contain less tin, making them very difficult for a beginner to use because more heat is required to melt the solder. A common solder is 40/60 which is well suited for all-around general use, but 60/40 melts easier, has more tin for a better joint and is preferred for electrical work.

Soldering Techniques

Successful soldering requires that the metals to be joined be heated to a temperature that will melt the solder — usually 360-460°F (182-238°C). Contrary to popular belief, the purpose of the soldering iron is not to melt the solder itself, but to heat the parts being soldered to a temperature high enough to melt the solder when it is touched to the work. Melting flux-cored solder on the soldering iron will usually destroy the effectiveness of the flux.

NOTE: *Soldering tips are made of copper for good heat conductivity, but must be "tinned" regularly for quick transference of heat to the project and to prevent the solder from sticking to the iron. To "tin" the iron, simply heat it and touch the flux-cored solder to the tip; the solder will flow over the hot tip. Wipe the excess off with a clean rag, but be careful as the iron will be hot.*

After some use, the tip may become pitted. If so, simply dress the tip smooth with a smooth file and "tin" the tip again. An old saying holds that "metals well cleaned are half soldered." Flux-cored solder will remove oxides but rust, bits of insulation and oil or grease must be removed with a wire brush or emery cloth. For maximum strength in soldered parts, the joint must start off clean and tight. Weak joints will result in gaps too wide for the solder to bridge. If a separate soldering flux is used, it should be brushed or swabbed on only those areas that are to be soldered. Most solders contain a core of flux and separate fluxing is unnecessary. Hold the work to be soldered firmly. It is best to solder on a wooden board, because a metal vise will only rob the piece to be soldered of heat and make it difficult to melt the solder. Hold the soldering tip with the broadest face against the work to be soldered. Apply solder under the tip close to the work, using enough solder to give a heavy film between the iron and the piece being soldered, while moving slowly and making sure the solder melts properly. Keep the work level or the solder will run to the lowest part and favor the thicker parts, because these require more heat to melt the solder. If the soldering tip overheats (the solder coating on the face of the tip burns up), it should be retinned. Once the soldering is completed, let the soldered joint stand until cool. Tape and seal all soldered wire splices after the repair has cooled.

Wire Harness and Connectors

The on-board computer (ECM) wire harness electrically connects the control unit to the various solenoids, switches and sensors used by the control system. Most connectors in the engine compartment or otherwise exposed to the elements are protected against moisture and dirt which could create oxidation and deposits on the terminals. This protection is important because of the very low voltage and current levels used by the computer and sensors. All connectors have a lock which secures the male and female terminals together, with a secondary lock holding the seal and terminal into the connector. Both terminal locks must be released when disconnecting ECM connectors.

These special connectors are weather-proof and all repairs require the use of a special terminal and the tool required to service it. This tool is used to remove the pin and sleeve terminals. If removal is attempted with an ordinary pick, there is a good chance that the terminal will be bent or deformed. Unlike standard blade type terminals, these terminals cannot be straightened once they are bent. Make certain that the connectors are properly seated and all of the sealing rings in place when connecting leads. On some models, a hinge-type flap provides a backup or secondary locking feature for the terminals. Most secondary locks are used to improve the connector reliability by retaining the terminals if the small terminal lock tangs are not positioned properly.

Molded-on connectors require complete replacement of the connection. This means splicing a new connector assembly into the harness. All splices in on-board computer systems should be soldered to insure proper contact.

Use care when probing the connections or replacing terminals in them as it is possible to short between opposite terminals. If this happens to the wrong terminal pair, it is possible to damage certain components. Always use jumper wires between connectors for circuit checking and never probe through weatherproof seals.

Open circuits are often difficult to locate by sight because corrosion or terminal misalignment are hidden by the connectors. Merely wiggling a connector on a sensor or in the wiring harness may correct the open circuit condition. This should always be considered when an open circuit or a failed sensor is indicated. Intermittent problems may also be caused by oxidized or loose connections. When using a circuit tester for diagnosis, always probe connections from the wire side. Be careful not to damage sealed connectors with test probes.

All wiring harnesses should be replaced with identical parts, using the same gauge wire and connectors. When signal wires are spliced into a harness, use wire with high temperature insulation only. With the low voltage and current levels found in the system, it is important that the best possible connection at all wire splices be made by soldering the splices together. It is seldom necessary to replace a complete harness. If replacement is necessary, pay close attention to insure proper harness routing. Secure the harness with suitable plastic wire clamps to prevent vibrations from causing the harness to wear in spots or contact any hot components.

NOTE: *Weatherproof connectors cannot be replaced with standard connectors. Instructions are provided with replacement connector and terminal packages. Some wire harnesses have mounting indicators (usually pieces of colored tape) to mark where the harness is to be secured.*

In making wiring repairs, it's important that you always replace damaged wires with wires that are the same gauge as the wire being replaced. The heavier the wire, the smaller the gauge number. Wires are color-coded to aid in identification and whenever possible the same color coded wire should be used for replacement. A wire stripping and crimping tool is necessary to install solderless terminal connectors. Test all crimps by pulling on the wires; it should not be possible to pull the wires out of a good crimp.

Wires which are open, exposed or otherwise damaged are repaired by simple splicing. Where possible, if the wiring harness is accessible and the damaged place in the wire can be located, it is best to open the harness and check for all possible damage. In an inaccessible harness, the wire must be bypassed with a new insert, usually taped to the outside of the old harness.

When replacing fusible links, be sure to use fusible link wire, NOT ordinary automotive wire. Make sure the fusible segment is of the same gauge and construction as the one being replaced and double the stripped end when crimping the terminal connector for a good contact. The melted (open) fusible link segment of the wiring harness should be cut off as close to the harness as possible, then a new segment spliced in as described. In the case of a damaged fusible link that feeds two harness wires, the harness connections should be replaced with two fusible link wires so that each circuit will have its own separate protection.

NOTE: *Most of the problems caused in the wiring harness are due to bad ground connections. Always check all vehicle ground connections for corrosion or looseness before performing any power feed checks to eliminate the chance of a bad ground affecting the circuit.*

Repairing Hard Shell Connectors

Unlike molded connectors, the terminal contacts in hard shell connectors can be replaced. Weatherproof hard-shell connectors with the leads molded into the shell have non-replaceable terminal ends. Replacement usually involves the use of a special terminal removal tool that depress the locking tangs (barbs) on the connector terminal and allow the connector to be removed from the rear of the shell. The connector shell should be replaced if it shows any evidence of burning, melting, cracks, or breaks. Replace individual terminals that are burnt, corroded, distorted or loose.

NOTE: *The insulation crimp must be tight to prevent the insulation from sliding back on the wire when the wire is pulled. The insulation must be visibly compressed under the crimp tabs, and the ends of the crimp should be turned in for a firm grip on the insulation.*

The wire crimp must be made with all wire strands inside the crimp. The terminal must be fully compressed on the wire strands with the ends of the crimp tabs turned in to make a firm grip on the wire. Check all connections with an ohmmeter to insure a good contact. There should be no measurable resistance between the wire and the terminal when connected.

Mechanical Test Equipment

Vacuum Gauge

Most gauges are graduated in inches of mercury (in.Hg), although a device called a manometer reads vacuum in inches of water (in. H_2O).

The normal vacuum reading usually varies between 18 and 22 in.Hg at sea level. To test engine vacuum, the vacuum gauge must be connected to a source of manifold vacuum. Many engines have a plug in the intake manifold which can be removed and replaced with an adapter fitting. Connect the vacuum gauge to the fitting with a suitable rubber hose or, if no manifold plug is available, connect the vacuum gauge to any device using manifold vacuum, such as EGR valves, etc. The vacuum gauge can be used to determine if enough vacuum is reaching a component to allow its actuation.

Hand Vacuum Pump

Small, hand-held vacuum pumps come in a variety of designs. Most have a built-in vacuum gauge and allow the component to be tested without removing it from the vehicle. Operate the pump lever or plunger to apply the correct amount of vacuum required for the test specified in the diagnosis routines. The level of vacuum in inches of Mercury (in.Hg) is indicated on the pump gauge. For some testing, an additional vacuum gauge may be necessary.

Intake manifold vacuum is used to operate various systems and devices on late model vehicles. To correctly diagnose and solve problems in vacuum control systems, a vacuum source is necessary for testing. In some cases, vacuum can be taken from the intake manifold when the engine is running, but vacuum is normally provided by a hand vacuum pump. These hand vacuum pumps have a built-in vacuum gauge that allow testing while the device is still attached to the component. For some tests, an additional vacuum gauge may be necessary.

HEATING AND AIR CONDITIONING

NOTE: *If a procedure requires that an air conditioning refrigerant line connection be loosened or disconnected, refer to Chapter 1 for the correct and safe way to discharge the system of refrigerant. The air conditioning lines are connected with special connectors, use care when removing or installing the lines. Refer to the illustration provided for air conditioning line coupling procedures.*

Blower Motor
REMOVAL AND INSTALLATION

1. Disconnect the negative battery cable.
2. Remove the under dash sound deadening panel from the passenger's side.
3. Remove the glove box assembly and brace.

4. Remove the cooling hose from the blower motor assembly.
5. Disconnect the electrical wiring connector from the blower motor.
6. Remove the mounting bolts and remove the blower motor. Separate the blower motor fan wheel from the motor shaft.
7. Install the blower motor fan wheel on the motor shaft.
8. Place the blower motor into position in the housing and secure it with the mounting bolts.
9. Connect the wiring to the blower motor. Install the glove box and brace. Install the sound panel.

Heater Core
REMOVAL AND INSTALLATION
Without Air Conditioning

1. Disconnect the negative battery cable. Drain the engine coolant to a level below the heater core.
CAUTION: *When draining the coolant, keep in mind that cats and dogs are attracted by the ethylene glycol antifreeze, and are quite likely to drink any that is left in an uncovered container or in puddles on the ground. This will prove fatal in sufficient quantity. Always drain the coolant into a sealable container. Coolant should be reused unless it is contaminated or several years old.*
2. Remove the instrument panel.
3. Disconnect and plug the heater hoses from the heater core.
4. Remove the main air duct from the heater case.
5. Remove the heater case mounting screws and pull the heater case straight back. Take care not to bend the heater core hose tubes.
6. Remove the heater core tube braces. Lift the heater core straight up and out of the case.

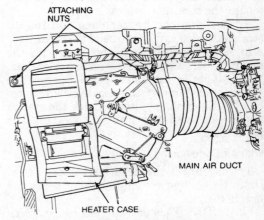

Heater case removal/installation-without AC

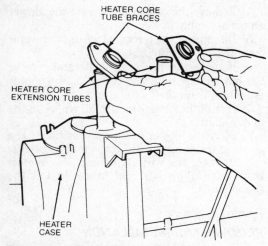

Remove/install extension tube braces

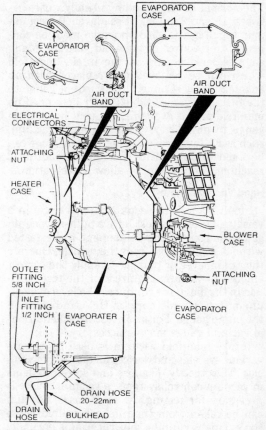

Evaporator case mounting

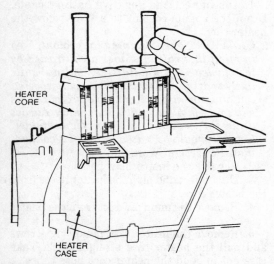

Remove/install the heater core

7. Place the heater core into the case and mount the core tube braces.

8. Position the heater case and install straight, taking care not to bend the core extension tubes. Secure the heater case with the mounting screws. Install the main heater duct.

9. Install the instrument panel. Connect the heater hose. Connect the negative battery cable. Fill the cooling system. Check the system for leaks, and the heating system for performance.

With Air Conditioning

1. Disconnect the negative battery cable. Drain the cooling system to a point below the heater core.

CAUTION: *When draining the coolant, keep in mind that cats and dogs are attracted by the ethylene glycol antifreeze, and are quite*

likely to drink any that is left in an uncovered container or in puddles on the ground. This will prove fatal in sufficient quantity. Always drain the coolant into a sealable container. Coolant should be reused unless it is contaminated or several years old.

2. Discharge the air conditioning system safely. Disconnect and plug the air conditioning lines at the evaporator case. Remove the carbon canister.

3. Remove the instrument panel. Disconnect the electrical connectors from the air conditioning relays at the top of the evaporator case.

4. From both ends of the evaporator case, remove the air duct bands. Remove the drain hose from the evaporator case.

5. Remove the evaporator case mounting nuts and carefully remove the evaporator case from the vehicle.

6. Disconnect the heater hose from the heater core, and plug them.

7. Remove the heater case mounting bolts. Pull the heater case straight back and remove it from the vehicle.

8. Remove the heater core extension tube

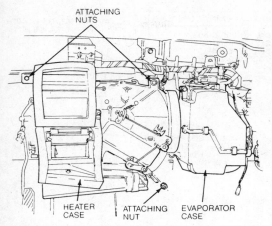

ATTACHING NUTS

HEATER CASE | ATTACHING NUT | EVAPORATOR CASE

Heater case mounting-with AC

braces. Pull the heater core straight up and out of the heater case.

9. Position the heater core in the heater case. Install the extension tube braces. Mount the heater case into the vehicle.

10. Put the evaporator case in position and secure the mounting nuts. Connect the air duct bands and the electrical connectors. Install the evaporator drain hose.

11. Connect the heater hoses and the air conditioning lines. Install the carbon canister.

12. Connect the negative battery cable. Fill the cooling system and charge the air conditioning system. Check all systems for operating performance. Check for coolant leaks.

Evaporator Case

REMOVAL AND INSTALLATION

1. Disconnect the negative battery cable.

2. Safely discharge the air conditioning system. Remove the carbon canister. Disconnect and cap the refrigerant lines to the evaporator.

3. Remove the instrument panel. Disconnect the electrical connectors from the controls on the top of the evaporator case. Remove the air duct bands. Remove the evaporator case drain hose.

4. Remove the evaporator case mounting nuts and remove the evaporator case from the vehicle.

5. Place the case in position and secure it with the mounting nuts.

6. Connect the duct bands and install the drain hose.

7. Connect the electrical wiring connectors to the controls on top of the evaporator case. Install the instrument panel.

8. Connect the air conditioning lines. Install the carbon canister.

9. Connect the negative battery cable. Charge the air conditioning system.

Evaporator Core

REMOVAL AND INSTALLATION

1. Disconnect the negative battery cable.

2. Safely discharge the air conditioning system. Remove the carbon canister. Disconnect and cap the refrigerant lines to the evaporator.

3. Remove the instrument panel. Disconnect the electrical connectors from the controls on the top of the evaporator case. Remove the air duct bands. Remove the evaporator case drain hose.

4. Remove the evaporator case mounting nuts and remove the evaporator case from the vehicle.

5. Remove the evaporator core cover and the core.

6. Install the evaporator core to the case and install the evaporator case.

RADIO

REMOVAL AND INSTALLATION

1. Disconnect the negative battery cable.

2. Remove the ash tray. Remove the selector trim panel (ATX), or the gearshift and boot trim panel (MTX).

3. Remove the cigar lighter connector. Disconnect the cigar lighter lamp by twisting the socket.

4. Remove the two screws attaching the radio to the instrument panel. Remove the radio. Disconnect the antenna cable and electrical connectors.

5. Connect the electrical connectors and antenna lead.

6. Place the radio into position and secure it with the mounting screws.

7. Install the cigar lighter lamp and connect the wiring to the lighter.

8. Install the gearshift/selector trim. Connect the negative battery cable.

WINDSHIELD WIPERS

Wiper Arm and Blade

REMOVAL AND INSTALLATION

1. For front wipers: Remove the wiper arm base cover/retaining cap by unscrewing it.

2. Remove the arm and blade assembly from the wiper pivot stud.

3. Install the wiper arm and blade on the wiper pivot and install the cover/retaining cap.

4. For rear wipers: Lift the cover on the base of the rear wiper arm. Unscrew the retaining

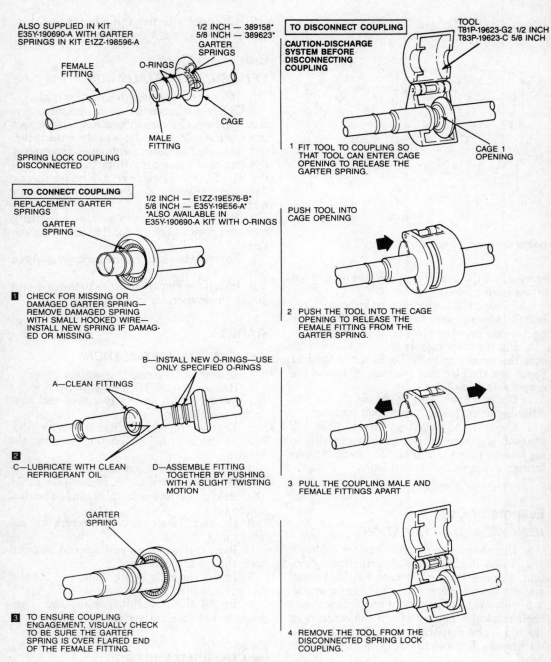

ALSO SUPPLIED IN KIT
E35Y-190690-A WITH GARTER
SPRINGS IN KIT E1ZZ-198596-A

1/2 INCH — 389158*
5/8 INCH — 389623*

FEMALE FITTING

O-RINGS

GARTER SPRINGS

MALE FITTING

CAGE

SPRING LOCK COUPLING
DISCONNECTED

TO CONNECT COUPLING

REPLACEMENT GARTER
SPRINGS

1/2 INCH — E1ZZ-19E576-B*
5/8 INCH — E35Y-19E56-A*
*ALSO AVAILABLE IN
E35Y-190690-A KIT WITH O-RINGS

GARTER SPRING

1 CHECK FOR MISSING OR
DAMAGED GARTER SPRING—
REMOVE DAMAGED SPRING
WITH SMALL HOOKED WIRE—
INSTALL NEW SPRING IF DAMAG-
ED OR MISSING.

B—INSTALL NEW O-RINGS—USE
ONLY SPECIFIED O-RINGS

A—CLEAN FITTINGS

2 C—LUBRICATE WITH CLEAN
REFRIGERANT OIL

D—ASSEMBLE FITTING
TOGETHER BY PUSHING
WITH A SLIGHT TWISTING
MOTION

GARTER SPRING

3 TO ENSURE COUPLING
ENGAGEMENT, VISUALLY CHECK
TO BE SURE THE GARTER
SPRING IS OVER FLARED END
OF THE FEMALE FITTING.

TO DISCONNECT COUPLING

CAUTION-DISCHARGE
SYSTEM BEFORE
DISCONNECTING
COUPLING

TOOL
T81P-19623-G2 1/2 INCH
T83P-19623-C 5/8 INCH

1 FIT TOOL TO COUPLING SO
THAT TOOL CAN ENTER CAGE
OPENING TO RELEASE THE
GARTER SPRING.

CAGE 1 OPENING

PUSH TOOL INTO
CAGE OPENING

2 PUSH THE TOOL INTO THE CAGE
OPENING TO RELEASE THE
FEMALE FITTING FROM THE
GARTER SPRING.

3 PULL THE COUPLING MALE AND
FEMALE FITTINGS APART

4 REMOVE THE TOOL FROM THE
DISCONNECTED SPRING LOCK
COUPLING.

AC line connectors

nut and remove the wiper arm and blade assembly.

5. Place the rear wiper arm and blade in position and secure the mounting nut. Close the cover.

ADJUSTMENTS

1. To adjust the sweep on the front wipers: Remove the arm and blade assembly. Turn the wiper switch on and allow the wiper pivots to go through two or three cycles. Turn the wiper switch off and allow the system to park. Install the wiper arm and blade assembly so there is ¾–1¼ in. of space from the bottom of the windshield.

2. To adjust the sweep of the rear wipers: Remove the rear wiper arm and blade assembly. Turn the rear wipers on and allow them to go through two or three cycles. Turn the switch off and allow them to park. Install the wiper

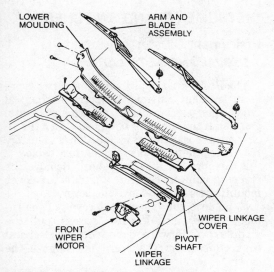

Front windshield wiper components

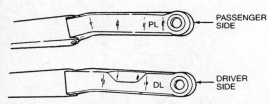

Wiper insert removal/installation

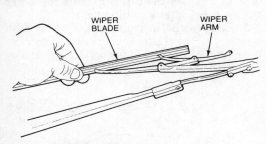

Wiper arm side position identification (right or left)

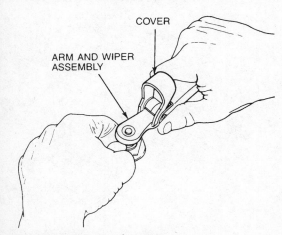

Remove/install rear wiper arm

arm and blade assembly so that there is ¾–1¼ in. of space from the bottom of the rear window.

NOTE: *The front wipers can operate in a summer or winter mode. The summer mode permits the wiper arm and blade assembly to park below the windshield. The winter mode allows the wiper arm and blade to park on the windshield. The summer/winter mode control connector is located on the driver's knee panel. The connector is marked summer or winter. Plug the wire on the connector desired.*

Windshield Wiper Motor
REMOVAL AND INSTALLATION
Front Wipers

1. Disconnect the negative battery cable.
2. Remove the windshield wiper arm and blades assemblies.
3. Disconnect the hose from the wiper washer jet nozzle.
4. Remove the lower cowl molding.
5. Remove the wiper linkage cover.
6. Disconnect the wiper linkage by pulling

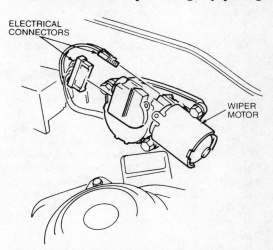

Remove/install front windshield wiper motor

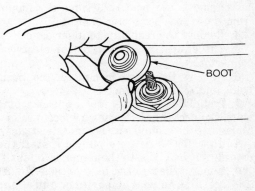

Remove/install rear motor boot

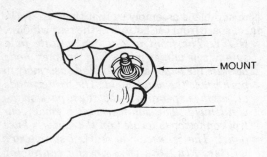

Remove/install rear motor mount

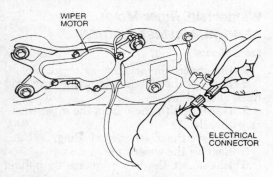

Remove/install rear wiper motor

off the wiper motor output arm. Disconnect the electrical connectors.

7. Remove the wiper motor mounting screws. Remove the wiper motor.

8. Install the wiper motor and attaching screws.

9. Connect the electrical wiring connectors. Attach the wiper linkage to the motor output arm. Install the wiper linkage cover. Install the lower molding, connect the washer nozzles and connect the negative battery cable.

10. Adjust and install the wiper arm and blade assemblies.

Rear Wiper

1. Disconnect the negative battery cable.

2. Remove the arm and blade assembly.

3. Remove the boot, nut, and the mount from the rear wiper motor pivot.

4. Remove the rear liftgate inner panel.

5. Disconnect the wiper motor electrical connector.

6. Remove the rear wiper motor mounting bolts, and remove the motor.

7. Install the rear wiper motor and attaching bolts. Connect the electrical wiring connectors. Make sure the ground wire is connected tightly.

8. Install the liftgate panel. Install the mount, nut and boot to the motor pivot shaft.

9. Connect the negative battery cable. Adjust and install the rear wiper arm and blade assembly.

INSTRUMENTS AND SWITCHES

Instrument Cluster

REMOVAL AND INSTALLATION

The Probe is equipped with one of two types of instrument cluster. A electro-mechanical (analog gauges), or an electronic cluster (digital gauges). If the vehicle is equipped with a turbocharger a boost gauge is included in the cluster.

1. Disconnect the negative battery cable.

2. Remove the steering wheel. Remove the steering column cover to instrument cover mounting screws. Remove the cover.

3. Remove the instrument cover to instrument cluster module cover screws, pull the module cover forward, disconnect the electrical connectors (from the rear) and remove the cover.

4. Remove the instrument cluster cover to dash screws and the cover. Remove the lower cluster panel screws and the panel.

5. Remove the instrument cluster to dash screws, pull the cluster forward and disconnect the electrical wiring connectors. On the analog

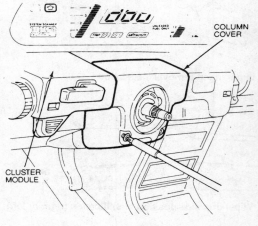

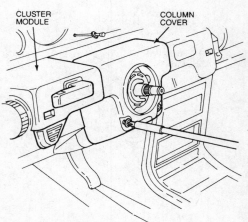

Remove/install the steering column cover

type, disconnect the speedometer cable. Remove the cluster.

6. Position the instrument cluster and connect the electrical connectors (and speedometer on analog type cluster). Push the cluster into place and install the mounting screws.

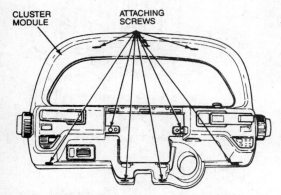

Remove/install the cluster module cover screws

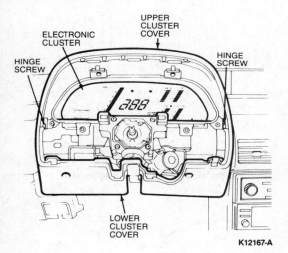

K12167-A

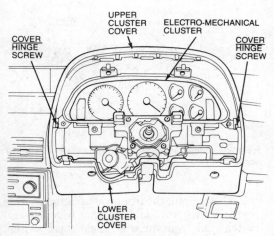

Lower cluster mounting screws

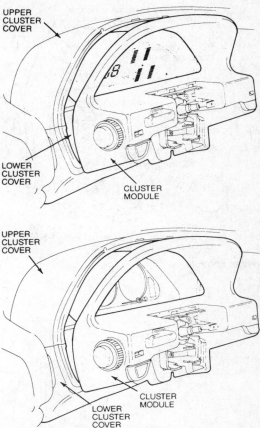

Remove/install the instrument cluster

7. Install the lower panel, cluster cover, module wiring and module cover, steering column and the steering wheel.

8. Connect the negative battery cable. Check instrument cluster gauges for operation.

Windshield Wiper Switch (Dash Mounted)

REMOVAL AND INSTALLATION

Front Wipers

1. Disconnect the negative battery cable. Remove the instrument cluster module cover.

2. Gently, pull the front washer/interval rate control switch/knob and the front wiper control switch/knob from the windshield wiper switch.

3. From the rear of the instrument cluster module, remove the windshield wiper switch retaining screws and the switch.

4. Install the front wiper/washer switch and retaining screws.

5. Install the front wiper control switch/knob. Install the front washer/interval rate control switch/knob. Install the module

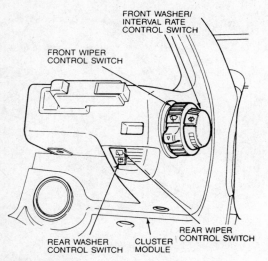

Wiper controls

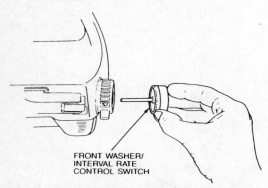

Remove/install the washer interval rate control switch

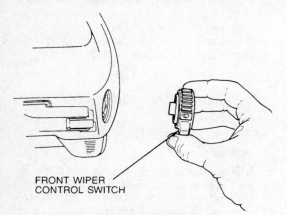

Remove/install from the washer control switch

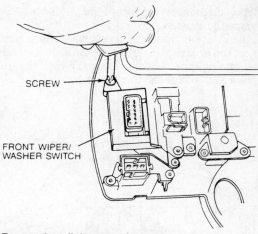

Remove/install the mounting screws

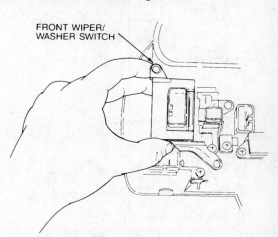

Remove/install the front wiper/washer switch

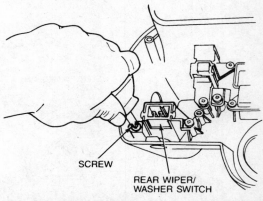

Remove/install rear washer/wiper switch mounting screws

cover and connect the negative battery cable. Check wiper/washer operation.

Rear Wiper

1. Disconnect the negative battery cable. Remove the instrument cluster module cover.

2. Gently, pull the front washer/interval rate control switch/knob and the front wiper control switch/knob from the windshield wiper switch.

3. From the rear of the instrument cluster

module, remove the windshield wiper switch retaining screws and the switch.

4. Remove the rear wiper/washer switch mounting screws. Depress the the mounting tangs on the control switch button and remove the switch button.

5. Remove the rear wiper/washer switch.

6. Install the rear wiper/washer switch. Install the control button.

7. Install the front wiper/washer switch and components.

8. Connect the negative battery cable. Check wiper/washer operation.

9. If the wiper interval relay needs replacement, reach behind the cluster and pull it from its mounting socket.

Headlight Switch
REMOVAL AND INSTALLATION

The headlight switch is located on the left side of the instrument panel. When the headlight switch is rotated to the 2nd position, all of the accessory lights are activated.

When the switch is rotated the the 3rd position, the headlight retractors will raise the headlights, and the lights are turned ON.

When the switch is rotated the the 4th posi-

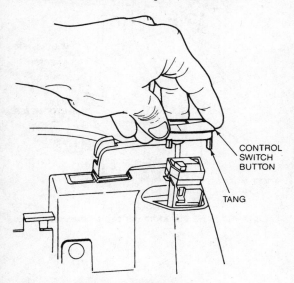

Remove/install control switch button

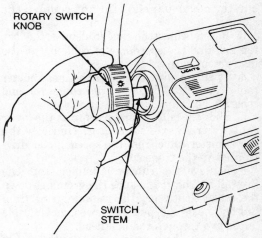

Remove/install rotary switch knob

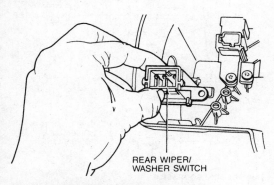

Remove/install rear wiper/washer switch

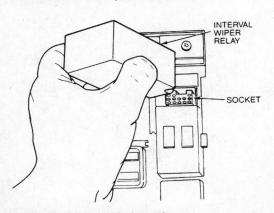

Remove/install interval wiper relay

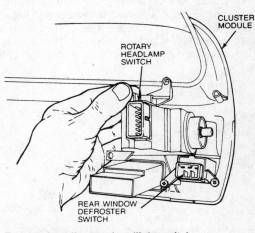

Remove/install rotary headlight switch

tion, the headlights will remain raised but the lights will turn OFF. The 4th position is used for servicing. The high beam switch is located on the turn signal switch control lever.

1. Disconnect the negative battery cable. Remove the turn signal switch assembly.

2. Remove the rotary switch knob from the switch shaft by gently pulling in away from the panel.

3. Remove the mounting screw and the switch assembly.

4. Install the rotary headlight switch and mounting screws. Install the control knob. Install the turn signal switch. Connect the negative battery cable. Check switch operation.

Speedometer Cable

REMOVAL AND INSTALLATION

Electro-Mechanical Type

1. Disconnect the negative battery cable.

2. Remove the upper and lower instrument cluster cover panels. (Do not remove the cluster).

3. Reach behind the cluster, depress the lock tab and pull the speedometer cable out of the instrument cluster.

4. Open the hood and locate the speedometer cable connector. Unscrew the connector and separate both upper and lower cables.

5. Slide the rubber boot back from the lower cable to transaxle connector. Unscrew the speedometer cable from the speedometer driven gear on the transaxle.

6. Remove the rubber grommet from the firewall bulkhead and slide the grommet down the cable. Gently pry the retaining ring from the bulkhead and pull the speedometer cable upper end through the bulkhead.

7. Insert the upper speedometer cable through the bulkhead into the vehicle.

8. Install the retaining ring and grommet into the bulkhead. Connect the upper and lower cable. Connect the lower cable to the driven gear assembly. Place the boot into position. Connect the upper cable to the rear of the

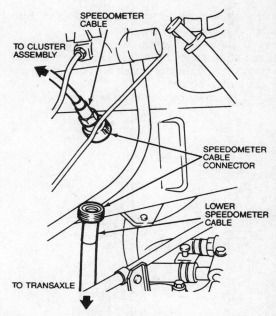

Upper and lower speedometer cable connection

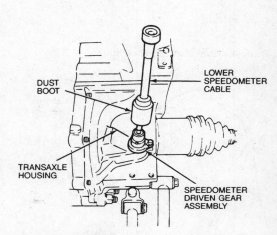

Lower cable connector

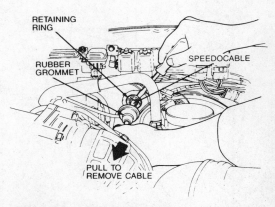

Bulkhead grommet and snapring

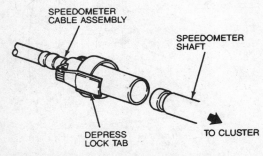

Depress the speedometer cable locking tab

speedometer. Install the upper and lower instrument cluster covers. Connect the negative battery cable. Check speedometer operation.

LIGHTING

Headlights

The headlamp system consists of two halogen headlamps mounted on retractable mechanisms, two optional fog lamps, a four-postion switch mounted on the left side of the instrument panel, and a high beam selector switch, located in the turn signal switch.

The four-position lighting switch controls the headlamps, parking lamps, side marker lamps, tail lamps, license plate lamps, cigar lighter lamp, and activates the panel lamp controller.

When the headlamp switch is rotated to the second postion, the parking lamps, side marker lamps, tail lamps, license plate lamps, cigar lighter lamp, and the instrument panel illumination lamps are activated.

When the headlamp switch is rotated to the third position, the headlamps are activated and the headlamp retractors lift the headlamps from the OFF position to the ON position.

When the headlamp switch is rotated to the fourth position, the headlamps will remain in the extended position, but all lamps including the headlamps will be extinguished. This service feature is beneficial for cleaning and service of the headlamp bulb. When the headlamp switch is rotated to the OFF postion, the headlamp retractors return the headlamps to their resting positions.

A manual control knob for the retractor is located beneath each headlamp retractor motor and is reached from under the front fascia. The retractor motor is mounted on a bracket that is attached to the radiator support.

The dimmer switch is located on the lower left side of the instrument panel. It can adjust the intensity of the instrument panel lamps using the thumbwheel control. The high beams are activated by gently pulling the turn signal lever toward the driver until the switch latches. Repeating this procedure will return headlamps to low beam operation.

The headlamp housing consists of a retractor hinge unit, mounting bracket, headlamp, locking collar, plastic bezel cover, and a headlamp lid. The high intensity halogen headlamp and the wiring connector are a single assembly. The headlamp is installed through the front of the mounting bracket and is held in position by a locking collar. The headlamp housing is mounted to the chassis by the retractor hinge unit.

The headlamp retractor motor is located under the tractor hinge unit. The motor pushes up and pulls down on the retractor hinge unit through a motor link assembly which attaches the headlamp housing to the retractor motor. Consequently, the headlamp is pulled to the retracted position without changing headlamp aim.

To operate the optional fog lamps, the low beams or the parking lamps must be on. The fog lamp switch is incorporated into the rotary light switch. The fog lamp system consists of the two fog lamps, a relay, the switch assembly, and a wiring assembly. If the high beams are activated, the fog lamps are automatically shut off.

On the headlamp circuit; battery voltage is applied at all times to the Headlight Relay and the Main Light Switch. With the Main Light Switch turned to HEAD, the Headlamp Relay is provided a ground. With the ground provided, the Headlamp Relay is energized and voltage is applied to the Dimmer Relay, the Headlight Checker (if equipped), and the Low Beam filament of the Dual Beam Headlamps.

With the Headlamps in Low Beam, the Headlamps can be shifted to High Beam by pulling on the Multi-Function Switch. This will energize the Dimmer Relay and supply voltage to the High Beam filament.

Flash-To-Pass can be operated with the Main Light Switch in OFF and the Retractors down. This is done by pulling up slightly on the Multi-Function Switch. This will activate the Headlamp Relay and apply voltage to the Headlamp Retractors. The Timer of the Multi-Function Switch will continue to apply voltage to the Retractors to maintain the Headlamps in the up position to allow flashing of the Headlamps without lowering the Retractors between flashes.

Battery voltage is also applied at all times from the Head Fuse to the coil of the Main Light Switch internal relay. Whenever the Main Light Switch is turned to HEAD, the internal relay's coil is grounded through the switch. With the coil grounded, the relay becomes energized, and the relay contacts are pulled closed to Position 1. When this occurs, battery voltage is applied to the Headlamp Retractor relays through the Head Fuse, Position 1 of the internal contacts, and the Position A side of the Headlamp Retractor mechanical switches. Since the Headlamp Retractor relay coils are permanently grounded, the relays are energized and their contacts are pulled closed as soon as battery voltage is applied. With the Headlamp Retractor relays energized and their contacts closed, battery voltage is applied to the Headlamp Retractor motors from the Retra

Fuse. As the Headlamps reach their full UP position, the mechanical switch in each Headlamp Retractor moves to Position B and opens the circuit between the Main Light Switch internal relay and the Headlamp Retractor relays. With battery voltage no longer applied, the Headlamp Retractor relays are de-energized, their contacts open, the circuits from the Retra Fuse to the Headlamp Retractors open, and the motors stop operating.

The Headlamp Retractor motors always rotate in the same direction. A cam assembly attached to the motor shaft moves the Headlamps into their UP and DOWN positions. When the Main Lamp Switch is turned to PARK or OFF, the ground is removed from the Main Light Switch internal relay coil. With the ground removed, the relay is de-energized and the contacts open to Position 2. Battery voltage is now applied to the Headlamp Retractor relays through the Head Fuse, Position 2 of the internal relay contacts, and the UP side of the Headlamp Retractor switches. This action again energizes the Headlamp Retractor relays, pulls the contacts closed, and closes circuits between the Retra Fuse and the Headlamp Retractor motors. The motors continue to operate until the Headlamps reach their full DOWN position and the mechanical switches in the Headlamp Retractors break the circuits by moving to Position A.

With the Main Light Switch turned to the HEAD or PARK and the Dimmer Switch in the low beam position, battery voltage is applied through the Head Fuse, and the closed contacts of the Headlamp and Dimmer Relays to energize the Foglamp Relay. With the contacts of the Foglamp Relay closed, battery voltage is applied through a fuse and the closed contacts of the Main Light switch to the Foglamp Switch. When the Foglamp Switch is ON, voltage is applied to the Foglamps.

REMOVAL AND INSTALLATION

CAUTION: *The halogen headlamp contains pressurized gas. It may shatter if the glass envelope is scratched or dropped. Handle the headlamp carefully. Keep the headlamp out of the reach of children.*

1. Extend the headlamps and set the rotary switch in the third detent position. The headlamps should remain extended with the lights out.
2. Disconnect the negative battery cable.
3. Remove the attaching screws from the bezel and remove the bezel.
4. Remove the lamp retaining collar and the headlamp as an assembly after disconnecting the wiring harness plug.
5. Install the wiring harness to the head-

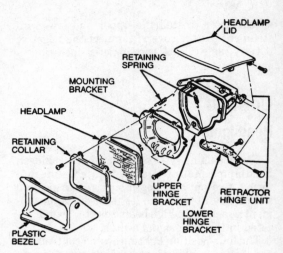

Headlamp beam removal/installation

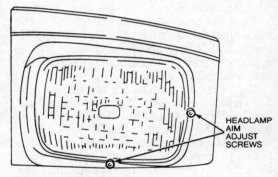

Headlamp alignment points

lamp. Position and secure the headlamp and retaining collar. Install the bezel. Connect the negative battery cable and place the headlamp switch in the second detent position. The lamp should light.

Signal and Marker Lights
REMOVAL AND INSTALLATION

Front Turn Signal and Parking Lamp

1. Remove the attaching screws and partially remove the front parking light lens.
2. Remove the bulb socket by turning it in a counterclockwise direction. Remove the bulb from the socket by carefully pushing it in and twisting it counterclockwise.
3. Install a new bulb in the socket and install the socket into the lens. Secure the lens in position.

Front Side Marker

1. Remove the attaching screws and partially remove the front side marker light lens.
2. Remove the bulb socket by turning it in a counterclockwise direction. Remove the bulb

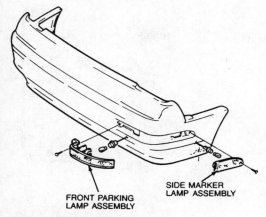

FRONT PARKING
LAMP ASSEMBLY

SIDE MARKER
LAMP ASSEMBLY

Turn signal and parking lamps

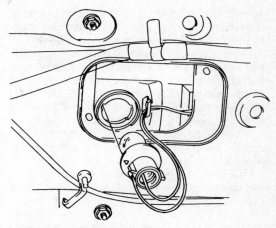

Lamp bulb removal/installation

from the socket by carefully pushing it in and twisting it counterclockwise.

3. Install a new bulb in the socket and install the socket into the lens. Secure the lens in position.

Rear Lamp/Marker Bulbs

1. Remove the plastic fasteners securing the rear trim panel. Remove the far right side upper trunk side garnish molding to gain access to the far right side bulb.

2. Carefully remove the socket of the bulb

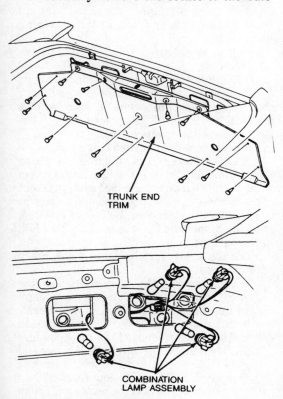

TRUNK END
TRIM

COMBINATION
LAMP ASSEMBLY

Tall lamp removal/installation

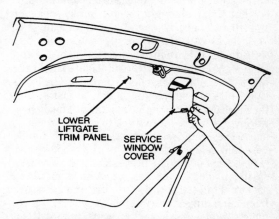

LOWER
LIFTGATE
TRIM PANEL

SERVICE
WINDOW
COVER

Highmount stoplight bulb removal/installation

that requires replacing. Push the bulb in and twist it counterclockwise to remove.

3. Install the new bulb. Install the trim and/or cover panel.

TRAILER WIRING

Wiring the car for towing is fairly easy. There are a number of good wiring kits available and these should be used, rather than trying to design your own. All trailers will need brake lights and turn signals as well as tail lights and side marker lights. Most states require extra marker lights for overly wide trailers. Also, most states have recently required back-up lights for trailers, and most trailer manufacturers have been building trailers with back-up lights for several years.

Additionally, some Class I, most Class II and just about all Class III trailers will have electric brakes.

Add to this number an accessories wire, to

operate trailer internal equipment or to charge the trailer's battery, and you can have as many as seven wires in the harness.

Determine the equipment on your trailer and buy the wiring kit necessary. The kit will contain all the wires needed, plus a plug adapter set which included the female plug, mounted on the bumper or hitch, and the male plug, wired into, or plugged into the trailer harness.

When installing the kit, follow the manufacturer's instructions. The color coding of the wires is standard throughout the industry.

One point to note, some domestic vehicles, and most imported vehicles, have separate turn signals. On most domestic vehicles, the brake lights and rear turn signals operate with the same bulb. For those vehicles with separate turn signals, you can purchase an isolation unit so that the brake lights won't blink whenever the turn signals are operated, or, you can go to your local electronics supply house and buy four diodes to wire in series with the brake and turn signal bulbs. Diodes will isolate the brake and turn signals. The choice is yours. The isolation units are simple and quick to install, but far more expensive than the diodes. The diodes, however, require more work to install properly, since they require the cutting of each bulb's wire and soldering in place of the diode.

One final point, the best kits are those with a spring loaded cover on the vehicle mounted socket. This cover prevents dirt and moisture from corroding the terminals. Never let the vehicle socket hang loosely. Always mount it securely to the bumper or hitch.

CIRCUIT PROTECTION

Fuse Block/Panel
Turn Signal/Hazard Flasher

The main fuse block is located inside the left side of the engine compartment near the battery. The interior fuse panel is located just above the left side kick panel. The turn signal/emergency flasher is located on the main relay box on the lower left hand corner. Remove of the fuses or flasher is by pulling out the defective and plugging a new replacement.

Fuse Link

The fuse link is a short length of special, Hypalon (high temperature) insulated wire, integral with the engine compartment wiring harness and should not be confused with standard wire. It is several wire gauges smaller than the circuit which it protects. Under no circumstances should a fuse link replacement repair

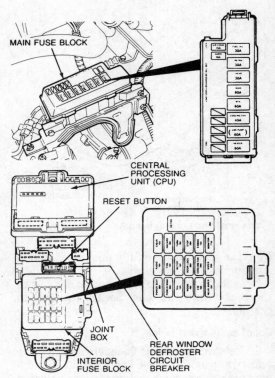

Fuse block/panel locations

be made using a length of standard wire cut from bulk stock or from another wiring harness.

To repair any blown fuse link use the following procedure:

1. Determine which circuit is damaged, its location and the cause of the open fuse link. If the damaged fuse link is one of three fed by a common No. 10 or 12 gauge feed wire, determine the specific affected circuit.

2. Disconnect the negative battery cable.

3. Cut the damaged fuse link from the wiring harness and discard it. If the fuse link is one of three circuits fed by a single feed wire, cut it out of the harness at each splice end and discard it.

4. Identify and procure the proper fuse link and butt connectors for attaching the fuse link to the harness.

5. To repair any fuse link in a 3-link group with one feed:

a. After cutting the open link out of the harness, cut each of the remaining undamaged fuse links close to the feed wire weld.

b. Strip approximately ½" of insulation from the detached ends of the two good fuse links. Then insert two wire ends into one end of a butt connector and carefully push one stripped end of the replacement fuse link into the same end of the butt connector and crimp all three firmly together.

Troubleshooting Basic Turn Signal and Flasher Problems

Most problems in the turn signals or flasher system, can be reduced to defective flashers or bulbs, which are easily replaced. Occasionally, problems in the turn signals are traced to the switch in the steering column, which will require professional service.

F = Front   R = Rear   • = Lights off   o = Lights on

Problem		Solution
Turn signals light, but do not flash		• Replace the flasher
No turn signals light on either side		• Check the fuse. Replace if defective. • Check the flasher by substitution • Check for open circuit, short circuit or poor ground
Both turn signals on one side don't work		• Check for bad bulbs • Check for bad ground in both housings
One turn signal light on one side doesn't work		• Check and/or replace bulb • Check for corrosion in socket. Clean contacts. • Check for poor ground at socket
Turn signal flashes too fast or too slow		• Check any bulb on the side flashing too fast. A heavy-duty bulb is probably installed in place of a regular bulb. • Check the bulb flashing too slow. A standard bulb was probably installed in place of a heavy-duty bulb. • Check for loose connections or corrosion at the bulb socket
Indicator lights don't work in either direction		• Check if the turn signals are working • Check the dash indicator lights • Check the flasher by substitution
One indicator light doesn't light		• On systems with 1 dash indicator: See if the lights work on the same side. Often the filaments have been reversed in systems combining stoplights with taillights and turn signals. Check the flasher by substitution • On systems with 2 indicators: Check the bulbs on the same side Check the indicator light bulb Check the flasher by substitution

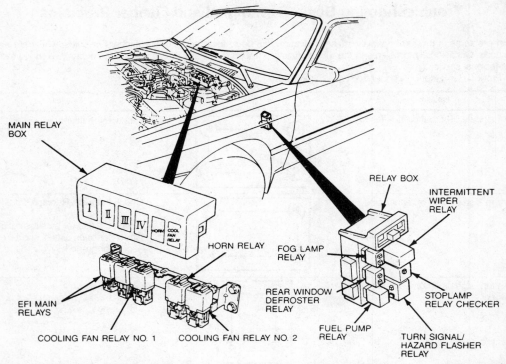

MAIN RELAY BOX

RELAY BOX

INTERMITTENT WIPER RELAY

HORN RELAY

FOG LAMP RELAY

EFI MAIN RELAYS

REAR WINDOW DEFROSTER RELAY

STOPLAMP RELAY CHECKER

COOLING FAN RELAY NO. 1

COOLING FAN RELAY NO. 2

FUEL PUMP RELAY

TURN SIGNAL/ HAZARD FLASHER RELAY

RELAY AND UNIT	LOCATION	NUMBER
Turn Signal/Hazard Flasher Relay	Under dash panel	—
Stop and Tail Lamp Checker Relay	Under dash panel	—
Intermittent Wiper Relay	Under dash panel	—
Fuel Pump Relay	Under dash panel	—
Rear Defroster Relay	Under dash panel	—
Fog Lamp Relay	Under dash panel	—
EFI Main Relay	On the bulkhead	I
EFI Main Relay	On the bulkhead	II
Cooling Fan Relay No. 1*	On the bulkhead	III
Horn Relay	On the bulkhead	—
Cooling Fan Relay No. 2	On the bulkhead	—

*Cooling Fan Relay No. 1 is only for models equipped with 4EAT

Relay box location

NOTE: *Care must be taken when fitting the three fuse links into the butt connector as the internal diameter is a snug it for three wires. Make sure to use a proper crimping tool. Pliers, side cutters, etc. will not apply the proper crimp to retain the wires and withstand a pull test.*

c. After crimping the butt connector to the three fuse links, cut the weld portion from the feed wire and strip approximately ½" of insulation from the cut end. Insert the stripped end into the open end of the butt connector and crimp very firmly.

d. To attach the remaining end of the re-

placement fuse link, strip approximately ½" of insulation from the wire end of the circuit from which the blown fuse link was removed, and firmly crimp a butt connector or equivalent to the stripped wire. Then, insert the end of the replacement link into the other end of the butt connector and crimp firmly.

e. Using rosin core solder with a consistency of 60 percent tin and 40 percent lead, solder the connectors and the wires at the repairs and insulate with electrical tape.

6. To replace any fuse link on a single circuit in a harness, cut out the damaged portion, strip approximately ½" of insulation from the two

Troubleshooting Basic Lighting Problems

Problem	Cause	Solution
Lights		
One or more lights don't work, but others do	• Defective bulb(s) • Blown fuse(s) • Dirty fuse clips or light sockets • Poor ground circuit	• Replace bulb(s) • Replace fuse(s) • Clean connections • Run ground wire from light socket housing to car frame
Lights burn out quickly	• Incorrect voltage regulator setting or defective regulator • Poor battery/alternator connections	• Replace voltage regulator • Check battery/alternator connections
Lights go dim	• Low/discharged battery • Alternator not charging • Corroded sockets or connections • Low voltage output	• Check battery • Check drive belt tension; repair or replace alternator • Clean bulb and socket contacts and connections • Replace voltage regulator
Lights flicker	• Loose connection • Poor ground • Circuit breaker operating (short circuit)	• Tighten all connections • Run ground wire from light housing to car frame • Check connections and look for bare wires
Lights "flare"—Some flare is normal on acceleration—if excessive, see "Lights Burn Out Quickly"	• High voltage setting	• Replace voltage regulator
Lights glare—approaching drivers are blinded	• Lights adjusted too high • Rear springs or shocks sagging • Rear tires soft	• Have headlights aimed • Check rear springs/shocks • Check/correct rear tire pressure
Turn Signals		
Turn signals don't work in either direction	• Blown fuse • Defective flasher • Loose connection	• Replace fuse • Replace flasher • Check/tighten all connections
Right (or left) turn signal only won't work	• Bulb burned out • Right (or left) indicator bulb burned out • Short circuit	• Replace bulb • Check/replace indicator bulb • Check/repair wiring
Flasher rate too slow or too fast	• Incorrect wattage bulb • Incorrect flasher	• Flasher bulb • Replace flasher (use a variable load flasher if you pull a trailer)
Indicator lights do not flash (burn steadily)	• Burned out bulb • Defective flasher	• Replace bulb • Replace flasher
Indicator lights do not light at all	• Burned out indicator bulb • Defective flasher	• Replace indicator bulb • Replace flasher

wire ends and attach the appropriate replacement fuse link to the stripped wire ends with two proper size butt connectors. Solder the connectors and wires and insulate the tape.

7. To repair any fuse link which has an eyelet terminal on one end such as the charging circuit, cut off the open fuse link behind the weld, strip approximately ½" of insulation from the cut end and attach the appropriate new eyelet fuse link to the cut stripped wire with an appropriate size butt connector. Solder the connectors and wires at the repair and insulate with tape.

8. Connect the negative battery cable to the battery and test the system for proper operation.

NOTE: *Do not mistake a resistor wire for a fuse link. The resistor wire is generally longer and has print stating, "Resistor: don't cut or splice."*

Troubleshooting Basic Dash Gauge Problems

Problem	Cause	Solution
Coolant Temperature Gauge		
Gauge reads erratically or not at all	• Loose or dirty connections • Defective sending unit	• Clean/tighten connections • Bi-metal gauge: remove the wire from the sending unit. Ground the wire for an instant. If the gauge registers, replace the sending unit.
	• Defective gauge	• Magnetic gauge: disconnect the wire at the sending unit. With ignition ON gauge should register COLD. Ground the wire; gauge should register HOT.
Ammeter Gauge—Turn Headlights ON (do not start engine). Note reaction		
Ammeter shows charge Ammeter shows discharge Ammeter does not move	• Connections reversed on gauge • Ammeter is OK • Loose connections or faulty wiring • Defective gauge	• Reinstall connections • Nothing • Check/correct wiring • Replace gauge
Oil Pressure Gauge		
Gauge does not register or is inaccurate	• On mechanical gauge, Bourdon tube may be bent or kinked	• Check tube for kinks or bends preventing oil from reaching the gauge
	• Low oil pressure	• Remove sending unit. Idle the engine briefly. If no oil flows from sending unit hole, problem is in engine.
	• Defective gauge	• Remove the wire from the sending unit and ground it for an instant with the ignition ON. A good gauge will go to the top of the scale.
	• Defective wiring	• Check the wiring to the gauge. If it's OK and the gauge doesn't register when grounded, replace the gauge.
	• Defective sending unit	• If the wiring is OK and the gauge functions when grounded, replace the sending unit
All Gauges		
All gauges do not operate	• Blown fuse • Defective instrument regulator	• Replace fuse • Replace instrument voltage regulator
All gauges read low or erratically	• Defective or dirty instrument voltage regulator	• Clean contacts or replace
All gauges pegged	• Loss of ground between instrument voltage regulator and car • Defective instrument regulator	• Check ground • Replace regulator
Warning Lights		
Light(s) do not come on when ignition is ON, but engine is not started	• Defective bulb • Defective wire	• Replace bulb • Check wire from light to sending unit
	• Defective sending unit	• Disconnect the wire from the sending unit and ground it. Replace the sending unit if the light comes on with the ignition ON.
Light comes on with engine running	• Problem in individual system • Defective sending unit	• Check system • Check sending unit (see above)

Fuse	Affect These Circuits
HEAD 30A (Main)	Headlight
BTN 60A (Main)	Front Fog Lamps, Glove Compartment Lamp, Parking Lamps, Front and Rear Marker Lamps, Tail Lamps, License Lamps, Illumination Lamps, Cargo Lamp, Stoplamps, High Mount Stop Lamp, Horn, Power Antenna, Turn and Hazard Flasher Lamps, Power Seat, Power Door Locks, 4EAT System, Sound Warning System, Heating and Air Conditioning (Electronic Control)
MAIN 80A (Main)	Charging System, Remote Control Mirror, Audio System, Cigar Lighter, Air Conditioner, Programmed Ride Control System, Front Wiper and Washer, Rear Wiper and Washer, Backup Lamps, Cruise Control System, Meter and Warning Lights, Electronically Controlled Power Steering System, Emission and Fuel Control System, Rear Window Defroster, Power Window, Ignition System, Vehicle Maintenance Monitor (VMM), System Scanner (Electronic Cluster)
RETRA 30A (Main)	Headlamp Retractors
ABS PUMP 60A (Main)	ABS Control System
FUEL INJ. 30A (Main)	Emission and fuel injection
AIR COND 15A (Main)	Air Conditioning Compressor, Magnetic Clutch Control System
AUDIO 10A (Main)	Audio System
COOLING FAN 40A (Main)	Cooling Fan System
HEATER 60A (Main)	Heater Control System

The fuses are color-coded by amp rating

Fuse Value Amps	Color Code
30	Pink
40	Green
60	Yellow
80	Black

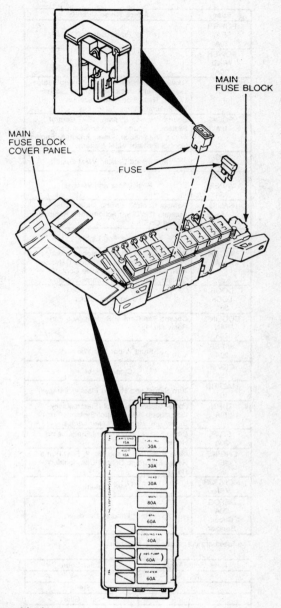

MAIN FUSE BLOCK

MAIN FUSE BLOCK COVER PANEL

FUSE

Main fuse block

Fuse	Affect These Circuits
POWER SEAT 30A	Power Seats
POWER WIND 30A	Power Windows
TAIL 15A	Glove Compartment Lamp, Parking Lamps, Side Marker Lamps, Tail Lamps, License Lamps, Rear Side Marker Lamps, Illumination Lamps
ROOM 10A	Sound Warning System, 4EAT Control System, Luggage Compartment Lamp, Audio, Illumination, Power Antenna, Engine Control System, VMM System
EIC 10A	Instrument Cluster, VMM System
REAR WIPER 15A	Rear Wiper and Washer
RADIO 15A	Remote Control Mirrors, Audio/Power Antenna (Up/Down Action when Radio is Turned On/Off)
FOG 15A	Front Fog Lights
METER 15A	Backup Lamps, Power Antenna, Sound Warning System, Rear Window Defroster, 4EAT Control System, Cruise Control System, Cooling Fan Control System
DOOR LOCK 30A	Power Door Locks
COOLING FAN 20A	Cooling Fan Control System (Add Fan Relay No. 1)
WIPER 20A	Front Wiper and Washer
CIGAR 15A	Cigar Lighter
HAZARD 10A	Turn Signal and Hazard Flasher Lamps
TURN 10A	Power Steering Control (Electronically Controlled), ABS Control System, Turn Signal and Hazard Flasher Lamps
STOP 20A	Brake Lamps, High Mount Brake Lamp, Horns
ENGINE 15A	Main Relay No. 1 and No. 2, Fuel Pump Relay, Electronic Control Unit, Ignition Relay
MONITOR 7.5A	VMM System
DEFOG 30A Circuit Breaker	Rear Window Defroster

The fuses are color-coded by amp rating

Fuse Value Amps	Color Code
7.5	Amber
10	Red
15	Light Blue
20	Yellow
30	Light Green

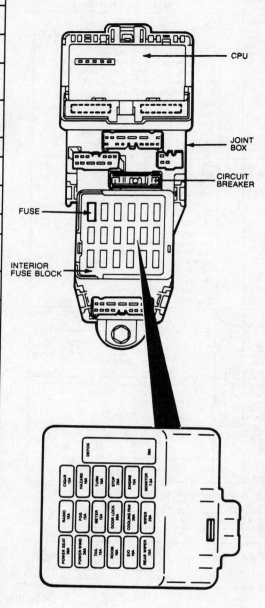

Fuse panel

Troubleshooting the Heater

Problem	Cause	Solution
Blower motor will not turn at any speed	• Blown fuse • Loose connection • Defective ground • Faulty switch • Faulty motor • Faulty resistor	• Replace fuse • Inspect and tighten • Clean and tighten • Replace switch • Replace motor • Replace resistor
Blower motor turns at one speed only	• Faulty switch • Faulty resistor	• Replace switch • Replace resistor
Blower motor turns but does not circulate air	• Intake blocked • Fan not secured to the motor shaft	• Clean intake • Tighten security
Heater will not heat	• Coolant does not reach proper temperature • Heater core blocked internally • Heater core air-bound • Blend-air door not in proper position	• Check and replace thermostat if necessary • Flush or replace core if necessary • Purge air from core • Adjust cable
Heater will not defrost	• Control cable adjustment incorrect • Defroster hose damaged	• Adjust control cable • Replace defroster hose

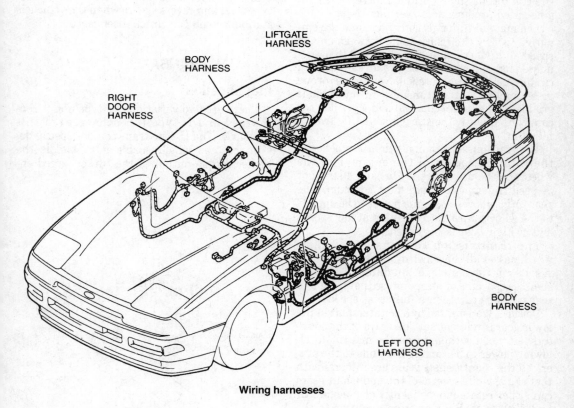

Wiring harnesses

Drive Train

7

UNDERSTANDING THE MANUAL TRANSMISSION

Because of the way an internal combustion engine breathes, it can produce torque, or twisting force, only within a narrow speed range. Most modern, overhead valve engines must turn at about 2,500 rpm to produce their peak torque. By 4,500 rpm they are producing so little torque that continued increases in engine speed produce no power increases.

The manual transmission and clutch are employed to vary the relationship between engine speed and the speed of the wheels so that adequate engine power can be produced under all circumstances. The clutch allows engine torque to be applied to the transmission input shaft gradually, due to mechanical slippage. The car can, consequently, be started smoothly from a full stop.

The transmission changes the ratio between the rotating speeds of the engine and the wheels by the use of gears. On cars, 4-speed or 5-speed transmissions are most common. The gear ratios allow full engine power to be applied to the wheels during acceleration at low speeds and at highway/passing speeds.

The transmission contains a mainshaft which passes all the way through the transmission, from the clutch to the differential. This shaft is separated at one point, so that front and rear portions can turn at different speeds.

Power is transmitted by a countershaft in the lower gears and reverse. The gears of the countershaft mesh with gears on the mainshaft, allowing power to be carried from one to the other. All the countershaft gears are integral with that shaft, while several of the mainshaft gears can either rotate independently of the shaft or be locked to it. Shifting from one gear to the next causes one of the gears to be freed from rotating with the shaft and locks another to it. Gears are locked and unlocked by internal dog clutches which slide between the center of the gear and the shaft. The forward gears usually employ synchronizers; friction members which smoothly bring gear and shaft to the same speed before the toothed dog clutches are engaged.

The clutch is operating properly if:

1. It will stall the engine when released with the vehicle held stationary.

2. The shift lever can be moved freely between 1st and reverse gears when the vehicle is stationary and the clutch disengaged.

MANUAL TRANSAXLE

Identification

There are two variations (G-type non-turbocharged and H-type turbocharged) of this transaxle. The H-type transaxle has special design features which enable it to handle the higher torque output of the turbocharged en-

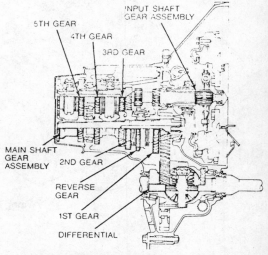

Non-turbo transaxle components

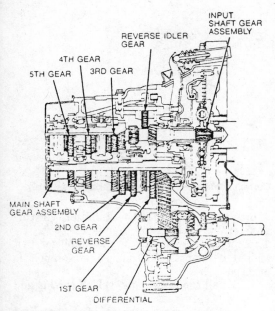

Turbo transaxle components

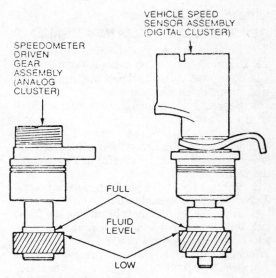

Checking transaxle fluid level

gine. Each transaxle has it own gear ratio which are engineered to match the varying performance characteristics of the two engine designs.

Both types have reverse gear synchromesh shifting and the 5th/reverse clutch hub assembly on the input shaft. The helical cut forward gears are in constant mesh with the corresponding gears on the opposing shaft. The forward gears are selected by means of a synchronizer mechanism. 3rd, 4th and 5th gears are mounted on the input shaft. First, 2nd and reverse gears have straight cut teeth and are engaged through the reverse idler gear by means of a synchronizer mechanism.

The turbocharged transaxle has 3 separate shift rods for 1st/2nd, 3rd/4th and 5th/reverse. Needle bearings are used on the turbocharged transaxle to reduce the sliding resistance of the forward gears.

Capacities

The 5-speed transaxle uses Dexron®II automatic transmission fluid. The capacity of the transaxle is 3.6 quarts or 3.35L for the G-type (non-turbocharged) and 3.9 quarts or 3.65L for the H-type (turbocharged).

Checking Fluid Level

1. Transaxle fluid level should only be checked after the vehicle has been standing on level ground for some time.

2. On vehicles equipped with a digital cluster, disconnect the harness from the vehicle speed sensor assembly located on the transaxle.

3. On vehicles equipped with an analog cluster, remove the speedometer cable dust cover and disconnect the cable from the speedometer driven gear.

4. After removing the retaining bolt, pull the gear case to remove it from the housing. Insert a suitable tool between the speedometer gear case and the clutch housing and use it to pry the gear case loose if necessary. On digital cluster vehicles, remove the vehicle speed sensor assembly in the same manner.

5. Check that the oil level is between the **F** and **L** on the dipstick.

6. Add the necessary amount of the specified oil through the gear case hole to correct the fluid level.

ON CAR SERVICES

Fluid Change and Refill

1. Park the vehicle on level ground and apply the parking brake.

2. Remove the speedometer driven gear assembly on vehicles equipped with an analog cluster or the vehicle speed sensor assembly on vehicles equipped with a digital cluster.

NOTE: *It may be necessary to raise and support the vehicle safely to gain access to the drain plug.*

3. Remove the drain plug and drain the oil into a suitable pan.

4. Replace the drain plug and torque to 29–43 ft. lbs. Then add the necessary amount of the specified oil through the speedometer gear case hole.

5. Start engine, road test and check for leaks.

Differential Oil Seals

REMOVAL AND INSTALLATION

1. Raise vehicle and safely support the vehicle. Drain oil from the transaxle assembly.

2. Remove the front wheels and remove the splash shields as necessary.

3. Separate the front stabilizer from the lower arm.

4. Remove the clinch bolt and pull the lower arm downward. Separate the knuckle from the lower arm ball joint. Be careful not to damage the ball joint dust boot.

5. Remove the cotter pin then disconnect the tie rod end with special tool.

6. Separate the halfshaft by pulling the front hub outward. Do not use too much force at once, increase the force gradually.

NOTE: *When removing the right side halfshaft remove the right joint shaft bracket.*

7. Do not allow the halfshaft joint to bent to its maximum extent as damage to the joint could result. Support the halfshaft using string or equivalent.

8. Remove the oil seal from the transaxle using a suitable tool.

9. Coat the new oil seal lip with transaxle oil. Tap the new seal until the oil seal installer or equivalent contacts the case.

10. Replace the halfshaft end clip. Insert the clip with the gap at the top of the groove.

11. Pull the front hub outward, then fit the halfshaft into the transaxle.

12. Insert the halfshaft into the transaxle by pushing on the wheel hub assembly. Be careful not to damage the oil seal when pushing on the wheel hub.

13. After installation is finished, pull the front hub slowly outward to check that the halfshaft is held securely by the clip.

14. Install the lower arm ball joint to the knuckle and tighten the clinch bolt to 32–40 ft. lbs.

15. Install the tie rod end and insert a new cotter pin. Tighten the tie rod end to 22–33 ft. lbs.

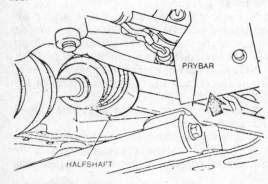

Removing the halfshaft

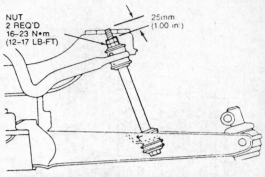

Correct adjustment of the stabilizer bolt assembly

16. Adjust and tighten the stabilizer. The correct torque for the stabilizer is 12–17 ft. lbs. The correct adjustment of the stabilizer bolt should be tighten so that 25mm of bolt is exposed.

17. Install the drain plug, splash shields and install wheel/tire assembly.

18. Add the correct quantity of the specified oil to the transaxle.

19. Start engine, road test and check for leaks.

Transaxle

REMOVAL AND INSTALLATION

NOTE: *The transaxle is removed separately from the engine.*

1. Disconnect the battery cables. Remove the battery and battery carrier.

2. Disconnect the main fuse block.

3. Disconnect the center distributor lead.

4. Disconnect the air flow meter connector and remove the air cleaner assembly.

5. On the turbocharged vehicles remove the inter cooler hose to throttle body and air cleaner to turbocharger. On non-turbocharged vehicles just remove the resonance chamber and bracket.

6. Disconnect the speedometer cable on analog cluster or harness on digital cluster.

7. Disconnect the grounds from the transaxle case.

8. Raise and safely support the vehicle. Remove the front wheels.

9. Remove the splash shields.

10. Drain the transaxle oil into a suitable pan.

11. Remove the slave cylinder from the transaxle.

12. Disconnect the tie rod ends using a suitable tool.

13. Remove the stabilizer bar control links.

14. Remove the bolts and nuts at the left and right lower arm ball joints.

15. Pull the lower arms downward to separate

TRANSAXLE PLUG

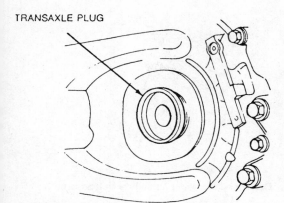

Install special tool to hold differential side gears

them from the knuckles. Do not damage the ball joint dust boots.

16. Separate the left halfshaft from the transaxle by prying with a bar or equivalent inserted between the shaft and the transaxle case. Be careful not to damage the oil seal.

17. Remove the joint shaft bracket.

18. Separate the right halfshaft together with the joint shaft by prying with a bar or equivalent inserted between the shaft and the transaxle case. Be careful not to damage the oil seal.

19. Install the special tools to hold the differential side gear in the proper position.

NOTE: *Failure to install the differential side gears holding tool may cause the differential side gears to become mispositioned.*

20. Remove the gusset plate to transaxle bolts.

21. Remove the extension bar and the control rod.

22. Remove the flywheel inspection cover.

23. Mark or tag the electrical connections if necessary and remove the starter and access brackets.

24. Support the engine with the engine support fixture or equivalent.

25. Remove the center transaxle mount and bracket.

26. Remove the left transaxle mount and bracket.

27. Remove the nut and bolt which attaches the right transaxle mount to the frame.

28. Remove the crossmember and the left side lower arm as an assembly.

29. Position a transmission jack under the transaxle and secure the transaxle to the jack.

30. Remove the transaxle mounting bolts.

31. Remove the transaxle from the vehicle. The engine must always be properly supported while the transaxle is out of the vehicle.

32. Apply a thin coating of clutch grease to the spline of the input shaft. Attach a safety device at 2 places on the transaxle and place a board on the jack and position the transaxle on it. The transaxle is not well balanced and be careful when positioning it on the jack.

33. Install the transaxle onto the engine. Tighten the transaxle mounting bolts to 66–86 ft. lbs.

34. Install the center transaxle mount and bracket. Tighten the bolts 27–40 ft. lbs. and the nuts to 47–66 ft. lbs. Do not install the nut which braces the throttle air hose bracket.

35. Install the left transaxle mount and tighten bolts on the mount to 27–38 ft. lbs. for non-turbocharged vehicles and 49–69 ft. lbs. for turbocharged vehicles. The retaining nuts on this mount are torque to 49–69 ft. lbs. for both engines.

36. Install the crossmember and the left side lower arm as an assembly. The tightening torque is 27–40 ft. lbs. on the bolts and 55–69 ft. lbs. on the nut.

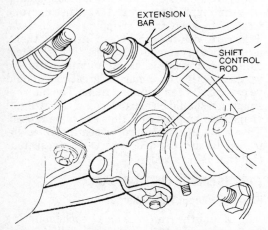

Remove the extension bar and control rod-transaxle removal

ENGINE-TO-TRANSAXLE BOLT

89–117 N•m
(66–86 LB-FT)

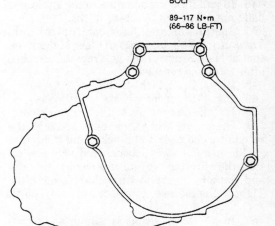

Mounting bolt locations

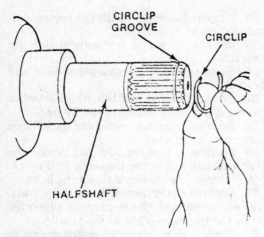

Always replace the circlip

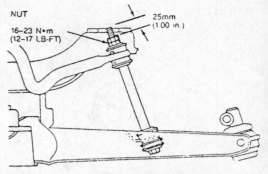

Correct adjustment of stabilizer bolt assembly

37. Install the right transaxle mount bolt and nut and tighten to 63–86 ft. lbs.
38. Install the starter, electrical connections and access brackets.
39. Install the flywheel inspection cover.
40. Install the slave cylinder.
41. Install the gusset plate to transaxle bolts and torque the bolts to 27–38 ft. lbs.
42. Replace the circlips at the end of each halfshafts.
43. Remove the special tools holding the differential side gears in the proper position and install the halfshafts.

NOTE: *After complete installation, pull the front hub outward to confirm that the halfshaft will not come out. Be careful not damage the oil seal.*

44. Attach the lower arm ball joints to the knuckle.
45. Install the tie rod ends and new cotter pins. Tighten the tie rod end bolts to 22–33 ft. lbs.
46. Install the bolts and nuts to the lower arm ball joints. Tighten to 32–40 ft. lbs.
47. Install the stabilizer bar control link. Tighten nut/bolt to 12–17 ft. lbs. Make sure, that at least 25mm of the bolt remains exposed after torque is reached.
48. Install the splash shields.
49. Install the front wheels.
50. Install the grounds to the transaxle case.
51. On non-turbocharged vehicles, install the resonance chamber and bracket and tighten to 69–95 inch lbs. On turbocharged vehicles, install the throttle body to intercooler air hose and the air cleaner to turbocharger air hose. Tighten the bracket to mount nut to 47–66 ft. lbs.
52. Install the air cleaner assembly and reconnect the air flow meter connector. The correct torque for the air cleaner assembly is 69–95 inch lbs.

53. Reconnect the center distributor lead.
54. Connect the main fuse block and tighten retaining bolts to 69–95 inch lbs.
55. Install the battery carrier and battery. Reconnect the battery cables.
56. Remove the engine support fixture or equivalent.
57. Add the correct quantity of the specified fluid.
58. Connect the speedometer cable on analog cluster equipped vehicles or harness for digital cluster equipped vehicles.
59. Start the engine, road test for proper operation and check for leaks.

Overhaul

Before Disassembly: When servicing the unit, it is recommended that as each part is disassembled, it is cleaned in solvent and dried with compressed air. Disassembly and reassembly of this unit and its parts must be done on a clean work bench. Also, before installing bolts into aluminum parts, always dip the threads into clean transmission oil. Anti-seize compound can also be used to prevent bolts from galling the aluminum and seizing. Always use a torque wrench to keep from stripping the threads. Take care with the seals when installing them, especially the smaller O-rings. The slightest damage can cause leaks. Aluminum parts are very susceptible to damage so great care should be exercised when handling them. The internal snaprings should be expanded and the external snaprings compressed if they are to be reused. This will help insure proper seating when installed. Be sure to replace any O-ring, gasket, or seal that is removed.

DISASSEMBLY OF TRANSAXLE

Engines Without Turbocharger

1. Mount the transaxle on a bench mounting fixture or equivalent.
2. Remove the drain plug and drain any remaining fluid from the transaxle.

3. Remove the bolts that secure the rear cover to the transaxle case. Tap the cover with a rubber or plastic mallet to loosen the gasket seal. Remove the rear cover. Shift the transaxle to 1st gear.

4. Use special tool to lock up the input shaft. Uncrimp the tabs and remove the locknuts.

5. Remove the input reverse synchronizer gear.

6. Remove the main reverse synchronizer gear.

7. Use a suitable tool to drive out the roll pin.

8. Remove the shift fork, synchronizer ring and clutch hub assembly.

9. Remove the synchronizer ring.

10. Remove the input 5th gear.

11. Remove the gear sleeve.

12. Remove the main 5th gear.

13. Remove the lock bolts, washer, guide bolt, springs and ball.

14. Tap the transaxle case lightly with a rub-ber or plastic hammer to loosen the gasket seal. Remove the transaxle case.

15. Remove the magnet.

16. Remove the reverse idler shaft and gear.

17. Remove the lock bolt from the gate.

18. Remove the clip and 5th and reverse shift rod.

19. Remove the gate.

20. Remove the pin.

21. Remove the crank lever shaft and assembly.

22. Align the ends of the interlock sleeve and control lever, then turn the shift rod counterclockwise.

23. Raise both shift forks and shift the clutch hub sleeves.

24. Lift the control end and remove the steel ball.

25. Remove the shift fork and shift rod assembly.

26. Remove the input shaft gear assembly.

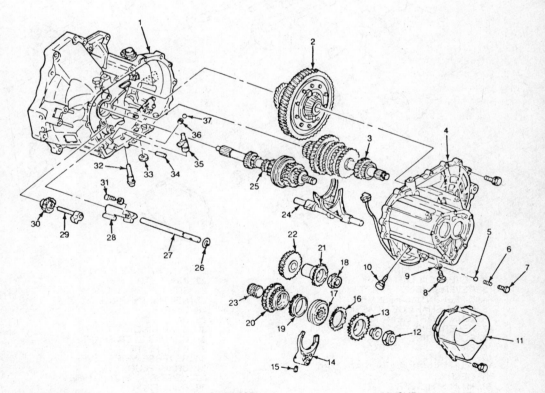

1.	CLUTCH HOUSING	14.	SHIFT FORK	26.	CLIP
2.	DIFFERENTIAL	15.	ROLL PIN	27.	SHIFT ROD (5TH AND
3.	MAIN SHAFT GEAR ASSEMBLY	16.	SYNCHRONIZER RING		REVERSE)
4.	TRANSAXLE CASE	17.	CLUTCH HUB ASSEMBLY	28.	GATE
5.	BALL	18.	LOCKNUT	29.	REVERSE IDLER SHAFT
6.	SPRING	19.	SYNCHRONIZER RING	30.	REVERSE IDLER GEAR
7.	LOCK BOLT	20.	INPUT 5TH GEAR	31.	LOCK BOLT
8.	GUIDE BOLT	21.	MAIN REVERSE	32.	CRANK LEVER SHAFT
9.	WASHER		SYNCHRONIZER GEAR	33.	MAGNET
10.	LOCK BOLT	22.	MAIN 5TH GEAR	34.	PIN
11.	REAR COVER	23.	GEAR SLEEVE	35.	CRANK LEVER ASSEMBLY
12.	LOCKNUT	24.	SHIFT FORK AND SHIFT ROD	36.	SPRING
13.	INPUT REVERSE		ASSEMBLY	37.	BALL
	SYNCHRONIZER GEAR	25.	INPUT SHAFT GEAR ASSEMBLY		

Exploded view of non-turbo transaxle

27. Remove the mainshaft gear assembly.
28. Remove the differential assembly.
29. Remove the input shaft bearing cups, diaphragm spring and adjustment shims.

30. Remove the input shaft seal using special tool or equivalent.
31. Remove the mainshaft bearing cups, adjustment shims, diaphragm spring and funnel.

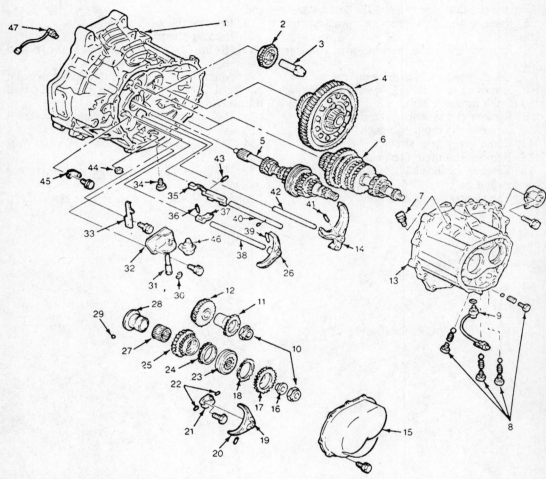

1.	CLUTCH HOUSING	24.	SYNCHRONIZER RING
2.	REVERSE IDLER GEAR	25.	INPUT 5TH GEAR
3.	REVERSE IDLER SHAFT	26.	SHIFT FORK (3RD/4TH)
4.	DIFFERENTIAL ASSEMBLY	27.	NEEDLE BEARING
5.	INPUT SHAFT GEAR ASSEMBLY	28.	SLEEVE
6.	MAIN SHAFT GEAR ASSEMBLY	29.	BALL
7.	REVERSE IDLER SHAFT SET BOLT	30.	SNAP RING
8.	BOLT, SPRING AND BALL	31.	CRANK LEVER SHAFT
9.	BACKUP LAMP SWITCH	32.	BASE PLATE
10.	LOCKNUT	33.	REVERSE SHIFT LEVER
11.	MAIN REVERSE SYNCHRONIZER	34.	DRAIN PLUG
	GEAR	35.	SHIFT ROD END (5TH/REV)
12.	MAIN 5TH GEAR	36.	ROLL PIN
13.	TRANSAXLE CASE	37.	SHIFT ROD END (3RD/4TH)
14.	SHIFT FORK (1ST/2ND)	38.	SHIFT ROD (3RD/4TH)
15.	REAR COVER	39.	ROLL PIN
16.	SLEEVE	40.	ROLL PIN
17.	INPUT REVERSE SYNCHRONIZER	41.	ROLL PIN
	GEAR	42.	SHIFT ROD (1ST/2ND)
18.	SYNCHRONIZER RING	43.	ROLL PIN
19.	ROLL PIN	44.	MAGNET
20.	SHIFT FORK (5TH AND REVERSE)	45.	LEVER SET SPRING
21.	INTERLOCK PLATE	46.	CRANK LEVER ASSEMBLY
22.	INTERLOCK PIN	47.	NEUTRAL SWITCH
23.	CLUTCH HUB ASSEMBLY		

Exploded view of turbo transaxle

32. Remove the guide plate and spacer.

33. Remove the change arm.

34. Remove the selector pin using a suitable tool.

35. Remove the change rod and boot.

36. Remove the spring.

37. Remove the reverse gate.

38. Remove the selector.

39. Remove the change arm oil seal using special tools or equivalent.

40. Remove the breather cover and breather.

41. Remove the speedometer driven gear assembly on vehicles equipped with analog cluster or vehicle speed sensor assembly from vehicles equipped with digital cluster from the case.

42. Remove the differential bearing cups using special tools or equivalent. Remove the adjustment shim(s).

43. Remove the reverse lever shaft and reverse lever.

44. Remove the neutral switch and gasket.

45. Remove the differential seals using special tools or equivalent.

Engines With Turbocharger

1. Mount the transaxle on a bench mounting fixture or equivalent.

2. Remove the drain plug and drain any remaining fluid from the transaxle.

3. Remove the bolts that secure the rear cover to the transaxle case. Tap the cover with a rubber or plastic mallet to loosen the gasket seal. Remove the rear cover.

4. Remove the roll pin with a suitable tool.

5. Shift the transaxle into 5th gear by pressing down the shift fork and rod.

6. Shift the transaxle into 1st gear.

7. Uncrimp the tabs and remove the locknuts.

8. Remove the sleeve.

9. Remove the input reverse synchronizer gear.

10. Remove the main reverse synchronizer gear.

11. Remove the shift fork, synchronizer ring and clutch hub assembly.

12. Remove the synchronizer ring and input 5th gear.

13. Remove the needle bearing.

14. Remove the sleeve.

15. Remove the ball.

16. Remove the main 5th gear.

17. Remove the interlock plate and bolts.

18. Remove the interlock pins.

19. Remove the backup light switch.

20. Remove the bolts, springs and balls.

21. Remove the transaxle case attaching bolts and the reverse idler shaft set bolt.

22. Tap the transaxle case lightly with a rubber or plastic hammer to loosen the gasket seal. Remove the transaxle case.

23. Remove the magnet.

24. Remove the reverse idler shaft.

25. Remove the reverse idler gear.

26. Remove the base plate assembly.

27. Remove the snapring, crank lever shaft and crank lever assembly from the base plate.

28. Remove the reverse shift lever.

29. Remove the lever set spring.

30. Remove the roll pin from the 3rd/4th shift fork and shift rod.

31. Remove the roll pin from the 3rd/4th shift rod end.

32. Remove the 3rd/4th shift fork, rod and rod end.

33. Remove the roll pin from the 1st/2nd shift fork and shift rod.

34. Remove the 1st/2nd shift rod and shift fork.

35. Remove the 5th/reverse shift rod and shift rod end. Remove the interlock pin from the 5th/reverse shift rod.

36. Remove the main and input shaft gear assemblies as complete units.

37. Remove the differential assembly.

38. Remove the neutral safety switch.

39. Remove the mainshaft bearing cups, adjustment shims, diaphragm spring and funnel.

40. Remove the input shaft bearing cups, diaphragm spring and adjustment shim(s).

41. Remove the differential bearing cups using special tools. Remove the adjustment shim(s).

42. Remove the input shaft seal using special tools.

NOTE: *When removing this seal be careful not to split or damage the transaxle case. If necessary use special tools.*

43. Remove the differential oil seals using special tools or equivalent.

44. Remove the change arm roll pin with suitable tool.

45. Remove the baffle plate, change arm and change rod.

46. Remove the change arm oil seal using special tools.

47. Remove the speedometer driven gear assembly on vehicles equipped with analog cluster or vehicle speed sensor assembly from vehicles equipped with digital cluster from the case.

48. Remove the oil passage, breather cover and breather.

Unit Disassembly and Assembly
INPUT SHAFT GEAR ASSEMBLY
Non-Turbo

NOTE: *The synchronizer rings are not interchangeable. Be sure to keep them in the order that they were removed.*

1. Press off the bearing cone 4th gear end

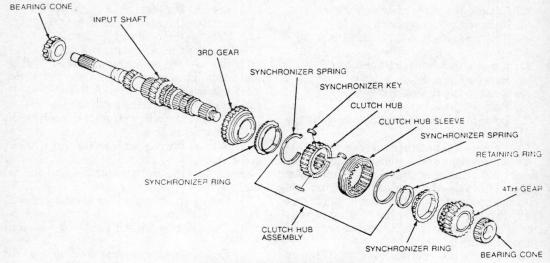

Non-turbo input shaft gear assembly

side using shaft protector and suitable tools. Hold the input shaft.

2. Remove the 4th gear and synchronizer ring.

3. Remove the retaining ring.

4. Press off the clutch hub assembly, synchronizer ring and 3rd gear using shaft protector and suitable tools. Hold the input shaft.

5. Press off the bearing cone 3rd gear end side using shaft protector and suitable tools.

6. Remove the synchronizer springs and keys from the clutch hub.

7. Remove the clutch hub from the clutch hub sleeve.

Turbo

NOTE: *The synchronizer rings are not interchangeable. Be sure to keep them in the order that they were removed.*

1. Press off the bearing cone 4th gear end side using shaft protector and suitable tools. Hold the input shaft.

2. Remove the 4th gear, needle bearing and sleeve.

3. Remove the ball and synchronizer ring.

4. Press off the clutch hub assembly, synchronizer ring and 3rd gear using shaft protector and suitable tools. Hold the input shaft.

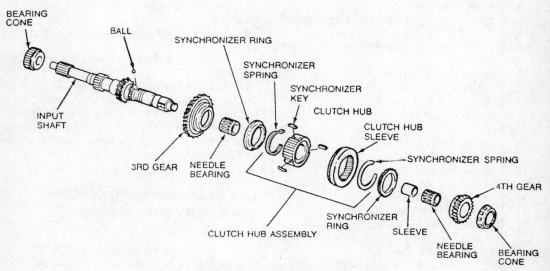

Turbo input shaft gear assembly

5. Remove the needle bearing.

6. Press off the bearing cone 3rd gear end side using shaft protector and suitable tools. Hold the input shaft.

7. Remove the synchronizer springs and keys from the clutch hub.

8. Remove the clutch hub from the clutch hub sleeve.

INSPECTION

Engines without Turbocharger

1. Check for worn or damaged synchronizer cone, hub sleeve coupling or gear teeth.

2. Check the input shaft gear runout. Check the runout by mounting the gear shaft in a lathe or V-blocks. The maximum allowable runout is 0.05mm.

3. The clearance between the 3rd and 2nd gears is 0.05–0.20mm. The maximum allowable clearance is 0.25mm.

4. The clearance between the 4th gear and bearing cone is 0.165–0.365mm. The maximum allowable clearance is 0.415mm.

Engines with Turbocharger

1. Check for worn or damaged synchronizer cone, hub sleeve coupling or gear teeth.

2. Check the input shaft gear runout. Check the runout by mounting the gear shaft in a lathe or V-blocks. The maximum allowable runout is 0.035mm.

3. Check the input shaft diameter and the inner gear diameter for correct specifications.

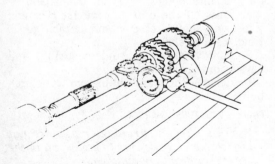

Checking input shaft for runout

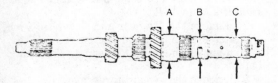

A: 41.80-41.99mm (1.646-1.653 inch)

B: 36.75-37.00mm (1.447-1.457 inch)

C: 36.17-36.20mm (1.424-1.425 inch)

Checking input shaft diameter-turbo

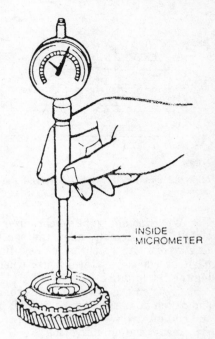

3rd: 47.00-47.02mm (1.850-1.851 inch)

4th: 47.00-47.02mm (1.850-1.851 inch)

5th: 43.00-43.02mm (1.693-1.694 inch)

Checking input shaft inner gear diameter-turbo

4. Check the clearance between the 3rd and input shaft gears it should be 0.15–0.26mm.

5. Check the clearance between the 4th gear and bearing cone it should be 0.15–0.26mm.

Assembly

ENGINES WITHOUT TURBOCHARGER

1. Slide the clutch hub into the clutch hub sleeve.

2. Install the synchronizer keys and springs. NOTE: *Whenever a bearing cone is removed, it must be replaced.*

3. Press on a new bearing cone 3rd gear end side using shaft protector and suitable tools.

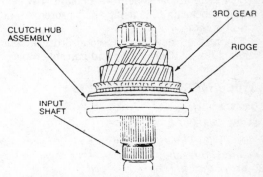

Installing the clutch hub assembly

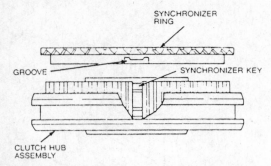

Align the synchronizer ring groove with the synchronizer key

4. When installing the synchronizer ring and clutch hub assembly, align the synchronizer ring groove and synchronizer key. Be sure to have the ridge facing the 3rd gear when installing the clutch hub assembly.

5. Press on the 3rd gear, synchronizer ring and clutch hub assembly using shaft protector and suitable tools.

6. Install the retaining ring.

7. Press on the synchronizer ring, 4th gear and new bearing cone using shaft protector and suitable tools.

ENGINES WITH TURBOCHARGER

1. Slide the clutch hub into the clutch hub sleeve.

2. Install the synchronizer keys and springs.

3. Lubricate needle bearing assembly with the specified transaxle fluid and install the needle bearing assembly.

4. When installing the synchronizer ring and clutch hub assembly, align the synchronizer ring groove and synchronizer key.

5. Press on the 3rd gear, synchronizer ring and clutch hub assembly using shaft protector and suitable tools.

6. Install the ball, sleeve and needle bearing. Lubricate the needle bearing assembly with the specified transaxle fluid before installing.

NOTE: *Whenever a bearing cone is removed, it must be replaced.*

7. Press on the synchronizer ring, 4th gear and new bearing cone using shaft protector and suitable tools.

8. Press on new bearing cone 3rd gear end side using shaft protector and suitable tools.

MAINSHAFT GEAR ASSEMBLY

Disassembly

ENGINES WITHOUT TURBOCHARGER

NOTE: *The synchronizer rings are not interchangeable. Be sure to keep them in the order that they were removed.*

1. Press off the bearing cone 4th gear end

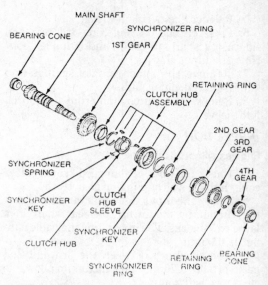

Mainshaft gear assembly; non-turbo

side using shaft protector and suitable tools. Hold the mainshaft.

2. Press off the 4th gear using shaft protector and suitable tools. Hold the mainshaft.

3. Remove the retaining ring.

4. Press off the 3rd and 2nd gears using shaft protector and suitable tools. Hold the mainshaft.

5. Remove the synchronizer ring.

6. Remove the retaining ring.

7. Press off the clutch hub assembly, synchronizer ring and 1st gear using shaft protector and suitable tools. Hold the mainshaft.

8. Press off the bearing cone 1st gear end side using shaft protector and suitable tools. Hold the mainshaft.

9. Remove the synchronizer springs and keys from the clutch hub.

10. Remove the clutch hub from the clutch hub sleeve.

ENGINES WITH TURBOCHARGER

NOTE: *The synchronizer rings are not interchangeable. Be sure to keep them in the order that they were removed.*

1. Press off the bearing cone 4th gear end side using shaft protector and suitable tools. Hold the mainshaft.

2. Remove the 4th gear and sleeve.

3. Remove the 3rd and 2nd gears.

4. Remove the needle bearing, sleeve and ball.

5. Remove the synchronizer gear.

6. Press off the clutch hub assembly, synchronizer ring and 1st gear using shaft protector and suitable tools. Hold the mainshaft.

7. Remove the needle bearing and thrust washer.

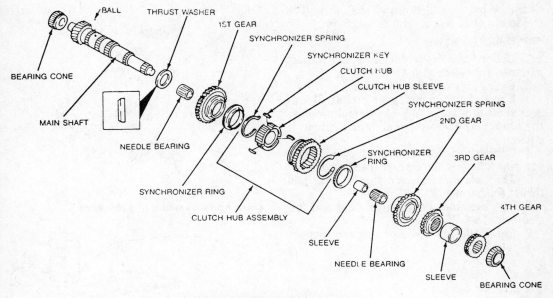

Mainshaft gear assembly; turbo

8. Press off the bearing cone 1st gear end side using shaft protector and suitable tools. Hold the mainshaft.

9. Remove the synchronizer springs and keys from the clutch hub.

10. Remove the clutch hub from the clutch hub sleeve.

Inspection

ENGINES WITHOUT TURBOCHARGER

1. Check for worn or damaged gear contact surfaces, splines or gear teeth.

2. Check for clogged oil passage.

3. Check the mainshaft gear runout. Mount gear shaft in a lathe or V-blocks and measure the runout. The maximum allowable runout is 0.015mm.

4. Check the clearance between the 1st gear and differential drive gear it should be 0.05–0.28mm. The maximum allowable clearance is 0.48mm.

5. Check the clearance between the 2nd and 3rd gears it should be 0.175–0.455mm. The maximum allowable clearance is 0.505mm.

6. Check the oil clearance between mainshaft and gears.

7. Measure the diameter of the gear shaft where the gear is installed. Measure the inside diameter of the gear. The difference between the two measurements is the clearance. If the clearance is more than allowable, replace the gear and/or shaft as necessary. The standard clearance should be 0.025–0.080mm.

8. Check the synchronizer ring engagement with gear. The ring must engage smoothly with gear.

9. Check the synchronizer ring clearance from the side of gear. Press the synchronizer ring uniformly against the gear and measure around the circumference. The standard clearance is 1.5mm. The minimum allowable clearance is 0.8mm.

10. Check clutch hub sleeve for excessive

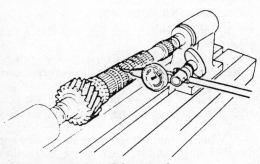

Checking the mainshaft for runout

Checking the mainshaft and gears for oil clearance; non-turbo

clearance between sleeve and shift fork. The maximum allowable clearance is 0.5mm.

ENGINES WITH TURBOCHARGER

1. Check for worn or damaged gear contact surfaces, splines or gear teeth.
2. Check for clogged oil passage.
3. Check the mainshaft gear runout. Mount gear shaft in a lathe or V-blocks and measure the runout. The maximum allowable runout is 0.03mm.
4. Check the mainshaft diameter and the inner gear diameter for correct specifications.
5. The clearance between the 1st gear and thrust washer is 0.13–0.35mm.
6. The clearance between the 2nd and 3rd gears is 0.15–0.26mm.
7. Check the synchronizer ring engagement

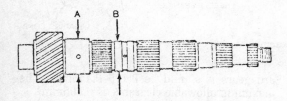

A: 42.80-42.99mm (1.685-1.689 inch)

B: 36.95-37.11mm (1.455-1.461 inch)

Checking the mainshaft diameter; turbo

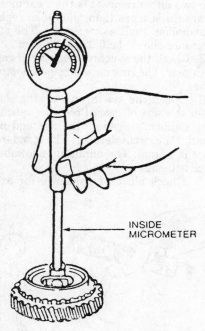

INSIDE MICROMETER

1st: 48.00-48.02mm (1.890-1.891 inch)

2nd: 50.00-50.02mm (1.968-1.969 inch)

Checking the mainshaft inner gear diameter; turbo

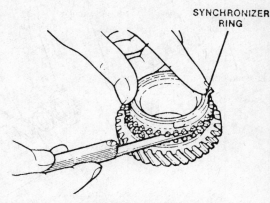

SYNCHRONIZER RING

Checking synchronizer ring clearance

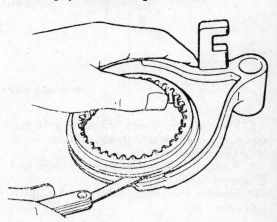

Checking the clutch hub sleeve to shift fork clearance

with gear. The ring must engage smoothly with gear.

8. Check the synchronizer ring clearance from the side of gear. Press the synchronizer ring uniformly against the gear and measure around the circumference. The standard clearance is 1.5mm. The minimum allowable clearance is 0.8mm.
9. Check clutch hub sleeve for excessive clearance between sleeve and shift fork. The maximum allowable clearance is 0.45mm.

Assembly

ENGINES WITHOUT TURBOCHARGER

1. Slide the clutch hub into the clutch hub sleeve.
2. Install the synchronizer keys and springs. NOTE: *Whenever a bearing cone is removed, it must be replaced.*
3. Press on the new bearing cone 1st gear end side using shaft protector and suitable tools.
4. When installing the synchronizer ring and clutch hub assembly, align the synchronizer ring groove and synchronizer key.

5. Press on the 1st gear, synchronizer ring and clutch hub assembly using shaft protector and suitable tools.

6. Install the retaining ring.

7. Press on the synchronizer ring, 2nd gear and 3rd gear using shaft protector and suitable tools.

8. Install the retaining ring.

9. Press on the 4th gear using shaft protector and suitable tools.

10. Press on the new bearing cone 4th gear end side using shaft protector and suitable tools.

ENGINES WITH TURBOCHARGER

1. Slide the clutch hub into the clutch hub sleeve.

2. Install the synchronizer keys and springs.

3. Install the thrust washer and needle bearing. Before installing the needle bearing lubricate the bearing with the specified transaxle fluid.

4. When installing the synchronizer ring and clutch hub assembly, align the synchronizer ring groove and synchronizer key.

5. Press on the 1st gear, synchronizer ring and clutch hub assembly using shaft protector and suitable tools.

6. Install the synchronizer ring.

7. Install the ball, sleeve and needle bearing. Before installing the needle bearing lubricate the bearing with the specified transaxle fluid.

8. Install the 2nd and 3rd gears.

9. Install the sleeve and 4th gear.

NOTE: *Whenever a bearing cone is removed, it must be replaced.*

10. Press on the new bearing cone, 4th gear end side using shaft protector and suitable tools. Make sure that the sleeve does not rotate.

11. Press on the new bearing cone, 1st gear end side using shaft protector and suitable tools.

DIFFERENTIAL

NOTE: *The differential assemblies are the same for both engines.*

Disassembly

1. Remove the knock or roll pin.

2. Remove the pinion shaft.

3. Remove the pinions and thrust washers by rotating them out of the gear case.

4. Remove the side gears and thrust washers.

5. Remove the bearing cone, speedometer drive gear end side using suitable tools.

6. Remove the speedometer drive gear.

7. Remove the bearing cone, ring gear end side using suitable tools.

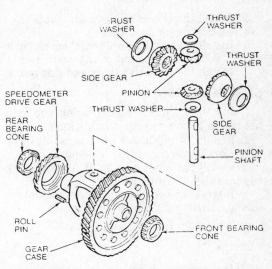

Exploded view of the differential assembly

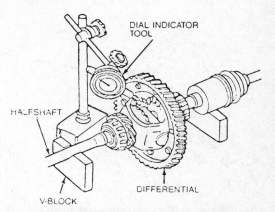

Checking the backlash in the differential assembly

Inspection

1. Check for damaged or worn gears.

2. Check for cracked or damaged gear case.

3. Check the side gear and pinion backlash.

   a. Install the left and right halfshafts into the differential.

   b. Support the halfshafts on V-blocks.

   c. Use dial indicator or equivalent with magnetic base/flex arm to measure the backlash of both pinion gears. If the backlash is more than allowable, select a thrust washer with a different thickness.

   d. The maximum allowable amount of backlash is 0–0.1mm.

Assembly

NOTE: *Whenever a bearing cone is removed, it must be replaced.*

1. Install the speedometer drive gear and new bearing cone using suitable tools.

2. Install the new bearing cone, ring gear end side using suitable tools.

3. Install the thrust washers and pinions.

4. Install the pinion shaft.

5. Install the knock or roll pin, them crimp it so that it cannot come out of the gear case.

6. Install the thrust washers and side gears.

SHIM SELECTION

1. Install the differential bearing cup into the clutch housing using suitable tools.

2. Install the oil funnel and mainshaft front bearing cup into the clutch housing.

3. Install the input gear shaft front bearing cup into the clutch housing.

4. Inspect the bearing cups after installation to make sure that they are fully seated.

INPUT SHAFT

1. Install the input shaft gear assembly into the clutch housing.

2. Place the rear bearing cup on the input shaft bearing.

3. Position shim selection gauge tool T88C–77000–CH3 (non-turbocharged) or T88C–77000–CH2 (turbocharged) on top of input shaft gear assembly.

4. Place the 6 collars part of special tool T87C–77000–J on the clutch housing at the correct positions.

NOTE: *The 2 halves of the shim selection gauge tool T88C–77000–CH2 (turbocharged)*

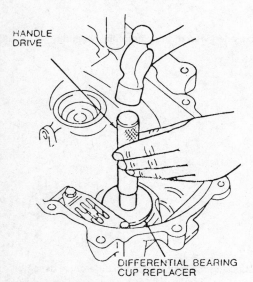

Installing the differential bearing cup

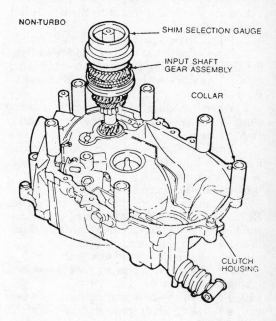

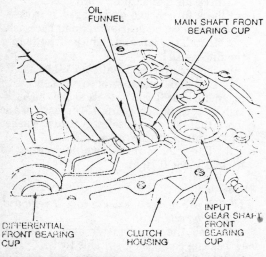

Installing the oil funnel and mainshaft front bearing cup into the clutch housing

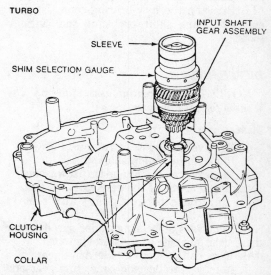

Installing special tool collars in the correct position

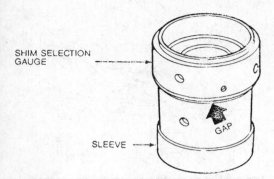

Eliminate the gap in the special tool before adjustment

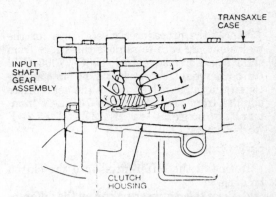

Lift the input shaft gear assembly equally on both sides

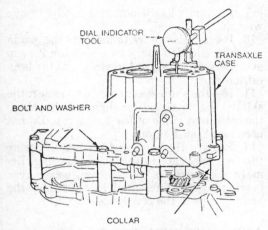

Check the endplay of the input shaft

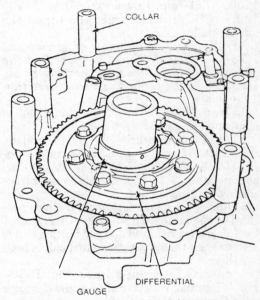

Install special tool collars on the differential assembly

must be turned to eliminate any gap between them before adjustment.

5. Place the transaxle case on the collars, then install the washers and bolts part of special tool T87C–77000–J. Tighten the non-turbocharged version to 13–14 ft. lbs. Tighten the turbocharged version to 27–38 ft. lbs.

6. Mount a dial indicator or equivalent, to check the endplay of the input shaft.

7. Rotate the input shaft gear assembly several times to help seat the bearings.

8. Adjust the dial indicator to **0** at the lowest point on the end of the input shaft. Do not disturb dial indicator tool until at least 3 endplay readings have been taken.

9. Raise the input shaft gear assembly by hand and read endplay. Lower the input shaft gear assembly.

10. The input shaft gear assembly must be lifted equally on both sides or it will tend to cock to one side, resulting in an incorrect reading.

11. Turn the input shaft gear assembly several times until dial indicator returns to **0**. Raise input shaft gear assembly by hand to take a second endplay measurement.

12. Repeat Step 11 to obtain at least 3 read-

ings within 0.1mm of each other. Average at least 3 of the measurements to obtain an endplay reading.

13. Subtract 0.7mm from the endplay reading to account for the thickness of the diaphragm spring which goes between the shim and the cup. This result is the final shim size.

14. From shim selection kit E92Z–7L172–A (non-turbocharged) or E92Z–7L172–C (turbocharged), select the shim(s) that is closest or slightly larger to the final shim size. Do not use more than 2 shims.

15. Remove the bolts and washers securing the transaxle case to the clutch housing. Remove the transaxle case, gauge, rear bearing cup and input shaft gear assembly. Do not remove the bearing cups in the clutch housing.

MAINSHAFT

Repeat the procedures given above for the mainshaft. Be sure to remove the sleeve from shim selection gauge tool T88C–77000–CH2 (turbocharged). There should be no gap between the gauge halves. Select the appropriate shim(s) from shim kit E92Z–7L172–A (non-turbocharged) or E92Z–7L172–B (turbocharged).

DIFFERENTIAL

1. Install the differential into the clutch housing.
2. Place the rear bearing cup on the differential bearing.
3. Position shim selection gauge tool T88C–77000–CH1 (non-turbocharged) or T88C–77000–CH2 (turbocharged) on top of the differential.
NOTE: *The 6 collars part of special tool T87C–77000–J should be placed on the clutch housing at the same locations as described in the input shaft shim selection procedure.*
4. Turn The 2 halves of the gauge tool to eliminate any gap between them.
5. Place the transaxle case on the collars, then install the washers and bolts part of special tool T87C–77000–J. Tighten the non-turbocharged to 13–14 ft. lbs. Tighten the turbocharged to 27–38 ft. lbs.
6. Adjust the gauge tool using the pins provided in special tool T87C–77000–J until all of the free play is removed and the bearing cup is seated. Then thread the gauge tool halves back together.
7. Insert the torque adapter tool T88C–77000–L through the transaxle case and engage the differential pinion shaft.
8. Attach a torque wrench to the tool.
9. Turn the gauge using the adjusting rods part of special tool T87C–77000–J until a read-

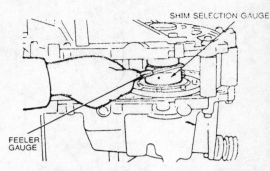

Use a feeler gauge to measure the gap in the shim selection gauge

ing of 4.3 inch lbs. is obtained on the torque wrench.
10. Use a feeler gauge to measure the gap in the shim selection gauge tool. Measure the gap at 4 spots, at 90 degree intervals. Use the largest measurement.
11. Use the shim selection chart to select the shim(s) that is closest (or slightly larger than) the measured value of the gauge gap. Do not use more than 2 shims.
12. Remove the bolts and washers securing the transaxle case to the clutch housing. Remove the transaxle case, collars, gauge, rear bearing cup and differential. Do not remove the bearing cups in the clutch housing.

ASSEMBLY OF TRANSAXLE

Engines Without Turbocharger

1. Install the neutral switch, gasket and backup light switch. Tighten to 14–22 ft. lbs.
2. Install the washer and drain plug and tighten to 29–43 ft. lbs.
3. Install the differential seals using suitable tools.
4. Install the input shaft seal using suitable tools.
NOTE: *Whenever the transaxle is assembled, the bearing preload must be adjusted. The input shaft, mainshaft and differential bearing preload can be adjusted by selecting shims to insert between the rear bearing cups and transaxle case. To determine the correct thickness shim, use shim selection information (at the end of this section) and shim selection part sets T87C–77000–J and T88C–77000–CH or equivalent.*
5. Install the adjustment shim(s) and rear differential bearing cup to the transaxle case using suitable tools.
6. Install the adjustment shim(s), diaphragm spring and input shaft bearing cup into the transaxle case. Install the diaphragm spring in the correct position.
7. Install the adjustment shim(s), diaphragm

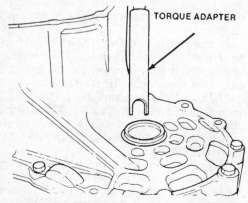

Insert the special tool to engage the differential pinion shaft

SHIM SELECTION

Part Number	Shim Thickness	
	in.	mm
NON-TURBOCHARGED ENGINE		
E92Z-4067-A	0.004	0.10
E92Z-4067-B	0.005	0.12
E92Z-4067-C	0.006	0.14
E92Z-4067-D	0.0063	0.16
E92Z-4067-E	0.007	0.18
E92Z-4067-F	0.008	0.20
E92Z-4067-G	0.010	0.25
E92Z-4067-H	0.012	0.30
E92Z-4067-J	0.014	0.35
E92Z-4067-K	0.016	0.40
E92Z-4067-L	0.018	0.45
E92Z-4067-N	0.020	0.50
E92Z-4067-P	0.022	0.55
E92Z-4067-Q	0.024	0.60
E92Z-4067-R	0.026	0.65
E92Z-4067-S	0.028	0.70
E92Z-4067-T	0.030	0.75
E92Z-4067-U	0.032	0.80
E92Z-4067-V	0.034	0.85
E92Z-4067-W	0.036	0.90
E92Z-4067-X	0.038	0.95
E92Z-4067-Y	0.040	1.00
E92Z-4067-Z	0.042	1.05
E92Z-4067-AA	0.044	1.10
E92Z-4067-AB	0.046	1.15
E92Z-4067-AC	0.048	1.20
TURBOCHARGED ENGINE		
E92Z-4067-AD	0.004	0.10
E92Z-4067-AE	0.005	0.12
E92Z-4067-AF	0.006	0.14
E92Z-4067-AG	0.0063	0.16
E92Z-4067-AH	0.008	0.20
E92Z-4067-AJ	0.010	0.25
E92Z-4067-AK	0.012	0.30
E92Z-4067-AL	0.014	0.35
E92Z-4067-AM	0.016	0.40
E92Z-4067-AN	0.018	0.45
E92Z-4067-AP	0.020	0.50
E92Z-4067-AR	0.022	0.55
E92Z-4067-AS	0.024	0.60
E92Z-4067-AT	0.026	0.65
E92Z-4067-AU	0.028	0.70
E92Z-4067-AV	0.030	0.75
E92Z-4067-AW	0.032	0.80

SHIM SELECTION

Part Number	Shim Thickness	
	in.	mm
E92Z-4067-AX	0.034	0.85
E92Z-4067-AY	0.036	0.90
E92Z-4067-AZ	0.038	0.95
E92Z-4067-BA	0.040	1.00
E92Z-4067-BB	0.042	1.05
E92Z-4067-BC	0.044	1.10
E92Z-4067-BD	0.046	1.15
E92Z-4067-BE	0.048	1.20

12. Install the change arm and tighten to 104–122 inch lbs.

13. Install the guide plate. Tighten the bolt above the spring to 69–100 inch lbs. Tighten the remaining bolts to 16–25 inch lbs.

14. Install the reverse lever and reverse lever shaft.

15. Install a new roll pin.

16. Install the speedometer driven gear assembly to the case on vehicles with analog cluster or vehicle speed sensor to the case on vehicles with digital cluster.

17. Install the magnet.

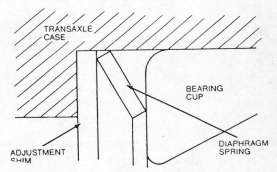

Installing the diaphragm spring in the correct position

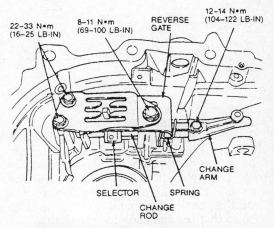

Installing the guide plate; non-turbo

spring and mainshaft bearing cup into the transaxle case. Install the diaphragm spring in the correct position.

8. Install the breather and breather cover.

9. Install the change rod seal using suitable tools.

10. Install the change rod and boot, spring, reverse gate and selector.

11. Install a new roll pin.

SPECIFICATIONS
TORQUE SPECIFICATIONS

	ft. lbs.	Nm		ft. lbs.	Nm
Gearshift housing assembly	60–84 ①	7–10	Right transaxle mount	63–86	85–117
Extension bar to transaxle	23–34	31–46	Flywheel inspection cover	69–95 ①	8–11
Shift control rod	60–84 ①	7–10	Slave cylinder	14–19	19–26
Transaxle case to clutch housing (non-turbo)	13–14	18–20	Gusset plate to transaxle	27–38	37–52
Transaxle case to clutch housing (turbo)	27–38	37–52	Neutral switch	14–22	20–29
Transaxle to engine	66–86	89–17	Backup lamp switch	14–22	20–29
Center transaxle mount bolts	27–40	36–54	Change arm (non-turbo)	104–122 ①	12–14
Center transaxle mount nuts	47–66	64–69	Rear cover	68–95 ①	8–11
Transaxle to left mount (non-turbo)	27–38	37–52	Reverse shift lever (turbo)	69–95 ①	8–11
Transaxle to left mount (turbo)	49–69	67–93	Reverse idler shaft (turbo)	13–19	18–26
Left mount to bracket	49–69	67–93	Interlock plate	13–19	18–26
Crossmember bolts	27–40	36–54	Locknuts (input and main shaft)	94–145	128–196
Crossmember nuts	55–69	75–93	① Inch lbs.		

SPECIAL TOOLS

Tool Number	Description	Tool Number	Description
T87C-77000-H	Differential seal replacer	D84L-1123-A	Bearing pulling attachment
T88C-7025-AH	Transaxle plug set	D87L-6000-A	Engine support bar
T88C-77000-CH	Shim selection set	T50T-100-A	Slide hammer
T88C-77000-EH	Differential bearing cone replacer	T53T-4621-B	Bearing cone replacer
T88C-77000-FH	Differential bearing cup replacer	T57L-500-B	Bench mounting fixture
T88C-7025-BH	Differential bearing cup installer	T57L-4621-B	Bearing cone replacer
T88C-7025-CH	Differential bearing cone replacer	T58L-101-B	Puller
T88C-7025-DH	Bearing cone replacer	T71P-4621-B	Puller plate
T88C-7025-EH	Pilot bearing installer	T73L-2196-A	Disc brake piston remover
T88C-7025-FH	Input shaft seal replacer	T74P-7137-K	Clutch aligner
T88C-77000-CH2	Shim selection gauge	T75L-1165-B	Bearing installation plate
T88C-7025-GH	Torque adapter	T75L-1165-DA	Bearing cone replacer
T88C-77000-CH3	Shim selection gauge	T77F-1102-A	Puller
D80L-100-A	Blind hole puller set	T77F-4220-B1	Puller
D80L-522-A	Gear and pulley puller	T77J-7025-G	Installer
D80L-625-3	Shaft protector	T78P-3504-N	Locknut pin remover
D80L-625-4	Shaft protector	T80T-4000-W	Handle driver
D80L-625-6	Shaft protector	T86P-70043-A	Puller jaws
D80L-630-3	Step plate	T87C-77000-D	Bearing cone replacer
D80L-630-4	Step plate	T87C-77000-J	Shim selection set
D80L-927-A	Push puller set	T88T-7025-B	Bearing cone replacer
D84L-1122-A	Bearing pulling attachment	TOOL-4201-C	Dial indicator tool
014-00210	Hi-Lift transmission jack	T77J-7025-B	Locknut staking tool

18. Install the differential.
19. Install the input and mainshaft.
20. Shift to 2nd gear and 4th gear and correctly position the shift fork and shift rod assembly.
21. Insert the spring seat and springs into the reverse lever shaft, then install the ball and hold it in place with a scraper knife or equivalent. Push the control end in a clockwise direction so that the ball goes into the shaft.
22. Position each clutch hub sleeve to the **N**

positon, then tap the shift rod from above so that the steel ball goes into the center groove. Swivel the control end until the ball goes into the groove detent.
23. Install the crank lever shaft and assembly.
24. Insert the pin.
25. Install the gate and 5th/reverse shift rod. Tighten the gate mounting bolt. Be sure to align the shift rod and gate mounting hole.

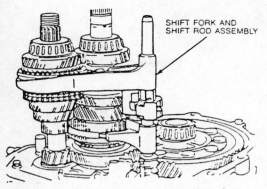

Positioning the shift fork and rod assembly for installation; non-turbo

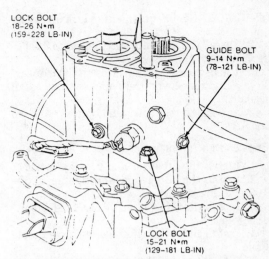

Installing the lock and guide bolt; non-turbo

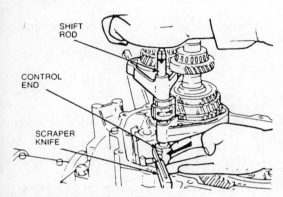

Install shift rod assembly; non-turbo

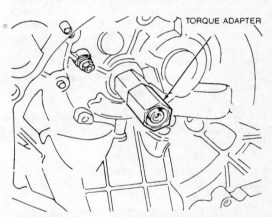

Lock up the input shaft with special tool; non-turbo

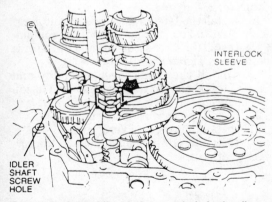

Face the reverse idler shaft screw hole in the direction shown; non-turbo

26. Install the reverse idler gear and shft.

27. Align the end of the interlock sleeve with the control lever. Position the reverse idler shaft screw hole.

28. Clean the contact surfaces on the clutch housing and transaxle case, then apply a thin coat of sealant.

29. Place the transaxle case on the clutch housing and tighten the attaching bolts to 27–38 ft. lbs.

30. Install 2 transaxle plugs or equivalent, between the differential side gears. Failure to install the transaxle plugs may allow the differential side gears to become mispositioned.

31. Install the lock bolt and tighten to 159–228 inch lbs.

32. Install the guide bolt and tighten to 78–121 inch lbs.

33. Install the ball, springs and lock bolt and tighten to 129–181 inch lbs.

34. Install the main 5th gear.

35. Install the gear sleeve.

36. Install the input 5th gear.

37. Install the synchronizer ring.

38. Install the shift fork, clutch hub assembly and synchronizer ring.

39. Install the roll pin.

40. Install the main reverse synchronizer gear.

41. Install the input reverse synchronizer gear.

42. Shift to 1st gear. Use torque adapter tool

T88C–7025–GH or equivalent to lock up the input shaft.

43. Install the locknuts and tighten to 94–145 ft. lbs. Stake the locknuts.

44. Clean the contact surfaces on the transaxle case and rear cover, than apply a thin coat of sealant.

45. Install the rear cover and tighten to 68–95 inch lbs.

Engines with Turbocharger

1. Install the breather and breather cover.

2. Install the oil passage and tighten to 69–100 inch lbs.

3. Install the differential oil seals using suitable tools.

4. Install the input shaft seal using suitable tools.

NOTE: *Whenever the transaxle is assembled, the bearing preload must be adjusted. The input shaft, mainshaft and differential bearing preload can be adjusted by selecting shims to insert between the rear bearing cups and transaxle case. To determine the correct thickness shim, use shim selection information (at the end of this section) and selection part sets T87C–77000–J and T88C–77000–CH or equivalent.*

5. Install the adjustment shim(s) and rear differential bearing cup into the transaxle case using suitable tools.

6. Install the adjustment shim(s), diaphragm spring and input shaft bearing cup into the transaxle case. Install the diaphragm spring in the correct position.

7. Install the adjustment shim(s), diaphragm spring and mainshaft bearing cup into the

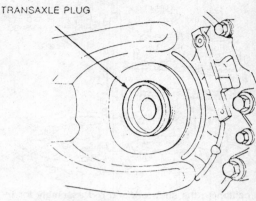

TRANSAXLE PLUG

Installing the transaxle plug

transaxle case. Install the diaphragm spring in the correct position.

8. Install the change arm oil seal using suitable tools.

9. Install the change rod and change arm.

10. Install the baffle plate and tighten to 87–113 inch lbs.

11. Install a new roll pin into the change arm. The roll pin length is 28mm.

12. Install the differential assembly.

13. Install the main and input shaft gear assemblies.

14. Install the interlock pin to the 5th/reverse shift rod.

15. Install the shift rod end and the 5th/reverse shift rod.

16. Install the 1st/2nd shift rod and shift fork.

17. Shift to 2nd gear and install the roll pin.

18. Install the lever set spring and the reverse shift lever. Tighten to 69–95 inch lbs.

19. Install the crank lever assembly and crank lever shaft into the base plate and install the snapring.

20. Install the base plate assembly.

21. Install the reverse idler gear.

22. Install the reverse idler shaft in the correct position.

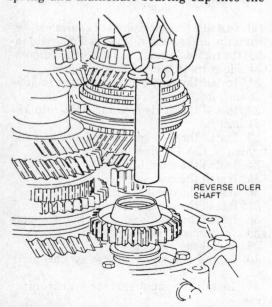

REVERSE IDLER SHAFT

Installing the reverse idler in the correct position; turbo

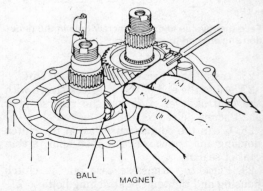

BALL MAGNET

Installing the ball with a magnet; turbo

23. Install the magnet.

24. Clean the contact surfaces on the clutch housing and transaxle case, then apply a thin coat of sealant.

25. Place the transaxle case on the clutch housing and tighten the attaching bolts to 27–38 ft. lbs.

26. Install 2 transaxle plugs or equivalent, between the differential side gears. Failure to install the transaxle plugs may allow the differential side gears to become mispositioned.

27. Install the right transaxle mount and tighten bolts to 58–86 ft. lbs.

28. Install the reverse idler shaft set bolt and tighten to 13–19 ft. lbs.

29. Install the balls, springs and bolts. Tighten to 14–22 ft. lbs.

30. Install the backup light switch and tighten to 14–22 ft. lbs.

31. Install the interlock pins.

32. Install the interlock plate and tighten to 13–19 ft. lbs.

33. Install the neutral switch and tighten to 14–22 ft. lbs.

34. Install the washer and drain plug and tighten to 29–43 ft. lbs.

35. Install the speedometer driven gear assembly to the case on vehicles with analog cluster or vehicle speed sensor to the case on vehicles with digital cluster.

36. Install the main 5th gear.

37. Install the ball.

38. Install the sleeve.

39. Lubricate the needle beaering assembly with the specified fluid and install the needle bearing.

40. Install the input 5th gear and synchronizer ring.

41. Install the shift fork, clutch hub assembly and synchronizer ring.

42. Install the main reverse synchronizer gear.

43. Install the input reverse synchronizer gear.

44. Install the sleeve.

45. Shift to 5th gear and then to 1st gear.

46. Install the locknuts and tighten to 94–145 ft. lbs. Stake the locknuts.

47. Install the roll pin.

48. Clean the contct surfaces on the transaxle case and rear cover, then apply a thin coat of sealant. Install the rear cover and tighten to 68–95 inch lbs.

Halfshafts

REMOVAL AND INSTALLATION

Left Side

1. Disconnect the negative battery cable. Raise and safely support the vehicle.

2. Remove the left front wheel, hub grease cup and the left splash shield.

3. Remove the stabilizer link assembly from the lower control arm.

4. Use a cape chisel and hammer and raise the staked portion of the hub nut.

5. Have an assistant apply the brakes and loosen, but do not remove, the hub nut.

6. Remove the lower ball joint to steering knuckle bolt. Pry the lower arm downward to separate the ball joint.

7. Pull the steering knuckle outward.

8. Position a pry bar between the halfshaft and transaxle case, carefully pry the halfshaft from the case while supporting the halfshaft.

9. Support the halfshaft. Remove the hub nut and slide the halfshaft from the steering knuckle.

NOTE: *If the halfshaft binds in the hub spline, use a plastic hammer to bump it out, or a wheel puller to press it out.*

10. Place transaxle plugs, or equivalents in the transaxle case to prevent dirt from entering, and the differential side gears from becoming mispositioned.

11. Install a new circlip on the differential end of the halfshaft.

12. Slide the halfshaft into position through the steering knuckle drive hub. Install a new hub nut, but do not completely tighten it at this time.

13. Remove the transaxle plug and slide the halfshaft into the transaxle case, slowly push in the halfshaft until the circlip snaps into place.

14. Install and torque the lower control arm ball joint to steering knuckle nut and bolt to 32–40 ft. lbs.

15. Install the stabilizer link assembly to the control arm. Install the splash shield and wheel. Torque the wheel nuts to 65–87 ft. lbs.

16. Lower the vehicle. Tighten the new hub nut to 116–174 ft. lbs. Stake the new nut with a blunt chisel.

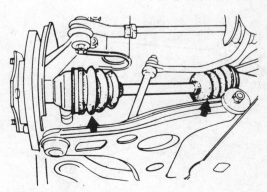

Halfshaft boots

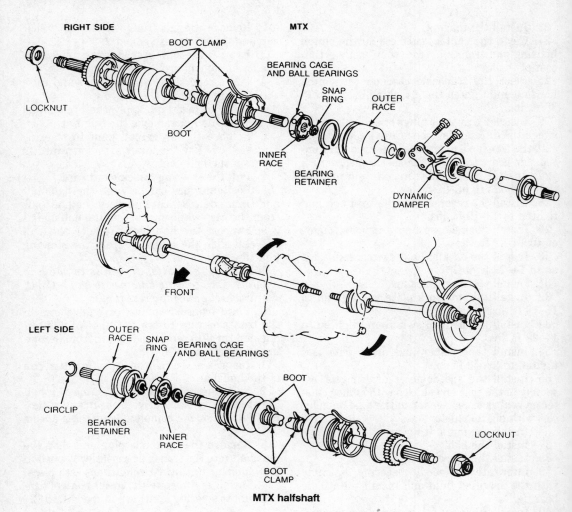

MTX halfshaft

Right Side

1. Disconnect the negative battery cable. Raise and safely support the vehicle.

2. Remove the left front wheel, hub grease cup and the left splash shield.

3. Remove the stabilizer link assembly from the lower control arm.

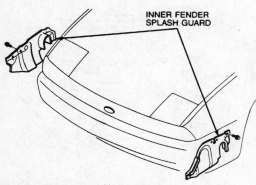

Remove/install splash shields

4. Use a cape chisel and hammer and raise the staked portion of the hub nut.

5. Have an assistant apply the brakes and loosen, but do not remove, the hub nut.

6. Remove the lower ball joint to steering knuckle bolt. Pry the lower arm downward to separate the ball joint. Remove the dynamic damper mounting from the engine mounting.

7. Pull the steering knuckle outward.

8. Position a pry bar between the halfshaft and transaxle case, carefully pry the halfshaft from the case while supporting the halfshaft.

9. Support the halfshaft. Remove the hub nut and slide the halfshaft from the steering knuckle.

NOTE: *If the halfshaft binds in the hub spline, use a plastic hammer to bump it out, or a wheel puller to press it out.*

10. Place transaxle plugs, or equivalents in the transaxle case to prevent dirt from entering, and the differential side gears from becoming mispositioned.

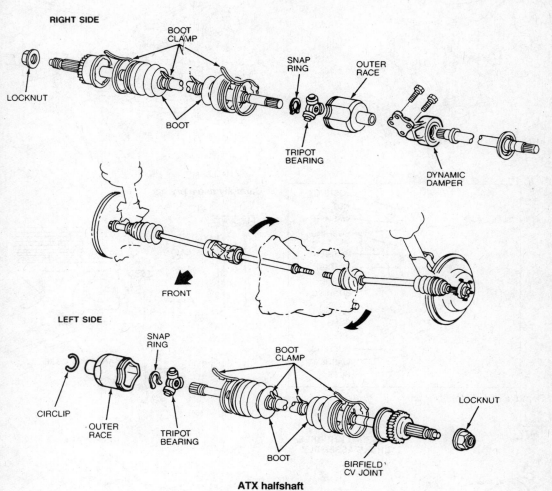

ATX

RIGHT SIDE

LOCKNUT

BOOT CLAMP

BOOT

SNAP RING

TRIPOT BEARING

OUTER RACE

DYNAMIC DAMPER

FRONT

LEFT SIDE

CIRCLIP

OUTER RACE

SNAP RING

TRIPOT BEARING

BOOT

BOOT CLAMP

LOCKNUT

BIRFIELD CV JOINT

ATX halfshaft

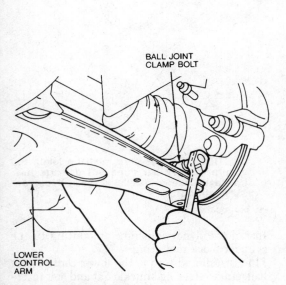

BALL JOINT CLAMP BOLT

LOWER CONTROL ARM

Remove/install ball joint

RIGHT HALFSHAFT

DYNAMIC DAMPER

MOUNTING BOLTS

PILOT BOLT

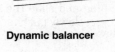

Dynamic balancer

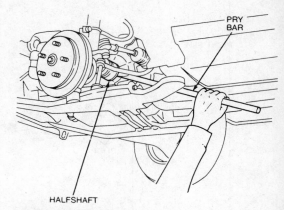

HALFSHAFT

Carefully use a pry bar

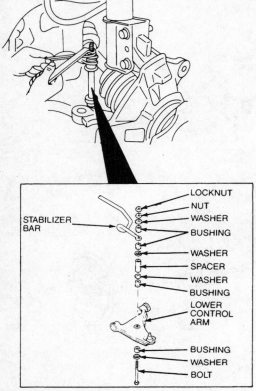

Remove/install stabilizer bar

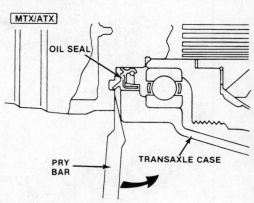

MTX/ATX

OIL SEAL

PRY BAR

TRANSAXLE CASE

Pry bar location

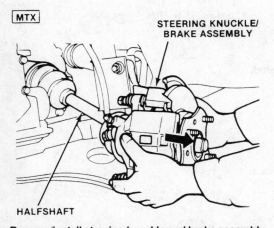

MTX

STEERING KNUCKLE/
BRAKE ASSEMBLY

HALFSHAFT

Remove/install steering knuckle and brake assembly

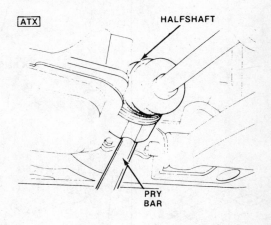

ATX

HALFSHAFT

PRY BAR

11. Install a new circlip on the differential end of the halfshaft.

12. Slide the halfshaft into position through the steering knuckle drive hub. Install a new hub nut, but do not completely tighten it at this time.

13. Remove the transaxle plug and slide the halfshaft into the transaxle case, slowly push in the halfshaft until the circlip snaps into place.

CAUTION: Extreme care must be taken to ensure the pry bar does not damage the transaxle case, transaxle oil seal, CV joint or CV joint boot.

Pry bar location

Install the dynamic damper mounting to the cylinder block mounting.

14. Install and torque the lower control arm ball joint to steering knuckle nut and bolt to 32–40 ft. lbs.

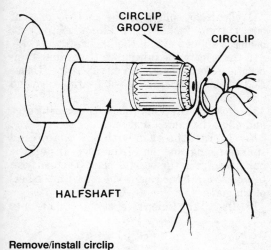

Remove/install circlip

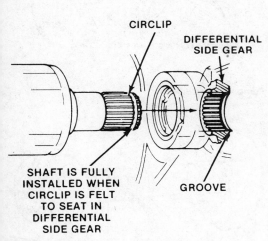

Circlip installation

15. Install the stabilizer link assembly to the control arm. Install the splash shield and wheel. Torque the wheel nuts to 65–87 ft. lbs.

16. Lower the vehicle. Tighten the new hub nut to 116–174 ft. lbs. Stake the new nut with a blunt chisel.

CV-JOINT OVERHAUL

Rzeppa Joint

1. CV-joint components are matched during manufacture and therefore cannot be interchanged with components from another CV-joint.

2. Clamp the halfshaft in a soft jawed vise. Do not allow the vise to contact the boot or boot clamps.

3. Remove the large boot clamp. After removing the clamp, roll the boot back over the shaft.

NOTE: *If this procedure is being done to just replace a damage boot, the grease should be checked at this time for contamination. Rub some grease between your fingers. If grit can be felt the grease is contaminated. A contaminated joint should be disassembled, cleaned and repacked.*

4. Remove the outer joint to shaft retaining ring. Before removing the bearing retainer, scribe mating marks on the shaft and retainer for installation alignment.

5. Remove the outer race. Paint alignment marks on the inner race and shaft for installation alignment.

6. Remove the inner race snapring from the end of the halfshaft. Remove the inner race, cage and ball bearings from the shaft as an assembly.

7. Carefully pry the ball bearing out of the

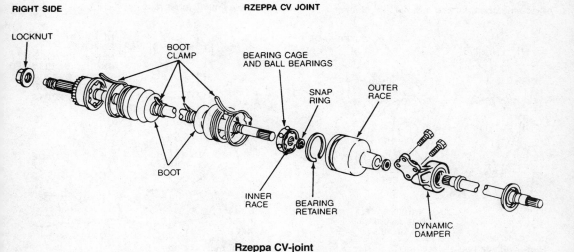

Rzeppa CV-joint

bearing cage. Do not scratch the bearing or cage surfaces. Match mark the inner race and bearing cage.

8. Rotate the inner race to align the bearing lands with the windows in the bearing cage. Remove the inner race through the large end of the cage.

9. Remove the small clamp and the boot from the halfshaft.

10. Clean and inspect all parts, use a rebuilding kit if necessary.

11. Tape the splines of the shaft to prevent boot cutting. Install the small end of the boot over the splined end of the halfshaft.

12. Lubricate the inner race (Use High Temperature Ford Constant Velocity Joint Grease E43Z-19590A, or equivalent), bearing cage and ball bearings.

13. Position the inner race in the bearing cage and align the match marks.

14. Install the race with the chamfered splines facing the end of the cage. Install the ball bearings in the bearing cage. The balls can be pressed into the cage windows with the heel of the hand.

15. Install the inner race, cage and balls onto

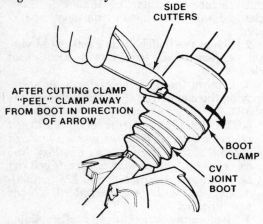

Remove the large boot clamp

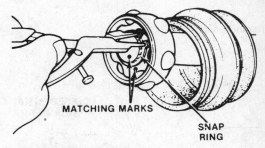

Remove/install snapring

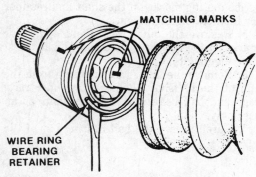

Place matchmarks and remove the retainer

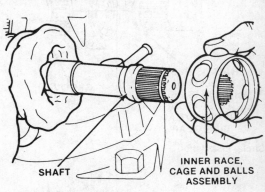

Remove/install inner race

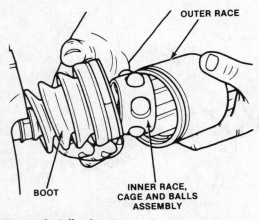

Remove/install outer race

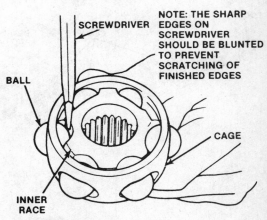

Pry out ball bearings

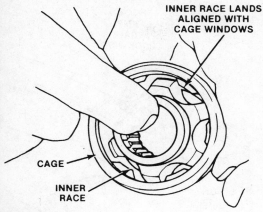

INNER RACE LANDS
ALIGNED WITH
CAGE WINDOWS

CAGE

INNER
RACE

Rotate inner race

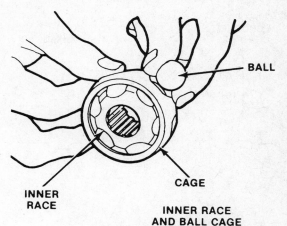

BALL

INNER
RACE

CAGE

INNER RACE
AND BALL CAGE
—ASSEMBLED

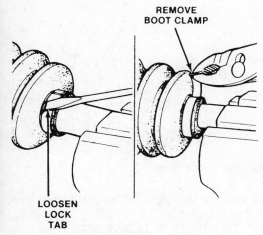

REMOVE
BOOT CLAMP

LOOSEN
LOCK
TAB

Remove the small boot clamp

SMALL
DIAMETER

Install the balls

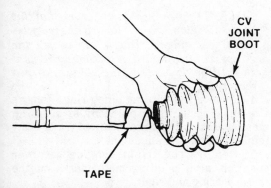

CV
JOINT
BOOT

TAPE

Tape splines before installing the boot

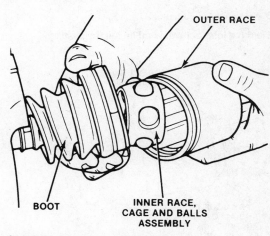

OUTER RACE

BOOT

INNER RACE,
CAGE AND BALLS
ASSEMBLY

Install the inner race, cage and balls

the halfshaft as an assembly. Make sure the chamfer on the bearing cage faces the snapring and that the match marks are aligned.

16. Install the inner race snapring. Lubricate (pack) the outer race with two ounces of the specified grease. Install the outer race and add an additional ounce of the specified grease. Install the wire retainer.

17. Position the boot, making sure it is fully seated in the grooves provided. Extend or compress the CV-joint as necessary to get the distance of 89mm of boot length. Do not allow the overall dimension to change until the boot clamps are installed.

18. Insert a dull tool under the edge of the large end of the boot to allow any trapped air to escape.

19. Install the new boot clamps. Work the CV-joint through its full range of travel. Twist the

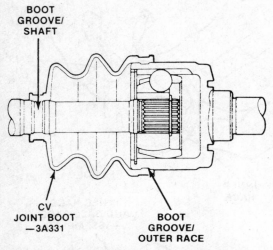

BOOT
GROOVE/
SHAFT

CV
JOINT BOOT
—3A331

BOOT
GROOVE/
OUTER RACE

Make sure the boot is fully seated in the grooves

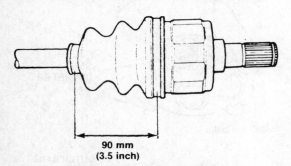

90 mm
(3.5 inch)

Hold the joint at 89mm and install the clamps

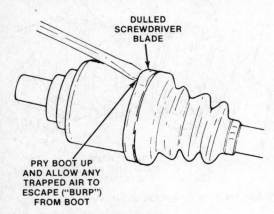

DULLED
SCREWDRIVER
BLADE

PRY BOOT UP
AND ALLOW ANY
TRAPPED AIR TO
ESCAPE ("BURP")
FROM BOOT

Insert blunt tool under boot edge

joint at various angles, the joint should flex, extend and compress smoothly.

Tripot Joint

1. CV joint components are matched during manufacture and therefore cannot be interchanged with components from another CV-joint.

2. Clamp the halfshaft in a soft jawed vise.

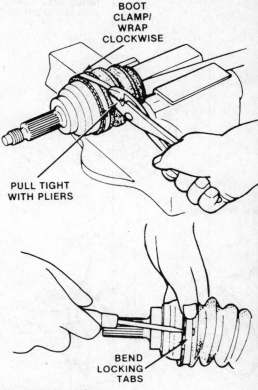

BOOT
CLAMP/
WRAP
CLOCKWISE

PULL TIGHT
WITH PLIERS

BEND
LOCKING
TABS

Install the boot clamps

Do not allow the vise to contact the boot or boot clamps.

3. Remove the large boot clamp. After removing the clamp, roll the boot back over the shaft.

NOTE: *The grease should be checked at this time for contamination. Rub some grease between your fingers. If grit can be felt the grease is contaminated. A contaminated joint should be disassembled, cleaned and repacked.*

4. Remove the wire retaining ring. Remove the outer race, after painting or scribing matchmarks on the outer race and tripot bearing for installation alignment.

5. Remove the tripot bearing retainer snapring, after painting matchmarks on the tripot bearing and shaft.

6. Use a brass drift and hammer and remove the bearing assembly from the shaft. Remove the small clamp and the boot.

7. After cleaning the splined end of the shaft, wrap tape around the end to prevent boot cutting at installation.

8. Clean and inspect all components. Lubricate all components with High Temperature Constsant Velocity Joint Grease, (Ford E43Z-19590A or equivalent).

9. Install the boot over the shaft, small end

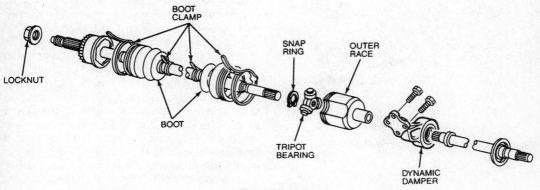

ATX
TRIPOT CV JOINT

RIGHT SIDE

BOOT
CLAMP

SNAP
RING

OUTER
RACE

LOCKNUT

BOOT

TRIPOT
BEARING

DYNAMIC
DAMPER

Tripot joint

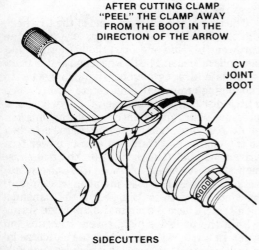

AFTER CUTTING CLAMP
"PEEL" THE CLAMP AWAY
FROM THE BOOT IN THE
DIRECTION OF THE ARROW

CV
JOINT
BOOT

SIDECUTTERS

Remove the boot clamps

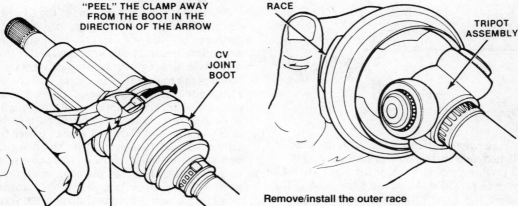

OUTER
RACE

TRIPOT
ASSEMBLY

Remove/install the outer race

TRIPOT
BEARING

OUTER
RACE

ALIGNMENT
MARKS

Matchmark the outer race and bearing

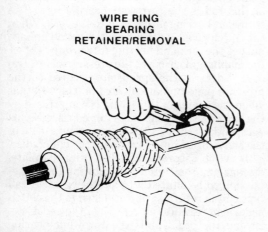

WIRE RING
BEARING
RETAINER/REMOVAL

Remove/install the wire retainer

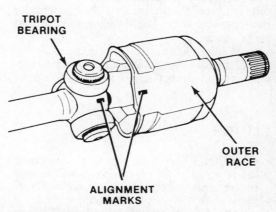

first. Install the tripot bearing on the shaft with
the matchmarks aligned. Use a brass drift and
hammer if necessary.

10. Install the snapring retainer. Fill the CV
outer race with 3.5 oz. of grease. Install the out-

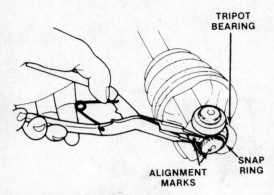

Matchmark the tripot bearing and shaft

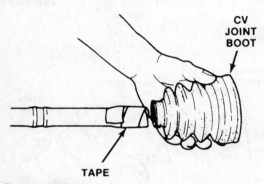

Tape the splines

er race over the tripot joint, with matchmarks aligned, and install the wire retainer ring.

11. Position the CV-joint boot into the grooves provided. Make sure the boot is fully seated.

12. Extend or compress the joint to achieve at total length of 89mm. Insert a blunt tool under the large end of the boot to allow any trapped air to escape.

13. Hold the joint at the required length and install the boot clamps. Work the joint into various positions to make sure it moves freely.

CLUTCH

CAUTION: *The clutch driven disc contains asbestos, which has been determined to be a cancer causing agent. Never clean clutch surfaces with compressed air! Avoid inhaling any dust from any clutch surface! When cleaning clutch surfaces, use a commercially available brake cleaning fluid.*

The purpose of the clutch is to disconnect and connect engine power at the transmission. A car at rest requires a lot of engine torque to get all that weight moving. An internal combustion engine does not develop a high starting torque

(unlike steam engines), so it must be allowed to operate without any load until it builds up enough torque to move the car. Torque increases with engine rpm. The clutch allows the engine to build up torque by physically disconnecting the engine from the transmission, relieving the engine of any load or resistance. The transfer of engine power to the transmission (the load) must be smooth and gradual; if it weren't, drive line components would wear out or break quickly. This gradual power transfer is made possible by gradually releasing the clutch pedal. The clutch disc and pressure plate are the connecting link between the engine and transmission. When the clutch pedal is released, the disc and plate contact each other (clutch engagement), physically joining the engine and transmission. When the pedal is pushed in, the disc and plate separate (the clutch is disengaged), disconnecting the engine from the transmission.

The clutch assembly consists of the flywheel, the clutch disc, the clutch pressure plate, the throwout bearing and fork, the actuating linkage and the pedal. The flywheel and clutch pressure plate (driving members) are connected to the engine crankshaft and rotate with it. The clutch disc is located between the flywheel and pressure plate, and splined to the transmission shaft. A driving member is one that is attached to the engine and transfers engine power to a driven member (clutch disc) on the transmission shaft. A driving member (pressure plate) rotates (drives) a driven member (clutch disc) on contact and, in so doing, turns the transmission shaft. There is a circular diaphragm spring within the pressure plate cover (transmission side). In a relaxed state (when the clutch pedal is fully released), this spring is convex; that is, it is dished outward toward the transmission. Pushing in the clutch pedal actuates an attached linkage rod. Connected to the other end of this rod is the throwout bearing fork. The throwout bearing is attached to the fork. When the clutch pedal is depressed, the clutch linkage pushes the fork and bearing forward to contact the diaphragm spring of the pressure plate. The outer edges of the spring are secured to the pressure plate and are pivoted on rings so that when the center of the spring is compressed by the throwout bearing, the outer edges bow outward and, by so doing, pull the pressure plate in the same direction – away from the clutch disc. This action separates the disc from the plate, disengaging the clutch and allowing the transmission to be shifted into another gear. A coil type clutch return spring attached to the clutch pedal arm permits full release of the pedal. Releasing the pedal pulls the throwout bearing away from the diaphragm spring resulting in a

Troubleshooting Basic Clutch Problems

Problem	Cause
Excessive clutch noise	Throwout bearing noises are more audible at the lower end of pedal travel. The usual causes are: • Riding the clutch • Too little pedal free-play • Lack of bearing lubrication A bad clutch shaft pilot bearing will make a high pitched squeal, when the clutch is disengaged and the transmission is in gear or within the first 2″ of pedal travel. The bearing must be replaced. Noise from the clutch linkage is a clicking or snapping that can be heard or felt as the pedal is moved completely up or down. This usually requires lubrication. Transmitted engine noises are amplified by the clutch housing and heard in the passenger compartment. They are usually the result of insufficient pedal free-play and can be changed by manipulating the clutch pedal.
Clutch slips (the car does not move as it should when the clutch is engaged)	This is usually most noticeable when pulling away from a standing start. A severe test is to start the engine, apply the brakes, shift into high gear and SLOWLY release the clutch pedal. A healthy clutch will stall the engine. If it slips it may be due to: • A worn pressure plate or clutch plate • Oil soaked clutch plate • Insufficient pedal free-play
Clutch drags or fails to release	The clutch disc and some transmission gears spin briefly after clutch disengagement. Under normal conditions in average temperatures, 3 seconds is maximum spin-time. Failure to release properly can be caused by: • Too light transmission lubricant or low lubricant level • Improperly adjusted clutch linkage
Low clutch life	Low clutch life is usually a result of poor driving habits or heavy duty use. Riding the clutch, pulling heavy loads, holding the car on a grade with the clutch instead of the brakes and rapid clutch engagement all contribute to low clutch life.

reversal of spring position. As bearing pressure is gradually released from the spring center, the outer edges of the spring bow outward, pushing the pressure plate into closer contact with the clutch disc. As the disc and plate move closer together, friction between the two increases and slippage is reduced until, when full spring pressure is applied (by fully releasing the pedal), The speed of the disc and plate are the same. This stops all slipping, creating a direct connection between the plate and disc which results in the transfer of power from the engine to the transmission. The clutch disc is now rotating with the pressure plate at engine speed and, because it is splined to the transmission shaft, the shaft now turns at the same engine speed. Understanding clutch operation can be rather difficult at first; if you're still confused after reading this, consider the following analogy. The action of the diaphragm spring can be compared to that of an oil can bottom. The bottom of an oil can is shaped very much like the clutch diaphragm spring and pushing in on the can bottom and then releasing it produces a similar effect. As mentioned earlier, the clutch pedal re-

turn spring permits full release of the pedal and reduces linkage slack due to wear. As the linkage wears, clutch free-pedal travel will increase and free-travel will decrease as the clutch wears. Free-travel is actually throwout bearing lash.

The diaphragm spring type clutches used are available in two different designs: flat diaphragm springs or bent spring. The bent fingers are bent back to create a centrifugal boost ensuring quick re-engagement at higher engine speeds. This design enables pressure plate load to increase as the clutch disc wears and makes low pedal effort possible even with a heavy-duty clutch. The throwout bearing used with the bent finger design is 1¼″ long and is shorter than the bearing used with the flat finger design. These bearings are not interchangeable. If the longer bearing is used with the bent finger clutch, free-pedal travel will not exist. This results in clutch slippage and rapid wear.

The transmission varies the gear ratio between the engine and rear wheels. It can be shifted to change engine speed as driving conditions and loads change. The transmission al-

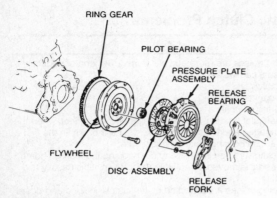

Clutch assembly components

lows disengaging and reversing power from the engine to the wheels.

The Probe clutch is a single plate, dry friction disc with a diaphragm-style spring pressure plate. The clutch disc has a splined hub which attaches the disc to the input shaft. The disc has friction material where it contacts the flywheel and pressure plate. Torsion springs on the disc help absorb engine torque pulses. The pressure plate applies pressure to the clutch disc, holding it tight against the surface of the flywheel. The diaphragm spring is located between two fulcrum rings riveted to the clutch cover. The clutch operating mechanism consists of a release bearing, fork and cylinder. The release fork and slave cylinder transfer pedal motion to the release bearing. In the engaged position, the diaphragm spring holds the pressure plate against the clutch disc, so engine

torque is transmitted to the input shaft. When the clutch pedal is depressed, the release bearing pushes the diaphragm spring center toward the flywheel. The diaphragm spring pivots the fulcrum, relieving the load on the pressure plate. Steel spring straps riveted to the clutch cover lift the pressure plate from the clutch disc, disengaging the engine drive from the transaxle and enabling the gears to be changed.

The hydraulic clutch control system consists of a fluid reservoir, master cylinder, slave cylinder and pressure line. The clutch master cylinder and reservoir are mounted on the firewall bulkhead. Fluid level is checked at the reservoir.

The clutch master cylinder converts mechanical clutch pedal movement into hydraulic fluid movement. The fluid pressure is transmitted down the pressure line to the slave cylinder. The slave cylinder is mounted on the transaxle. It converts the hydraulic fluid movement to mechanical movement, allowing the release fork and bearing to engage and disengage the clutch.

ADJUSTMENTS

Pedal Height

1. To determine if pedal height adjustment is required, measure the distance between the

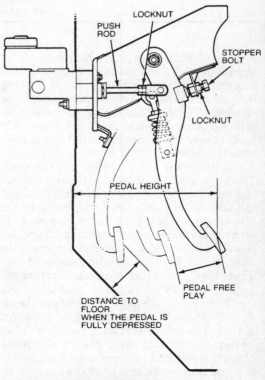

1. PRESSURE LINE
2. PRESSURE PLATE ASSEMBLY
3. RELEASE BEARING
4. DISC ASSEMBLY
5. SPRING
6. CLUTCH PEDAL
7. CLUTCH MASTER CYLINDER
   AND RESERVOIR
8. RELEASE FORK
9. SLAVE CYLINDER

Clutch hydraulic system

Clutch pedal height and freeplay

firewall and the center of the clutch pedal pad. The distance should be 216.5–221.5mm.

2. To adjust, if the distance is not within specifications; remove the lower dash panel and air ducts.

3. Loosen the locknut on the clutch pedal stopper bolt and turn the stopper bolt until the pedal height is correct.

4. Tighten the locknut and install the air ducts and dash panel.

Pedal Freeplay

1. Measure the clutch pedal freeplay. Freeplay should be between 5.0–13.0mm.

2. If adjustment is required, remove the lower dash panel and the air ducts.

3. Loosen the locknut on the clutch master cylinder connecting rod. Turn the rod, in the required direction, until the freeplay is within specifications.

4. Measure the distance from the floor to the center of the clutch pedal pad when the pedal is fully depressed. The distance should be 68.5mm or more. Tighten the locknut. Install the air ducts and dash panel.

Driven Disc and Pressure Plate
REMOVAL AND INSTALLATION

1. Remove the transaxle.

2. Lock the flywheel with an appropriate tool. Insert a dowel, or special clutch disc aligning tool, through the center of the clutch plate into the clutch pilot bearing on the flywheel. This will support the assembly when the pressure plate mounting bolts are removed.

3. Remove the pressure plate mounting bolts, loosen them each a little at a time in rotation.

4. Remove the pressure plate. Remove the clutch driven disc and alignment tool.

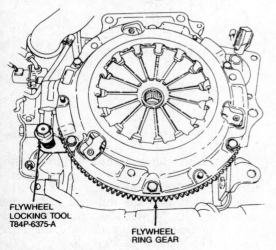

Clutch and flywheel

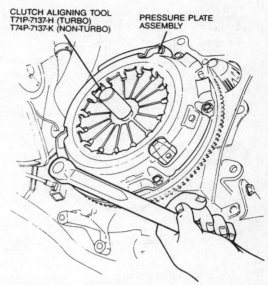

Remove/install the clutch assembly

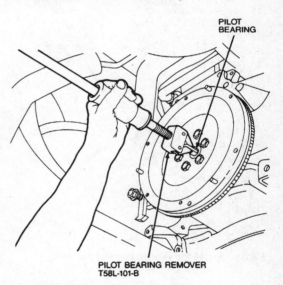

Pilot bearing removal

5. Inspect the clutch pilot bearing. Inspect the flywheel surface. Service as required.

6. If the flywheel needs servicing, loosen and remove the mounting bolts. Support the flywheel before removing the last bolt. The flywheel is heavy, if it drops it, or you could be damaged.

7. Remove the release bearing from the transaxle. Remove the clutch fork.

8. Clean and inspect all components. Replace as required.

9. Apply grease to the contact tip areas of the clutch release fork and the release bearing. Install the fork in position on the transaxle. Install the release bearing on the fork.

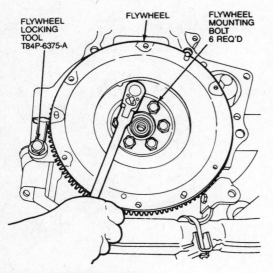

Remove/install the flywheel

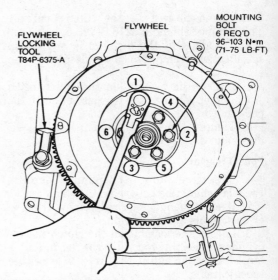

Tighten the flywheel bolts in sequence

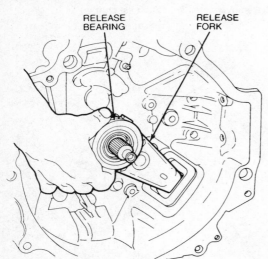

Remove/install the release bearing and fork

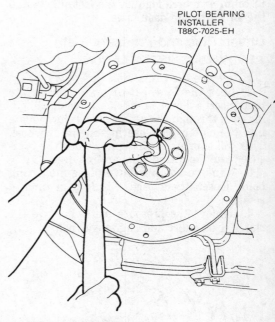

Install the pilot bearing

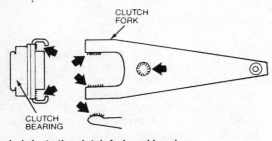

Lubricate the clutch fork and bearing

10. Attach the flywheel to the crankshaft, if removed. Tighten the bolts in sequence to 71–75 ft. lbs. Install the pilot bearing if removed.

11. Clean the splines of the old clutch disc, if reused. Apply an small amount of grease to the splines of the clutch disc and input shaft of the transaxle.

12. Install the clutch disc on the flywheel with the spring hub facing out. Hold the disc in position with the proper aligning tool. Place the pressure plate over the disc and install the mounting bolts. Tighten the mounting bolts a little at a time, in sequence until the final torque of each bolt is 13–20 ft. lbs.

13. Install the transaxle.

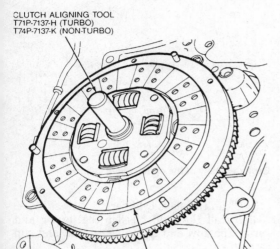

Clutch plate alignment

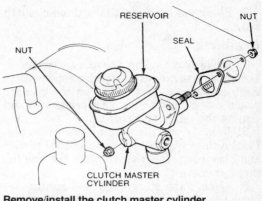

Remove/install the clutch master cylinder

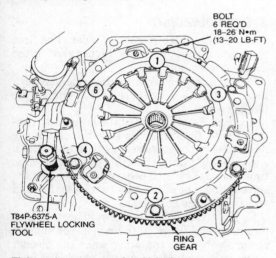

Tighten the pressure plate bolts in sequence

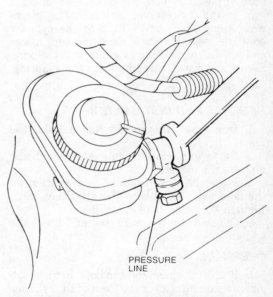

Pressure line on the clutch master cylinder

Clutch Master Cylinder

REMOVAL AND INSTALLATION

1. If the vehicle is equipped with ABS (anti-lock brakes), remove the ABS relay box.

2. Disconnect the pressure line to the master cylinder. Take care not to spill brake fluid on painted surfaces. It will remove the paint. If fluid is spilled, rinse with clear water as quickly as possible.

3. Remove the mounting nuts and the clutch master cylinder.

4. Place the master cylinder on the mounting studs and secure it with the nuts. Tighten the mounting nuts to 14–19 ft. lbs.

5. Connect the pressure line and tighten the nut.

6. Install the ABS box, if equipped.

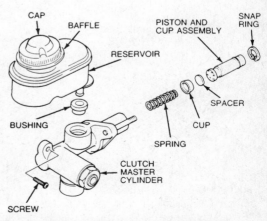

Exploded view of the clutch master cylinder

7. Bleed the air from the hydraulic clutch system.

OVERHAUL

1. While overhauling the master cylinder, work in a clean area and keep all components as clean as possible. Press down on the cylinder piston assembly with an appropriate tool and remove the retaining snapring.

2. Remove the piston and cup assembly. Place a clean rag over the front of the cylinder and blow compressed air through the line fitting to remove.

3. Remove the spacer, cup and spring. Remove the reservoir attaching screw, the reservoir and mounting bushing.

4. Clean all components. Inspect the cylinder bore. If pitted, replace the complete cylinder.

5. Install the reservoir and mounting grommet. Apply clean brake fluid to the cylinder bore and assembly the spring, new cup, spacer and new piston and cup assembly into the bore. Secure the piston assembly with the snapring.

Clutch Slave Cylinder

REMOVAL AND INSTALLATION

1. Disconnect the pressure line and plug the line.

2. Remove the slave cylinder attaching bolts. Remove the cylinder.

3. Place the slave cylinder into position on the transaxle and secure the attaching bolts. Tighten the bolts to 14–19 ft. lbs.

4. Connect the pressure line and bleed the system.

OVERHAUL

1. Pull off the push rod and boot. Remove the piston assembly. Cover the front of the cylinder with a clean rag. Blow compressed air through the line fitting to remove.

2. Remove the spring, bleeder cap and ball.

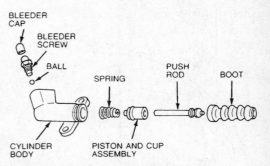

Exploded view of the clutch slave cylinder

3. Clean the slave cylinder.

4. Install the ball, bleeder cap, screw and spring (narrow end facing the piston and cup assembly).

5. Install a new piston and cup assembly. Install the rod and boot.

SYSTEM BLEEDING

1. Fill the clutch master cylinder. The fluid level must be at ¾ full or higher during the bleeding operation.

2. Remove the bleeder cap from the slave cylinder. Attach a vinyl hose to the end of the bleeder screw.

3. Place the other end of the hose into a container with fluid in it. Be sure the end of the hose is below the surface of the container fluid.

4. Slowly pump the clutch pedal several times. Hold the clutch pedal down and open the slave cylinder bleeder screw to release the fluid and air into the container.

5. Tighten the bleeder screw. Repeat the procedure several times, until no more air bubbles are present in the container when the bleeder screw is opened. Make sure to check the fluid level in the master cylinder after each bleeder screw opening. Check clutch operation, bleed the system again, if necessary.

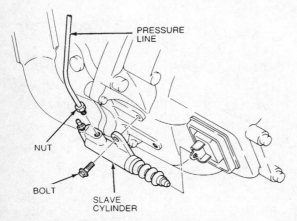

Remove/install the clutch slave cylinder

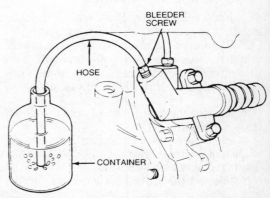

Bleeding the air from the clutch hydraulic system

AUTOMATIC TRANSAXLE

Understanding Automatic Transmissions

The automatic transmission allows engine torque and power to be transmitted to the rear wheels within a narrow range of engine operating speeds. The transmission will allow the engine to turn fast enough to produce plenty of power and torque at very low speeds, while keeping it at a sensible rpm at high vehicle speeds. The transmission performs this job entirely without driver assistance. The transmission uses a light fluid as the medium for the transmission of power. This fluid also works in the operation of various hydraulic control circuits and as a lubricant. Because the transmission fluid performs all of these three functions, trouble within the unit can easily travel from one part to another. For this reason, and because of the complexity and unusual operating principles of the transmission, a very sound understanding of the basic principles of operation will simplify troubleshooting.

THE TORQUE CONVERTER

The torque converter replaces the conventional clutch. It has three functions:

1. It allows the engine to idle with the vehicle at a standstill, even with the transmission in gear.

2. It allows the transmission to shift from range to range smoothly, without requiring that the driver close the throttle during the shift.

3. It multiplies engine torque to an increasing extent as vehicle speed drops and throttle opening is increased. This has the effect of making the transmission more responsive and reduces the amount of shifting required.

The torque converter is a metal case which is shaped like a sphere that has been flattened on opposite sides. It is bolted to the rear end of the engine's crankshaft. Generally, the entire metal case rotates at engine speed and serves as the engine's flywheel.

The case contains three sets of blades. One set is attached directly to the case. This set forms the torus or pump. Another set is directly connected to the output shaft, and forms the turbine. The third set is mounted on a hub which, in turn, is mounted on a stationary shaft through a one-way clutch. This third set is known as the stator.

A pump, which is driven by the converter hub at engine speed, keeps the torque converter full of transmission fluid at all times. Fluid flows continuously through the unit to provide cooling.

Under low-speed acceleration, the torque converter functions as follows:

The torus is turning faster than the turbine. It picks up fluid at the center of the converter and, through centrifugal force, slings it outward. Since the outer edge of the converter moves faster than the portions at the center, the fluid picks up speed.

The fluid then enters the outer edge of the turbine blades. It then travels back toward the center of the converter case along the turbine blades. In impinging upon the turbine blades, the fluid loses the energy picked up in the torus.

If the fluid were now to immediately be returned directly into the torus, both halves of the converter would have to turn at approximately the same speed at all times, and torque input and output would both be the same.

In flowing through the torus and turbine, the fluid picks up two types of flow, or flow in two separate directions. It flows through the turbine blades, and it spins with the engine. The stator, whose blades are stationary when the vehicle is being accelerated at low speeds, converts one type of flow into another. Instead of allowing the fluid to flow straight back into the torus, the stator's curved blades turn the fluid almost 90 degrees toward the direction of rotation of the engine. Thus the fluid does not flow as fast toward the torus, but is already spinning when the torus picks it up. This has the effect of allowing the torus to turn much faster than the turbine. This difference in speed may be compared to the difference in speed between the smaller and larger gears in any gear train. The result is that engine power output is higher, and engine torque is multiplied.

As the speed of the turbine increases, the fluid spins faster and faster in the direction of engine rotation. As a result, the ability of the stator to redirect the fluid flow is reduced. Under cruising conditions, the stator is eventually forced to rotate on its one-way clutch in the direction of engine rotation. Under these conditions, the torque converter begins to behave almost like a solid shaft, with the torus and turbine speeds being almost equal.

THE PLANETARY GEARBOX

The ability of the torque converter to multiply engine torque is limited. Also, the unit tends to be more efficient when the turbine is rotating at relatively high speeds. Therefore, a planetary gearbox is used to carry the power output of the turbine to the driveshaft.

Planetary gears function very similarly to conventional transmission gears. However, their construction is different in that three elements make up one gear system, and, in that all three elements are different from one another.

The three elements are: an outer gear that is shaped like a hoop, with teeth cut into the inner surface; a sun gear, mounted on a shaft and located at the very center of the outer gear; and a set of three planet gears, held by pins in a ring-like planet carrier, meshing with both the sun gear and the outer gear. Either the outer gear or the sun gear may be held stationary, providing more than one possible torque multiplication factor for each set of gears. Also, if all three gears are forced to rotate at the same speed, the gearset forms, in effect, a solid shaft.

Most modern automatics use the planetary gears to provide either a single reduction ratio of about 1.8:1, or two reduction gears: a low of about 2.5:1, and an intermediate of about 1.5:1. Bands and clutches are used to hold various portions of the gearsets to the transmission case or to the shaft on which they are mounted. Shifting is accomplished, then, by changing the portion of each planetary gearset which is held to the transmission case or to the shaft.

THE SERVOS AND ACCUMULATORS

The servos are hydraulic pistons and cylinders. They resemble the hydraulic actuators used on many familiar machines, such as bulldozers. Hydraulic fluid enters the cylinder, under pressure, and forces the piston to move to engage the band or clutches.

The accumulators are used to cushion the engagement of the servos. The transmission fluid must pass through the accumulator on the way to the servo. The accumulator housing contains a thin piston which is sprung away from the discharge passage of the accumulator. When fluid passes through the accumulator on the way to the servo, it must move the piston against spring pressure, and this action smooths out the action of the servo.

THE HYDRAULIC CONTROL SYSTEM

The hydraulic pressure used to operate the servos comes from the main transmission oil pump. This fluid is channeled to the various servos through the shift valves. There is generally a manual shift valve which is operated by the transmission selector lever and an automatic shift valve for each automatic upshift the transmission provides: i.e., two-speed automatics have a low-high shift valve, while three-speeds have a 1-2 valve, and a 2-3 valve.

There are two pressures which effect the operation of these valves. One is the governor pressure which is affected by vehicle speed. The other is the modulator pressure which is affected by intake manifold vacuum or throttle position. Governor pressure rises with an increase in vehicle speed, and modulator pressure rises as the throttle is opened wider. By responding to these two pressures, the shift valves cause the upshift points to be delayed with increased throttle opening to make the best use of the engine's power output.

Most transmissions also make use of an auxiliary circuit for downshifting. This circuit may be actuated by the throttle linkage or the vacuum line which actuates the modulator, or by a cable or solenoid. It applies pressure to a special downshift surface on the shift valve or valves.

The transmission modulator also governs the line pressure, used to actuate the servos. In this way, the clutches and bands will be actuated with a force matching the torque output of the engine.

Application

The 4EAT electronically controlled automatic transaxle is installed in the Probe.

Fluid Pan

REMOVAL AND INSTALLATION

1. Disconnect the negative battery cable. Raise and safely support the front of the vehicle.
2. Drain the transaxle fluid. Remove the pan mounting bolts and the pan.
3. Clean all gasket mounting surfaces.
4. Install the pan using a new gasket. Tighten the mounting bolts to 69–95 in. lbs.

ADJUSTMENTS

Kickdown Cable

NOTE: *A pressure gauge Ford tool T57L-77820 and adapter D87C-77000A, or equivalents are required.*

1. Remove the splash shield next to the left front tire.
2. Remove the square head plug (marked L) and install the adapter and pressure gauge. Turn the kickdown cable locknuts to the furthest point from the throttle cam (loosen the cable completely).
3. Shift the transaxle into PARK and warm up the engine. Operate the engine between 700–800 rpm.

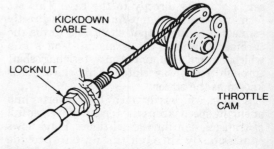

Kickdown cable adjustment

4. Turn the locknuts toward the throttle cam until the line pressure begins to exceed 63–66 psi. Turn the locknuts away from the throttle cam until a pressure of 63–66 psi is maintained.

5. Tighten the locknuts. Turn off the engine. Remove the pressure gauge and install the square head plug.

Neutral Safety Switch

The neutral safety switch is located on the top left side of the transaxle.

REMOVAL AND INSTALLATION

1. Disconnect the negative battery cable.

2. Remove the shift lever to neutral safely switch nut and lever.

3. Remove the switch mounting bolts. Remove the switch.

4. Disconnect the electrical wiring connectors from the switch.

5. Connect the wiring to the switch. Place the switch in position and start the mounting bolts. Place a small drill bit through the alignment hole in the switch, into the hole in the transaxle case. Tighten the mounting bolts to 22–29 ft. lbs. Connect the lever and nut. Connect the negative battery cable.

Transaxle

REMOVAL AND INSTALLATION

NOTE: *The transaxle is removed separately from the engine.*

1. Disconnect the battery cables. Remove the battery and battery carrier.

2. Disconnect the main fuse block.

3. Disconnect the center distributor lead.

4. Disconnect the air flow meter connector and remove the air cleaner assembly.

5. Remove the resonance chamber and bracket.

6. Disconnect the speedometer cable on analog cluster or harness on digital cluster. Disconnect the five transaxle control electrical connectors and separate the transaxle wiring harness from the mounting clips.

7. Disconnect the two ground wires from the transaxle case. Disconnect the range selector cable from the transaxle case. Disconnect the kickdown cable.

8. Raise and safely support the vehicle. Remove the front wheels.

9. Remove the splash shields.

10. Drain the transaxle fluid into a suitable pan.

11. Disconnect the oil cooler lines and plug them.

12. Disconnect the tie rod ends using a suitable tool.

13. Remove the stabilizer bar control links.

14. Remove the bolts and nuts at the left and right lower arm ball joints.

15. Pull the lower arms downward to separate them from the knuckles. Do not damage the ball joint dust boots.

16. Separate the left halfshaft from the transaxle by prying with a bar or equivalent inserted between the shaft and the transaxle case. Be careful not to damage the oil seal.

17. Remove the right joint shaft bracket.

18. Separate the right halfshaft together with the joint shaft by prying with a bar or equivalent inserted between the shaft and the transaxle case. Be careful not to damage the oil seal.

19. Install the special tools to hold the differential side gear in the proper position.

NOTE: *Failure to install the differential side gears holding tool may cause the differential side gears to become mispositioned.*

20. Remove the gusset plate to transaxle bolts.

21. Remove the torque converter cover. Remove the torque converter to engine flexplate mounting nuts

22. Mark or tag the electrical connections if necessary and remove the starter and access brackets.

23. Support the engine with the engine support fixture or equivalent.

24. Remove the center transaxle mount and bracket.

25. Remove the left transaxle mount and bracket.

26. Remove the nut and bolt which attaches the right transaxle mount to the frame.

27. Remove the crossmember and the left side lower arm as an assembly.

28. Position a transmission jack under the transaxle and secure the transaxle to the jack.

29. Remove the transaxle mounting bolts.

30. Remove the transaxle from the vehicle. Pull the transaxle away slowly from the engine. Place a pry bar between the converter and engine flexplate. Pry the converter carefully away from the engine. Lower the transaxle. The engine must always be properly supported while the transaxle is out of the vehicle.

31. Attach a safety device at 2 places on the transaxle and place a board on the jack and position the transaxle on it. The transaxle is not well balanced and be careful when positioning it on the jack. Make sure the converter is pushed back and in the correct mounted position.

32. Raise the transaxle on the jack and align the converter mounting studs with the engine flexpalte. Install the transaxle onto the engine. Tighten the transaxle mounting bolts to 66–86 ft. lbs.

33. Install the center transaxle mount and

bracket. Tighten the bolts 27–40 ft. lbs. and the nuts to 47–66 ft. lbs. Do not install the nut which braces the throttle air hose bracket.

34. Install the left transaxle mount and tighten bolts on the mount to 46–69 ft. lbs. vehicles. The retaining nut on this mount is torqued to 63–86 ft. lbs.

35. Install the crossmember and the left side lower arm as an assembly. The tightening torque is 27–40 ft. lbs. on the bolts and 55–69 ft. lbs. on the nut.

36. Install the right transaxle mount bolt and nut and tighten to 63–86 ft. lbs.

37. Install the starter, electrical connections and access brackets.

38. Install the converter mounting nuts tighten them to 32–45 ft. lbs.

39. Install the converter cover.

40. Install the gusset plate to transaxle bolts and torque the bolts to 27–38 ft. lbs.

41. Replace the circlips at the end of each halfshafts.

42. Remove the special tools holding the differential side gears in the proper position and install the halfshafts.

NOTE: *After complete installation, pull the front hub outward to confirm that the halfshaft will not come out. Be careful not damage the oil seal.*

43. Attach the lower arm ball joints to the knuckle.

44. Install the tie rod ends and new cotter pins. Tighten the tie rod end bolts to 22–33 ft. lbs.

45. Install the bolts and nuts to the lower arm ball joints. Tighten to 32–40 ft. lbs.

46. Install the stabilizer bar control link. Tighten nut/bolt to 12–17 ft. lbs. Make sure, that at least 25mm of the bolt remains exposed after torque is reached.

47. Install the splash shields.

48. Install the front wheels.

49. Install the two ground wires to the transaxle case. Connect the kickdown cable, the range selector cable and the transaxle control harness. Connect the speedometer.

50. Install the resonance chamber and bracket and tighten to 69–95 inch lbs.

51. Install the air cleaner assembly and reconnect the air flow meter connector. The correct

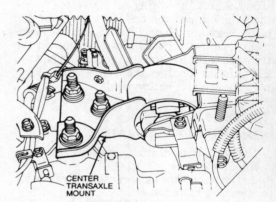
Remove/install the center transaxle mount

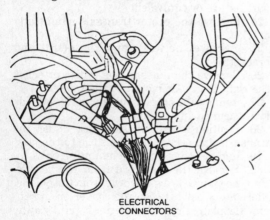
Auto transaxle wiring connections

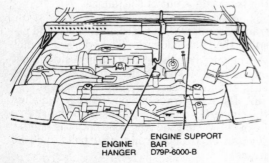
Engine hanger installation

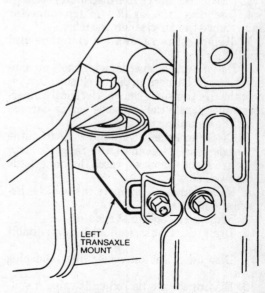
Remove/install the left transaxle mount

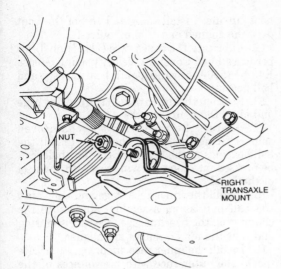

Remove/install the right transaxle mount

torque for the air cleaner assembly is 69–95 inch lbs.

52. Connect the center distributor lead.

53. Connect the main fuse block and tighten retaining bolts to 69–95 inch lbs.

54. Install the battery carrier and battery. Connect the battery cables.

55. Remove the engine support fixture or equivalent.

56. Add the correct quantity of the specified fluid.

57. Start the engine, road test for proper operation and check for leaks.

Halfshafts

REMOVAL AND INSTALLATION

Left Side

1. Disconnect the negative battery cable. Raise and safely support the vehicle.

2. Remove the left front wheel, hub grease cup and the left splash shield.

3. Remove the stabilizer link assembly from the lower control arm.

4. Use a cape chisel and hammer and raise the staked portion of the hub nut.

5. Have an assistant apply the brakes and loosen, but do not remove, the hub nut.

6. Remove the lower ball joint to steering knuckle bolt. Pry the lower arm downward to separate the ball joint.

7. Pull the steering knuckle outward.

8. Position a pry bar between the halfshaft and transaxle case, carefully pry the halfshaft from the case while supporting the halfshaft.

9. Support the halfshaft. Remove the hub nut and slide the halfshaft from the steering knuckle.

NOTE: *If the halfshaft binds in the hub spline, use a plastic hammer to bump it out, or a wheel puller to press it out.*

10. Place transaxle plugs, or equivalents in the transaxle case to prevent dirt from entering, and the differential side gears from becoming mispositioned.

11. Install a new circlip on the differential end of the halfshaft.

12. Slide the halfshaft into position through the steering knuckle drive hub. Install a new hub nut, but do not completely tighten it at this time.

13. Remove the transaxle plug and slide the halfshaft into the transaxle case, slowly push in the halfshaft until the circlip snaps into place.

14. Install and torque the lower control arm ball joint to steering knuckle nut and bolt to 32–40 ft. lbs.

15. Install the stabilizer link assembly to the control arm. Install the splash shield and wheel. Torque the wheel nuts to 65–87 ft. lbs.

16. Lower the vehicle. Tighten the new hub nut to 116–174 ft. lbs. Stake the new nut with a blunt chisel.

Right Side

1. Disconnect the negative battery cable. Raise and safely support the vehicle.

2. Remove the left front wheel, hub grease cup and the left splash shield.

3. Remove the stabilizer link assembly from the lower control arm.

4. Use a cape chisel and hammer and raise the staked portion of the hub nut.

5. Have an assistant apply the brakes and loosen, but do not remove, the hub nut.

6. Remove the lower ball joint to steering knuckle bolt. Pry the lower arm downward to separate the ball joint. Remove the dynamic damper mounting from the engine mounting.

7. Pull the steering knuckle outward.

8. Position a pry bar between the halfshaft and transaxle case, carefully pry the halfshaft from the case while supporting the halfshaft.

9. Support the halfshaft. Remove the hub nut and slide the halfshaft from the steering knuckle.

NOTE: *If the halfshaft binds in the hub spline, use a plastic hammer to bump it out, or a wheel puller to press it out.*

10. Place transaxle plugs, or equivalents in the transaxle case to prevent dirt from entering, and the differential side gears from becoming mispositioned.

11. Install a new circlip on the differential end of the halfshaft.

12. Slide the halfshaft into position through the steering knuckle drive hub. Install a new

hub nut, but do not completely tighten it at this time.

13. Remove the transaxle plug and slide the halfshaft into the transaxle case, slowly push in the halfshaft until the circlip snaps into place. Install the dynamic damper mounting to the cylinder block mounting.

14. Install and torque the lower control arm ball joint to steering knuckle nut and bolt to 32–40 ft. lbs.

15. Install the stabilizer link assembly to the control arm. Install the splash shield and wheel. Torque the wheel nuts to 65–87 ft. lbs.

16. Lower the vehicle. Tighten the new hub nut to 116–174 ft. lbs. Stake the new nut with a blunt chisel.

CV-JOINT OVERHAUL

Rzeppa Joint

1. CV-joint components are matched during manufacture and therefore cannot be interchanged with components from another CV-joint.

2. Clamp the halfshaft in a soft jawed vise. Do not allow the vise to contact the boot or boot clamps.

3. Remove the large boot clamp. After removing the clamp, roll the boot back over the shaft.

NOTE: *If this procedure is being done to just replace a damage boot, the grease should be checked at this time for contamination. Rub some grease between your fingers. If grit can be felt the grease is contaminated. A contaminated joint should be disassembled, cleaned and repacked.*

4. Remove the outer joint to shaft retaining ring. Before removing the bearing retainer, scribe mating marks on the shaft and retainer for installation alignment.

5. Remove the outer race. Paint alignment marks on the inner race and shaft for installation alignment.

6. Remove the inner race snapring from the end of the halfshaft. Remove the inner race, cage and ball bearings from the shaft as an assembly.

7. Carefully pry the ball bearing out of the bearing cage. Do not scratch the bearing or cage surfaces. Match mark the inner race and bearing cage.

8. Rotate the inner race to align the bearing lands with the windows in the bearing cage. Remove the inner race through the large end of the cage.

9. Remove the small clamp and the boot from the halfshaft.

10. Clean and inspect all parts, use a rebuilding kit if necessary.

11. Tape the splines of the shaft to prevent boot cutting. Install the small end of the boot over the splined end of the halfshaft.

12. Lubricate the inner race (Use High Temperature Ford Constant Velocity Joint Grease E43Z-19590A, or equivalent), bearing cage and ball bearings.

13. Position the inner race in the bearing cage and align the match marks.

14. Install the race with the chamfered splines facing the end of the cage. Install the ball bearings in the bearing cage. The balls can be pressed into the cage windows with the heel of the hand.

15. Install the inner race, cage and balls onto the halfshaft as an assembly. Make sure the chamfer on the bearing cage faces the snapring and that the match marks are aligned.

16. Install the inner race snapring. Lubricate (pack) the outer race with two ounces of the specified grease. Install the outer race and add an additional ounce of the specified grease. Install the wire retainer.

17. Position the boot, making sure it is fully seated in the grooves provided. Extend or compress the CV-joint as necessary to get the distance of 89mm of boot length. Do not allow the overall dimension to change until the boot clamps are installed.

18. Insert a dull tool under the edge of the large end of the boot to allow any trapped air to escape.

19. Install the new boot clamps. Work the CV-joint through its full range of travel. Twist the joint at various angles, the joint should flex, extend and compress smoothly.

Tripot Joint

1. CV joint components are matched during manufacture and therefore cannot be interchanged with components from another CV-joint.

2. Clamp the halfshaft in a soft jawed vise. Do not allow the vise to contact the boot or boot clamps.

3. Remove the large boot clamp. After removing the clamp, roll the boot back over the shaft.

NOTE: *The grease should be checked at this time for contamination. Rub some grease between your fingers. If grit can be felt the grease is contaminated. A contaminated joint should be disassembled, cleaned and repacked.*

4. Remove the wire retaining ring. Remove the outer race, after painting or scribing matchmarks on the outer race and tripot bearing for installation alignment.

5. Remove the tripot bearing retainer snapring, after painting matchmarks on the tripot bearing and shaft.

6. Use a brass drift and hammer and remove the bearing assembly from the shaft. Remove the small clamp and the boot.

7. After cleaning the splined end of the shaft, wrap tape around the end to prevent boot cutting at installation.

8. Clean and inspect all components. Lubricate all components with High Temperature Constsant Velocity Joint Grease, (Ford E43Z-19590A or equivalent).

9. Install the boot over the shaft, small end first. Install the tripot bearing on the shaft with the matchmarks aligned. Use a brass drift and hammer if necessary.

10. Install the snapring retainer. Fill the CV outer race with 3.5 oz. of grease. Install the outer race over the tripot joint, with matchmarks aligned, and install the wire retainer ring.

11. Position the CV-joint boot into the grooves provided. Make sure the boot is fully seated.

12. Extend or compress the joint to achieve at total length of 89mm. Insert a blunt tool under the large end of the boot to allow any trapped air to escape.

13. Hold the joint at the required length and install the boot clamps. Work the joint into various positions to make sure it moves freely.

Suspension and Steering

8

FRONT SUSPENSION

The front suspension consists of MacPherson struts and a single wishbone lower control arm. Strut towers located in the wheel wells locate the upper ends of the MacPherson struts. If the vehicle is equipped with programmed ride control (PRC), the PRC actuator bolts to the top of the strut mounting block which houses a rubber mounted strut bearing. The upper end of the coil spring rides in a heavy rubber spring seat. A forged steering knuckle bolts to the shock absorber. The lower ball joint is pressed into the control arm and is attached to the steering knuckle. The wide stance control arms are supported by rubber bushings at each end.

Troubleshooting Basic Steering and Suspension Problems

Problem	Cause	Solution
Hard steering (steering wheel is hard to turn)	• Low or uneven tire pressure • Loose power steering pump drive belt • Low or incorrect power steering fluid • Incorrect front end alignment • Defective power steering pump • Bent or poorly lubricated front end parts	• Inflate tires to correct pressure • Adjust belt • Add fluid as necessary • Have front end alignment checked/adjusted • Check pump • Lubricate and/or replace defective parts
Loose steering (too much play in the steering wheel)	• Loose wheel bearings • Loose or worn steering linkage • Faulty shocks • Worn ball joints	• Adjust wheel bearings • Replace worn parts • Replace shocks • Replace ball joints
Car veers or wanders (car pulls to one side with hands off the steering wheel)	• Incorrect tire pressure • Improper front end alignment • Loose wheel bearings • Loose or bent front end components • Faulty shocks	• Inflate tires to correct pressure • Have front end alignment checked/adjusted • Adjust wheel bearings • Replace worn components • Replace shocks
Wheel oscillation or vibration transmitted through steering wheel	• Improper tire pressures • Tires out of balance • Loose wheel bearings • Improper front end alignment • Worn or bent front end components	• Inflate tires to correct pressure • Have tires balanced • Adjust wheel bearings • Have front end alignment checked/adjusted • Replace worn parts
Uneven tire wear	• Incorrect tire pressure • Front end out of alignment • Tires out of balance	• Inflate tires to correct pressure • Have front end alignment checked/adjusted • Have tires balanced

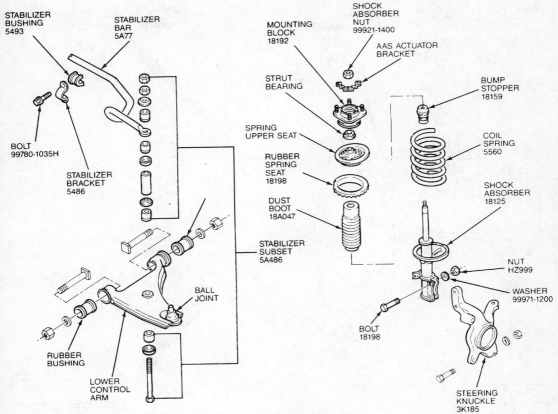

Front suspension components

Body lean on turns is controlled by a hollow stabilizer bar that connects to both lower control arms.

If the vehicle is not equipped with PRC, the struts used are the conventional non-adjustable type and cannot be interchanged with the PRC type. Also, PRC actuators will be absent from the strut mounting block.

The PRC system feature provides for the selection of SOFT, NORM, or SPORT suspension dampening. This selection is based on driving conditions in addition to the driver's selection of ride control mode.

Battery voltage is applied to the Programmed Ride Control Module and the Programmed Ride Control Switch through a fuse whenever the Ignition Switch is in START or RUN. The Programmed Ride Control Module receives inputs from the Steering Angle Sensor, the Vehicle Speed Sensor, and the Programmed Ride Control Switch. The Steering Angle Sensor also provides an input to the Programmed Ride Control Module for determination of lateral forces exerted on the vehicle but is not driver controlled through the selection made at the Programmed Ride Control Switch. Upon sensing inputs from these sensors, the module applies voltage to the Actuators located at the adjustable struts.

MacPherson Struts

REMOVAL AND INSTALLATION

1. Raise and safely support the front of the vehicle with the suspension hanging.
2. Remove the wheel assembly.
3. Raise the hood. Remove the rubber cap from the strut mounting block. If equipped with PRC, disconnect the control module connector.
4. Put an alignment mark on the inside of the strut mounting block and the chassis strut tower for installation alignment.
5. Remove the PRC module, if equipped.
6. Remove the anti-lock brake harness and bracket, if equipped.
7. Remove the brake caliper. Remove the brake hose from the strut mounting.
8. Remove the bolts that mount the strut to the steering knuckle.
9. Remove the vane airflow meter. Remove

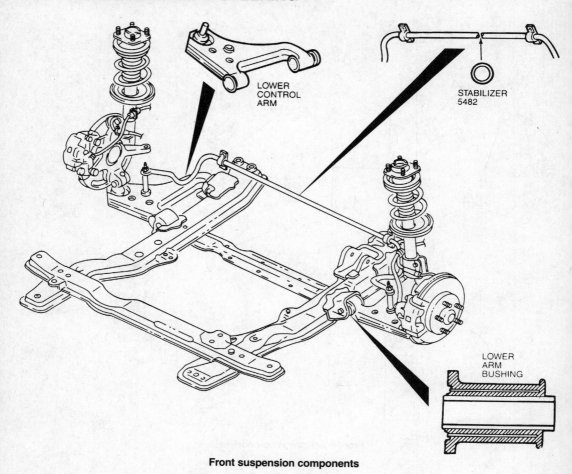

LOWER
CONTROL
ARM

STABILIZER
5482

LOWER
ARM
BUSHING

Front suspension components

the ignition coil mounting bracket from the strut mount.

10. Remove the strut mounting bolts from the strut tower and remove the strut.

11. Service the strut as required. Place the upper strut mount into position on the strut tower. Be sure the alignment marks match.

12. Install the strut mounting bolts and tight-en them to 34–46 ft. lbs. Install the ignition coil bracket, and the vane airflow meter. Install the PRC control module and anti-lock harness if equipped.

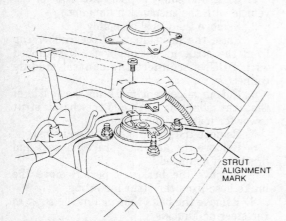

STRUT
ALIGNMENT
MARK

Make a strut alignment locator mark

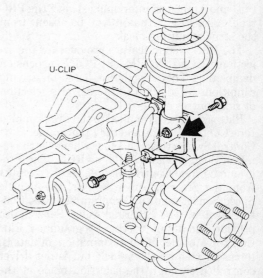

U-CLIP

Remove/install strut to steering knuckle

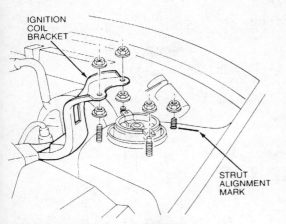

Remove/install the ignition coil bracket

IGNITION COIL BRACKET

STRUT ALIGNMENT MARK

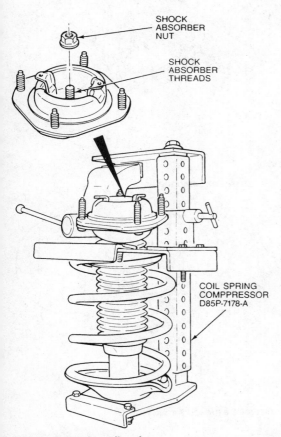

SHOCK ABSORBER NUT

SHOCK ABSORBER THREADS

COIL SPRING COMPPRESSOR D85P-7178-A

Compressing the coil spring

OVERHAUL

1. Place the strut assembly in a vise. Loosen, but do not remove the shock mounting nut.

2. Install a safe suitable spring compressor and compress the coil spring.

3. Remove the shock mounting nut. Gradually release the coil spring compressor pressure. Take care not to damage the shock mounting threads.

4. Remove the PRC control module (if equipped), the strut mounting block, upper spring seat, dust boot, bump stopper and the coil spring from the shock absorber.

5. Install the parts on the shock, install the mounting block so that the notch on the block is 180° from the knuckle mounting bracket.

6. Compress the coil spring and install the mounting nut. Torque the nut to 47–69 ft. lbs. Gradually release the coil spring pressure.

7. Install the strut assembly.

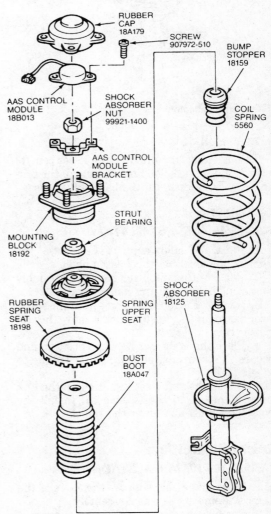

RUBBER CAP 18A179

SCREW 907972-510

BUMP STOPPER 18159

AAS CONTROL MODULE 18B013

SHOCK ABSORBER NUT 99921-1400

AAS CONTROL MODULE BRACKET

COIL SPRING 5560

STRUT BEARING

MOUNTING BLOCK 18192

RUBBER SPRING SEAT 18198

SPRING UPPER SEAT

SHOCK ABSORBER 18125

DUST BOOT 18A047

Shock mounting components

13. Install the rubber cap over the strut. Install the steering knuckle to strut mounting bolts and tighten them to 69–86 ft. lbs.

14. Install the brake caliper and secure the brake line to the strut bracket.

15. Install the wheel assembly and lower the vehicle.

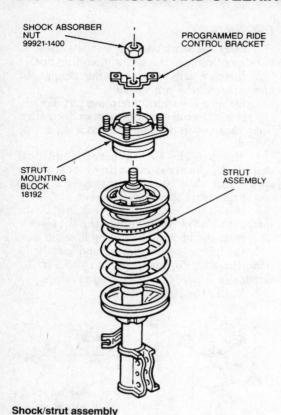

Shock/strut assembly

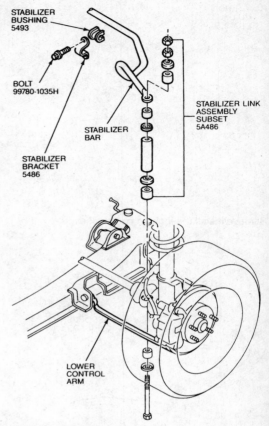

Stabilizer bar components

Lower Ball Joint

The ball joint, mounted on the lower control arm, is not serviceable. Replacement of the control arm is necessary if the ball joint is worn.

Stabilizer Bar

REMOVAL AND INSTALLATION

1. Raise and safely support the front of the vehicle. Remove the wheel assembly.
2. Remove the stabilizer bar link assembly mounting bolts from the control arm.
3. Remove the mounting bolt from the stabilizer bar mounting bushing and remove the stabilizer bar.
4. Place the stabilizer bar into position and secure the mounting bushing bolts. Torque to 27–40 ft. lbs.
5. Install the stabilizer link, tighten the link until 20mm of thread is exposed. Install the wheel assembly and lower the vehicle.

Lower Control Arm

REMOVAL AND INSTALLATION

1. Raise and safely support the front of the vehicle. Remove the wheel assembly.
2. Remove the brake caliper and support it out of the way.

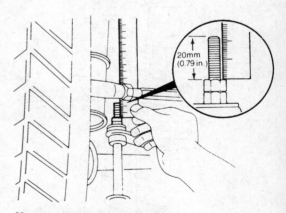

Measure exposed thread length

3. Remove the stabilizer link assembly.
4. Remove the ball joint clamp bolt from the steering knuckle and separate the ball joint from the knuckle.
5. Remove the harmonic damper from the chassis frame. (Left side on ATX models only).
6. Remove the control arm to chassis mounting bolts and remove the control arm.
7. Place the control arm in position on the

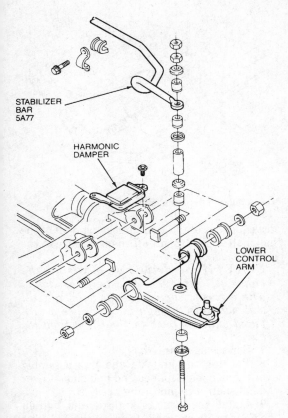

STABILIZER
BAR
5A77

HARMONIC
DAMPER

LOWER
CONTROL
ARM

Lower control arm components

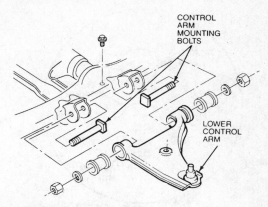

CONTROL
ARM
MOUNTING
BOLTS

LOWER
CONTROL
ARM

Remove/install the control arm

chassis and install the mounting bolts. Tighten the mounting bolts to 69–93 ft. lbs.

8. Install the harmonic damper. Install the ball joint stud to the steering knuckle. Tighten the bolt to 32–40 ft. lbs.

9. Install the stabilizer link assembly. Allow 20mm of thread to be exposed.

10. Install the brake caliper. Install the wheel assembly. Lower the vehicle.

Steering Knuckle
REMOVAL AND INSTALLATION

1. Raise and safely support the front of the vehicle. Remove the wheel assembly.

2. Raise the staked part of the halfshaft hub retaining nut, and remove the nut.

3. Remove the stabilizer link from the control arm.

4. Remove the tie rod end nut. Separate the tie rod end from the steering knuckle. Remove the brake caliper, adapter and disc rotor. Hang the caliper out of the way with wire.

5. Remove the ball joint to steering knuckle mounting bolt. Pry downward on the control arm to separate the steering knuckle.

6. Remove the steering knuckle to strut mounting bolts. Slide the steering knuckle and

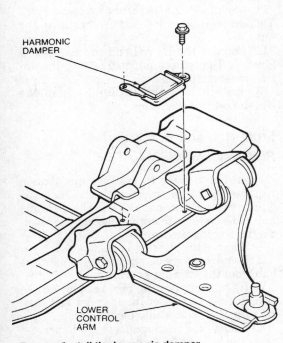

HARMONIC
DAMPER

LOWER
CONTROL
ARM

Remove/install the harmonic damper

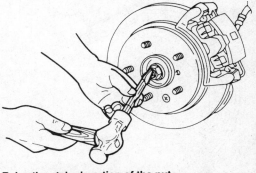

Raise the staked portion of the nut

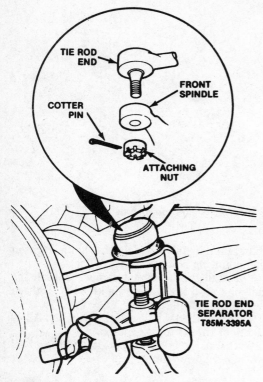

Separate the tie rod end from the knuckle

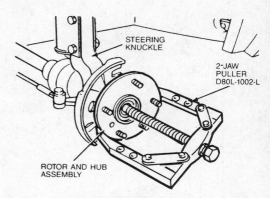

Use a puller if the halfshaft is stuck

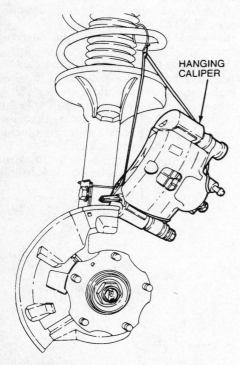

Suspend the caliper

drive hub out of the strut bracket and off of the halfshaft. Pull straight off so no damage to the grease seals occurs.

NOTE: *If the drive hub binds on the halfshaft, tap the end of the halfshaft lightly with a plastic hammer. If the halfshaft still will not slide through the hub, use a two-jawed puller to push the halfshaft from the hub.*

7. Service as required.

8. Position the knuckle and hub assembly over the halfshaft splined end and slide it over the halfshaft into mounting position.

9. Install the strut to knuckle and tighten the bolts to 69–86 ft. lbs. Connect the ball joint to the knuckle and tighten the mounting bolt to 32–40 ft. lbs.

10. Install the brake rotor. Install the brake caliper and adapter.

11. Mount a new halfshaft hub retaining nut. Tighten the nut to 116–174 ft. lbs. Stake the nut.

12. Connect the tie rod end to the steering knuckle. Tighten the nut to 22–36 ft. lbs. Install a new cotter pin.

13. Install the stabilizer link. Install the wheel. Lower the vehicle.

Front Hub and Bearing

REMOVAL AND INSTALLATION

Front hub bearing removal and installation requires the use of special tools such as a hydraulic press. Remove the steering knuckle and hub and have an automotive machine shop handle the bearing service.

1. Remove the steering knuckle.

2. Remove the grease seal and press the drive hub from the steering knuckle.

3. If the inner bearing race remains on the hub, grind a section of the race flat and then split the race with a chisel and hammer.

4. Remove the bearing snapring retainer and press the bearing from the hub.

5. During press operations, take care not to damage the disc brake dust shield. It should be left mounted unless it has been damaged.

6. Clean all components and inspect the hub and knuckle for cracks, wear, and scoring. Replace as necessary.

7. Press the bearing into position in the steering knuckle. Install the retaining snapring.

8. Lubricate the grease seal lip and install the seal.

9. Press the drive hub through the bearing. Install the steering knuckle.

Front End Alignment

CASTER

Front caster adjustment is not a separate procedure, rather front caster should fall within specification when the front camber is adjusted.

CAMBER

Camber is always set before any other adjustments. Camber can cause both pull and tire wear if it is not set correctly.

Camber adjustment is done by rotating the strut bearing to one of three positions, which changes the offset of the top of the strut. When the strut bearing is in position A; Camber angle is 27° and caster is 0. When in position B; Camber angle is 27° and caster is plus 28°. When in

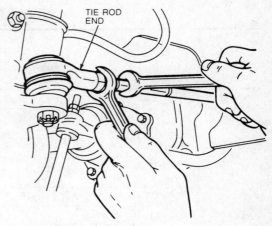

Loosen/tighten the locknut

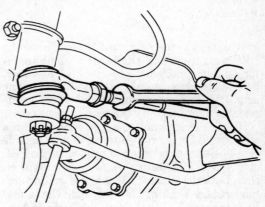

Turn the tie rod

position C; Camber angle is 0 and caster is plus 28°.

TOE

1. If the toe-in needs adjustment (toe is the difference in width between the front of the wheel assemblies and rear of the wheel assemblies at their centers.

2. If adjustment is required, loosen the locknuts at the tie rod ends. The right and left tie rod are equally threaded.

3. Turn the tie rod in or out as required to reach specification, but turn equally on both sides. One turn of the tie rod equals about 7mm.

4. After adjustment is completed, tighten the tie rod end locknuts.

REAR SUSPENSION

The rear suspension is fully independent utilizing rear MacPherson struts at each wheel. If the vehicle is equipped with programmed ride

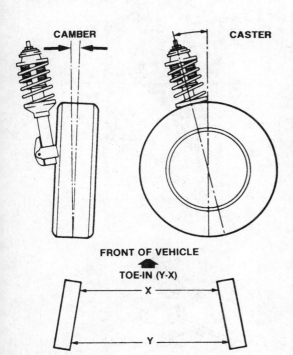

Caster, camber, toe

Wheel Alignment

| Year | Model | | Caster | | Camber | | Toe-in (in.) | Steering Axis Inclination (deg.) |
			Range (deg.)	Preferred Setting (deg.)	Range (deg.)	Preferred Setting (deg.)		
1989–90	Probe GL	Front	0.47P–1.97P	1.22P	0.47N–1.03P	0.28P	0–0.24	12.78
		Rear	—	—	0.25N–1.25P	0.50P	0.12N–0.12P	—
	Probe LX	Front	0.47P–1.97P	1.22P	0.47N–1.03P	0.28P	0–0.24	12.78
		Rear	—	—	0.25N–1.25P	0.50P	0.12N–0.12P	—
	Probe GT	Front	0.47P–1.97P	1.22P	0.47N–1.03P	0.28P	0–0.24	12.78
		Rear	—	—	0.25N–1.25P	0.50P	0.12N–0.12P	—

N Negative
P Positive

control (PRC), the rear strut towers locate the PRC actuators and the strut assemblies. A forged rear spindle bolts to the shock absorber, double rear lateral links, and a single trailing arm. It is these components and a rear cross-member that make up the rear suspension.

If the vehicle is not equipped with PRC, the struts used are the conventional non-adjustable type and cannot be interchanged with the PRC struts. The PRC actuators are not present either. Both the lateral links and the trailing arm have rubber bushings at each end. The lateral links are attached to the rear subframe and the spindle with a common bolt and nut assembly at each end. The trailing arm bolts to the shock absorber and a bracket on the floor pan. Never try to straight a damage rear suspension component. Always replace with a new part.

Lateral links, trailing arms, and spindles are normally replaced only if damaged. If a suspension part has been damaged, have the underbody dimensions checked. If the underbody dimensions are not correct, the body will have to be straightened before install new suspension parts.

MacPherson Strut

REMOVAL AND INSTALLATION

1. Raise and safely support the rear of the vehicle. Remove the wheel assembly.
2. Remove the upper trunk side garnish and lower side trim to gain access to the top of the strut,
3. Disconnect and remove the PRC module, if equipped. Remove the ABS (anti-skid brake) harness and bracket, if equipped.
4. Remove the rear brake drum and backing plate, or rear disc caliper and rotor assembly. Remove the brake hose from the strut bracket.

5. Loosen the trailing arm bolt. Remove the spindle to shock mounting bolts.
6. Remove the upper strut mounting nuts and remove the strut.

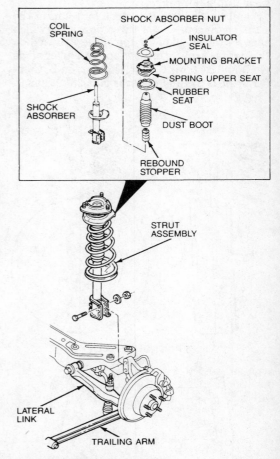

Rear strut assembly components

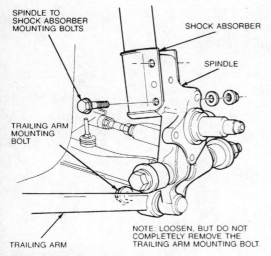

NOTE: LOOSEN, BUT DO NOT COMPLETELY REMOVE THE TRAILING ARM MOUNTING BOLT.

Remove/install shock to spindle

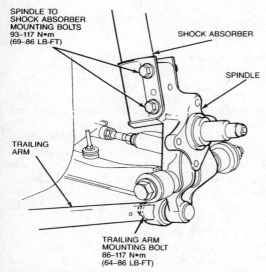

Shock installation

7. Position the strut and secure the upper mounting nuts. Tighten them to 34–46 ft. lbs.

8. Install the ABS harness and PRC module, if equipped.

9. Install the trim removed for upper strut access.

10. Install the spindle to shock mounting bolts. Tighten to 69–86 ft. lbs. Tighten the trailing arm bolt to 64–86 ft. lbs.

11. Install the rear brake backing plate and drum or caliper and rotor. Connect the brake line bracket.

12. Install the wheel assembly. Lower the vehicle.

OVERHAUL

Refer to the front strut overhaul procedure in the previous Front Suspension section.

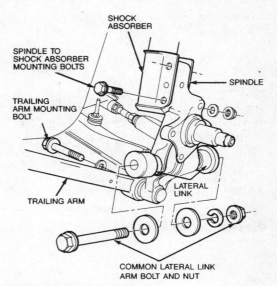

COMMON LATERAL LINK ARM BOLT AND NUT

Remove/install spindle

Spindle

REMOVAL AND INSTALLATION

1. Raise and safely support the rear of the vehicle. Remove the wheel assembly.

2. Remove the brake drum and backing plate, or the caliper and rotor assembly.

3. Loosen, but do not completely remove the spindle to shock absorber mounting bolts.

4. Remove the common lateral link arm bolt and nut from the spindle.

5. Remove the trailing arm mounting bolt at the spindle. Remove the spindle to shock mounting bolts, and remove the spindle.

6. Position the spindle onto the shock and install the mounting bolts. Tighten the bolts to 69–86 ft. lbs.

7. Install the lateral link arm bolt and nut through the spindle and tighten to 64–86 ft. lbs.

8. Install the trailing arm mounting bolt and tighten to 64–86 ft. lbs.

9. Install the rear brakes. Install the wheel assembly. Lower the vehicle.

Lateral Link, Trailing Arm and Rear Crossmember

REMOVAL AND INSTALLATION

1. Remove the rear wheel spindle. Remove the stabilizer bar.

2. Remove the nut from the rear lateral link mounting bolt at the rear crossmember and remove the lateral link. The common mounting bolt, the bolt and front lateral link cannot be removed at this time because of lack of clearance.

3. Remove the parking brake attaching bolts from the trailing arm assembly. Remove the

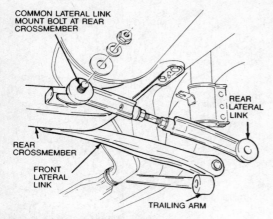

Remove/install rear lateral link

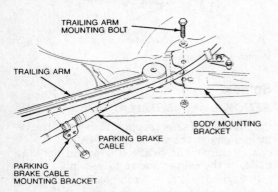

Remove/install trailing arm

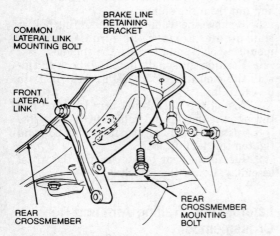

Remove/install crossmember and front lateral link

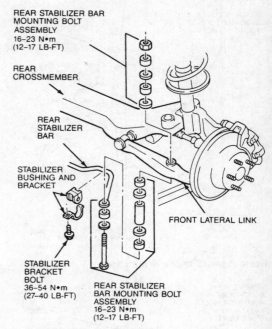

Remove/install rear stabilizer bar

trailing arm body mounting bracket bolt. Remove the trailing arm.

4. Remove the exhaust mounting bolts and the brake line retaining bracket from the rear crossmember. Remove the mounting bolts from the end of the crossmember. Remove the rear crossmember and front lateral link as an assembly.

5. Remove the common link mounting bolt from the rear crossmember. Remove the front lateral link from the crossmember.

6. Install the front lateral link to the crossmember and install the common mounting bolt. Install the rear crossmember onto the vehicle and install the mounting bolts. Install the exhaust mounting bolts, and the brake line bracket. Torque the crossmember mounting bolts to 27–40 ft. lbs.

7. Position the trailing arm to the body mounting bracket and install the mounting bolt. Tighten the bolt to 46–69 ft. lbs. Install the parking brake cable attaching bolts.

8. Position the rear lateral link onto the common mounting bolt and install the mounting nut. Tighten the nut to 64–86 ft. lbs.

9. Install the rear stabilizer bar. Install the rear spindle.

Rear Wheel Bearings

REMOVAL AND INSTALLATION

1. Raise and safely support the rear of the vehicle. Remove the wheel assembly.

2. Remove the center hub cover. Use a chisel and unstake the hub nut. Remove and discard the hub nut.

3. Remove the brake drum or rotor assembly.

4. Pry the grease seal from the brake drum. Remove the snapring that retains the rear wheel bearing. Press the bearing from the hub.

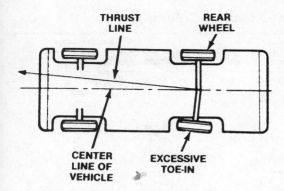

NOTE: THE THRUST LINE IS THE PATH BOTH REAR WHEELS TAKE AS THEY ROLL DOWN THE ROAD.

Rear end thrust line

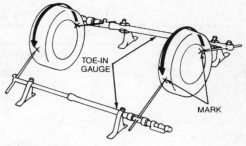

Toe-in adjustment

5. Press a new bearing into position and install the snapring.

6. Lubricate the lips of a new grease retainer and install the retainer,

7. Install the drum or rotor assembly. Install a new hub retaining bolt and tighten it to 73–101 ft. lbs. Stake the nut using a blunt chisel.

8. Install the hub cover. Install the wheel assembly. Lower the vehicle.

Rear End Alignment

Rear end alignment should be checked whenever front end alignment is serviced. If the rear toe and tracking are not set correctly, accelerated tire wear may occur. The thrust line of the rear wheels may also be affected. The thrust line is the path the rear wheels take as they roll down the road. Ideally, the thrust line should align perfectly with the center line of the vehicle. If, the thrust line is not correct, the vehicle will slightly understeer in one direction and oversteer in the other. It will also affect wheel centering. Check the rear toe when ever alignment is performed. Rear toe adjustment is performed much like front toe adjustment, except, in some cases, the measurement reading is reversed depending on the gauge used.

STEERING

The non-electronically controlled power rack and pinion steering gear has an integral valving and power assist system.

The valve body is an integral part of the steering gear housing. The pressure line and return line from the pump attach at the valve body. A rotary valve directs high pressure hydraulic fluid through external oil lines to the correct side of the rack piston.

A spring loaded pressure pad assembly is used to keep the rack in constant contact with the pinion. Rubber boots at each end of the rack seal out dust, dirt and contaminants.

The steering gear housing is mounted on bulkhead with a rubber bushing and mounting bracket at each end. The mounting brackets are attached to the bulkhead with three bolts at each bracket.

The Variable Assist Power Steering (VAPS) feature automatically adjusts power steering pressure. VAPS provides light steering effort during low speed and parking maneuvers and higher steering effort at higher speeds for improved road feel. The VAPS system consists of VAPS, Control Unit, Steering Angle Sensor, Vehicle Speed Sensor, Solenoid Valve, Test Connector, and Inter-Connecting Wiring.

The Variable Assist Power Steering System is completely automatic, with no driver operated controls. The system continuously monitors steering wheel angle and vehicle speed to determine when to adjust steering system pressure. The system opens a solenoid valve to provide full power assist at vehicle speeds less than 6.2 mph or when the steering wheel is turned more than 45° to the right or left. The system reduces power assist under other conditions.

The VAPS Control Unit has a special feature which should be noted before performing any VAPS diagnostic procedures. A slide switch located on the VAPS Control Unit allows for 10 percent harder steering effort or a 10 percent lighter steering effort from normal production setting. Note the position of this switch before proceeding with diagnostics.

Steering Wheel

REMOVAL AND INSTALLATION

1. Disconnect the negative battery cable.

2. Remove the steering wheel horn pad by removing the mounting screws from the rear of the steering wheel. Disconnect the wiring from the horn pad.

3. Remove the steering wheel mounting nut. Place matchmarks on the steering wheel and the shaft for installation alignment.

Troubleshooting the Steering Column

Problem	Cause	Solution
Will not lock	· Lockbolt spring broken or defective	· Replace lock bolt spring
High effort (required to turn ignition key and lock cylinder)	· Lock cylinder defective · Ignition switch defective · Rack preload spring broken or deformed · Burr on lock sector, lock rack, housing, support or remote rod coupling · Bent sector shaft · Defective lock rack · Remote rod bent, deformed · Ignition switch mounting bracket bent · Distorted coupling slot in lock rack (tilt column)	· Replace lock cylinder · Replace ignition switch · Replace preload spring · Remove burr · Replace shaft · Replace lock rack · Replace rod · Straighten or replace · Replace lock rack
Will stick in "start"	· Remote rod deformed · Ignition switch mounting bracket bent	· Straighten or replace · Straighten or replace
Key cannot be removed in "off-lock"	· Ignition switch is not adjusted correctly · Defective lock cylinder	· Adjust switch · Replace lock cylinder
Lock cylinder can be removed without depressing retainer	· Lock cylinder with defective retainer · Burr over retainer slot in housing cover or on cylinder retainer	· Replace lock cylinder · Remove burr
High effort on lock cylinder between "off" and "off-lock"	· Distorted lock rack · Burr on tang of shift gate (automatic column) · Gearshift linkage not adjusted	· Replace lock rack · Remove burr · Adjust linkage
Noise in column	· One click when in "off-lock" position and the steering wheel is moved (all except automatic column) · Coupling bolts not tightened · Lack of grease on bearings or bearing surfaces · Upper shaft bearing worn or broken · Lower shaft bearing worn or broken · Column not correctly aligned · Coupling pulled apart · Broken coupling lower joint · Steering shaft snap ring not seated · Shroud loose on shift bowl. Housing loose on jacket—will be noticed with ignition in "off-lock" and when torque is applied to steering wheel.	· Normal—lock bolt is seating · Tighten pinch bolts · Lubricate with chassis grease · Replace bearing assembly · Replace bearing. Check shaft and replace if scored. · Align column · Replace coupling · Repair or replace joint and align column · Replace ring. Check for proper seating in groove. · Position shroud over lugs on shift bowl. Tighten mounting screws.
High steering shaft effort	· Column misaligned · Defective upper or lower bearing · Tight steering shaft universal joint · Flash on I.D. of shift tube at plastic joint (tilt column only) · Upper or lower bearing seized	· Align column · Replace as required · Repair or replace · Replace shift tube · Replace bearings
Lash in mounted column assembly	· Column mounting bracket bolts loose · Broken weld nuts on column jacket · Column capsule bracket sheared	· Tighten bolts · Replace column jacket · Replace bracket assembly

Troubleshooting the Steering Column (cont.)

Problem	Cause	Solution
Lash in mounted column assembly (cont.)	• Column bracket to column jacket mounting bolts loose	• Tighten to specified torque
	• Loose lock shoes in housing (tilt column only)	• Replace shoes
	• Loose pivot pins (tilt column only)	• Replace pivot pins and support
	• Loose lock shoe pin (tilt column only)	• Replace pin and housing
	• Loose support screws (tilt column only)	• Tighten screws
Housing loose (tilt column only)	• Excessive clearance between holes in support or housing and pivot pin diameters	• Replace pivot pins and support
	• Housing support-screws loose	• Tighten screws
Steering wheel loose—every other tilt position (tilt column only)	• Loose fit between lock shoe and lock shoe pivot pin	• Replace lock shoes and pivot pin
Steering column not locking in any tilt position (tilt column only)	• Lock shoe seized on pivot pin	• Replace lock shoes and pin
	• Lock shoe grooves have burrs or are filled with foreign material	• Clean or replace lock shoes
	• Lock shoe springs weak or broken	• Replace springs
Noise when tilting column (tilt column only)	• Upper tilt bumpers worn	• Replace tilt bumper
	• Tilt spring rubbing in housing	• Lubricate with chassis grease
One click when in "off-lock" position and the steering wheel is moved	• Seating of lock bolt	• None. Click is normal characteristic sound produced by lock bolt as it seats.
High shift effort (automatic and tilt column only)	• Column not correctly aligned	• Align column
	• Lower bearing not aligned correctly	• Assemble correctly
	• Lack of grease on seal or lower bearing areas	• Lubricate with chassis grease
Improper transmission shifting— automatic and tilt column only	• Sheared shift tube joint	• Replace shift tube
	• Improper transmission gearshift linkage adjustment	• Adjust linkage
	• Loose lower shift lever	• Replace shift tube

Troubleshooting the Ignition Switch

Problem	Cause	Solution
Ignition switch electrically inoperative	• Loose or defective switch connector	• Tighten or replace connector
	• Feed wire open (fusible link)	• Repair or replace
	• Defective ignition switch	• Replace ignition switch
Engine will not crank	• Ignition switch not adjusted properly	• Adjust switch
Ignition switch wil not actuate mechanically	• Defective ignition switch	• Replace switch
	• Defective lock sector	• Replace lock sector
	• Defective remote rod	• Replace remote rod
Ignition switch cannot be adjusted correctly	• Remote rod deformed	• Repair, straighten or replace

Troubleshooting the Turn Signal Switch

Problem	Cause	Solution
Turn signal will not cancel	• Loose switch mounting screws • Switch or anchor bosses broken • Broken, missing or out of position detent, or cancelling spring	• Tighten screws • Replace switch • Reposition springs or replace switch as required
Turn signal difficult to operate	• Turn signal lever loose • Switch yoke broken or distorted • Loose or misplaced springs • Foreign parts and/or materials in switch • Switch mounted loosely	• Tighten mounting screws • Replace switch • Reposition springs or replace switch • Remove foreign parts and/or material • Tighten mounting screws
Turn signal will not indicate lane change	• Broken lane change pressure pad or spring hanger • Broken, missing or misplaced lane change spring • Jammed wires	• Replace switch • Replace or reposition as required • Loosen mounting screws, reposition wires and retighten screws
Turn signal will not stay in turn position	• Foreign material or loose parts impeding movement of switch yoke • Defective switch	• Remove material and/or parts • Replace switch
Hazard switch cannot be pulled out	• Foreign material between hazard support cancelling leg and yoke	• Remove foreign material. No foreign material impeding function of hazard switch—replace turn signal switch.
No turn signal lights	• Inoperative turn signal flasher • Defective or blown fuse • Loose chassis to column harness connector • Disconnect column to chassis connector. Connect new switch to chassis and operate switch by hand. If vehicle lights now operate normally, signal switch is inoperative • If vehicle lights do not operate, check chassis wiring for opens, grounds, etc.	• Replace turn signal flasher • Replace fuse • Connect securely • Replace signal switch • Repair chassis wiring as required
Instrument panel turn indicator lights on but not flashing	• Burned out or damaged front or rear turn signal bulb • If vehicle lights do not operate, check light sockets for high resistance connections, the chassis wiring for opens, grounds, etc. • Inoperative flasher • Loose chassis to column harness connection • Inoperative turn signal switch • To determine if turn signal switch is defective, substitute new switch into circuit and operate switch by hand. If the vehicle's lights operate normally, signal switch is inoperative.	• Replace bulb • Repair chassis wiring as required • Replace flasher • Connect securely • Replace turn signal switch • Replace turn signal switch
Stop light not on when turn indicated	• Loose column to chassis connection • Disconnect column to chassis connector. Connect new switch into system without removing old.	• Connect securely • Replace signal switch

Troubleshooting the Turn Signal Switch (cont.)

Problem	Cause	Solution
Stop light not on when turn indicated (cont.)	Operate switch by hand. If brake lights work with switch in the turn position, signal switch is defective. • If brake lights do not work, check connector to stop light sockets for grounds, opens, etc.	• Repair connector to stop light circuits using service manual as guide
Turn indicator panel lights not flashing	• Burned out bulbs • High resistance to ground at bulb socket • Opens, ground in wiring harness from front turn signal bulb socket to indicator lights	• Replace bulbs • Replace socket • Locate and repair as required
Turn signal lights flash very slowly	• High resistance ground at light sockets • Incorrect capacity turn signal flasher or bulb • If flashing rate is still extremely slow, check chassis wiring harness from the connector to light sockets for high resistance • Loose chassis to column harness connection • Disconnect column to chassis connector. Connect new switch into system without removing old. Operate switch by hand. If flashing occurs at normal rate, the signal switch is defective.	• Repair high resistance grounds at light sockets • Replace turn signal flasher or bulb • Locate and repair as required • Connect securely • Replace turn signal switch
Hazard signal lights will not flash—turn signal functions normally	• Blow fuse • Inoperative hazard warning flasher • Loose chassis-to-column harness connection • Disconnect column to chassis connector. Connect new switch into system without removing old. Depress the hazard warning lights. If they now work normally, turn signal switch is defective. • If lights do not flash, check wiring harness "K" lead for open between hazard flasher and connector. If open, fuse block is defective	• Replace fuse • Replace hazard warning flasher in fuse panel • Conect securely • Replace turn signal switch • Repair or replace brown wire or connector as required

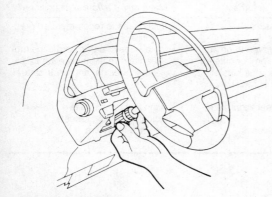

Remove/install horn pad

4. Use a steering wheel puller and remove the steering wheel.

5. Service as required. Align the matchmarks and place the steering wheel on the steering column shaft.

6. Install the wheel hub mounting nut. Tighten to 29–36 ft. lbs.

7. Connect the horn wire and install the horn pad. Connect the negative battery cable.

Turn Signal Switch
REMOVAL AND INSTALLATION

1. Remove the negative battery cable. Remove the horn pad and the steering wheel.

Troubleshooting the Manual Steering Gear

Problem	Cause	Solution
Hard or erratic steering	• Incorrect tire pressure	• Inflate tires to recommended pressures
	• Insufficient or incorrect lubrication	• Lubricate as required (refer to Maintenance Section)
	• Suspension, or steering linkage parts damaged or misaligned	• Repair or replace parts as necessary
	• Improper front wheel alignment	• Adjust incorrect wheel alignment angles
	• Incorrect steering gear adjustment	• Adjust steering gear
	• Sagging springs	• Replace springs
Play or looseness in steering	• Steering wheel loose	• Inspect shaft spines and repair as necessary. Tighten attaching nut and stake in place.
	• Steering linkage or attaching parts loose or worn	• Tighten, adjust, or replace faulty components
	• Pitman arm loose	• Inspect shaft splines and repair as necessary. Tighten attaching nut and stake in place
	• Steering gear attaching bolts loose	• Tighten bolts
	• Loose or worn wheel bearings	• Adjust or replace bearings
	• Steering gear adjustment incorrect or parts badly worn	• Adjust gear or replace defective parts
Wheel shimmy or tramp	• Improper tire pressure	• Inflate tires to recommended pressures
	• Wheels, tires, or brake rotors out-of-balance or out-of-round	• Inspect and replace or balance parts
	• Inoperative, worn, or loose shock absorbers or mounting parts	• Repair or replace shocks or mountings
	• Loose or worn steering or suspension parts	• Tighten or replace as necessary
	• Loose or worn wheel bearings	• Adjust or replace bearings
	• Incorrect steering gear adjustments	• Adjust steering gear
	• Incorrect front wheel alignment	• Correct front wheel alignment
Tire wear	• Improper tire pressure	• Inflate tires to recommended pressures
	• Failure to rotate tires	• Rotate tires
	• Brakes grabbing	• Adjust or repair brakes
	• Incorrect front wheel alignment	• Align incorrect angles
	• Broken or damaged steering and suspension parts	• Repair or replace defective parts
	• Wheel runout	• Replace faulty wheel
	• Excessive speed on turns	• Make driver aware of conditions
Vehicle leads to one side	• Improper tire pressures	• Inflate tires to recommended pressures
	• Front tires with uneven tread depth, wear pattern, or different cord design (i.e., one bias ply and one belted or radial tire on front wheels)	• Install tires of same cord construction and reasonably even tread depth, design, and wear pattern
	• Incorrect front wheel alignment	• Align incorrect angles
	• Brakes dragging	• Adjust or repair brakes
	• Pulling due to uneven tire construction	• Replace faulty tire

Troubleshooting the Power Steering Gear

Problem	Cause	Solution
Hissing noise in steering gear	• There is some noise in all power steering systems. One of the most common is a hissing sound most evident at standstill parking. There is no relationship between this noise and performance of the steering. Hiss may be expected when steering wheel is at end of travel or when slowly turning at standstill.	• Slight hiss is normal and in no way affects steering. Do not replace valve unless hiss is extremely objectionable. A replacement valve will also exhibit slight noise and is not always a cure. Investigate clearance around flexible coupling rivets. Be sure steering shaft and gear are aligned so flexible coupling rotates in a flat plane and is not distorted as shaft rotates. Any metal-to-metal contacts through flexible coupling will transmit valve hiss into passenger compartment through the steering column.
Rattle or chuckle noise in steering gear	• Gear loose on frame	• Check gear-to-frame mounting screws. Tighten screws to 88 N·m (65 foot pounds) torque.
	• Steering linkage looseness	• Check linkage pivot points for wear. Replace if necessary.
	• Pressure hose touching other parts of car	• Adjust hose position. Do not bend tubing by hand.
	• Loose pitman shaft over center adjustment NOTE: A slight rattle may occur on turns because of increased clearance off the "high point." This is normal and clearance must not be reduced below specified limits to eliminate this slight rattle.	• Adjust to specifications
	• Loose pitman arm	• Tighten pitman arm nut to specifications
Squawk noise in steering gear when turning or recovering from a turn	• Damper O-ring on valve spool cut	• Replace damper O-ring
Poor return of steering wheel to center	• Tires not properly inflated • Lack of lubrication in linkage and ball joints	• Inflate to specified pressure • Lube linkage and ball joints
	• Lower coupling flange rubbing against steering gear adjuster plug	• Loosen pinch bolt and assemble properly
	• Steering gear to column misalignment	• Align steering column
	• Improper front wheel alignment • Steering linkage binding • Ball joints binding • Steering wheel rubbing against housing	• Check and adjust as necessary • Replace pivots • Replace ball joints • Align housing
	• Tight or frozen steering shaft bearings	• Replace bearings
	• Sticking or plugged valve spool	• Remove and clean or replace valve
	• Steering gear adjustments over specifications	• Check adjustment with gear out of car. Adjust as required.
	• Kink in return hose	• Replace hose
Car leads to one side or the other (keep in mind road condition and wind. Test car in both directions on flat road)	• Front end misaligned • Unbalanced steering gear valve NOTE: If this is cause, steering effort will be very light in direction of lead and normal or heavier in opposite direction	• Adjust to specifications • Replace valve

Troubleshooting the Power Steering Gear (cont.)

Problem	Cause	Solution
Momentary increase in effort when turning wheel fast to right or left	• Low oil level • Pump belt slipping • High internal leakage	• Add power steering fluid as required • Tighten or replace belt • Check pump pressure. (See pressure test)
Steering wheel surges or jerks when turning with engine running especially during parking	• Low oil level • Loose pump belt • Steering linkage hitting engine oil pan at full turn • Insufficient pump pressure • Pump flow control valve sticking	• Fill as required • Adjust tension to specification • Correct clearance • Check pump pressure. (See pressure test). Replace relief valve if defective. • Inspect for varnish or damage, replace if necessary
Excessive wheel kickback or loose steering	• Air in system • Steering gear loose on frame • Steering linkage joints worn enough to be loose • Worn poppet valve • Loose thrust bearing preload adjustment • Excessive overcenter lash	• Add oil to pump reservoir and bleed by operating steering. Check hose connectors for proper torque and adjust as required. • Tighten attaching screws to specified torque • Replace loose pivots • Replace poppet valve • Adjust to specification with gear out of vehicle • Adjust to specification with gear out of car
Hard steering or lack of assist	• Loose pump belt • Low oil level **NOTE:** Low oil level will also result in excessive pump noise • Steering gear to column misalignment • Lower coupling flange rubbing against steering gear adjuster plug • Tires not properly inflated	• Adjust belt tension to specification • Fill to proper level. If excessively low, check all lines and joints for evidence of external leakage. Tighten loose connectors. • Align steering column • Loosen pinch bolt and assemble properly • Inflate to recommended pressure
Foamy milky power steering fluid, low fluid level and possible low pressure	• Air in the fluid, and loss of fluid due to internal pump leakage causing overflow	• Check for leak and correct. Bleed system. Extremely cold temperatures will cause system aeriation should the oil level be low. If oil level is correct and pump still foams, remove pump from vehicle and separate reservoir from housing. Check welsh plug and housing for cracks. If plug is loose or housing is cracked, replace housing.
Low pressure due to steering pump	• Flow control valve stuck or inoperative • Pressure plate not flat against cam ring	• Remove burrs or dirt or replace. Flush system. • Correct
Low pressure due to steering gear	• Pressure loss in cylinder due to worn piston ring or badly worn housing bore • Leakage at valve rings, valve body-to-worm seal	• Remove gear from car for disassembly and inspection of ring and housing bore • Remove gear from car for disassembly and replace seals

Troubleshooting the Power Steering Pump

Problem	Cause	Solution
Chirp noise in steering pump	• Loose belt	• Adjust belt tension to specification
Belt squeal (particularly noticeable at full wheel travel and stand still parking)	• Loose belt	• Adjust belt tension to specification
Growl noise in steering pump	• Excessive back pressure in hoses or steering gear caused by restriction	• Locate restriction and correct. Replace part if necessary.
Growl noise in steering pump (particularly noticeable at stand still parking)	• Scored pressure plates, thrust plate or rotor • Extreme wear of cam ring	• Replace parts and flush system • Replace parts
Groan noise in steering pump	• Low oil level • Air in the oil. Poor pressure hose connection.	• Fill reservoir to proper level • Tighten connector to specified torque. Bleed system by operating steering from right to left—full turn.
Rattle noise in steering pump	• Vanes not installed properly • Vanes sticking in rotor slots	• Install properly • Free up by removing burrs, varnish, or dirt
Swish noise in steering pump	• Defective flow control valve	• Replace part
Whine noise in steering pump	• Pump shaft bearing scored	• Replace housing and shaft. Flush system.
Hard steering or lack of assist	• Loose pump belt • Low oil level in reservoir **NOTE:** Low oil level will also result in excessive pump noise • Steering gear to column misalignment • Lower coupling flange rubbing against steering gear adjuster plug • Tires not properly inflated	• Adjust belt tension to specification • Fill to proper level. If excessively low, check all lines and joints for evidence of external leakage. Tighten loose connectors. • Align steering column • Loosen pinch bolt and assemble properly • Inflate to recommended pressure
Foaming milky power steering fluid, low fluid level and possible low pressure	• Air in the fluid, and loss of fluid due to internal pump leakage causing overflow	• Check for leaks and correct. Bleed system. Extremely cold temperatures will cause system aeriation should the oil level be low. If oil level is correct and pump still foams, remove pump from vehicle and separate reservoir from body. Check welsh plug and body for cracks. If plug is loose or body is cracked, replace body.
Low pump pressure	• Flow control valve stuck or inoperative • Pressure plate not flat against cam ring	• Remove burrs or dirt or replace. Flush system. • Correct
Momentary increase in effort when turning wheel fast to right or left	• Low oil level in pump • Pump belt slipping • High internal leakage	• Add power steering fluid as required • Tighten or replace belt • Check pump pressure. (See pressure test)
Steering wheel surges or jerks when turning with engine running especially during parking	• Low oil level • Loose pump belt • Steering linkage hitting engine oil pan at full turn • Insufficient pump pressure	• Fill as required • Adjust tension to specification • Correct clearance • Check pump pressure. (See pressure test). Replace flow control valve if defective.

Troubleshooting the Power Steering Pump (cont.)

Problem	Cause	Solution
Steering wheel surges or jerks when turning with engine running especially during parking (cont.)	• Sticking flow control valve	• Inspect for varnish or damage, replace if necessary
Excessive wheel kickback or loose steering	• Air in system	• Add oil to pump reservoir and bleed by operating steering. Check hose connectors for proper torque and adjust as required.
Low pump pressure	• Extreme wear of cam ring • Scored pressure plate, thrust plate, or rotor • Vanes not installed properly • Vanes sticking in rotor slots • Cracked or broken thrust or pressure plate	• Replace parts. Flush system. • Replace parts. Flush system. • Install properly • Freeup by removing burrs, varnish, or dirt • Replace part

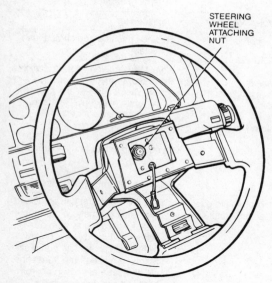

Remove/install steering wheel mounting nut

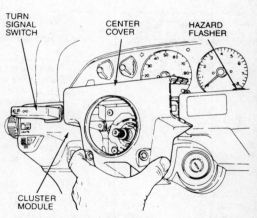

Remove/install center steering column cover

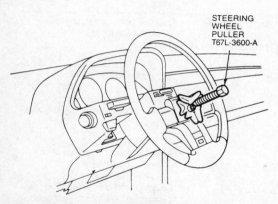

Use a puller to remove the steering wheel

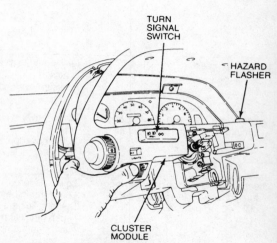

Remove/install cluster module

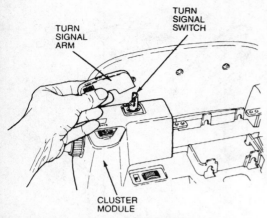

Remove/install turn signal switch lever

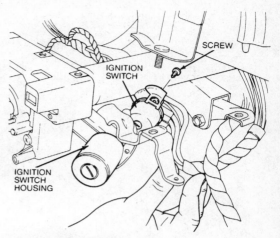

Remove/install ignition switch

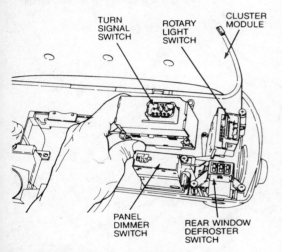

Remove/install turn signal switch

2. Remove the attaching screws securing the center steering column cover and remove the cover.

3. Remove the cluster module mounting screws. Pull the module forward and remove the electrical connectors. Remove the cluster module.

4. Remove the turn signal lever mounting screw from the arm and remove the arm.

5. Remove the switch mounting screws and remove the switch.

6. Position the turn signal switch and attach it with the mounting screws. Install the control lever.

7. Install the module. Install the center column cover. Install the steering wheel and connect the negative battery cable.

Ignition Switch
REMOVAL AND INSTALLATION

1. Disconnect the negative battery cable.
2. Remove the upper steering column

mounting bolts and allow the column to hang down.

3. Remove the steering column pivot lock assembly. (See Steering Column service). Remove the screw securing the ignition switch to the ignition switch housing.

4. Disconnect the four snap connectors located to the left of the steering column. Remove the protective loom from the ignition switch wires.

5. Note the positions of each wire in the four-terminal connector for installation position. Disconnect the two wires going to the warning buzzer (green wire and red/orange wire), by pushing the tang with a paper clip or similiar tool.

6. Connect the warning buzzer wires. Install the protective loom around the ignition switch wires. Connect the four snap connectors.

7. Install the switch to the switch housing.

8. Install the steering column pivot lock and the column mounting bolts. Connect the negative battery cable.

Steering Column
REMOVAL AND INSTALLATION

1. Disconnect the negative battery cable. Remove the steering wheel.

2. Remove the steering column cover.

3. Remove the instrument cover. Pull the instrument cover forward and disconnect the electrical connectors. Remove the ignition light bulb.

4. Loosen the cover hinge screws and cluster cover mounting screws. Remove the cover. Remove the lower panel and the lap and defroster ducts.

5. Disconnect the four electrical connectors at the turn signal assmebly.

6. Remove the lower column connector U-

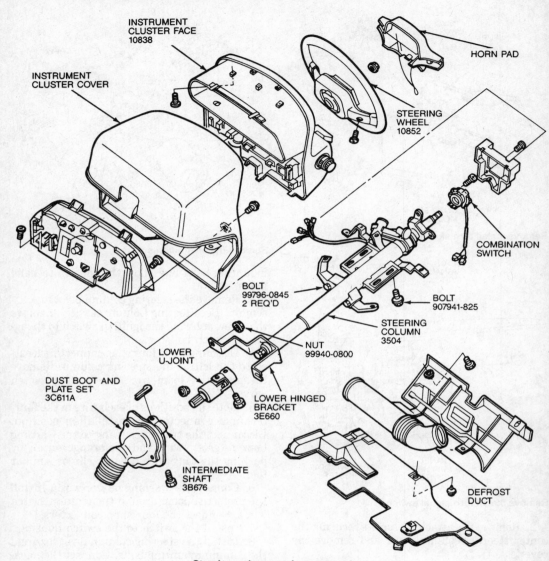

INSTRUMENT
CLUSTER FACE
10838

INSTRUMENT
CLUSTER COVER

HORN PAD

STEERING
WHEEL
10852

COMBINATION
SWITCH

BOLT
99796-0845
2 REQ'D

BOLT
907941-825

STEERING
COLUMN
3504

NUT
99940-0800

LOWER
U-JOINT

LOWER HINGED
BRACKET
3E660

DUST BOOT AND
PLATE SET
3C611A

INTERMEDIATE
SHAFT
3B676

DEFROST
DUCT

Steering column and components

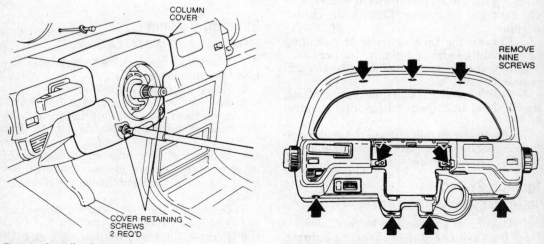

COLUMN
COVER

REMOVE
NINE
SCREWS

COVER RETAINING
SCREWS
2 REQ'D

Remove/install column cover

Remove/install instrument cover

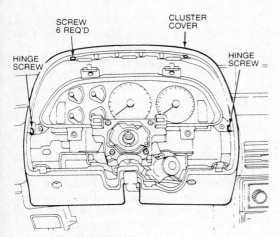

Remove/install cluster cover

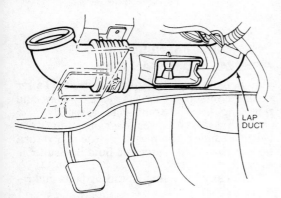

Remove/install air ducts

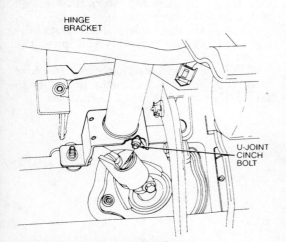

Remove/install upper cinch bolt

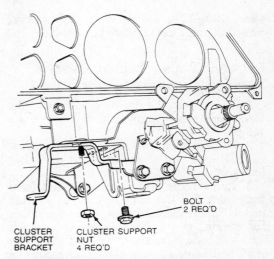

Remove/install cluster support bracket

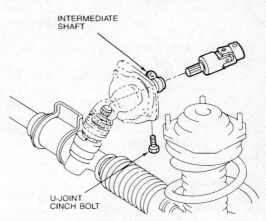

Remove/install lower cinch bolt

joint upper cinch bolt. Remove the steering column upper mounting nuts from the hinge bracket. Remove the cluster support nuts, and the two nuts and four bolts from the upper column brackets. Remove the steering shaft assembly.

7. Lift the boot from the intermediate shaft U-joint at the steering rack. Remove the lower U-joint cinch bolt. Remove the four nuts from the intermediate shaft dust cover assembly and remove the intermediate shaft and dust cover.

8. Have an assistant hold the intermediate shaft and dust cover assembly, guide the lower U-joint onto the steering rack pinion. Tighten the cinch bolt to 13–20 ft. lbs.

9. Install the dust cover mounting bolts.

10. Have an assistant hold the steering column, guide the column into the intermediate shaft. Install the hinge bracket nuts, but do not tighten. Install the four bolts to the upper column bracket. Tighten the nuts to 12–17 ft. lbs. Tighten the bolts to 12–17 ft. lbs.

11. Install the cluster nuts. Tighten them to 6.5–10 ft. lbs. Install the upper cinch bolt to 13–20 ft. lbs.

12. Connect the electrical connectors at the turn signal. Position the cluster cover and attach. Connect the electrical connectors and install the ignition bulb. Install the instrument

cover. Install the column cover and steering wheel. Connect the negative battery cable.

Rack and Pinion Steering Gear
REMOVAL AND INSTALLATION

1. Disconnect the negative battery cable. Raise and safely support the front of the vehicle.

2. Remove the front wheel assemblies. Separate the tie rod ends from the steering knuckles.

3. Remove the plastic splash shield from both sides. Put the cinch bolt at the steering rack U-joint into position for removal and lock the steering wheel. Pull the steering column dust boot back, place matchmarks on the pinion shaft and lower steering column intermediate shaft universal joint. Remove the clamp bolt.

4. Disconnect the two hydraulic lines from the steering gear assembly. Position the lines out of the way.

5. Remove the steering gear mounting bolts, there are six.

6. Lower the steering gear until it rests on the crossmember.

7. Carefully slide the steering gear toward the right side of the vehicle until the left tie rod clears the left lower control arm. Slide the gear assembly to the left and remove it from the vehicle.

8. Place the steering gear into position. Have an assistant guide the pinion shaft into the intermediate shaft after aligning the matchmarks. Install the mounting bolts. Tighten to 27–40 ft. lbs.

9. Install the clamp bolt and tighten to 13–20 ft. lbs.

10. Install the hydraulic lines. Connect the tie rod ends. Install the splash shields and the front wheel assemblies. Lower the vehicle.

11. Connect the negative battery cable. Check the power steering fluid level. Add fluid as required.

12. Perform start up sequence as follows: Disconnect the coil wire. Crank the engine with the starter. Add power steering fluid until the level is constant. When cranking the engine, move the steering wheel from side to side. The wheels must be on the ground when turning the steering wheel from lock to lock. Start the engine after connecting the coil wire. Rotate the steering wheel from lock to lock several times. Turn off the engine and check the power steering fluid level. Add fluid as necessary. Disconnect the negative battery cable. Depress the brake pedal for at least five seconds to erase failure codes. Connect the negative battery cable.

Power Steering Pump
REMOVAL AND INSTALLATION

1. Remove the right front splash shield after raising and supporting the vehicle safely, and removing the right front wheel assembly.

2. Remove the power steering pump drive belt. Disconnect the pressure hose and return hose at the pump. Catch the fluid in a suitable container.

3. Remove the pump mounting bolts and remove the pump.

4. Install the pump and mounting bolts. Connect the pressure and return lines. Install and tension the drive belt.

5. Install the right splash shield. Install the right front wheel assembly and lower the vehicle.

6. Fill the power steering pump reservoir with fluid. Perform the startup procedure as described in Step 12 of the Steering Gear.

BRAKE SYSTEM

Operation

The hydraulic system is composed of the master cylinder, the brake lines, the brake pressure distributing valve, and the wheel cylinders (drum brakes) and/or calipers (disc brakes).

The master cylinder/reservoir serves as a brake fluid reservoir and as a hydraulic pump. Brake fluid is stored in the two sections of the master cylinder. The front half of the master cylinder holds the fluid that is used to activate the rear brakes. The rear half of the master cylinder holds the fluid that activates the front brakes. This tandem master cylinder is required by federal law as a safety device. Since the front hydraulic system is independent of the rear system, a fluid leak in one system would only cause that system to fail, allowing the older system to stop the car.

When the brake pedal is depressed, it moves a piston mounted in the bottom of the master cylinder. The movement of this piston creates hydraulic pressure in the master cylinder. This pressure is carried to the wheel cylinders or calipers by the brake lines.

On the way to the wheels, the brake fluid passes through the combination (pressure differential) valve. The valve is connected between the front and rear brake lines. Each of the brake lines is connected to one of the upright sides of the valve. The brake fluid passes through each of the upright sides inside the valve and leaves at the bottom of the sides where the outgoing brake lines pick up the fluid and carry it on to the wheels. A piston is mounted in the crossbar section. It is held centered in the valve by the brake fluid in each of the upright sides. If a leak should develop in either the front or rear brake system, fluid pressure in the portion of the pressure differential valve which corresponds to that system would drop. This

would cause the piston in the crossbar of the valve to move toward that section of the valve, since the normal fluid pressure in the other side of the valve would now be dominant.

When the hydraulic pressure reaches the wheels, after the pedal has been depressed, it enters the wheel cylinders or calipers. Here it comes into contact with a piston or pistons. The hydraulic pressure causes the piston(s) to move, which moves the brake shoes or pads (disc brakes), causing them to come into contact with the drums or rotors (disc brakes). Friction between the brake shoes and the drums causes the car to slow down. There is a relationship between the amount of pressure that is applied to the brake pedal and the amount of force which moves the brake shoes against the drums. Therefore, the harder the brake pedal is depressed, the quicker the car should stop.

Since a hydraulic system operates on fluids, air is a natural enemy. Air in the system retards the passage of hydraulic pressure from the master cylinder to the wheels. Anytime a hydraulic component below the master cylinder is opened or removed, the system must be bled (of air) to ensure proper operation.

The wheel cylinders used with drum brakes are composed of a cylinder with a polished inside bore, which is mounted on the brake shoe backing plate, two boots, two pistons, two cups, a spring, and a bleeder screw. When hydraulic pressure enters the wheel cylinder, it contacts the two cylinder cups. The cups seal the cylinder and prevent fluid from leaking out. The hydraulic pressure forces the cups outward. The cups in turn force the pistons outward. The pistons contact the brake shoes and the hydraulic pressure in the wheel cylinders overcomes the pressure of the brake springs, causing the shoes to contact the brake drum. When the brake pedal is released, the brake shoe return springs pull the brake shoes away from the drum. This

Troubleshooting the Brake System

Problem	Cause	Solution
Low brake pedal (excessive pedal travel required for braking action.)	• Excessive clearance between rear linings and drums caused by inoperative automatic adjusters	• Make 10 to 15 alternate forward and reverse brake stops to adjust brakes. If brake pedal does not come up, repair or replace adjuster parts as necessary.
	• Worn rear brakelining	• Inspect and replace lining if worn beyond minimum thickness specification
	• Bent, distorted brakeshoes, front or rear	• Replace brakeshoes in axle sets
	• Air in hydraulic system	• Remove air from system. Refer to Brake Bleeding.
Low brake pedal (pedal may go to floor with steady pressure applied.)	• Fluid leak in hydraulic system	• Fill master cylinder to fill line; have helper apply brakes and check calipers, wheel cylinders, differential valve tubes, hoses and fittings for leaks. Repair or replace as necessary.
	• Air in hydraulic system	• Remove air from system. Refer to Brake Bleeding.
	• Incorrect or non-recommended brake fluid (fluid evaporates at below normal temp).	• Flush hydraulic system with clean brake fluid. Refill with correct-type fluid.
	• Master cylinder piston seals worn, or master cylinder bore is scored, worn or corroded	• Repair or replace master cylinder
Low brake pedal (pedal goes to floor on first application—o.k. on subsequent applications.)	• Disc brake pads sticking on abutment surfaces of anchor plate. Caused by a build-up of dirt, rust, or corrosion on abutment surfaces	• Clean abutment surfaces
Fading brake pedal (pedal height decreases with steady pressure applied.)	• Fluid leak in hydraulic system	• Fill master cylinder reservoirs to fill mark, have helper apply brakes, check calipers, wheel cylinders, differential valve, tubes, hoses, and fittings for fluid leaks. Repair or replace parts as necessary.
	• Master cylinder piston seals worn, or master cylinder bore is scored, worn or corroded	• Repair or replace master cylinder
Decreasing brake pedal travel (pedal travel required for braking action decreases and may be accompanied by a hard pedal.)	• Caliper or wheel cylinder pistons sticking or seized	• Repair or replace the calipers, or wheel cylinders
	• Master cylinder compensator ports blocked (preventing fluid return to reservoirs) or pistons sticking or seized in master cylinder bore	• Repair or replace the master cylinder
	• Power brake unit binding internally	• Test unit according to the following procedure: (a) Shift transmission into neutral and start engine (b) Increase engine speed to 1500 rpm, close throttle and fully depress brake pedal (c) Slow release brake pedal and stop engine (d) Have helper remove vacuum check valve and hose from power unit. Observe for backward movement of brake pedal. (e) If the pedal moves backward, the power unit has an internal bind—replace power unit

Troubleshooting the Brake System (cont.)

Problem	Cause	Solution
Spongy brake pedal (pedal has abnormally soft, springy, spongy feel when depressed.)	• Air in hydraulic system • Brakeshoes bent or distorted • Brakelining not yet seated with drums and rotors • Rear drum brakes not properly adjusted	• Remove air from system. Refer to Brake Bleeding. • Replace brakeshoes • Burnish brakes • Adjust brakes
Hard brake pedal (excessive pedal pressure required to stop vehicle. May be accompanied by brake fade.)	• Loose or leaking power brake unit vacuum hose • Incorrect or poor quality brakelining • Bent, broken, distorted brakeshoes • Calipers binding or dragging on mounting pins. Rear brakeshoes dragging on support plate.	• Tighten connections or replace leaking hose • Replace with lining in axle sets • Replace brakeshoes • Replace mounting pins and bushings. Clean rust or burrs from rear brake support plate ledges and lubricate ledges with molydisulfide grease. **NOTE:** If ledges are deeply grooved or scored, do not attempt to sand or grind them smooth—replace support plate.

	• Caliper, wheel cylinder, or master cylinder pistons sticking or seized
	• Power brake unit vacuum check valve malfunction
		• Repair or replace parts as necessary
		
		• Test valve according to the following procedure:
		  (a) Start engine, increase engine speed to 1500 rpm, close throttle and immediately stop engine
		  (b) Wait at least 90 seconds then depress brake pedal
		  (c) If brakes are not vacuum assisted for 2 or more applications, check valve is faulty

	• Power brake unit has internal bind	• Test unit according to the following procedure:
		  (a) With engine stopped, apply brakes several times to exhaust all vacuum in system
		  (b) Shift transmission into neutral, depress brake pedal and start engine
		  (c) If pedal height decreases with foot pressure and less pressure is required to hold pedal in applied position, power unit vacuum system is operating normally. Test power unit. If power unit exhibits a bind condition, replace the power unit.

	• Master cylinder compensator ports (at bottom of reservoirs) blocked by dirt, scale, rust, or have small burrs (blocked ports prevent fluid return to reservoirs). • Brake hoses, tubes, fittings clogged or restricted • Brake fluid contaminated with improper fluids (motor oil, transmission fluid, causing rubber components to swell and stick in bores • Low engine vacuum	• Repair or replace master cylinder **CAUTION:** Do not attempt to clean blocked ports with wire, pencils, or similar implements. Use compressed air only. • Use compressed air to check or unclog parts. Replace any damaged parts. • Replace all rubber components, combination valve and hoses. Flush entire brake system with DOT 3 brake fluid or equivalent. • Adjust or repair engine

Troubleshooting the Brake System (cont.)

Problem	Cause	Solution
Grabbing brakes (severe reaction to brake pedal pressure.)	• Brakelining(s) contaminated by grease or brake fluid	• Determine and correct cause of contamination and replace brakeshoes in axle sets
	• Parking brake cables incorrectly adjusted or seized	• Adjust cables. Replace seized cables.
	• Incorrect brakelining or lining loose on brakeshoes	• Replace brakeshoes in axle sets
	• Caliper anchor plate bolts loose	• Tighten bolts
	• Rear brakeshoes binding on support plate ledges	• Clean and lubricate ledges. Replace support plate(s) if ledges are deeply grooved. Do not attempt to smooth ledges by grinding.
	• Incorrect or missing power brake reaction disc	• Install correct disc
	• Rear brake support plates loose	• Tighten mounting bolts
Dragging brakes (slow or incomplete release of brakes)	• Brake pedal binding at pivot	• Loosen and lubricate
	• Power brake unit has internal bind	• Inspect for internal bind. Replace unit if internal bind exists.
	• Parking brake cables incorrrectly adjusted or seized	• Adjust cables. Replace seized cables.
	• Rear brakeshoe return springs weak or broken	• Replace return springs. Replace brakeshoe if necessary in axle sets.
	• Automatic adjusters malfunctioning	• Repair or replace adjuster parts as required
	• Caliper, wheel cylinder or master cylinder pistons sticking or seized	• Repair or replace parts as necessary
	• Master cylinder compensating ports blocked (fluid does not return to reservoirs).	• Use compressed air to clear ports. Do not use wire, pencils, or similar objects to open blocked ports.
Vehicle moves to one side when brakes are applied	• Incorrect front tire pressure	• Inflate to recommended cold (reduced load) inflation pressure
	• Worn or damaged wheel bearings	• Replace worn or damaged bearings
	• Brakelining on one side contaminated	• Determine and correct cause of contamination and replace brakelining in axle sets
	• Brakeshoes on one side bent, distorted, or lining loose on shoe	• Replace brakeshoes in axle sets
	• Support plate bent or loose on one side	• Tighten or replace support plate
	• Brakelining not yet seated with drums or rotors	• Burnish brakelining
	• Caliper anchor plate loose on one side	• Tighten anchor plate bolts
	• Caliper piston sticking or seized	• Repair or replace caliper
	• Brakelinings water soaked	• Drive vehicle with brakes lightly applied to dry linings
	• Loose suspension component attaching or mounting bolts	• Tighten suspension bolts. Replace worn suspension components.
	• Brake combination valve failure	• Replace combination valve
Chatter or shudder when brakes are applied (pedal pulsation and roughness may also occur.)	• Brakeshoes distorted, bent, contaminated, or worn	• Replace brakeshoes in axle sets
	• Caliper anchor plate or support plate loose	• Tighten mounting bolts
	• Excessive thickness variation of rotor(s)	• Refinish or replace rotors in axle sets
Noisy brakes (squealing, clicking, scraping sound when brakes are applied.)	• Bent, broken, distorted brakeshoes	• Replace brakeshoes in axle sets
	• Excessive rust on outer edge of rotor braking surface	• Remove rust

Troubleshooting the Brake System (cont.)

Problem	Cause	Solution
Noisy brakes (squealing, clicking, scraping sound when brakes are applied.) (cont.)	• Brakelining worn out—shoes contacting drum of rotor	• Replace brakeshoes and lining in axle sets. Refinish or replace drums or rotors.
	• Broken or loose holddown or return springs	• Replace parts as necessary
	• Rough or dry drum brake support plate ledges	• Lubricate support plate ledges
	• Cracked, grooved, or scored rotor(s) or drum(s)	• Replace rotor(s) or drum(s). Replace brakeshoes and lining in axle sets if necessary.
	• Incorrect brakelining and/or shoes (front or rear).	• Install specified shoe and lining assemblies
Pulsating brake pedal	• Out of round drums or excessive lateral runout in disc brake rotor(s)	• Refinish or replace drums, re-index rotors or replace

forces the pistons back toward the center of the wheel cylinder. Wheel cylinders can fail in two ways; they can leak or lock up. Leaking wheel cylinders are caused either by defective cups or irregularities in the wheel cylinder bore. Frozen wheel cylinders are caused by foreign matter getting into the cylinders and preventing the pistons from sliding freely.

The calipers used with the disc brakes contain a piston, piston seal, piston dust boot, and bleeder screw. When hydraulic pressure enters the caliper, the piston is forced outward causing the disc brake pad to come into contact with the rotor. When the brakes are applied, the piston seal, mounted on the caliper housing, becomes slightly distorted in the direction of the rotor. When the brakes are released, the piston seal moves back to its normal position and, at the same time, pulls the piston back away from the brake pad. This allows the brake pads to move away from the rotor. Calipers can fail in three ways, two of these being caused by defective piston seals. When a piston seal becomes worn, it can allow brake fluid to leak out to contaminate the pad and rotor. If a piston seal becomes weak, it can fail to pull the piston away from the brake shoe when the brakes are released, allowing the brake pad to drag on the rotor when the car is being driven. If foreign material enters the caliper housing, it can prevent the piston from sliding freely, causing the brakes to stick on the rotor.

Clean, high-quality brake fluid, meeting DOT 3 specs, is essential to the proper operation of the brake system. Always buy the highest quality brake fluid available. If the brake fluid should become contaminated, it should be drained and flushed, and the master cylinder filled with new fluid. Never reuse brake fluid. Any brake fluid that is removed from the brake system should be discarded.

Since the hydraulic system is sealed, there must be a leak somewhere in the system if the master cylinder is repeatedly low on fluid.

The hydraulic brake system, on the Probe is a diagonally split system with a dual master cylinder. The left front and right rear are one one brake circuit while the right front and left rear are on another brake circuit.

A dual proportioning valve regulates hydraulic pressure in the brake circuit. When the brake pedal is applied, full brake circuit pressure passes through the proportioning valve to the rear brake circuit until the valves's split point is reached. Above the split point, the proportioning valve begins to reduce hydraulic pressure to the rear brake circuit, creating a balanced braking condition between the front and rear wheels while maintaining balanced hydraulic pressure at each rear wheel. Double walled steel tubing extends from the master cylinder pressure fitting to the rear cylinders and front calipers. Flexible hoses make the final connections between the body mounted brake tubes and the suspension mounted brake assemblies.

Adjustments
PEDAL HEIGHT AND FREE-PLAY

1. Check the distance from the center of the pedal pad to the floor. The distance should be 222–227mm.

2. Adjust the pedal height by adjusting the stoplight switch position. Loosen the switch locknut and turn the switch in the required direction for the adjustment necessary. Tighten the locknut when the pedal height is correct.

3. To check pedal freelay, pump the brakes several times to relieve booster pressure. Gently press down the brake pedal by hand. Freeplay should be 4–7mm.

4. Adjust the freeplay by loosening the lock-

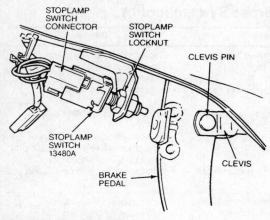

Adjust the brake pedal height

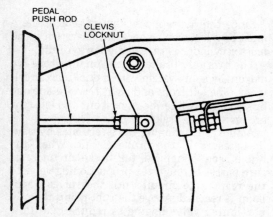

Adjust the brake pedal freeplay

nut on the brake pedal pushrod and turning the rod in the necessary direction. When the correct freeplay is reached, tighten the pushrod locknut.

Stoplight Switch

REMOVAL AND INSTALLATION

1. Disconnect the wiring connector to the switch.
2. Loosen and remove the locknut. Remove the switch.
3. Place the switch in the mounting bracket. Perform a pedal height adjustment. Connect the wiring connector to the stoplight switch.

Master Cylinder

REMOVAL AND INSTALLATION

Except ABS

1. Disconnect the fluid level sensor wiring. Use a tubing flare wrench, remove and plug the lines from the master cylinder. Plug the master cylinder tubing ports also.

2. Remove the master cylinder mounting nuts and the master cylinder assembly.
3. Service as required. Place the master cylinder in position and secure the mounting nuts. If the master cylinder is dry, bench bleed the cylinder before installation.
4. Connect the brake lines to the master cylinder. Fill the reservoir with new, clean brake fluid and bleed the system.

OVERHAUL

This is a tedious, time-consuming job. You can save yourself a lot of trouble by buying a rebuilt master cylinder from your dealer or a parts supply house. The small difference in cost between a rebuilding kit and a rebuilt part usually makes it more economical, in terms of time and work, to buy the rebuilt part.

1. Remove the master cylinder from the car.
2. Remove the reservoir cap and drain the brake fluid. Discard this fluid. Remove the reservoir mounting screw, gently pry upward on the reservoir to remove it from the master cylinder.
3. Mount the master upside down in a soft jawed vise.
4. Push in on the primary piston and remove the stopper screw and washer from the bottom of the master cylinder. Remove the front snapring and then remove the primary and secondary piston assemblies from the master cylinder bore.
5. Discard all used rubber parts and gaskets. These parts should be replaced with the new components included in the rebuilding kit.
6. Clean all the parts in clean brake fluid. Do not use mineral oil or alcohol for cleaning.
7. Check the cylinder bore and piston for wear, scoring, corrosion, or any other damage. If damaged, replace the master cylinder.
8. Check the piston-to-cylinder bore clearance; it should measure 0.15mm. If greater clearance exists, replace the piston, the cylinder, or both.
9. Assemble the master cylinder. Soak all of the components in clean brake fluid before assembling them. Install the reservoir and retaining screw.
10. Clamp the master cylinder in a vise by one of its flanges. Fill the reservoirs with fresh fluid, and pump the piston with a screwdriver until fluid squirts from the outlet ports. Install the master cylinder and bleed the system.

Power Brake Booster

Power brakes operate just as standard brake systems except in the actuation of the master cylinder pistons. A vacuum diaphragm is located on the front of the master cylinder and as-

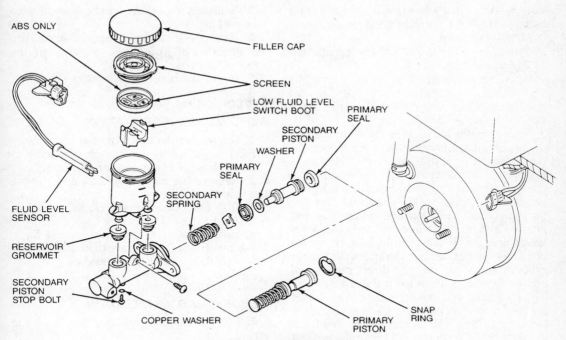

ABS ONLY

FILLER CAP

SCREEN

LOW FLUID LEVEL
SWITCH BOOT

PRIMARY
SEAL

SECONDARY
PISTON

WASHER

PRIMARY
SEAL

SECONDARY
SPRING

FLUID LEVEL
SENSOR

RESERVOIR
GROMMET

SECONDARY
PISTON
STOP BOLT

COPPER WASHER

PRIMARY
PISTON

SNAP
RING

Brake master cylinder assembly

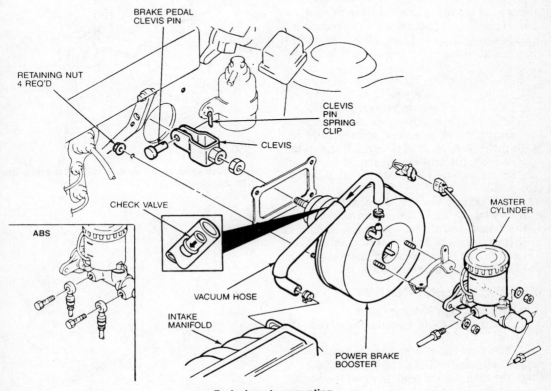

BRAKE PEDAL
CLEVIS PIN

RETAINING NUT
4 REQ'D

CLEVIS
PIN
SPRING
CLIP

CLEVIS

CHECK VALVE

MASTER
CYLINDER

ABS

VACUUM HOSE

INTAKE
MANIFOLD

POWER BRAKE
BOOSTER

Brake booster mounting

sists the driver in applying the brakes, reducing both the effort and travel he must put into moving the brake pedal.

The vacuum diaphragm housing is connected to the intake manifold by a vacuum hose. A check valve is placed at the point where the hose enters the diaphragm housing, so that during periods of low manifold vacuum brake assist vacuum will not be lost.

Depressing the brake pedal closes off the vacuum source and allows atmospheric pressure to enter on one side of the diaphragm. This causes the master cylinder pistons to move and apply the brakes. When the brake pedal is released, vacuum is applied to both sides of the diaphragm, and return springs return the diaphragm and master cylinder pistons to the released position. If the vacuum fails, the brake pedal rod will butt against the end of the master cylinder actuating rod, and direct mechanical application will occur as the pedal is depressed. The hydraulic and mechanical problems that apply to conventional brake systems also apply to power brakes, and should be checked for if the tests below do not reveal the problem. Test for a system vacuum leak as described below:

1. Operate the engine at idle with the transmission in Neutral without touching the brake pedal for at least one minute.

2. Turn off the engine, and wait one minute.

3. Test for the presence of assist vacuum by depressing the brake pedal and releasing it several times. Light application will produce less and less pedal travel, if vacuum was present. If there is no vacuum, air is leaking into the system somewhere.

4. Test for system operation as follows:

5. Pump the brake pedal (with engine off) until the supply vacuum is entirely gone.

6. Put a light, steady pressure on the pedal.

7. Start the engine, and operate it at idle with the transmission in Neutral. If the system is operating, the brake pedal should fall toward the floor if constant pressure is maintained on the pedal.

NOTE: *Power brake systems may be tested for hydraulic leaks just as ordinary systems are tested, except that the engine should be idling with the transmission in Neutral (manual) or Park (automatic) with the wheels blocked throughout the test.*

REMOVAL AND INSTALLATION

1. Remove the master cylinder.

2. Disconnect the vacuum line from the booster.

3. Remove the pin connecting the power brake operating rod and the brake pedal.

4. From under the dash, remove the booster mounting nuts. Remove the booster.

5. Replace the packing on the firewall with new packing.

6. If the check valve was removed, make sure the direction of installation marking on the valve is followed.

7. Install the booster and master cylinder.

Proportioning Valve

REMOVAL AND INSTALLATION

1. Disconnect the brake lines at the valve.
NOTE: *Use a flare nut wrench, if possible, to avoid damage to the lines and fittings.*

2. Remove the mounting bolts and remove the valve.
NOTE: *Do not disassemble the valve, replace with a new one if necessary.*

3. Install the valve and connect the lines. Make sure the brake lines are tight. Fill the system with fluid and bleed the brakes.

Caliper Hoses

REMOVAL AND INSTALLATION

1. Remove the hose retaining clip from the strut.

2. Remove the brake line fitting from the hose at the junction, using appropriate flare

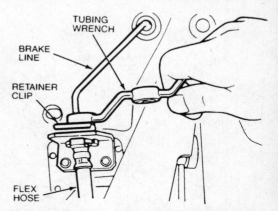

Use a flare wrench and remove/install the brake line to brake hose fitting

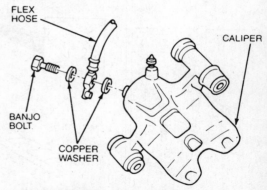

Brake hose connection at the caliper

wrenches. Remove the mounting clip from the bracket.

3. Remove the banjo bolt/fitting from the caliper end of the brake hose. Remove the fitting, hose and two copper sealing washers.

4. Mount the caliper end of the hose with a washer on each side of the hose connection. Install and tighten the banjo bolt/fitting.

5. Connect the brake hose and steel line. Tighten the fitting with a pair of flare wrenches. Do not kink the hose. Secure the fitting connection with the mounting clip. Secure the hose to the strut bracket. Bleed the system.

System Bleeding

The brakes should be bled whenever a brake line, caliper, wheel cylinder, or master cylinder has been removed or when the brake pedal is low or soft. The bleeding sequence is, right rear wheel, left front wheel, left rear wheel, and right front wheel.

1. Check the master cylinder fluid level. If necessary, add fluid to bring the level up.

2. Remove the bleeder cap at the wheel cylinder or caliper. Connect a rubber hose to the bleeder and immerse the other end in a glass container half filled with brake fluid.

3. Have an assistant depress the brake pedal to the floor, and then pause until the fluid flow stops and the bleeder nipple is closed.

4. Allow the pedal to return and repeat the procedure until a steady, bubble-free flow is seen.

5. Tighten the bleeder valve and replace the cap. Move on to the next wheel in sequence.

NOTE: *Frequently check the master cylinder level during this procedure. If the reservoir goes dry, air will enter the system and it will have to be rebled.*

FRONT DISC BRAKES

CAUTION: *Brake pads contain asbestos fibers. Asbestos has been determined to be a cancer-causing agent. Never clean brake surfaces with compressed air! Avoid inhaling any dust from any brake surface! When cleaning brake surfaces, use a commercially available cleaning fluid.*

Front Disc Brake Pads
INSPECTION

The brake pad thickness can usually be checked by removing the front (or rear, models equipped) wheel, and looking a cutout at the top of the brake caliper. Replace the pads if uneven wear (inner and outer pads) is determined. Always replace the brake pads as a set (both wheels).

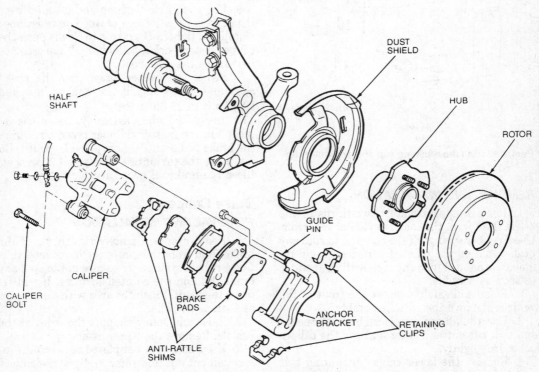

Front disc brake components

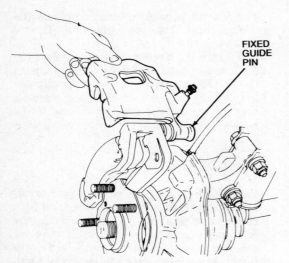

Pivot the caliper assembly on the fixed guide pin

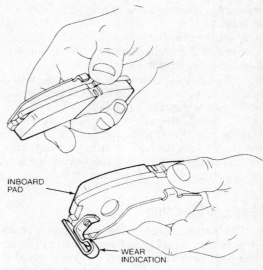

Clip to pad installation

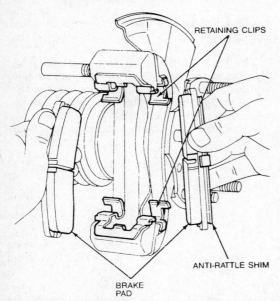

Remove/install the retaining clip and anti-rattle clip

REMOVAL AND INSTALLATION

1. Remove approximately two-thirds of the brake fluid from the master cylinder reservoir. Use a rubber syringe. Take care not to spill any brake fluid on the painted surfaces. It will remove the paint. Flush the area with clear water as soon as possible.

2. Raise and safely support the front of the vehicle. Remove the wheel assembly.

3. Use a small pry bar placed between the inspection cut out and rotor and pry the caliper outboard slightly.

4. Remove the lower caliper mounting bolt and swing the caliper upward off of the rotor,

pivoting the caliper on the upper fixed guide pin.

5. Identify the anti-rattle clips for installation position. Remove the brake pads from the caliper anchor and remove the retaining clips.

6. Install the retaining clips on the brake pads.

7. Install the brake pads in the caliper anchor. The pad equipped with the wear indicator is the outboard pad.

8. Use a suitable C-clamp and install it over the caliper. Place a block of wood on the caliper piston and tighten the clamp to slowly push the caliper piston back into its bore. Take care not to damage the dust boot.

9. Swing the caliper down over the brake pads and rotor. Install the anchor bolt and tighten it to 23-30 ft. lbs.

10. Install the wheel assembly. Lower the vehicle. Fill the master cylinder reservoir. Pump the brake pedal until a firm pedal is gained. Do not move the car until a firm pedal is present. Bleed the brakes if necessary.

Brake Caliper
REMOVAL AND INSTALLATION

1. Remove approximately two-thirds of the brake fluid from the master cylinder reservoir. Use a rubber syringe. Take care not to spill any brake fluid on the painted surfaces. It will remove the paint. Flush the area with clear water as soon as possible.

2. Raise and safely support the front of the vehicle. Remove the wheel assembly.

3. Use a small pry bar placed between the inspection cut out and rotor and pry the caliper outboard slightly.

4. Remove the lower caliper mounting bolt and swing the caliper upward off of the rotor, pivoting the caliper on the upper fixed guide pin.

5. Identify the anti-rattle clips for installation position. Remove the brake pads from the caliper anchor and remove the retaining clips.

6. Disconnect the banjo bolt/fitting from the caliper.

7. Slide the caliper off of the fixed guide pin.

8. Service the caliper as required.

9. Install the caliper on the fixed guide pin and install it over the anchor, pads and rotor. Make sure the caliper piston is fully seated in the caliper bore.

10. Install and tighten the anchor bolt to 23-30 ft. lbs.

11. Connect the brake line. Fill the system with fluid and bleed the brakes.

12. Install the wheel assembly. Lower the vehicle. Do not move the vehicle until a firm brake pedal is present.

OVERHAUL

1. Disconnect the brake hose from the caliper. Open the bleeder screw and allow the brake fluid to drain form the caliper through the brake hose connector hole. Remove the caliper assembly from the car.

2. Remove the caliper guide bushing and dust boots.

3. Remove the snapring and discard the piston dust boot.

4. Apply low pressure compressed air to the brake line hose in the caliper, and force the piston out of its bore. Keep your fingers out of the way of the piston, as it often will pop out with considerable force.

5. Remove the seal from the piston, being careful to avoid scratching the piston surface.

6. Clean all parts in alcohol. Discard all rubber parts.

7. Replace the piston if if appears worn, damaged or pitted. Replace all rubber parts.

8. Coat the piston and bore with clean brake fluid.

9. Coat the piston seal with rubber grease. Install it on the piston.

10. Insert the piston into the bore, being careful to avoid twisting the seal.

11. Apply silicone grease to the new dust boot and install it and the snapring.

12. Install the caliper and brake hose. Coat the pin bolt threads with clean brake fluid and tighten the anchor bolt. Bleed the system.

Disc Rotor

REMOVAL AND INSTALLATION

1. Remove the wheel assembly.

2. Remove the caliper and anchor bracket, suspend the assembly out of the way with wire.

3. Remove the rotor retaining screw and the rotor from the drive hub.

4. Inspect the rotor. Resurface or replace as required. If the wheel bearing needs to be serviced, refer to Chapter 7.

5. Install the rotor on the drive hub and install the retaining screw.

6. Install the caliper and anchor assembly. Install the wheel assembly.

REAR DISC BRAKES

CAUTION: *Brake pads contain asbestos fibers. Asbestos has been determined to be a cancer-causing agent. Never clean brake surfaces with compressed air! Avoid inhaling*

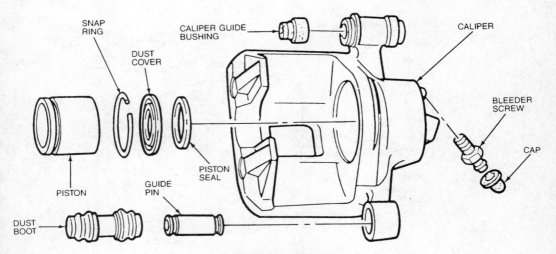

Front caliper components

any dust from any brake surface! When clean-ing brake surfaces, use a commercially avail-able cleaning fluid.

Rear Brake Pads

INSPECTION

The brake pad thickness can usually be checked by removing the front (or rear, models equipped) wheel, and looking a cutout at the top of the brake caliper. Replace the pads if uneven wear (inner and outer pads) is determined. Al-ways replace the brake pads as a set (both wheels).

REMOVAL AND INSTALLATION

1. Remove approximately two-thirds of the brake fluid from the master cylinder. Use a rub-ber syringe to remove the fluid.
2. Raise and safely support the rear of the ve-hicle. Remove the wheel assembly.
3. Loosen the parking brake cable housing adjusting nut. Remove the cable housing from the bracket and parking brake lever.
4. Pry the caliper slightly outboard. Remove the caliper retaining bolt. Pivot the caliper away from the adapter and brake pads.
5. Remove the caliper and support it out of the way.
6. Remove the V-spring from the disc pads. Remove the disc pads, anti-rattle shims and re-taining clips.
7. Install the pad retaining clips. Position the anti-rattle shims on the disc pads. Position the pads into the caliper anchor bracket. Install the V-spring.
8. Rotate the caliper piston clockwise with special tool T75P-2588B, or equivalent, to low-er the piston into the caliper bore.

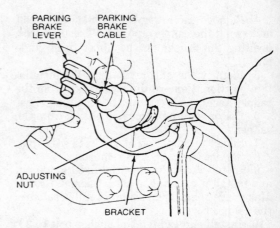

Loosen/tighten the parking brake cable adjusting nut

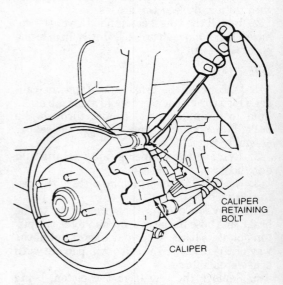

Remove/install the caliper retaining bolt

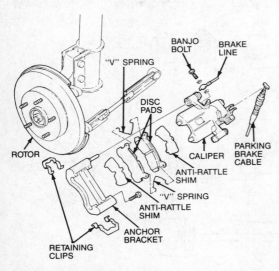

Rear disc brake components

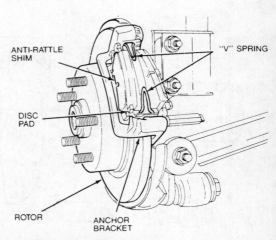

Remove/install shim and clip

9. Lubricate the guide pin bushings with high temperature grease. Install the caliper on the guide pin and install it over the pads, adapter and rotor. Secure the anchor bolt to 12-17 ft. lbs.

10. Bleed the brakes after filling the master cylinder. Install the wheel assembly. Lower the vehicle. Do not move the vehicle until a firm brake pedal is present.

Brake Caliper

REMOVAL AND INSTALLATION

1. Remove approximately two-thirds of the brake fluid from the master cylinder. Use a rubber syringe to remove the fluid.

2. Raise and safely support the rear of the vehicle. Remove the wheel assembly.

3. Loosen the parking brake cable housing adjusting nut. Remove the cable housing from the bracket and parking brake lever.

4. Pry the caliper slightly outboard. Remove the caliper retaining bolt. Pivot the caliper away from the adapter and brake pads.

5. Remove the brake hose and caliper from the vehicle.

6. Service the caliper as required and install the caliper.

7. Remove the V-spring from the disc pads. Remove the disc pads, anti-rattle shims and retaining clips.

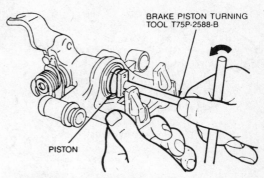

Remove/install the brake caliper piston

8. Install the pad retaining clips. Position the anti-rattle shims on the disc pads. Position the pads into the caliper anchor bracket. Install the V-spring.

9. Rotate the caliper piston clockwise with special tool T75P-2588B, or equivalent, to lower the piston into the caliper bore.

10. Lubricate the guide pin bushings with high temperature grease. Install the caliper on the guide pin and install it over the pads, adapter and rotor. Secure the anchor bolt to 12-17 ft. lbs.

11. Bleed the brakes after filling the master cylinder. Install the wheel assembly. Lower the vehicle. Do not move the vehicle until a firm brake pedal is present.

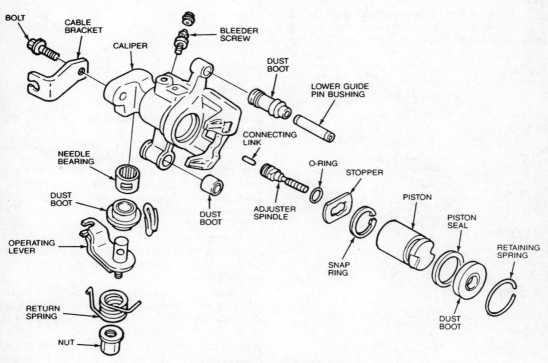

Rear brake caliper components

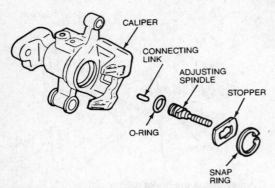

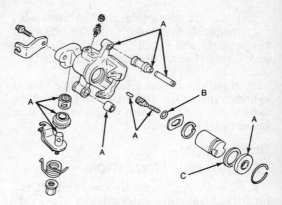

Remove/install connecting link, adjusting spindle, stopper and snapring

A—ORANGE COLORED GREASE
B—WHITE COLORED GREASE
C—RED COLORED GREASE

NOTE: APPLY THE GREASE SUPPLIED IN THE SEAL KIT TO THE POINTS SHOWN IN THE FIGURE.

Lubricate the components

OVERHAUL

1. Disconnect the brake hose from the caliper. Open the bleeder screw and allow the brake fluid to drain form the caliper through the brake hose connector hole. Remove the rear brake caliper.

2. Remove the caliper guide bushing and dust boots. Remove the piston dust cover retainer snapring. Use special tool T75P-2588B and turn the caliper piston counterclockwise to remove the piston from the adjuster spindle and caliper bore.

3. Remove the piston seal from the caliper piston. Take care not to scratch the piston surface.

4. Remove the stopper retaining snapring, the adjusting spindle, stopper and connecting link. Separate the adjuster spindle and the stop-

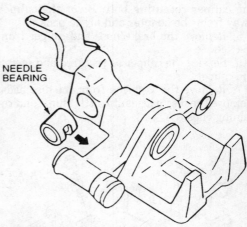

Align the needle bearing

per. Remove the O-ring from the adjuster spindle.

5. Remove the parking brake return spring, operating lever nut, and lockwasher.

6. Mark the relationship between the operating lever and shaft. Remove the operating lever from the shaft. Remove the seal, shaft and needle bearing from the caliper.

7. Clean all components. Lubricate the needle bearings with the lubricant provided in the rebuilding kit. Align the opening in the bearing with the bore in the caliper housing. Install the needle bearings.

8. Install the operating shaft. operating lever (aligning the matchmarks), lockwasher nut. Install the connecting link into the operating shaft.

9. Install the O-ring onto the adjuster spindle. Position the stopper onto the adjuster spindle so that the pins align with the caliper hous-

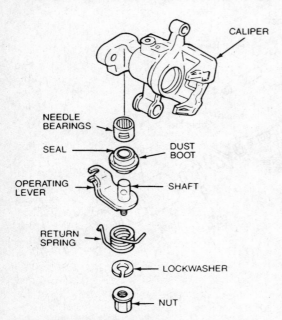

Remove/install the components

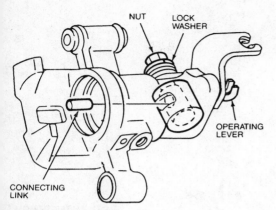

Component installation

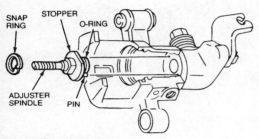

Component installation

ing. Install the adjuster spindle and the stopper into the caliper. Install the stopper snapring. Make sure the operating lever and adjuster spindle move freely. Install the brake return spring.

10. Install the square cut piston seal into the groove on the piston. Lubricate the seal and piston. Rotate the piston clockwise onto the adjusting spindle, using the special tool. Align the grooves in the piston with the opening in the caliper.

11. Install the dust boot and snapring.

12. Install the upper guide pin dust boot and lower guide pin bushing. Install the guide pin bushings. Install the caliper. Fill the master cylinder. Bleed the brake. Do not move the vehicle until a firm brake pedal is present.

Rotor
REMOVAL AND INSTALLATION

1. Remove the wheel assembly. Remove the two anchor mounting bolts and remove the caliper and anchor assembly. Support the caliper assembly out of the way.

2. Unstake the retaining nut with a chisel. Remove the nut and washer. Remove the rotor.

3. Install the rotor. Install the washer and new hub retaining nut. Stake the nut. Install the caliper and anchor assembly. Install the

wheel assembly. Do not move the vehicle until a firm brake pedal is present.

4. If rear wheel bearing service is required, see Chapter 7.

REAR DRUM BRAKES

CAUTION: *Brake shoes contain asbestos, which has been determined to be a cancer causing agent. Never clean the brake surfaces with compressed air! Avoid inhaling any dust from any brake surface! When cleaning brake surfaces, use a commercially available cleaning fluid.*

Brake Drum
REMOVAL AND INSTALLATION

1. Remove the wheel cover and loosen the lug nuts.

2. Jack up the rear of the car and support with jackstands. Remove the lug nuts and the rear wheels.

3. Loosen and remove the axle nut, slide the drum from the spindle.

4. Inspect the drum for grooves, have it machined or replaced as necessary.

5. Install the drum.

Brake Shoes
REMOVAL AND INSTALLATION

1. Remove the brake drum. Remove the brake shoe return springs and anti-rattle spring.

2. Remove the brake shoe hold-down springs. Push the springs in and twist the spring to disengage it from the hold-down pin.

3. Remove the rear brake shoe from the parking brake strut. Remove the front brake shoe.

4. Unless they are broken, leave the parking brake strut, adjuster mechanism and adjuster spring in place.

5. Clean the backing plate and lubricate the brake shoe contact points on the backing plate. Position the rear brake shoe on the parking brake strut. Install the hold-down spring and pin. Position the front shoe against the parking brake strut and install the hold-down spring and pin.

6. Install the brake return springs. Insert a screwdriver between the knurled quadrant and parking brake strut. Twist the screwdriver until the quadrant just touches the backing plate. Install the brake drum.

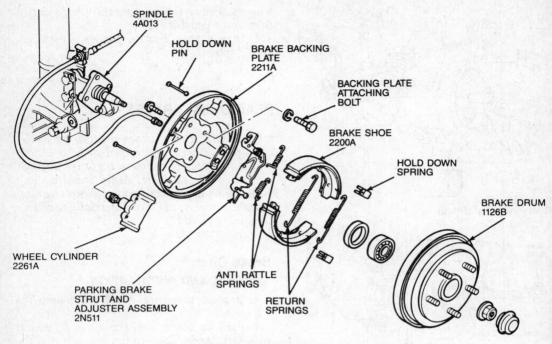

Rear drum brake components

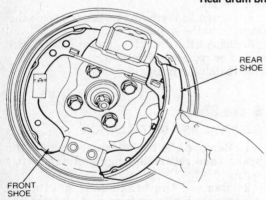

Remove/install the rear brake shoe from the parking brake strut

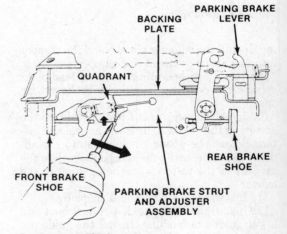

Quadrant positioning

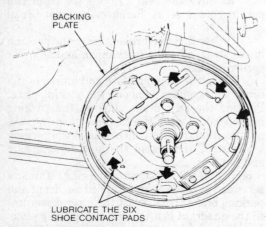

Backing plate lubrication points

Wheel Cylinder
OVERHAUL

Since the piston travel in the wheel cylinder changes when new brake shoes are installed, it is possible for previously good wheel cylinders to start leaking after new brakes are installed. Therefore, to save yourself the expense of having to replace new brakes that become saturated with brake fluid and the aggravation of having to take everything apart again, it is strongly recommended that wheel cylinders be rebuilt every time new brake shoes are installed. This is especially true for cars with high mileage.

CHILTON'S
AUTO BODY REPAIR TIPS

Tools and Materials • Step-by-Step Illustrated Procedures
How To Repair Dents, Scratches and Rust Holes
Spray Painting and Refinishing Tips

With a little practice, basic body repair procedures can be mastered by any do-it-yourself mechanic. The step-by-step repairs shown here can be applied to almost any type of auto body repair.

TOOLS & MATERIALS

You may already have basic tools, such as hammers and electric drills. Other tools unique to body repair — body hammers, grinding attachments, sanding blocks, dent puller, half-round plastic file and plastic spreaders — are relatively inexpensive and can be obtained wherever auto parts or auto body repair parts are sold. Portable air compressors and paint spray guns can be purchased or rented.

Auto Body Repair Kits

The best and most often used products are available to the do-it-yourselfer in kit form, from major manufacturers of auto body repair products. The same manufacturers also merchandise the individual products for use by pros.

Kits are available to make a wide variety of repairs, including holes, dents and scratches and fiberglass, and offer the advantage of buying the materials you'll need for the job. There is little waste or chance of materials going bad from not being used. Many kits may also contain basic body-working tools such as body files, sanding blocks and spreaders. Check the contents of the kit before buying your tools.

BODY REPAIR TIPS

Safety

Many of the products associated with auto body repair and refinishing contain toxic chemicals. Read all labels before opening containers and store them in a safe place and manner.

• Wear eye protection (safety goggles) when using power tools or when performing any operation that involves

the removal of any type of material.

• Wear lung protection (disposable mask or respirator) when grinding, sanding or painting.

Sanding

1 Sand off paint before using a dent puller. When using a non-adhesive sanding disc, cover the back of the disc with an overlapping layer or two of masking tape and trim the edges. The disc will last considerably longer.

2 Use the circular motion of the sanding disc to grind *into* the edge of the repair. Grinding or sanding away from the jagged edge will only tear the sandpaper.

3 Use the palm of your hand flat on the panel to detect high and low spots. Do not use your fingertips. Slide your hand slowly back and forth.

WORKING WITH BODY FILLER

Mixing The Filler

Cleanliness and proper mixing and application are extremely important. Use a clean piece of plastic or glass or a disposable artist's palette to mix body filler.

1 Allow plenty of time and follow directions. No useful purpose will be served by adding more hardener to make it cure (set-up) faster. Less hardener means more curing time, but the mixture dries harder; more hardener means less curing time but a softer mixture.

2 Both the hardener and the filler should be thoroughly kneaded or stirred before mixing. Hardener should be a solid paste and dispense like thin toothpaste. Body filler should be smooth, and free of lumps or thick spots.

Getting the proper amount of hardener in the filler is the trickiest part of preparing the filler. Use the same amount of hardener in cold or warm weather. For contour filler (thick coats), a bead of hardener twice the diameter of the filler is about right. There's about a 15% margin on either side, but, if in doubt use less hardener.

3 Mix the body filler and hardener by wiping across the mixing surface, picking the mixture up and wiping it again. Colder weather requires longer mixing times. Do not mix in a circular motion; this will trap air bubbles which will become holes in the cured filler.

Applying The Filler

1 For best results, filler should not be applied over ¼″ thick.

Apply the filler in several coats. Build it up to above the level of the repair surface so that it can be sanded or grated down.

The first coat of filler must be pressed on with a firm wiping motion.

Apply the filler in one direction only. Working the filler back and forth will either pull it off the metal or trap air bubbles.

REPAIRING DENTS

Before you start, take a few minutes to study the damaged area. Try to visualize the shape of the panel before it was damaged. If the damage is on the left fender, look at the right fender and use it as a guide. If there is access to the panel from behind, you can reshape it with a body hammer. If not, you'll have to use a dent puller. Go slowly and work the metal a little at a time. Get the panel as straight as possible before applying filler.

1 This dent is typical of one that can be pulled out or hammered out from behind. Remove the headlight cover, headlight assembly and turn signal housing.

2 Drill a series of holes ½ the size of the end of the dent puller along the stress line. Make some trial pulls and assess the results. If necessary, drill more holes and try again. Do not hurry.

3 If possible, use a body hammer and block to shape the metal back to its original contours. Get the metal back as close to its original shape as possible. Don't depend on body filler to fill dents.

4 Using an 80-grit grinding disc on an electric drill, grind the paint from the surrounding area down to bare metal. Use a new grinding pad to prevent heat buildup that will warp metal.

5 The area should look like this when you're finished grinding. Knock the drill holes in and tape over small openings to keep plastic filler out.

6 Mix the body filler (see Body Repair Tips). Spread the body filler evenly over the entire area (see Body Repair Tips). Be sure to cover the area completely.

7 Let the body filler dry until the surface can just be scratched with your fingernail. Knock the high spots from the body filler with a body file ("Cheesegrater"). Check frequently with the palm of your hand for high and low spots.

8 Check to be sure that trim pieces that will be installed later will fit exactly. Sand the area with 40-grit paper.

9 If you wind up with low spots, you may have to apply another layer of filler.

10 Knock the high spots off with 40-grit paper. When you are satisfied with the contours of the repair, apply a thin coat of filler to cover pin holes and scratches.

11 Block sand the area with 40-grit paper to a smooth finish. Pay particular attention to body lines and ridges that must be well-defined.

12 Sand the area with 400 paper and then finish with a scuff pad. The finished repair is ready for priming and painting (see Painting Tips).

Materials and photos courtesy of Ritt Jones Auto Body, Prospect Park, PA.

REPAIRING RUST HOLES

There are many ways to repair rust holes. The fiberglass cloth kit shown here is one of the most cost efficient for the owner because it provides a strong repair that resists cracking and moisture and is relatively easy to use. It can be used on large and small holes (with or without backing) and can be applied over contoured areas. Remember, however, that short of replacing an entire panel, no repair is a guarantee that the rust will not return.

1 Remove any trim that will be in the way. Clean away all loose debris. Cut away all the rusted metal. But be sure to leave enough metal to retain the contour or body shape.

2 Grind away all traces of rust with a 24-grit grinding disc. Be sure to grind back 3-4 inches from the edge of the hole down to bare metal and be sure all traces of paint, primer and rust are removed.

3 Block sand the area with 80 or 100 grit sandpaper to get a clear, shiny surface and feathered paint edge. Tap the edges of the hole inward with a ball peen hammer.

4 If you are going to use release film, cut a piece about 2-3" larger than the area you have sanded. Place the film over the repair and mark the sanded area on the film. Avoid any unnecessary wrinkling of the film.

5 Cut 2 pieces of fiberglass matte to match the shape of the repair. One piece should be about 1" smaller than the sanded area and the second piece should be 1" smaller than the first. Mix enough filler and hardener to saturate the fiberglass material (see Body Repair Tips).

6 Lay the release sheet on a flat surface and spread an even layer of filler, large enough to cover the repair. Lay the smaller piece of fiberglass cloth in the center of the sheet and spread another layer of filler over the fiberglass cloth. Repeat the operation for the larger piece of cloth.

7 Place the repair material over the repair area, with the release film facing outward. Use a spreader and work from the center outward to smooth the material, following the body contours. Be sure to remove all air bubbles.

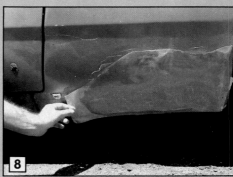

8 Wait until the repair has dried tack free and peel off the release sheet. The ideal working temperature is 60° 90° F. Cooler or warmer temperatures or high humidity may require additional curing time. Wait longer, if in doubt.

Sand and feather-edge the entire area. The initial sanding can be [d]one with a sanding disc on an electric [d]rill if care is used. Finish the sanding [w]ith a block sander. Low spots can be [fil]led with body filler; this may require [s]everal applications.

10 When the filler can just be scratched with a fingernail, [k]nock the high spots down with a body [fil]e and smooth the entire area with 80-[gr]it. Feather the filled areas into the sur[r]ounding areas.

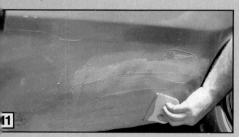

11 When the area is sanded smooth, mix some topcoat and hardener [an]d apply it directly with a spreader. [Th]is will give a smooth finish and pre[ve]nt the glass matte from showing [th]rough the paint.

12 Block sand the topcoat smooth with finishing sandpaper (200 grit), and 400 grit. The repair is ready for masking, priming and painting (see Painting Tips).

Materials and photos courtesy Marson Corporation, Chelsea, Massachusetts

PAINTING TIPS

Preparation

1 SANDING — Use a 400 or 600 grit wet or dry sandpaper. Wet-sand the area with a 1/4 sheet of sandpaper soaked in clean water. Keep the paper wet while sanding. Sand the area until the repaired area tapers into the original finish.

2 CLEANING — Wash the area to be painted thoroughly with water and a clean rag. Rinse it thoroughly and wipe the surface dry until you're sure it's completely free of dirt, dust, fingerprints, wax, detergent or other foreign matter.

3 MASKING — Protect any areas you don't want to overspray by covering them with masking tape and newspaper. Be careful not get fingerprints on the area to be painted.

4 PRIMING — All exposed metal should be primed before painting. Primer protects the metal and provides an excellent surface for paint adhesion. When the primer is dry, wet-sand the area again with 600 grit wet-sandpaper. Clean the area again after sanding.

Painting Techniques

Paint applied from either a spray gun or a spray can (for small areas) will provide good results. Experiment on an old piece of metal to get the right combination before you begin painting.

SPRAYING VISCOSITY (SPRAY GUN ONLY) — Paint should be thinned to spraying viscosity according to the directions on the can. Use only the recommended thinner or reducer and the same amount of reduction regardless of temperature.

AIR PRESSURE (SPRAY GUN ONLY) — This is extremely important. Be sure you are using the proper recommended pressure.

TEMPERATURE — The surface to be painted should be approximately the same temperature as the surrounding air. Applying warm paint to a cold surface, or vice versa, will completely upset the paint characteristics.

THICKNESS — Spray with smooth strokes. In general, the thicker the coat of paint, the longer the drying time. Apply several thin coats about 30 seconds apart. The paint should remain wet long enough to flow out and no longer; heavier coats will only produce sags or wrinkles. Spray a light (fog) coat, followed by heavier color coats.

DISTANCE — The ideal spraying distance is 8″-12″ from the gun or can to the surface. Shorter distances will produce ripples, while greater distances will result in orange peel, dry film and poor color match and loss of material due to overspray.

OVERLAPPING — The gun or can should be kept at right angles to the surface at all times. Work to a wet edge at an even speed, using a 50% overlap and direct the center of the spray at the lower or nearest edge of the previous stroke.

RUBBING OUT (BLENDING) FRESH PAINT — Let the paint dry thoroughly. Runs or imperfections can be sanded out, primed and repainted.

Don't be in too big a hurry to remove the masking. This only produces paint ridges. When the finish has dried for at least a week, apply a small amount of fine grade rubbing compound with a clean, wet cloth. Use lots of water and blend the new paint with the surrounding area.

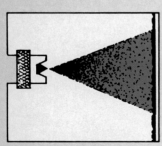

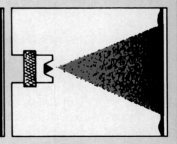

WRONG

Thin coat. Stroke too fast, not enough overlap, gun too far away.

CORRECT

Medium coat. Proper distance, good stroke, proper overlap.

WRONG

Heavy coat. Stroke too slow, too much overlap, gun too close.

NOTE: *Most wheel cylinders can be rebuilt while mounted in position on the brake backing plate. However, if the cylinder must be removed, disconnect the brake line and unbolt the cylinder after the brake shoes have be removed.*

1. Remove the brake shoes.

2. Place a bucket or some old newspapers under the brake backing plate to catch the brake fluid that will run out of the wheel cylinder. Disconnect the brake line and remove the cylinder mounting bolts. Remove the cylinder from the backing plate.

3. Remove the boots from the ends of the wheel cylinder.

4. Push one piston toward the center of the cylinder to force the opposite piston and cup out the other end of the cylinder. Reach in the open end of the cylinder and push the spring, cup, and piston out of the cylinder.

5. Remove the bleeder screw from the rear of the cylinder.

6. Inspect the inside of the wheel cylinder. If it is scored in any way, the cylinder must be honed with a wheel cylinder hone or fine emery paper, and finished with crocus cloth if emery paper is used. If the inside of the cylinder is excessively worm, the cylinder will have to be replaced, as only 0.08mm of material can be removed from the cylinder walls. Whenever honing or cleaning wheel cylinders, keep a small amount of brake fluid in the cylinder to serve as a lubricant.

7. Clean any foreign matter from the pistons. The sides of the pistons must be smooth for the wheel cylinders to operate properly.

8. Clean the cylinder bore with alcohol and a lint-free rag. Pull the rag through the bore several times to remove all foreign matter and dry the cylinder.

9. Install the bleeder screw and the return spring in the cylinder.

10. Coat new cylinder cups with new brake fluid and install them in the cylinder. Make sure they are square in the bore or they will leak.

11. Install the pistons in the cylinder after coating them with new brake fluid.

12. Coat the insides of the boots with new brake fluid and install them on the cylinder. Reinstall the wheel cylinder. Install and bleed the brakes.

ANTI-LOCK BRAKE SYSTEM

The ABS Anti-Lock Brake System functions by releasing and applying fluid pressure to the wheel calipers during braking. ABS does not function under normal braking conditions nor does it affect front to rear brake proportioning. When one or more wheels approaches a slip condition, ABS automatically senses the slip and activates pressure control function.

Through its pre-progamming, the control unit decides which wheel or wheel's brake pressures need modulation. Once the decision is made, the control unit sends appropriate signals to the solenoid valves located in the actuation assembly. As a result, the control valves then modulate the fluid pressure which results in a pressure reduction at the caliper to prevent further lock-up. The components of the ABS are: Master cylinder, Actuator assembly, Solenoid valves, Control valves, Fluid Reservoir, Control unit, Wheel sensors and, Proportioning valve.

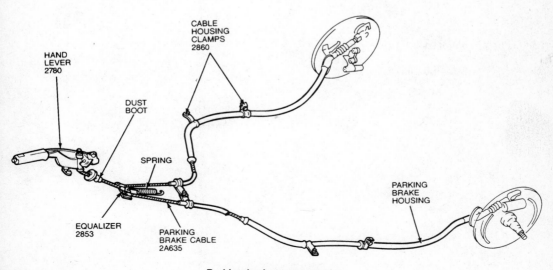

CABLE HOUSING CLAMPS 2860

HAND LEVER 2780

DUST BOOT

SPRING

EQUALIZER 2853

PARKING BRAKE CABLE 2A635

PARKING BRAKE HOUSING

Parking brake components

NOTE: *Servicing the ABS is usually beyond the resources of the car owner. Have the system serviced by a capable and equipped service dealer.*

PARKING BRAKE

Cable

ADJUSTMENT

1. The normal parking brake adjustment is made at the hand lever between the seats. Remove the attaching screws in the center console and remove the console.

2. Tighten the parking brake adjusting nut on the left side of the lever to shorten the equalizer cable. Tighten the nut until it takes seven to ten notches to fully set the parking brake.

3. Install the center console.

Parking Brake Cables

REMOVAL AND INSTALLATION

1. Remove the parking brake return spring at each backing plate with a pair of needlenose pliers.

2. Remove the attaching bolts from the park-

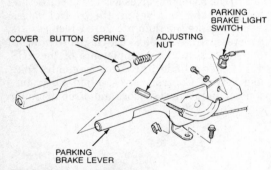

Parking brake control lever

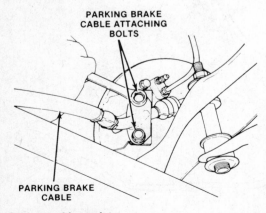

Cable attaching points

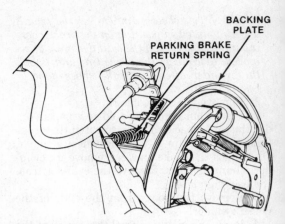

Remove/install cable return spring

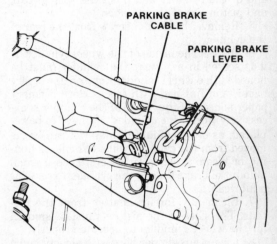

Remove/install the cable from the levers

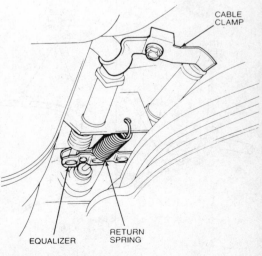

Equalizer assembly

Brake Specifications
All measurements in inches unless noted

| Year | Model | Lug Nut Torque (ft. lbs.) | Master Cylinder Bore | Brake Disc | | Standard Brake Drum Diameter | Minimum Lining Thickness | |
				Minimum Thickness	Maximum Runout		Front	Rear
1989–90	Probe GL	65–87	0.875	0.860 ③	0.003	9.0	0.120	0.040 ②
	Probe LX	65–87	0.875	0.860 ③	0.003	9.0	0.120	0.040 ②
	Probe GT	65–87	0.875	0.860 ③	0.003	10.0 ①	0.120	②

① Rear disc
② Rear disc pad—0.040 in.
③ Rear disc pad—0.350 in.

ing brake cable housing and pull it away from the backing plate.

3. Disconnect the parking brake cables from the backing plate levers. Unbolt the housing clamp from the rear trailing arm.

4. Unbolt the cable housing clamp from the body. Remove the cable clamp securing both cables from the body. Disconnect the cable return spring from the parking brake equalizer. Remove the cable from the equalizer.

5. Install the two cable ends into the parking brake equalizer. Install the cable housing support clamps on the body. Install the cable housing support to each trailing arm.

6. Connect the parking brake cables to the backing plate parking brake levers. Position the parking brake cable against the backing plate and install the attaching bolts. Adjust the cable.

Body

10

EXTERIOR

Doors

REMOVAL AND INSTALLATION

1. Open the door and remove the door check pin. Use a pin punch to raise the pin.
2. Remove the electrical wire boot, that the courtesy light wires run through, from the vehicle body mounting.
3. Disconnect the electrical wiring connector that is behind the body mounted boot.
4. Place a padded support under the door edge, or have an assistant support the door. Scribe the hinge location and remove the mounting bolts from the door hinges. Remove the door. There may be some shims behind the hinges. Make note of the number and their location for installation.
5. Service the components as required.
6. If the electrical wiring and boot were removed from the door, install the wiring through the door boot and secure the boot.
7. Place the door in position, supported by an assistant or padded support. Put any shims that were removed back into their previous positions. Install the mounting bolts. Tighten them just enough to support the door, but loose enough so that the door mounting position can be shifted. Slide the door around until the hinge scribe marks are aligned. Tighten the mounting bolts so that the door cannot move.
8. Check the fit and alignment of the door with the fender. Shims can be added or removed to make the surface areas even. Check the spacing around the door, adjust as necessary to make it even. Check the door swing, make sure there is no bind on interference with adjacent panels.
9. Tighten the mounting bolts to 31 ft. lbs. after desired door position is reached.
10. Connect the electrical wiring connector

and install the body boot. Install the door check pin.

ADJUSTMENT

1. The door hinges provide sufficient adjustment to correct most door misalignment conditions. The holes of the hinge and/or the hinge attaching points are enlarged or elongated to provide for hinge and door alignment. Do not cover up a poor door alignment with a striker adjustment.
2. Open the door. If there is excessive play in the hinges, replace them.
3. To adjust the door, loosen the hinge bolts just enough to permit movement of the door.

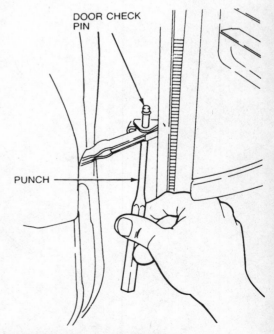

DOOR CHECK PIN

PUNCH →

Remove/install the door check pin

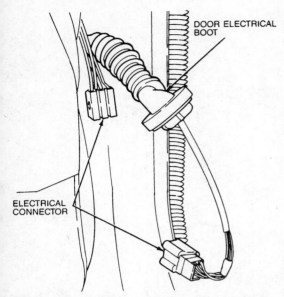

Remove/install the boot and electrical wiring connector

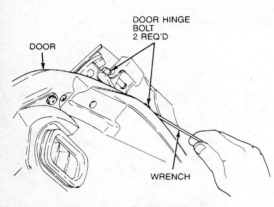

Loosen the hinge bolts for door adjustment

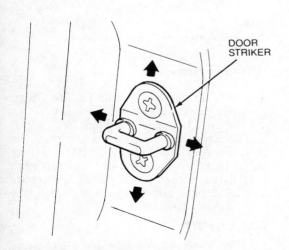

Door striker adjustment positions

4. Move the door/hinge to the proper alignment position. Tighten the hinge bolts to 31 ft. lbs. Check the door alignment and movement. Make sure the door does not bind and there is no interference with adjacent panels.

5. Repeat the operation until alignment is satisfactory. Check the striker for proper door position when closed.

6. The striker can be adjusted laterally and vertically as well as fore and aft. The striker should not be adjusted to correct door sag.

7. Check whether the door can be closed easily and if there is any play evident. If the door doesn't close easily then loosen the striker screws and adjust the striker by moving it up or down or side to side.

8. Inspect the rear alignment of the door in relation to the body. If there is a problem, adjust the striker position.

Hood

REMOVAL AND INSTALLATION

1. Open the hood and support it in the up position. Scribe the hood hinge locations on the hood panel.

2. Place protective covers on both fenders.

3. Disconnect the engine underhood light electrical connectors.

4. Have an assistant support the hood. Remove the hood to hinge mounting bolts. DO NOT let the hood slip downward when the bolts are loosened.

5. Remove the hood.

6. Place the hood into position on the hinges with an assistants help.

7. Install the hinge to hood mounting bolts tighten them, but leave the bolts loose enough

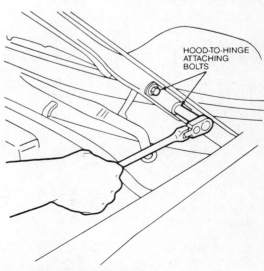

Hood to hinge mounting bolts

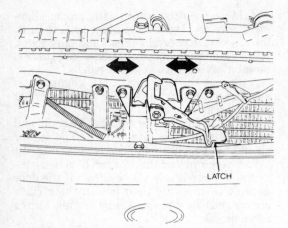

Hood latch adjustment

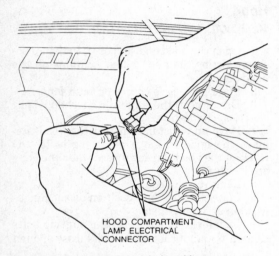

Disconnect/connect the underhood lamp

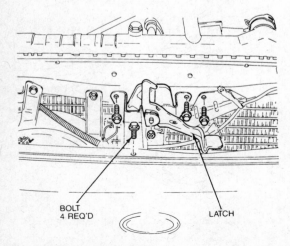

Hood latch mounting bolts

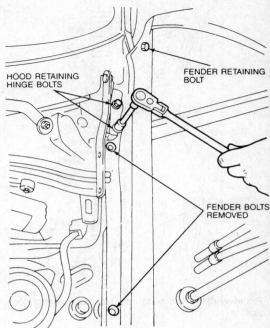

Remove/install hood hinge

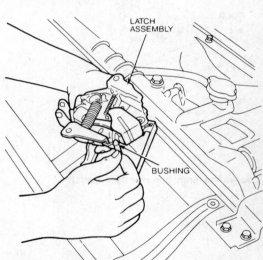

Remove/install hood latch

to permit shifting of the hood position. Align the scribe marks and tighten the bolts.

8. Connect the under hood light connector,

9. Remove the fender covers and close the hood. Check hood alignment and for even spacing between both fenders, the cowl and grill. Loosen the hood mounting bolts and adjust hood alignment and as required. Adjust the hood latch if necessary.

ADJUSTMENT

1. The hood can be adjusted front to rear and side to side by loosening the two hood to hinge

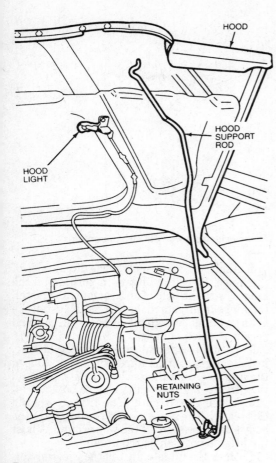

Remove/install hood support

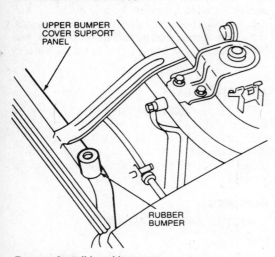

Remove/install hood bumpers

attaching bolts at each hinge. Position the hood as required and tighten the bolts.

2. The hood latch can be moved from side to side to align with the hood. Always align the hood first, then the latch.

3. The latch can be moved up or down to align the hood surface with the fenders.

4. Loosen the hood latch mounting bolts enough to slide the latch. Move the latch to the position desired and tighten the mounting bolts.

Rear Liftgate

REMOVAL AND INSTALLATION

1. The liftgate assembly pivots on two removable hinges assisted by two gas support cylinders. The liftgate hinges are accessible when the liftgate is opened and the upper trim is removed. Liftgate requires the help of an assistant.

2. Disconnect the negative battery cable.

3. Raise the liftgate. Remove the upper and lower liftgate trim panels.

4. Disconnect the rear window defroster electrical connector. Remove the rear wiper arm and blade assembly. Remove the rear wiper motor. Remove the electrical wiring boot from

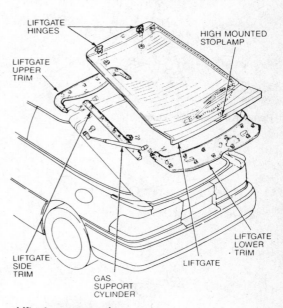

Liftgate components

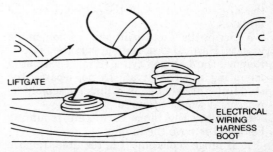

Remove/install the electrical boot and wiring connector

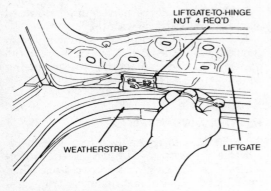

Remove/install hinge nuts

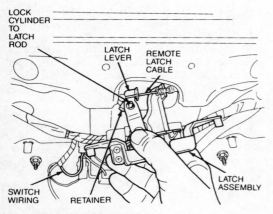

Remove/install liftgate latch

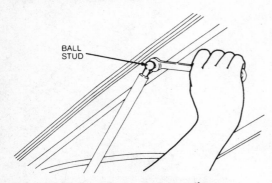

Remove/install upper gas strut mountings

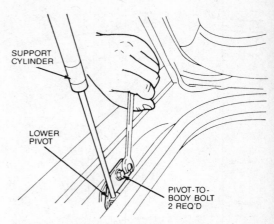

Remove/install lower gas strut mountings

8. Apply silicone sealant to the liftgate side of the hinge. Place the liftgate in position on the hinges, with the help of an assistant, and install the hinge to liftgate mounting bolts. Install the bolts just tight enough to secure the liftgate and permit position shiftng.

9. With the assistant supporting the liftgate, install the gas cylinder upper mounting studs to the liftgate. Align the scribed hinge marks, on the liftgate, and tighten the hinge bolts.

10. Close the liftgate. The liftgate should close easily. The space around the liftgate to the body should be even all the way around. Adjust the liftgate position as required.

11. Open the liftgate. Install the wiper motor. Run the electrical wiring into the liftgate and secure the boot. Connect the rear defroster wiring. Install the upper and lower trim panels. Close the liftgate and install the wiper arm and blade assembly. Connect the negative battery cable.

ADJUSTMENT

The liftgate can be adjusted up and down by the use of shims, or side to side by the use of the elongated holes at the liftgate hinge. The liftgate should be adjusted for an even, parallel fit with liftgate openings and the surrounding panels.

Bumpers

REMOVAL AND INSTALLATION

Front

1. Remove the front bumper cover by: Remove the battery assembly and the headlight assemblies to gain access to the front bumper cover attaching bolts.

2. Disconnect the marker and parking light electrical connectors. Remove the shoulder bolt from the upper corner of the bumper assembly cover. Remove the two retaining nuts from the

the liftgate and remove the wiring from the liftgate.

5. Scribe the hinge to liftgate position on the liftgate. Have an assistant support the liftgate. Remove the two gas cylinder to liftgate stud mounting from the liftgate. Do not separate the stud from the cylinder, or cylinder assembly replacement will be required.

6. Remove the hinge to liftgate mounting bolts and remove the liftgate.

7. If hinge replacement is required, remove the headliner enough to gain access to the hinge to body mounting bolts.

bumper cover to the front fenders on each side. Remove the screw from under the inside of the front fenders.

3. Remove the bumper assembly cover bracket mounting bolts and the brackets. Remove the screws securing the fender shields and remove the shields. Remove the two bolts that secure the bumper assembly cover to each fender from underneath. Remove the screws and clips and the bolts that secure the bumper cover to the bumper reinforcement. Remove the cover.

4. Remove the four bumper to isolator and bracket mounting nuts. Remove the bumper.

5. Install the bumper to the isolators and install the bumper cover.

Rear

1. Remove the rear bumper cover by: Remove the trunk end trim and lower trunk side trim. Remove all of the lamps from the vehicle.

Remove both license plate cover retaining screws and remove the cover.

2. Remove the one nut located under the license plate cover. Remove the cover retaining nuts located inside the trunk. Remove the two screws under each side of the bumper cover assembly. Remove the mounting screws from the backside of the bumper. Remove the screws in both clips that retain the cover at each upper corner. Slide the bumper cover away from the back of the vehicle and remove it.

3. Remove the bumper side track mounting screws and the side track. Depress the tangs on each clip securing the set plates and remove the plates. Remove the screws retaining the bumper slides and remove the slides.

4. Remove the eight bolts that secure the bumper to the stay brackets. Remove the bumper.

5. Install the bumper to the stay brackets and install the bumper cover.

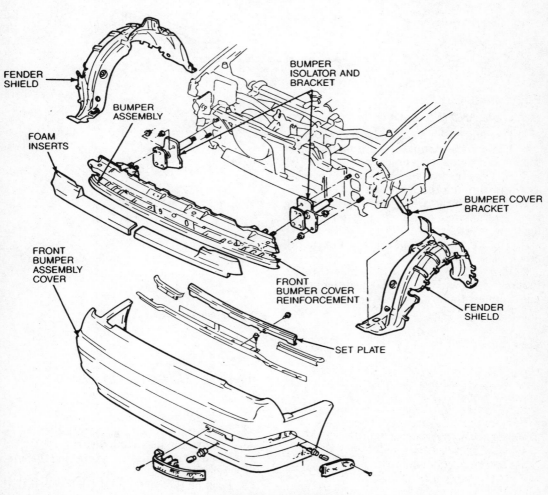

Front bumper and components

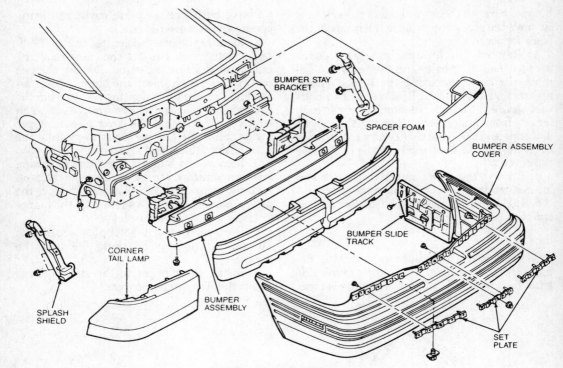

Rear bumper and components

Fog Lamps

REMOVAL AND INSTALLATION

1. Disconnect the negative battery cable.
2. Remove the mounting nut from the top of the fog lamp mounting bracket.
3. Remove the fog lamp housing and bracket as a unit through the front fascia.
4. Remove the attaching screws from the fog lamp lens retaining brackets and remove the fog lamp lens assembly.
5. Install the lens assembly mounting brackets.
6. Position the fog lamp assembly through the front facia and secure the upper mounting nut. Connect the negative battery cable.

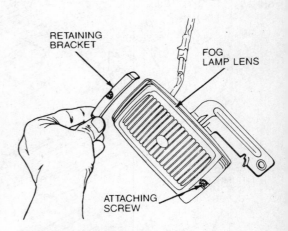

Fog lamp retaining bracket

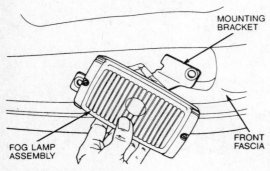

Fog lamp mounting

Outside Mirrors

REMOVAL AND INSTALLATION

Manual

1. Remove the control knob cover.
2. Remove the retaining screw and knob.
3. Remove the inside mirror trim.
4. Remove the mounting screws and the mirror assembly.
5. Position the mirror on the door and install the mounting screws.

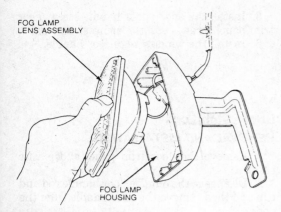

Fog lamp lens replacement

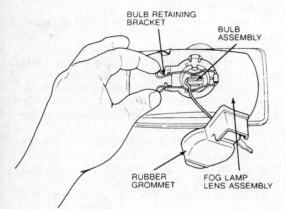

Remove/install fog lamp bulb

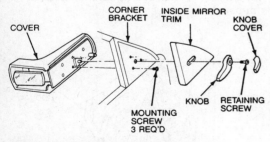

Remove/install manual outside mirror

6. Install the interior mirror trim.
7. Install the knob and retaining screw.
8. Install the control knob cover.

Electric

1. Disconnect the negative battery cable.
2. Remove the access cover.
3. Remove the three mounting screws.
4. Remove the mirror assembly and disconnect the wiring connector.
5. Connect the wiring connector.
6. Position the mirror on the door and install the mounting screws.

7. Install the access cover. Connect the negative battery cable.

Antenna

REPLACEMENT

1. Open the liftgate. Remove the right lower trunk side trim and the upper trunk side garnish.
2. Disconnect the antenna cable. Remove the antenna mounting bolt.
3. Remove the antenna tip. Unscrew and remove the bezel. Remove the bezel mount.
4. Note how and where the drain tube is mounted. Remove the antenna support and the antenna.
5. Attach the antenna support. Install the antenna bezel mount by aligning the bezel mount tab with the hole slot.

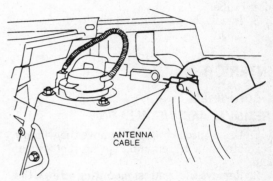

Remove/install antenna cable

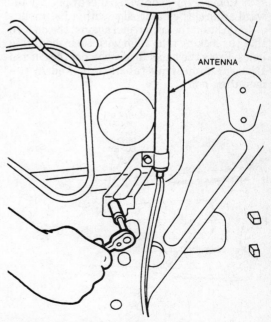

Remove/install antenna attaching bolt

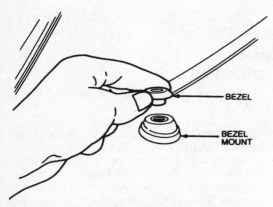

Antenna bezel and bezel and bezel mount

6. Install the antenna bezel. Install the antenna tip. Install the antenna attaching bolt.
7. Connect the antenna cable. Position the drain tube.
8. Install the garnish and side trim.

INTERIOR

Door Panels

REMOVAL AND INSTALLATION

1. Use a special tool and remove the window regulator handle retaining spring (horseshoe) clip.
2. Remove the armrest mounting screws, the inside door handle retaining screw and trim panel screws.
3. Remove the door trim panel by prying outward around the outer edge with a flat tool.
4. Position the trim panel against the door so that the locking tabs align with their mounting holes. Press the panel firmly against the door so that the mounting tabs are locked in the mounting holes.

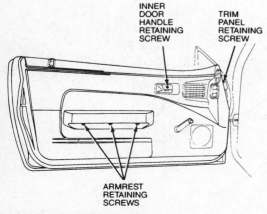

Remove/install door trim panel

5. Install the inside door handle screw, door trim panel screws, and the armrest screws.
6. Install the window regulator handle.

Door Latch/Lock

REMOVAL AND INSTALLATION

1. Remove the door trim panel and plastic sheet.
2. Disengage the outside door handle rod and clip and then remove the door handle from the door.
3. Remove the clip attaching the lock cylinder rod to the lock cylinder.
4. Remove the clip from the actuator motor, if electric.
5. Remove the push-button rod to latch.
6. Remove the clip attaching the outside door handle rod to the latch assembly.
7. Remove the screws attaching the latch assembly to the door. Remove the latch assembly with the remote control link and lock cylinder rod.
8. Place the latch assembly, with the remote control link and lock cylinder rod attached, in position on the inside of the door frame. Install and tighten the mounting screws.
9. Connect the outside door handle rod, the actuator motor rod, the lock cylinder rod and the remote control link.
10. Check the latch operation. Install the door trim panel.

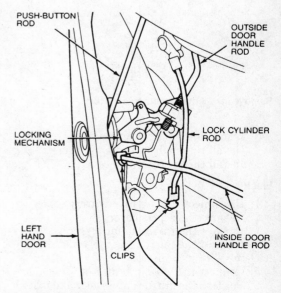

Remove/install door latch/lock

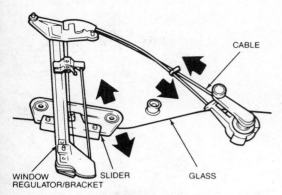

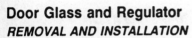

Window regulator assembly

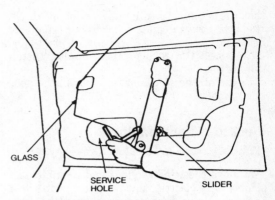

Remove/install door window glass

Door Glass and Regulator
REMOVAL AND INSTALLATION

1. The front door windows are regulated by two encased cables. The cables are attached from the regulator to a slider bracket. When the regulator handle is operated, the cables move the slider bracket up or down. The slider bracket then moves the window to the desired position. The cables are secured by nylon fasteners inside the door. Lubrication of the cables is not necessary.

2. Remove the door trim panel.

3. Remove the upper stops retaining bolts and remove the stops.

4. Remove the door mirror.

5. Remove the corner bracket mounting bolts.

6. Position the door glass so that the bolts securing the window glass can be removed through the door service hole. Remove the bolts.

7. Remove the glass upwards along the glass guide Tilt as necessary to remove.

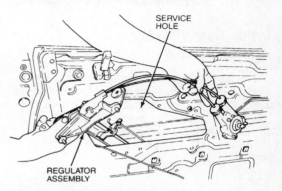

Remove/install regulator assembly

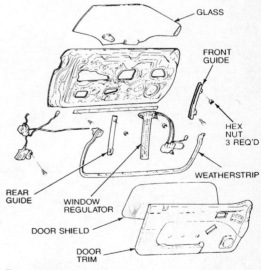

Door components

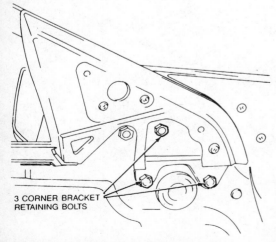

Window glass corner mounting bracket

8. Remove the regulator retaining nuts and remove the regulator through the service hole.

9. Install the regulator through the service hole and secure the mounting nuts.

10. Insert the glass carefully into position in the door glass channels.

11. Position the door glass and regulator so

that the mounting bolts may be installed. Install a tighten the glass to regulator mounting bolts.

12. Install the corner bracket bolts. Install the mirror.

13. Install the stop brackets. Install the door trim panel.

Electric Window Motor
REMOVAL AND INSTALLATION

Remove the window glass and regulator assembly. The electric window motor is attached to the regulator. Removing/installing the motor mounting bolts is the additional step required.

Inside Rear View Mirror
REPLACEMENT

The inside mirror assembly is held in position, on the windshield mounted bracket, by an allen screw. Loosen the allen screw and slide the mirror off of the mounting bracket. Slide the mirror onto the mounting bracket and tighten the allen screw.

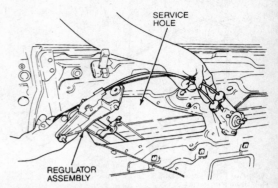

Electric window regulator and motor

Seats
REMOVAL AND INSTALLATION
Front

Two types of seats are used. The standard seat has only two adjustments. Forward and rearward slide, and seat back angle. The deluxe seat has the standard adjustments plus four additional.

The front seats are secured to the floor by three bolts and one nut. The nut should be in-

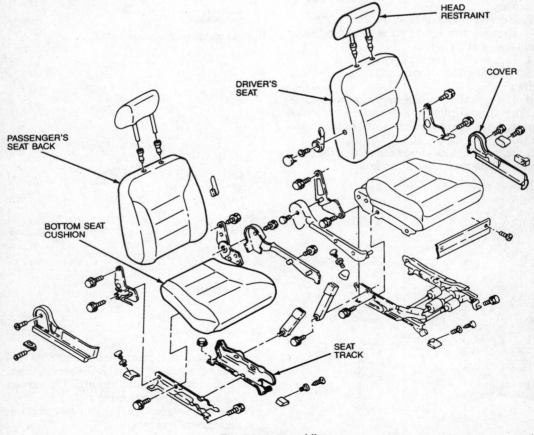

Front seat assemblies

stalled first, before installing the bolts. This ensures that the seat frame is correctly seated to the floor box section.

Rear

The rear seats are equipped with folding seat backs. The seat backs pivot on hinges bolted to the floor.

The seat cushion is secured to the floor by metal pins that lock into floor brackets. The pins are part of the seat cushion frame.

To remove the seat cushion a screwdriver is placed under the cushion to release the retaining locks on each end of the cushion. The folding back is lowered and the pivot hinge mounting bolts are removed to allow seat back removal and installation. The seat cushion is installed by putting the cushion in position and pressing back and down on the front.

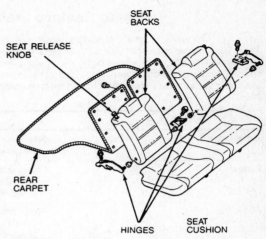

Rear seat assembly

Power Seat Motor/Track Assembly
REMOVAL AND INSTALLATION

1. Remove the seat assembly and place it upside down on a suitable working surface.
2. Remove the front trim cover. Remove the slide lifter switch handle, the recliner lever handle, and the left trim cover.
3. Disconnect the slide lifter switch electrical connector.
4. Remove the right side trim cover, and the seat cushion.
5. Remove the four bolts (two per side), retaining the recliner knuckles to the power seat track.
6. Service the power seat track as required.
7. Install the recliner knuckles, seat cushion, right trim cover, electrical connector, left trim panel, recliner handle, slide lifter switch handle and front trim cover.
8. Install the seat.

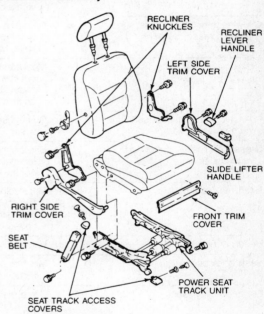

Power seat components

How to Remove Stains from Fabric Interior

For rest results, spots and stains should be removed as soon as possible. Never use gasoline, lacquer thinner, acetone, nail polish remover or bleach. Use a 3′ x 3″ piece of cheesecloth. Squeeze most of the liquid from the fabric and wipe the stained fabric from the outside of the stain toward the center with a lifting motion. Turn the cheesecloth as soon as one side becomes soiled. When using water to remove a stain, be sure to wash the entire section after the spot has been removed to avoid water stains. Encrusted spots can be broken up with a dull knife and vacuumed before removing the stain.

Type of Stain	How to Remove It
Surface spots	Brush the spots out with a small hand brush or use a commercial preparation such as K2R to lift the stain.
Mildew	Clean around the mildew with warm suds. Rinse in cold water and soak the mildew area in a solution of 1 part table salt and 2 parts water. Wash with upholstery cleaner.
Water stains	Water stains in fabric materials can be removed with a solution made from 1 cup of table salt dissolved in 1 quart of water. Vigorously scrub the solution into the stain and rinse with clear water. Water stains in nylon or other synthetic fabrics should be removed with a commercial type spot remover.
Chewing gum, tar, crayons, shoe polish (greasy stains)	Do not use a cleaner that will soften gum or tar. Harden the deposit with an ice cube and scrape away as much as possible with a dull knife. Moisten the remainder with cleaning fluid and scrub clean.
Ice cream, candy	Most candy has a sugar base and can be removed with a cloth wrung out in warm water. Oily candy, after cleaning with warm water, should be cleaned with upholstery cleaner. Rinse with warm water and clean the remainder with cleaning fluid.
Wine, alcohol, egg, milk, soft drink (non-greasy stains)	Do not use soap. Scrub the stain with a cloth wrung out in warm water. Remove the remainder with cleaning fluid.
Grease, oil, lipstick, butter and related stains	Use a spot remover to avoid leaving a ring. Work from the outisde of the stain to the center and dry with a clean cloth when the spot is gone.
Headliners (cloth)	Mix a solution of warm water and foam upholstery cleaner to give thick suds. Use only foam—liquid may streak or spot. Clean the entire headliner in one operation using a circular motion with a natural sponge.
Headliner (vinyl)	Use a vinyl cleaner with a sponge and wipe clean with a dry cloth.
Seats and door panels	Mix 1 pint upholstery cleaner in 1 gallon of water. Do not soak the fabric around the buttons.
Leather or vinyl fabric	Use a multi-purpose cleaner full strength and a stiff brush. Let stand 2 minutes and scrub thoroughly. Wipe with a clean, soft rag.
Nylon or synthetic fabrics	For normal stains, use the same procedures you would for washing cloth upholstery. If the fabric is extremely dirty, use a multi-purpose cleaner full strength with a stiff scrub brush. Scrub thoroughly in all directions and wipe with a cotton towel or soft rag.

Mechanic's Data

11

1":254mm
TAX
10.16mm
Liter
Parts
Overhaul

General Conversion Table

Multiply By	To Convert	To	
		LENGTH	
2.54	Inches	Centimeters	.3937
25.4	Inches	Millimeters	.03937
30.48	Feet	Centimeters	.0328
.304	Feet	Meters	3.28
.914	Yards	Meters	1.094
1.609	Miles	Kilometers	.621
		VOLUME	
.473	Pints	Liters	2.11
.946	Quarts	Liters	1.06
3.785	Gallons	Liters	.264
.016	Cubic inches	Liters	61.02
16.39	Cubic inches	Cubic cms.	.061
28.3	Cubic feet	Liters	.0353
		MASS (Weight)	
28.35	Ounces	Grams	.035
.4536	Pounds	Kilograms	2.20
—	To obtain	From	Multiply by

Multiply By	To Convert	To	
		AREA	
.645	Square inches	Square cms.	.155
.836	Square yds.	Square meters	1.196
		FORCE	
4.448	Pounds	Newtons	.225
.138	Ft./lbs.	Kilogram/meters	7.23
1.36	Ft./lbs.	Newton-meters	.737
.112	In./lbs.	Newton-meters	8.844
		PRESSURE	
.068	Psi	Atmospheres	14.7
6.89	Psi	Kilopascals	.145
		OTHER	
1.104	Horsepower (DIN)	Horsepower (SAE)	.9861
.746	Horsepower (SAE)	Kilowatts (KW)	1.34
1.60	Mph	Km/h	.625
.425	Mpg	Km/1	2.35
—	To obtain	From	Multiply by

Tap Drill Sizes

National Coarse or U.S.S.

Screw & Tap Size	Threads Per Inch	Use Drill Number
No. 5	40	39
No. 6	32	36
No. 8	32	29
No. 10	24	25
No. 12	24	17
$\frac{1}{4}$	20	8
$\frac{5}{16}$	18	F
$\frac{3}{8}$	16	$\frac{5}{16}$
$\frac{7}{16}$	14	U
$\frac{1}{2}$	13	$\frac{27}{64}$
$\frac{9}{16}$	12	$\frac{31}{64}$
$\frac{5}{8}$	11	$\frac{17}{32}$
$\frac{3}{4}$	10	$\frac{21}{32}$
$\frac{7}{8}$	9	$\frac{49}{64}$

National Coarse or U.S.S.

Screw & Tap Size	Threads Per Inch	Use Drill Number
1	8	$\frac{7}{8}$
$1\frac{1}{8}$	7	$\frac{63}{64}$
$1\frac{1}{4}$	7	$1\frac{7}{54}$
$1\frac{1}{2}$	6	$1\frac{11}{32}$

National Fine or S.A.E.

Screw & Tap Size	Threads Per Inch	Use Drill Number
No. 5	44	37
No. 6	40	33
No. 8	36	29
No. 10	32	21

National Fine or S.A.E.

Screw & Tap Size	Threads Per Inch	Use Drill Number
No. 12	28	15
$\frac{1}{4}$	28	3
$\frac{6}{16}$	24	1
$\frac{3}{8}$	24	Q
$\frac{7}{16}$	20	W
$\frac{1}{2}$	20	$\frac{29}{64}$
$\frac{9}{16}$	18	$\frac{33}{64}$
$\frac{5}{8}$	18	$\frac{37}{64}$
$\frac{3}{4}$	16	$\frac{11}{16}$
$\frac{7}{8}$	14	$\frac{13}{16}$
$1\frac{1}{8}$	12	$1\frac{3}{64}$
$1\frac{1}{4}$	12	$1\frac{11}{64}$
$1\frac{1}{2}$	12	$1\frac{27}{64}$

Drill Sizes In Decimal Equivalents

Inch	Decimal	Wire	mm
1/64	.0156		.39
	.0157		.4
	.0160	78	
	.0165		.42
	.0173		.44
	.0177		.45
	.0180	77	
	.0181		.46
	.0189		.48
	.0197		.5
	.0200	76	
	.0210	75	
	.0217		.55
	.0225	74	
	.0236		.6
	.0240	73	
	.0250	72	
	.0256		.65
	.0260	71	
	.0276		.7
	.0280	70	
	.0292	69	
	.0295		.75
	.0310	68	
1/32	.0312		.79
	.0315		.8
	.0320	67	
	.0330	66	
	.0335		.85
	.0350	65	
	.0354		.9
	.0360	64	
	.0370	63	
	.0374		.95
	.0380	62	
	.0390	61	
	.0394		1.0
	.0400	60	
	.0410	59	
	.0413		1.05
	.0420	58	
	.0430	57	
	.0433		1.1
	.0453		1.15
3/64	.0465	56	
	.0469		1.19
	.0472		1.2
	.0492		1.25
	.0512		1.3
	.0520	55	
	.0531		1.35
	.0550	54	
	.0551		1.4
	.0571		1.45
	.0591		1.5
	.0595	53	
	.0610		1.55
1/16	.0625		1.59
	.0630		1.6
	.0635	52	
	.0650		1.65
	.0669		1.7
	.0670	51	
	.0689		1.75
	.0700	50	
	.0709		1.8
	.0728		1.85

Inch	Decimal	Wire	mm
	.0730	49	
	.0748		1.9
	.0760	48	
	.0768		1.95
5/64	.0781		1.98
	.0785	47	
	.0787		2.0
	.0807		2.05
	.0810	46	
	.0820	45	
	.0827		2.1
	.0846		2.15
	.0860	44	
	.0866		2.2
	.0886		2.25
	.0890	43	
	.0906		2.3
	.0925		2.35
	.0935	42	
3/32	.0938		2.38
	.0945		2.4
	.0960	41	
	.0965		2.45
	.0980	40	
	.0981		2.5
	.0995	39	
	.1015	38	
	.1024		2.6
	.1040	37	
	.1063		2.7
	.1065	36	
	.1083		2.75
7/64	.1094		2.77
	.1100	35	
	.1102		2.8
	.1110	34	
	.1130	33	
	.1142		2.9
	.1160	32	
	.1181		3.0
	.1200	31	
	.1220		3.1
1/8	.1250		3.17
	.1260		3.2
	.1280		3.25
	.1285	30	
	.1299		3.3
	.1339		3.4
	.1360	29	
	.1378		3.5
	.1405	28	
9/64	.1406		3.57
	.1417		3.6
	.1440	27	
	.1457		3.7
	.1470	26	
	.1476		3.75
	.1495	25	
	.1496		3.8
	.1520	24	
	.1535		3.9
	.1540	23	
5/32	.1562		3.96
	.1570	22	
	.1575		4.0
	.1590	21	
	.1610	20	

Inch	Decimal	Wire & Letter	mm
	.1614		4.1
	.1654		4.2
	.1660	19	
	.1673		4.25
	.1693		4.3
	.1695	18	
11/64	.1719		4.36
	.1730	17	
	.1732		4.4
	.1770	16	
	.1772		4.5
	.1800	15	
	.1811		4.6
	.1820	14	
	.1850	13	
	.1850		4.7
	.1870		4.75
3/16	.1875		4.76
	.1890	12	
	.1890		4.8
	.1910	11	
	.1929		4.9
	.1935	10	
	.1960	9	
	.1969		5.0
	.1990	8	
	.2008		5.1
	.2010	7	
13/64	.2031		5.16
	.2040	6	
	.2047		5.2
	.2055	5	
	.2067		5.25
	.2087		5.3
	.2090	4	
	.2126		5.4
	.2130	3	
	.2165		5.5
7/32	2188		5.55
	.2205		5.6
	.2210	2	
	.2244		5.7
	.2264		5.75
	.2280	1	
	.2283		5.8
	.2323		5.9
	.2340	A	
15/64	.2344		5.95
	.2362		6.0
	.2380	B	
	.2402		6.1
	.2420	C	
	.2441		6.2
	.2460	D	
	.2461		6.25
	.2480		6.3
1/4	.2500	E	6.35
	.2520		6.
	.2559		6.5
	.2570	F	
	.2598		6.6
	.2610	G	
	.2638		6.7
17/64	.2656		6.74
	.2657		6.75
	.2660	H	
	.2677		6.8

Inch	Decimal	Letter	mm
	.2717		6.9
	.2720	I	
	.2756		7.0
	.2770	J	
	.2795		7.1
	.2810	K	
9/32	.2812		7.14
	.2835		7.2
	.2854		7.25
	.2874		7.3
	.2900	L	
	.2913		7.4
	.2950	M	
	.2953		7.5
19/64	.2969		7.54
	.2992		7.6
	.3020	N	
	.3031		7.7
	.3051		7.75
	.3071		7.8
	.3110		7.9
5/16	.3125		7.93
	.3150		8.0
	.3160	O	
	.3189		8.1
	.3228		8.2
	.3230	P	
	.3248		8.25
	.3268		8.3
21/64	.3281		8.33
	.3307		8.4
	.3320	Q	
	.3346		8.5
	.3386		8.6
	.3390	R	
	.3425		8.7
11/32	.3438		8.73
	.3445		8.75
	.3465		8.8
	.3480	S	
	.3504		8.9
	.3543		9.0
	.3580	T	
	.3583		9.1
23/64	.3594		9.12
	.3622		9.2
	.3642		9.25
	.3661		9.3
	.3680	U	
	.3701		9.4
	.3740		9.5
3/8	.3750		9.52
	.3770	V	
	.3780		9.6
	.3819		9.7
	.3839		9.75
	.3858		9.8
	.3860	W	
	.3898		9.9
25/64	.3906		9.92
	.3937		10.0
	.3970	X	
	.4040	Y	
13/32	.4062		10.31
	.4130	Z	
	.4134		10.5
27/64	.4219		10.71

Inch	Decimal	mm
7/16	.4331	11.0
	.4375	11.11
	.4528	11.5
29/64	.4531	11.51
15/32	.4688	11.90
	.4724	12.0
31/64	.4844	12.30
	.4921	12.5
1/2	.5000	12.70
	.5118	13.0
33/64	.5156	13.09
17/32	.5312	13.49
	.5315	13.5
35/64	.5469	13.89
	.5512	14.0
9/16	.5625	14.28
	.5709	14.5
37/64	.5781	14.68
	.5906	15.0
19/32	.5938	15.08
39/64	.6094	15.47
	.6102	15.5
5/8	.6250	15.87
	.6299	16.0
41/64	.6406	16.27
	.6496	16.5
21/32	.6562	16.66
	.6693	17.0
43/64	.6719	17.06
11/16	.6875	17.46
	.6890	17.5
45/64	.7031	17.85
	.7087	18.0
23/32	.7188	18.25
	.7283	18.5
47/64	.7344	18.65
	.7480	19.0
3/4	.7500	19.05
49/64	.7656	19.44
	.7677	19.5
25/32	.7812	19.84
	.7874	20.0
51/64	.7969	20.24
	.8071	20.5
13/16	.8125	20.63
	.8268	21.0
53/64	.8281	21.03
27/32	.8438	21.43
	.8465	21.5
55/64	.8594	21.82
	.8661	22.0
7/8	.8750	22.22
	.8858	22.5
57/64	.8906	22.62
	.9055	23.0
29/32	.9062	23.01
	.9219	23.41
59/64	.9252	23.5
15/16	.9375	23.81
	.9449	24.0
61/64	.9531	24.2
	.9646	24.5
31/64	.9688	24.6
	.9843	25.0
63/64	.9844	25.0
1	1.0000	25.4

AIR/FUEL RATIO: The ratio of air to gasoline by weight in the fuel mixture drawn into the engine.

AIR INJECTION: One method of reducing harmful exhaust emissions by injecting air into each of the exhaust ports of an engine. The fresh air entering the hot exhaust manifold causes any remaining fuel to be burned before it can exit the tailpipe.

ALTERNATOR: A device used for converting mechanical energy into electrical energy.

AMMETER: An instrument, calibrated in amperes, used to measure the flow of an electrical current in a circuit. Ammeters are always connected in series with the circuit being tested.

AMPERE: The rate of flow of electrical current present when one volt of electrical pressure is applied against one ohm of electrical resistance.

ANALOG COMPUTER: Any microprocessor that uses similar (analogous) electrical signals to make its calculations.

ARMATURE: A laminated, soft iron core wrapped by a wire that converts electrical energy to mechanical energy as in a motor or relay. When rotated in a magnetic field, it changes mechanical energy into electrical energy as in a generator.

ATMOSPHERIC PRESSURE: The pressure on the Earth's surface caused by the weight of the air in the atmosphere. At sea level, this pressure is 14.7 psi at 32°F (101 kPa at 0°C).

ATOMIZATION: The breaking down of a liquid into a fine mist that can be suspended in air.

AXIAL PLAY: Movement parallel to a shaft or bearing bore.

BACKFIRE: The sudden combustion of gases in the intake or exhaust system that results in a loud explosion.

BACKLASH: The clearance or play between two parts, such as meshed gears.

BACKPRESSURE: Restrictions in the exhaust system that slow the exit of exhaust gases from the combustion chamber.

BAKELITE: A heat resistant, plastic insulator material commonly used in printed circuit boards and transistorized components.

BALL BEARING: A bearing made up of hardened inner and outer races between which hardened steel ball roll.

BALLAST RESISTOR: A resistor in the primary ignition circuit that lowers voltage after the engine is started to reduce wear on ignition components.

BEARING: A friction reducing, supportive device usually located between a stationary part and a moving part.

BIMETAL TEMPERATURE SENSOR: Any sensor or switch made of two dissimilar types of metal that bend when heated or cooled due to the different expansion rates of the alloys. These types of sensors usually function as an on/off switch.

BLOWBY: Combustion gases, composed of water vapor and unburned fuel, that leak past the piston rings into the crankcase during normal engine operation. These gases are removed by the PCV system to prevent the buildup of harmful acids in the crankcase.

BRAKE PAD: A brake shoe and lining assembly used with disc brakes.

BRAKE SHOE: The backing for the brake lining. The term is, however, usually applied to the assembly of the brake backing and lining.

BUSHING: A liner, usually removable, for a bearing; an anti-friction liner used in place of a bearing.

BYPASS: System used to bypass ballast resistor during engine cranking to increase voltage supplied to the coil.

CALIPER: A hydraulically activated device in a disc brake system, which is mounted straddling the brake rotor (disc). The caliper contains at least one piston and two brake pads. Hydraulic pressure on the piston(s) forces the pads against the rotor.

CAMSHAFT: A shaft in the engine on which are the lobes (cams) which operate the valves. The camshaft is driven by the crankshaft, via a belt, chain or gears, at one half the crankshaft speed.

CAPACITOR: A device which stores an electrical charge.

CARBON MONOXIDE (CO): a colorless, odorless gas given off as a normal byproduct of combustion. It is poisonous and extremely dangerous in confined areas, building up slowly to toxic levels without warning if adequate ventilation is not available.

CARBURETOR: A device, usually mounted on the intake manifold of an engine, which mixes the air and fuel in the proper proportion to allow even combustion.

CATALYTIC CONVERTER: A device installed in the exhaust system, like a muffler, that converts harmful byproducts of combustion into carbon dioxide and water vapor by means of a heat-producing chemical reaction.

CENTRIFUGAL ADVANCE: A mechanical method of advancing the spark timing by using flyweights in the distributor that react to centrifugal force generated by the distributor shaft rotation.

CHECK VALVE: Any one-way valve installed to permit the flow of air, fuel or vacuum in one direction only.

CHOKE: A device, usually a moveable valve, placed in the intake path of a carburetor to restrict the flow of air.

CIRCUIT: Any unbroken path through which an electrical current can flow. Also used to describe fuel flow in some instances.

CIRCUIT BREAKER: A switch which protects an electrical circuit from overload by opening the circuit when the current flow exceeds a predetermined level. Some circuit breakers must be reset manually, while other reset automatically

COIL (IGNITION): A transformer in the ignition circuit which steps of the voltage provided to the spark plugs.

COMBINATION MANIFOLD: An assembly which includes both the intake and exhaust manifolds in one casting.

COMBINATION VALVE: A device used in some fuel systems that routes fuel vapors to a charcoal storage canister instead of venting them into the atmosphere. The valve relieves fuel tank pressure and allows fresh air into the tank as fuel level drops to prevent a vapor lock situation.

COMPRESSION RATIO: The comparison of the total volume of the cylinder and combustion chamber with the piston at BDC and the piston at TDC.

CONDENSER: 1. An electrical device which acts to store an electrical charge, preventing voltage surges.
2. A radiator-like device in the air conditioning system in which refrigerant gas condenses into a liquid, giving off heat.

CONDUCTOR: Any material through which an electrical current can be transmitted easily.

CONTINUITY: Continuous or complete circuit. Can be checked with an ohmmeter.

COUNTERSHAFT: An intermediate shaft which is rotated by a mainshaft and transmits, in turn, that rotation to a working part.

CRANKCASE: The lower part of an engine in which the crankshaft and related parts operate.

CRANKSHAFT: The main driving shaft of an engine which receives reciprocating motion from the pistons and converts it to rotary motion.

CYLINDER: In an engine, the round hole in the engine block in which the piston(s) ride.

CYLINDER BLOCK: The main structural member of an engine in which is found the cylinders, crankshaft and other principal parts.

CYLINDER HEAD: The detachable portion of the engine, fastened, usually, to the top of the cylinder block, containing all or most of the combustion chambers. On overhead valve engines, it contains the valves and their operating parts. On overhead cam engines, it contains the camshaft as well.

DEAD CENTER: The extreme top or bottom of the piston stroke.

DETONATION: An unwanted explosion of the air fuel mixture in the combustion chamber caused by excess heat and compression, advanced timing, or an overly lean mixture. Also referred to as "ping".

DIAPHRAGM: A thin, flexible wall separating two cavities, such as in a vacuum advance unit.

DIESELING: A condition in which hot spots in the combustion chamber cause the engine to run on after the key is turned off.

DIFFERENTIAL: A geared assembly which allows the transmission of motion between drive axles, giving one axle the ability to turn faster than the other.

DIODE: An electrical device that will allow current to flow in one direction only.

DISC BRAKE: A hydraulic braking assembly consisting of a brake disc, or rotor, mounted on an axle, and a caliper assembly containing, usually two brake pads which are activated by hydraulic pressure. The pads are forced against the sides of the disc, creating friction which slows the vehicle.

DISTRIBUTOR: A mechanically driven device on an engine which is responsible for electrically firing the spark plug at a predetermined point of the piston stroke.

DOWEL PIN: A pin, inserted in mating holes in two different parts allowing those parts to maintain a fixed relationship.

DRUM BRAKE: A braking system which consists of two brake shoes and one or two wheel cylinders, mounted on a fixed backing plate, and a brake drum, mounted on an axle, which revolves around the assembly. Hydraulic action applied to the wheel cylinders forces the shoes outward against the drum, creating friction and slowing the vehicle.

DWELL: The rate, measured in degrees of shaft rotation, at which an electrical circuit cycles on and off.

ELECTRONIC CONTROL UNIT (ECU): Ignition module, module, amplifier or igniter. See Module for definition.

ELECTRONIC IGNITION: A system in which the timing and firing of the spark plugs is controlled by an electronic control unit, usually called a module. These systems have not points or condenser.

ENDPLAY: The measured amount of axial movement in a shaft.

ENGINE: A device that converts heat into mechanical energy.

EXHAUST MANIFOLD: A set of cast passages or pipes which conduct exhaust gases from the engine.

FEELER GAUGE: A blade, usually metal, of precisely predetermined thickness, used to measure the clearance between two parts. These blades usually are available in sets of assorted thicknesses.

F-Head: An engine configuration in which the intake valves are in the cylinder head, while the camshaft and exhaust valves are located in the cylinder block. The camshaft operates the intake valves via lifters and pushrods, while it operates the exhaust valves directly.

FIRING ORDER: The order in which combustion occurs in the cylinders of an engine. Also the order in which spark is distributed to the plugs by the distributor.

FLATHEAD: An engine configuration in which the camshaft and all the valves are located in the cylinder block.

FLOODING: The presence of too much fuel in the intake manifold and combustion chamber which prevents the air/fuel mixture from firing, thereby causing a no-start situation.

FLYWHEEL: A disc shaped part bolted to the rear end of the crankshaft. Around the outer perimeter is affixed the ring gear. The starter drive engages the ring gear, turning the flywheel, which rotates the crankshaft, imparting the initial starting motion to the engine.

FOOT POUND (ft.lb. or sometimes, ft. lbs.): The amount of energy or work needed to raise an item weighing one pound, a distance of one foot.

FUSE: A protective device in a circuit which prevents circuit overload by breaking the circuit when a specific amperage is present. The device is constructed around a strip or wire of a lower amperage rating than the circuit it is designed to protect. When an amperage higher than that stamped on the fuse is present in the circuit, the strip or wire melts, opening the circuit.

GEAR RATIO: The ratio between the number of teeth on meshing gears.

GENERATOR: A device which converts mechanical energy into electrical energy.

HEAT RANGE: The measure of a spark plug's ability to dissipate heat from its firing end. The higher the heat range, the hotter the plug fires.

HUB: The center part of a wheel or gear.

HYDROCARBON (HC): Any chemical compound made up of hydrogen and carbon. A major pollutant formed by the engine as a byproduct of combustion.

HYDROMETER: An instrument used to measure the specific gravity of a solution.

INCH POUND (in.lb. or sometimes, in. lbs.): One twelfth of a foot pound.

INDUCTION: A means of transferring electrical energy in the form of a magnetic field. Principle used in the ignition coil to increase voltage.

INJECTION PUMP: A device, usually mechanically operated, which meters and delivers fuel under pressure to the fuel injector.

INJECTOR: A device which receives metered fuel under relatively low pressure and is activated to inject the fuel into the engine under relatively high pressure at a predetermined time.

INPUT SHAFT: The shaft to which torque is applied, usually carrying the driving gear or gears.

INTAKE MANIFOLD: A casting of passages or pipes used to conduct air or a fuel/air mixture to the cylinders.

JOURNAL: The bearing surface within which a shaft operates.

KEY: A small block usually fitted in a notch between a shaft and a hub to prevent slippage of the two parts.

MANIFOLD: A casting of passages or set of pipes which connect the cylinders to an inlet or outlet source.

MANIFOLD VACUUM: Low pressure in an engine intake manifold formed just below the throttle plates. Manifold vacuum is highest at idle and drops under acceleration.

MASTER CYLINDER: The primary fluid pressurizing device in a hydraulic system. In automotive use, it is found in brake and hydraulic clutch systems and is pedal activated, either directly or, in a power brake system, through the power booster.

MODULE: Electronic control unit, amplifier or igniter of solid state or integrated design which controls the current flow in the ignition primary circuit based on input from the pickup coil. When the module opens the primary circuit, the high secondary voltage is induced in the coil.

NEEDLE BEARING: A bearing which consists of a number (usually a large number) of long, thin rollers.

OHM: (Ω) The unit used to measure the resistance of conductor to electrical flow. One ohm is the amount of resistance that limits current flow to one ampere in a circuit with one volt of pressure.

OHMMETER: An instrument used for measuring the resistance, in ohms, in an electrical circuit.

OUTPUT SHAFT: The shaft which transmits torque from a device, such as a transmission.

OVERDRIVE: A gear assembly which produces more shaft revolutions than that transmitted to it.

OVERHEAD CAMSHAFT (OHC): An engine configuration in which the camshaft is mounted on top of the cylinder head and operates the valve either directly or by means of rocker arms.

OVERHEAD VALVE (OHV): An engine configuration in which all of the valves are located in the cylinder head and the camshaft is located in the cylinder block. The camshaft operates the valves via lifters and pushrods.

OXIDES OF NITROGEN (NOx): Chemical compounds of nitrogen produced as a byproduct of combustion. They combine with hydrocarbons to produce smog.

OXYGEN SENSOR: Used with the feedback system to sense the presence of oxygen in the exhaust gas and signal the computer which can reference the voltage signal to an air/fuel ratio.

PINION: The smaller of two meshing gears.

PISTON RING: An open ended ring which fits into a groove on the outer diameter of the piston. Its chief function is to form a seal between the piston and cylinder wall. Most automotive pistons have three rings: two for compression sealing; one for oil sealing.

PRELOAD: A predetermined load placed on a bearing during assembly or by adjustment.

PRIMARY CIRCUIT: Is the low voltage side of the ignition system which consists of the ignition switch, ballast resistor or resistance wire, bypass, coil, electronic control unit and pick-up coil as well as the connecting wires and harnesses.

PRESS FIT: The mating of two parts under pressure, due to the inner diameter of one being smaller than the outer diameter of the other, or vice versa; an interference fit.

RACE: The surface on the inner or outer ring of a bearing on which the balls, needles or rollers move.

REGULATOR: A device which maintains the amperage and/or voltage levels of a circuit at predetermined values.

RELAY: A switch which automatically opens and/or closes a circuit.

RESISTANCE: The opposition to the flow of current through a circuit or electrical device, and is measured in ohms. Resistance is equal to the voltage divided by the amperage.

RESISTOR: A device, usually made of wire, which offers a preset amount of resistance in an electrical circuit.

RING GEAR: The name given to a ring-shaped gear attached to a differential case, or affixed to a flywheel or as part a planetary gear set.

ROLLER BEARING: A bearing made up of hardened inner and outer races between which hardened steel rollers move.

ROTOR: 1. The disc-shaped part of a disc brake assembly, upon which the brake pads bear; also called, brake disc.
2. The device mounted atop the distributor shaft, which passes current to the distributor cap tower contacts.

SECONDARY CIRCUIT: The high voltage side of the ignition system, usually above 20,000 volts. The secondary includes the ignition coil, coil wire, distributor cap and rotor, spark plug wires and spark plugs.

SENDING UNIT: A mechanical, electrical, hydraulic or electromagnetic device which transmits information to a gauge.

SENSOR: Any device designed to measure engine operating conditions or ambient pressures and temperatures. Usually electronic in nature and designed to send a voltage signal to an on-board computer, some sensors may operate as a simple on/off switch or they may provide a variable voltage signal (like a potentiometer) as conditions or measured parameters change.

SHIM: Spacers of precise, predetermined thickness used between parts to establish a proper working relationship.

SLAVE CYLINDER: In automotive use, a device in the hydraulic clutch system which is activated by hydraulic force, disengaging the clutch.

SOLENOID: A coil used to produce a magnetic field, the effect of which is produce work.

SPARK PLUG: A device screwed into the combustion chamber of a spark ignition engine. The basic construction is a conductive core inside of a ceramic insulator, mounted in an outer conductive base. An electrical charge from the spark plug wire travels along the conductive core and jumps a preset air gap to a grounding point or points at the end of the conductive base. The resultant spark ignites the fuel/air mixture in the combustion chamber.

SPLINES: Ridges machined or cast onto the outer diameter of a shaft or inner diameter of a bore to enable parts to mate without rotation.

TACHOMETER: A device used to measure the rotary speed of an engine, shaft, gear, etc., usually in rotations per minute.

THERMOSTAT: A valve, located in the cooling system of an engine, which is closed when cold and opens gradually in response to engine heating, controlling the temperature of the coolant and rate of coolant flow.

TOP DEAD CENTER (TDC): The point at which the piston reaches the top of its travel on the compression stroke.

TORQUE: The twisting force applied to an object.

TORQUE CONVERTER: A turbine used to transmit power from a driving member to a driven member via hydraulic action, providing changes in drive ratio and torque. In automotive use, it links the driveplate at the rear of the engine to the automatic transmission.

TRANSDUCER: A device used to change a force into an electrical signal.

TRANSISTOR: A semi-conductor component which can be actuated by a small voltage to perform an electrical switching function.

TUNE-UP: A regular maintenance function, usually associated with the replacement and adjustment of parts and components in the electrical and fuel systems of a vehicle for the purpose of attaining optimum performance.

TURBOCHARGER: An exhaust driven pump which compresses intake air and forces it into the combustion chambers at higher than atmospheric pressures. The increased air pressure allows more fuel to be burned and results in increased horsepower being produced.

VACUUM ADVANCE: A device which advances the ignition timing in response to increased engine vacuum.

VACUUM GAUGE: An instrument used to measure the presence of vacuum in a chamber.

VALVE: A device which control the pressure, direction of flow or rate of flow of a liquid or gas.

VALVE CLEARANCE: The measured gap between the end of the valve stem and the rocker arm, cam lobe or follower that activates the valve.

VISCOSITY: The rating of a liquid's internal resistance to flow.

VOLTMETER: An instrument used for measuring electrical force in units called volts. Voltmeters are always connected parallel with the circuit being tested.

WHEEL CYLINDER: Found in the automotive drum brake assembly, it is a device, actuated by hydraulic pressure, which, through internal pistons, pushes the brake shoes outward against the drums.

A: Ampere

AC: Alternating current

A/C: Air conditioning

A-h: Ampere hour

AT: Automatic transmission

ATDC: After top dead center

μA: Microampere

bbl: Barrel

BDC: Bottom dead center

bhp: Brake horsepower

BTDC: Before top dead center

BTU: British thermal unit

C: Celsius (Centigrade)

CCA: Cold cranking amps

cd: Candela

cm^2: Square centimeter

cm^3, cc: Cubic centimeter

CO: Carbon monoxide

CO_2: Carbon dioxide

cu.in., in^3: Cubic inch

CV: Constant velocity

Cyl.: Cylinder

DC: Direct current

ECM: Electronic control module

EFE: Early fuel evaporation

EFI: Electronic fuel injection

EGR: Exhaust gas recirculation

Exh.: Exhaust

F: Fahrenheit

F: Farad

pF: Picofarad

μF: Microfarad

FI: Fuel injection

ft.lb., ft. lb., ft. lbs.: foot pound(s)

gal: Gallon

g: Gram

HC: Hydrocarbon

HEI: High energy ignition

HO: High output

hp: Horsepower

Hyd.: Hydraulic

Hz: Hertz

ID: Inside diameter

in.lb.; in. lb.; in. lbs: inch pound(s)

Int.: Intake

K: Kelvin

kg: Kilogram

kHz: Kilohertz

km: Kilometer

km/h: Kilometers per hour

$k\Omega$: Kilohm

kPa: Kilopascal

kV: Kilovolt

kW: Kilowatt

l: Liter

l/s: Liters per second

m: Meter

mA: Milliampere

mg: Milligram

mHz: Megahertz

mm: Millimeter

mm^2: Square millimeter

m^3: Cubic meter

$M\Omega$: Megohm

m/s: Meters per second

MT: Manual transmission

mV: Millivolt

μm: Micrometer

N: Newton

N-m: Newton meter

NOx: Nitrous oxide

OD: Outside diameter

OHC: Over head camshaft

OHV: Over head valve

Ω: Ohm

PCV: Positive crankcase ventilation

psi: Pounds per square inch

pts: Pints

qts: Quarts

rpm: Rotations per minute

rps: Rotations per second

R-12: A refrigerant gas (Freon)

SAE: Society of Automotive Engineers

SO_2: Sulfur dioxide

T: Ton

t: Megagram

TBI: Throttle Body Injection

TPS: Throttle Position Sensor

V: 1. Volt; 2. Venturi

μV: Microvolt

W: Watt

∞: Infinity

<: Less than

>: Greater than

Index

Chilton's Repair & Tune-Up Guides

The Complete line covers domestic cars, imports, trucks, vans, RV's and 4-wheel drive vehicles.

RTUG Title	Part No.
AMC 1975-82	7199
Covers all U.S. and Canadian models	
Aspen/Volare 1976-80	6637
Covers all U.S. and Canadian models	
Audi 1970-73	5902
Covers all U.S. and Canadian models.	
Audi 4000/5000 1978-81	7028
Covers all U.S. and Canadian models including turbocharged and diesel engines	
Barracuda/Challenger 1965-72	5807
Covers all U.S. and Canadian models	
Blazer/Jimmy 1969-82	6931
Covers all U.S. and Canadian 2- and 4-wheel drive models, including diesel engines	
BMW 1970-82	6844
Covers U.S. and Canadian models	
Buick/Olds/Pontiac 1975-85	7308
Covers all U.S. and Canadian full size rear wheel drive models	
Cadillac 1967-84	7462
Covers all U.S. and Canadian rear wheel drive models	
Camaro 1967-81	6735
Covers all U.S. and Canadian models	
Camaro 1982-85	7317
Covers all U.S. and Canadian models	
Capri 1970-77	6695
Covers all U.S. and Canadian models	
Caravan/Voyager 1984-85	7482
Covers all U.S. and Canadian models	
Century/Regal 1975-85	7307
Covers all U.S. and Canadian rear wheel drive models, including turbocharged engines	
Champ/Arrow/Sapporo 1978-83	7041
Covers all U.S. and Canadian models	
Chevette/1000 1976-86	6836
Covers all U.S. and Canadian models	
Chevrolet 1968-85	7135
Covers all U.S. and Canadian models	
Chevrolet 1968-79 Spanish	7082
Chevrolet/GMC Pick-Ups 1970-82 Spanish	7468
Chevrolet/GMC Pick-Ups and Suburban 1970-86	6936
Covers all U.S. and Canadian 1/2, 3/4 and 1 ton models, including 4-wheel drive and diesel engines	
Chevrolet LUV 1972-81	6815
Covers all U.S. and Canadian models	
Chevrolet Mid-Size 1964-86	6840
Covers all U.S. and Canadian models of 1964-77 Chevelle, Malibu and Malibu SS; 1974-77 Laguna; 1978-85 Malibu; 1970-86 Monte Carlo; 1964-84 El Camino, including diesel engines	
Chevrolet Nova 1986	7658
Covers all U.S. and Canadian models	
Chevy/GMC Vans 1967-84	6930
Covers all U.S. and Canadian models of 1/2, 3/4, and 1 ton vans, cutaways, and motor home chassis, including diesel engines	
Chevy S-10 Blazer/GMC S-15 Jimmy 1982-85	7383
Covers all U.S. and Canadian models	
Chevy S-10/GMC S-15 Pick-Ups 1982-85	7310
Covers all U.S. and Canadian models	
Chevy II/Nova 1962-79	6841
Covers all U.S. and Canadian models	
Chrysler K- and E-Car 1981-85	7163
Covers all U.S. and Canadian front wheel drive models	
Colt/Challenger/Vista/Conquest 1971-85	7037
Covers all U.S. and Canadian models	
Corolla/Carina/Tercel/Starlet 1970-85	7036
Covers all U.S. and Canadian models	
Corona/Cressida/Crown/Mk.II/Camry/Van 1970-84	7044
Covers all U.S. and Canadian models	
Corvair 1960-69	6691
Covers all U.S. and Canadian models	
Corvette 1953-62	6576
Covers all U.S. and Canadian models	
Corvette 1963-84	6843
Covers all U.S. and Canadian models	
Cutlass 1970-85	6933
Covers all U.S. and Canadian models	
Dart/Demon 1968-76	6324
Covers all U.S. and Canadian models	
Datsun 1961-72	5790
Covers all U.S. and Canadian models of Nissan Patrol; 1500, 1600 and 2000 sports cars; Pick-Ups; 410, 411, 510, 1200 and 240Z	
Datsun 1973-80 Spanish	7083
Datsun/Nissan F-10, 310, Stanza, Pulsar 1977-86	7196
Covers all U.S. and Canadian models	
Datsun/Nissan Pick-Ups 1970-84	6816
Covers all U.S and Canadian models	
Datsun/Nissan Z & ZX 1970-86	6932
Covers all U.S. and Canadian models	
Datsun/Nissan 1200, 210, Sentra 1973-86	7197
Covers all U.S. and Canadian models	
Datsun/Nissan 200SX, 510, 610, 710, 810, Maxima 1973-84	7170
Covers all U.S. and Canadian models	
Dodge 1968-77	6554
Covers all U.S. and Canadian models	
Dodge Charger 1967-70	6486
Covers all U.S. and Canadian models	
Dodge/Plymouth Trucks 1967-84	7459
Covers all 1/2, 3/4, and 1 ton 2- and 4-wheel drive U.S. and Canadian models, including diesel engines	
Dodge/Plymouth Vans 1967-84	6934
Covers all 1/2, 3/4, and 1 ton U.S. and Canadian models of vans, cutaways and motor home chassis	
D-50/Arrow Pick-Up 1979-81	7032
Covers all U.S. and Canadian models	
Fairlane/Torino 1962-75	6320
Covers all U.S. and Canadian models	
Fairmont/Zephyr 1978-83	6965
Covers all U.S. and Canadian models	
Fiat 1969-81	7042
Covers all U.S. and Canadian models	
Fiesta 1978-80	6846
Covers all U.S. and Canadian models	
Firebird 1967-81	5996
Covers all U.S. and Canadian models	
Firebird 1982-85	7345
Covers all U.S. and Canadian models	
Ford 1968-79 Spanish	7084
Ford Bronco 1966-83	7140
Covers all U.S. and Canadian models	
Ford Bronco II 1984	7408
Covers all U.S. and Canadian models	
Ford Courier 1972-82	6983
Covers all U.S. and Canadian models	
Ford/Mercury Front Wheel Drive 1981-85	7055
Covers all U.S. and Canadian models Escort, EXP, Tempo, Lynx, LN-7 and Topaz	
Ford/Mercury/Lincoln 1968-85	6842
Covers all U.S. and Canadian models of FORD Country Sedan, Country Squire, Crown Victoria, Custom, Custom 500, Galaxie 500, LTD through 1982, Ranch Wagon, and XL; MERCURY Colony Park, Commuter, Marquis through 1982, Gran Marquis, Monterey and Park Lane; LINCOLN Continental and Towne Car	
Ford/Mercury/Lincoln Mid-Size 1971-85	6696
Covers all U.S. and Canadian models of FORD Elite, 1983-85 LTD, 1977-79 LTD II, Ranchero, Torino, Gran Torino, 1977-85 Thunderbird; MERCURY 1972-85 Cougar,	

continued on next page

RTUG Title	Part No.	RTUG Title	Part No.
1983-85 Marquis, Montego, 1980-85 XR-7; LINCOLN 1982-85 Continental, 1984-85 Mark VII, 1978-80 Versailles		Mercedes-Benz 1974-84 Covers all U.S. and Canadian models	6809
Ford Pick-Ups 1965-86 Covers all ½, ¾ and 1 ton, 2- and 4-wheel drive U.S. and Canadian pick-up, chassis cab and camper models, including diesel engines	6913	Mitsubishi, Cordia, Tredia, Starion, Galant 1983-85 Covers all U.S. and Canadian models	7583
		MG 1961-81 Covers all U.S. and Canadian models	6780
Ford Pick-Ups 1965-82 Spanish	7469	Mustang/Capri/Merkur 1979-85 Covers all U.S. and Canadian models	6963
Ford Ranger 1983-84 Covers all U.S. and Canadian models	7338	Mustang/Cougar 1965-73 Covers all U.S. and Canadian models	6542
Ford Vans 1961-86 Covers all U.S. and Canadian ½, ¾ and 1 ton van and cutaway chassis models, including diesel engines	6849	Mustang II 1974-78 Covers all U.S. and Canadian models	6812
		Omni/Horizon/Rampage 1978-84 Covers all U.S. and Canadian models of DODGE omni, Miser, 024, Charger 2.2; PLYMOUTH Horizon, Miser, TC3, TC3 Tourismo; Rampage	6845
GM A-Body 1982-85 Covers all front wheel drive U.S. and Canadian models of BUICK Century, CHEVROLET Celebrity, OLDSMOBILE Cutlass Ciera and PONTIAC 6000	7309		
		Opel 1971-75 Covers all U.S. and Canadian models	6575
GM C-Body 1985 Covers all front wheel drive U.S. and Canadian models of BUICK Electra Park Avenue and Electra T-Type, CADILLAC Fleetwood and deVille, OLDSMOBILE 98 Regency and Regency Brougham	7587	Peugeot 1970-74 Covers all U.S. and Canadian models	5982
		Pinto/Bobcat 1971-80 Covers all U.S. and Canadian models	7027
		Plymouth 1968-76 Covers all U.S. and Canadian models	6552
		Pontiac Fiero 1984-85 Covers all U.S. and Canadian models	7571
GM J-Car 1982-85 Covers all U.S. and Canadian models of BUICK Skyhawk, CHEVROLET Cavalier, CADILLAC Cimarron, OLDSMOBILE Firenza and PONTIAC 2000 and Sunbird	7059	Pontiac Mid-Size 1974-83 Covers all U.S. and Canadian models of Ventura, Grand Am, LeMans, Grand LeMans, GTO, Phoenix, and Grand Prix	7346
GM N-Body 1985-86 Covers all U.S. and Canadian models of front wheel drive BUICK Somerset and Skylark, OLDSMOBILE Calais, and PONTIAC Grand Am	7657	Porsche 924/928 1976-81 Covers all U.S. and Canadian models	7048
		Renault 1975-85 Covers all U.S. and Canadian models	7165
		Roadrunner/Satellite/Belvedere/GTX 1968-73 Covers all U.S. and Canadian models	5821
GM X-Body 1980-85 Covers all U.S. and Canadian models of BUICK Skylark, CHEVROLET Citation, OLDSMOBILE Omega and PONTIAC Phoenix	7049	RX-7 1979-81 Covers all U.S. and Canadian models	7031
		SAAB 99 1969-75	5988
		SAAB 900 1979-85 Covers all U.S. and Canadian models	7572
GM Subcompact 1971-80 Covers all U.S. and Canadian models of BUICK Skyhawk (1975-80), CHEVROLET Vega and Monza, OLDSMOBILE Starfire, and PONTIAC Astre and 1975-80 Sunbird	6935	Snowmobiles 1976-80 Covers all Arctic Cat, John Deere, Kawasaki, Polaris, Ski-Doo and Yamaha	6978
		Subaru 1970-84 Covers all U.S. and Canadian models	6982
Granada/Monarch 1975-82 Covers all U.S. and Canadian models	6937	Tempest/GTO/LeMans 1968-73 Covers all U.S. and Canadian models	5905
Honda 1973-84 Covers all U.S. and Canadian models	6980	Toyota 1966-70 Covers all U.S. and Canadian models of Corona, MkII, Corolla, Crown, Land Cruiser, Stout and Hi-Lux	5795
International Scout 1967-73 Covers all U.S. and Canadian models	5912		
Jeep 1945-87 Covers all U.S. and Canadian CJ-2A, CJ-3A, CJ-3B, CJ-5, CJ-6, CJ-7, Scrambler and Wrangler models	6817	Toyota 1970-79 Spanish	7467
		Toyota Celica/Supra 1971-85 Covers all U.S. and Canadian models	7043
		Toyota Trucks 1970-85 Covers all U.S. and Canadian models of pick-ups, Land Cruiser and 4Runner	7035
Jeep Wagoneer, Commando, Cherokee, Truck 1957-86 Covers all U.S. and Canadian models of Wagoneer, Cherokee, Grand Wagoneer, Jeepster, Jeepster Commando, J-100, J-200, J-300, J-10, J20, FC-150 and FC-170	6739		
		Valiant/Duster 1968-76 Covers all U.S. and Canadian models	6326
		Volvo 1956-69 Covers all U.S. and Canadian models	6529
		Volvo 1970-83 Covers all U.S. and Canadian models	7040
Laser/Daytona 1984-85 Covers all U.S. and Canadian models	7563	VW Front Wheel Drive 1974-85 Covers all U.S. and Canadian models	6962
Maverick/Comet 1970-77 Covers all U.S. and Canadian models	6634	VW 1949-71 Covers all U.S. and Canadian models	5796
Mazda 1971-84 Covers all U.S. and Canadian models of RX-2, RX-3, RX-4, 808, 1300, 1600, Cosmo, GLC and 626	6981	VW 1970-79 Spanish	7081
		VW 1970-81 Covers all U.S. and Canadian Beetles, Karmann Ghia, Fastback, Squareback, Vans, 411 and 412	6837
Mazda Pick-Ups 1972-86 Covers all U.S. and Canadian models	7659		
Mercedes-Benz 1959-70 Covers all U.S. and Canadian models	6065		
Mereceds-Benz 1968-73 Covers all U.S. and Canadian models	5907		

Chilton's Repair & Tune-Up Guides are available at your local retailer or by mailing a check or money order for **$13.95** plus **$3.25** to cover postage and handling to:

Chilton Book Company
Dept. DM
Radnor, PA 19089

NOTE: When ordering be sure to include your name & address, book part No. & title.